THE LOGICAL ACCESSORY

INSTRUCTOR'S MANUAL TO ACCOMPANY CRITICAL THINKING, FOURTH EDITION

Brooke Noel Moore and Richard Parker

California State University, Chico

Mayfield Publishing Company
Mountain View, California
London • Toronto

International Standard Book Number: 1-55934-340-0

Manufactured in the United States of America

Mayfield Publishing Company
1280 Villa Street
Mountain View, CA 94041

Contents

Introduction

Welcome to the fourth edition of *The Logical Accessory*. We hope the resources provided here will help make your elementary course in logic or critical thinking easier and more pleasant to teach. This book includes answers for all the exercises in *Critical Thinking* that are not answered in the answer section of the text itself. It also includes substantial banks of additional exercises, with answers, for each chapter of the text (Chapters 5 and 6 are combined). Finally, the book includes some tips and suggestions that have come from our own experience with this material and that of several correspondents who have used previous editions.

This edition of *Critical Thinking* contains a chapter contributed by Nina Rosenstand and Anita Silvers (Chapter 13), covering both legal and aesthetic reasoning.

We've included a Pre- and Post-Test in the back pages of this book through three editions. It's still there, and we've also kept the Quick Quiz Question Bank that follows this introduction. The bank contains questions for each chapter in the text, all of them multiple-choice and easily gradable by machine. We think this bank can be useful in any number of ways. For example, you might use four or five (or eight or ten) of these questions to create a quick-to-grade (by hand, possibly) reading quiz for each chapter, just to make sure students are keeping up on their reading assignments. But you might also combine several chapters' worth of questions for a machine-gradable major exam. We aren't convinced that a critical thinking course can be effectively graded *entirely* in this fashion, but we also realize that more and more students are being crowded into sections and that such policies limit the instructor's options. We've begun giving a lot of multiple-choice quizzes ourselves.

Once again, if there are things you like about the text (or this accompaniment, or any of the rest of the package), we hope you'll let us or Mayfield Publishing Company know. Similarly, if there are things you think we can make better, send us your suggestions. We enjoy hearing from you.

Quick Quiz Question Bank

In this section, you'll find 130 multiple-choice questions, grouped ten per *CT* chapter. If you need short, easily graded quizzes on the chapters, this is a place to find them, courtesy of the efforts of Dan Barnett. Combine several chapters' worth, and the result is the basis for a machine-gradable exam over several chapters. We've begun using these both ways, and the results have been good. We hope you find them helpful. (Asterisks indicate correct answers.)

Chapter 1

1. "Critical thinking" is another name for logic.

    A. True

    *B. False

2. A single argument can have several conclusions.

    A. True

    *B. False

3. In the broadest sense, _____ is just any matter that is in dispute, in doubt, or simply "up for review."

    A. Logic

    B. Critical thinking

    *C. An issue

    D. A premise

4. Does this passage contain an argument? "Details of the murder came from dozens of interviews with Chico Mendes's neighbors, relatives, and bodyguards; testimony given by witnesses during pretrial hearings; transcripts of interviews conducted by the local and federal police; and the autopsy report" (Andrew Revkin, *The Burning Season*).

    A. Yes

    *B. No

5. Does this passage contain an argument? "The English word 'rubber' was derived from one of its first uses in Great Britain—to rub off unwanted pencil marks from a sheet of paper" (Andrew Revkin, *The Burning Season*).

    A. Yes

    *B. No

6. Consider the following argument: "Thinking of buying a house outside your present location? <u>You should avoid asking an agent where you live to make a referral in the new area.</u> This is because an agent who receives a referral from someone else in the business is often expected to compensate the referrer with 20% of his commission and that makes some salespeople overanxious to make referrals to agents they may not know well" (adapted from Ralph Warner, Ira Serkes, and George Devine, *How to Buy a House in California: Strategies for Beating the Affordability Gap*). The underlined sentence is

   A. A premise

   *B. The conclusion

7. What is the issue in the following argument? "It is an error to imagine that evolution signifies a constant tendency to increased perfection. That process undoubtedly involves a constant remodeling of the organism in adaptation to new conditions; but it depends on the nature of those conditions whether the direction of the modification effected shall be upward or downward" (T. H. Huxley, *Struggle for Existence in Human Society*).

   *A. Whether evolution signifies a constant tendency to increased perfection

   B. Whether evolution is true or false

   C. Whether evolution's direction is upward or downward

   D. Whether organisms can adapt to new surroundings

   E. Whether T. H. Huxley is a credible expert

8. Other than conveying factual information, what other purpose(s) might the following claim have? "In a lifetime, the average American will throw away 600 times his or her adult weight in garbage" (from *15 Simple Things Californians Can Do To Recycle,* by the EarthWorks Group and the California Department of Conservation's Division of Recycling).

   A. To alert the reader that an ordinary activity (creation of garbage) can have potentially profound consequences for the present (and the future)

   B. To provide a reason for citizens to become involved in recycling programs

   C. To provide an example of the "throwaway" society

   *D. All of the above

   E. None of the above

9. Consider the following passage: "All U.S. presidents have been women. George Bush was a U.S. president. Therefore, George Bush is a woman!" If the passage is an argument, does the conclusion follow from the premises as given?

   *A. Yes

   B. No

   C. The passage is not an argument

3

10. Consider the following passage: "<u>God governs the world</u>, not by irresistible force, but (by) persuasive argument and reason, controlling it into compliance with his eternal purposes" (Plutarch, *Phocion*). The underlined words are

   A. A premise

   B. The conclusion

   *C. Neither a premise nor a conclusion

Chapter 2

1. "Swaying in the breeze, Lin saw the American flag." What kind of ambiguity, if any, does this statement contain?

   A. Semantical ambiguity

   *B. Syntactical ambiguity

   C. No ambiguity

2. "Lin followed the ostrich in his pajamas." This statement contains

   A. Semantical ambiguity

   *B. Syntactical ambiguity

   C. No ambiguity

3. "If George Washington and Benjamin Franklin were the fathers of our country, they certainly must have had many children!" This statement contains

   *A. Semantical ambiguity

   B. Syntactical ambiguity

   C. No ambiguity

4. Consider the following passage: "The winter-run chinook salmon is almost extinct. Therefore, this winter-run chinook salmon you just caught is almost extinct." The argument makes use of what fallacy?

   A. Composition

   *B. Division

   C. No fallacy

5. Consider the following passage: "Each member of the local symphony society is over eighty years old. Therefore, the symphony society must be over eighty years old." What fallacy does this argument rely on?

   *A. Composition

   B. Division

   C. No fallacy

6. A term that is vague in one context may not be vague in another context.
    *A. True
    B. False

7. All ambiguous claims are vague claims.
    A. True
    *B. False

8. "Restaurant patrons should eat the vegetables only when they're steamed." What kind of ambiguity, if any, does this statement contain?
    A. Semantical ambiguity
    B. Syntactical ambiguity
    C. No ambiguity
    *D. Both A and B

9. "Mars is what I mean by a planet." What kind of definition is this?
    *A. Definition by example
    B. Definition by synonym
    C. Analytical definition

10. The emotive force of terms is part of their literal meaning.
    A. True
    *B. False

Chapter 3

1. Suppose a study was conducted to find out how long Hollywood actors spent on the job during a normal workday. Suppose further that the study found that the most common workday was eleven hours. This kind of average is called the
    A. Mean
    B. Median
    *C. Mode

2. Suppose a study was conducted to find out how long Hollywood actors spent on the job during a normal workday. Suppose further that researchers determined the average number of hours worked by adding up all the hours worked by those in the study and dividing that number by the number of people studied. This kind of average is called the
    *A. Mean
    B. Median
    C. Mode

3. Suppose a study was conducted to find out how long Hollywood actors spent on the job during a normal workday. Suppose it was determined that ten hours was the "halfway" point in the study: that is, half of the actors worked more than ten hours, and half worked fewer than ten hours a day. This kind of average is called the

    A. Mean

  *B. Median

    C. Mode

4. Novelist Saul Bellow won the Nobel prize in literature in 1976. This fact alone means Bellow's suggestions on funding allocations for the U.S. space program ought to be seriously considered.

    A. True

  *B. False

5. It is improper to dismiss a factual claim unless it can be disproved through direct observation.

    A. True

  *B. False

6. Suppose you wanted to find out more information about an alleged insider stock-trading scandal within Time Warner, Inc., which was accused of illegalities by the publisher of *Newsweek*. Which of the sources listed below would likely be the most credible?

    A. *Time* magazine (owned by Time Warner)

    B. *Newsweek* magazine

  *C. The *Wall Street Journal*

    D. The *National Enquirer*

7. It is always unwise to accept unsupported informative claims.

    A. True

  *B. False

8. A person who reports an observation can be regarded as credible unless there is some specific reason for believing otherwise.

  *A. True

    B. False

9. Suppose you read in the politically left periodical *The Progressive* the claim that the staff of former president Ronald Reagan manipulated the release of the U.S. hostages from captivity in Iran to coincide with the day of Reagan's inauguration. You realize the report may be biased against Reagan. How should a critical thinker respond?

   A. Declare the claim probably true

   B. Declare the claim probably false

   *C. Suspend judgment on the claim until more information is available

10. Suppose you read in the *Weekly World News* tabloid that Adolf Hitler is still alive. How should a critical thinker respond?

   A. Declare the claim probably true

   *B. Declare the claim probably false

   C. Suspend judgment on the claim until more information is available

Chapter 4

1. "The Macintosh computer display was located in the campus free speech area; many who watched the product demonstrations seemed interested in computers." What slanter is being used here?

   A. Downplayer

   B. Proof surrogate

   C. Hyperbole

   D. Euphemism

   *E. No slanter

2. "I simply won't go into health clubs; they're full of people who are nothing but a bunch of braggarts in fashionable gym clothes." What slanter is being used here?

   A. Loaded question

   *B. Stereotype

   C. Weaseler

   D. Proof surrogate

   E. None of the above

3. "If the university president is so dedicated to improving education, why are students worse off now than when she took office?" What slanter is being used here?

   A. Downplayer

   B. Euphemism

   *C. Loaded question

   D. Hyperbole

   E. No slanter

4. "David Letterman is the funniest man in America (as opinion polls show)." What is the phrase in parentheses?

   A. Innuendo

   *B. Proof surrogate

   C. Dysphemism

   D. Hyperbole

   E. None of the above

5. Saddam Hussein called his hostages "guests." What slanter did he use?

   A. Innuendo

   B. Downplayer

   C. Weaseler

   *D. Euphemism

   E. There is no slanter being used

6. "Several recent studies show that Tylenol is really more effective against headache pain than Motrin." What slanter is being used here?

   A. Hyperbole

   B. Weaseler

   *C. Proof surrogate

   D. Dysphemism

   E. None of the above

7. "A lawsuit is a machine which you go into as a pig and come out as a sausage" (adapted from Ambrose Bierce). What slanter is being used here?

   A. Weaseler

   *B. Persuasive comparison

   C. Downplayer

   D. Euphemism

   E. Proof surrogate

8. An ad that brings out pleasurable feelings in us as we watch it on television is thus giving us a good reason to buy that particular product or service.

   A. True

   *B. False

9. According to the text, most of the news in the newspapers and on television and radio is news that has been given to reporters, not news that has been dug up by a reporter's investigations.

   *A. True

   B. False

10. "That painting by Picasso is overpriced." What slanter is being used here?

    A. Loaded question

    B. Proof surrogate

    C. Stereotype

    D. Downplayer

   *E. No slanter

Chapter 5

1. A fallacy is any bad argument in which the reasons advanced for a claim fail to warrant its acceptance.

   *A. True

    B. False

2. Appeals to pity are always irrelevant.

    A. True

   *B. False

3. Several types of pseudoreasoning are used as smokescreens to draw the listener or reader away from the point at issue.

   *A. True

    B. False

4. There are some instances in which what people think to be true actually determines what is true.

   *A. True

    B. False

5. "Sure, driving after you've been drinking can get you into trouble with the law, but provided you're careful I don't think there's anything wrong with it. After all, everyone does it, right?" What kind of pseudoreasoning is being used here?

    A. Subjectivist fallacy

   *B. Appeal to common practice

    C. Appeal to pity

    D. Apple polishing

6. "Hey, Gert! Get a load of this: Reid thinks the L.A. Lakers will actually win the NBA Championship against the Chicago Bulls! Can you beat that?" What kind of pseudoreasoning is being used here?

   A. Appeal to belief

   B. Peer pressure

   *C. Horse laugh

   D. Appeal to pity

7. "Mr. Barnett, I'm here to discuss my grade, but before I do I'd like to compliment you on your choice of suspenders. I think they really give you a distinguished look! Gosh, I'm so proud just to be in your class!" What kind of pseudoreasoning is being used here?

   *A. Apple polishing

   B. Appeal to pity

   C. Peer pressure

   D. Two wrongs make a right

8. "There must be intelligent life on other planets; otherwise, human beings would be all alone in the vast reaches of space, and I just couldn't stand the loneliness!" What kind of pseudoreasoning is being used here?

   A. Appeal to pity

   B. Appeal to common practice

   C. Two wrongs make a right

   *D. Wishful thinking

   E. Scare tactics

9. "The Soviets have no reason to criticize the United States for producing the kind of pollution that leads to acid rain, because it was the Soviets, you remember, who polluted the world with radiation in the Chernobyl nuclear disaster." What kind of pseudoreasoning is being used here?

   A. Appeal to pity

   *B. Two wrongs make a right

   C. Peer pressure

   D. Appeal to belief

   E. Appeal to spite

10. "Ms. Soleil, this report says you are a poor typist. It looks as if the company will have to let you go."

"But don't you realize I have seven children to feed and an ex-husband who won't pay child support?"

"Hmmm. Well, on second thought, though you are still a poor typist, perhaps the company can find another position for you. Let me check with the training supervisor."

Was the personnel official buying into pseudoreasoning by offering another job to Ms. Soleil?

A. Yes, the personnel director was buying into "appeal to pity" pseudoreasoning.

*B. No, the personnel director was not buying into "appeal to pity" pseudoreasoning.

Chapter 6

1. Considerations about a person's credibility are irrelevant to the question of whether that person's premises establish his or her conclusion.

   *A. True

   B. False

2. Personal attack is an instance of ad hominem "reasoning."

   *A. True

   B. False

3. "If you experiment frequently with certain highly addictive drugs, the first thing you know you'll be seriously dependent on them." This is an example of slippery slope pseudoreasoning.

   A. True

   *B. False

4. "Why do I spend so much money on books? Well, if I didn't spend the money on books, I'd be an ignoramus—and I know which of those I prefer!" What kind of pseudoreasoning is being used here?

   *A. False dilemma

   B. Slippery slope

   C. Genetic fallacy

   D. Begging the question

5. "Of course Coach Pigslop would come out in favor of more money for athletics! Since he's the coach, he stands to benefit from bigger budgets!" What kind of pseudoreasoning does this passage use?

    A. False dilemma

    B. Straw man

    C. Begging the question

    *D. Circumstantial ad hominem

6. "If we vote in gun control, first thing you know some goon squad will begin confiscating all our guns!"

    *A. Slippery slope

    B. False dilemma

    C. Burden of proof

    D. Ad hominem

7. "Did you hear what Senator Dreul is arguing for? He wants an increase in the social security tax! What he really means is that he wants hard-working taxpayers to send in their entire paychecks so the government can decide how to spend the money. But taking away all our money violates the Constitution, and that means Senator Dreul's argument is no good!" What kind of pseudoreasoning is being used here?

    A. Ad hominem

    B. Begging the question

    *C. Straw man

    D. False dilemma

8. "When compared to paramedics, firefighters have a much faster response time to emergencies. The reasons for this are that firefighters have much more extensive in-the-field experience and are generally located within urban areas. In addition, paramedics have a much slower response time to emergencies." What kind of pseudoreasoning is being used here?

    A. Straw man

    *B. Begging the question

    C. Genetic fallacy

    D. Slippery slope

9. "Since what is these days called 'performance art' began as a joke, it follows that any requests for government grants for 'performance art' projects should be rejected as without value." What kind of pseudoreasoning is being used here?

    *A. Genetic fallacy

    B. Begging the question

    C. Slippery slope

    D. Straw man

10. Chen visits the doctor at the campus health center and is told that he is seriously overweight and must go on a diet. But Chen rejects this advice on the grounds that the doctor is also overweight and is not doing anything about it. If Chen is indulging in pseudoreasoning, what kind?

   A. Straw man

   B. Genetic fallacy

   C. Begging the question

   *D. Pseudorefutation

   E. No pseudoreasoning

Chapter 7

1. "The school cafeteria is closed because somebody set off a stink bomb inside." This passage is best interpreted as

   A. An argument

   *B. An explanation

   C. Neither an argument nor an explanation

2. "Critical-thinking textbooks contain many examples of explanations." This passage is best interpreted as

   A. An argument

   B. An explanation

   *C. Neither an argument nor an explanation

3. "Jo has a grade point average of 4.0—trust me on this, because I sneaked a peek at the school's computer, and that's what it said." This passage is best interpreted as

   *A. An argument

   B. An explanation

   C. Neither an argument nor an explanation

4. "The senator voted for the big defense appropriations bill because she did not want to anger her constituents, many of whom are employed by the military." This explanation is best interpreted as a

   A. Physical explanation

   *B. Behavioral explanation

   C. Functional explanation

5. "Why did the Senate vote on that military appropriations bill?" "The Senate's vote on appropriations bills is part of the money allocation process mandated by the U.S. Constitution." This passage is best interpreted as a

    A. Physical explanation

    B. Behavioral explanation

    *C. Functional explanation

6. "How did the senator's vote get registered? Pressure on the button on the senator's desk brought two electrical contacts together, completed a circuit, and registered her yes vote on the tote board." This passage is best interpreted as a

    *A. Physical explanation

    B. Behavioral explanation

    C. Functional explanation

7. "Ostriches cannot fly because they are not equipped to leave the ground under their own power." What is the problem with this explanation?

    A. It is not testable.

    B. It is not reliable.

    *C. It is circular.

    D. There is no problem with this explanation.

8. Explanatory comparisons are also called explanatory analogies.

    *A. True

    B. False

9. Carron explained that his ability to memorize the lines of the play came from long practice and from a newly awakened capacity to read the minds of the other actors. How might this explanation be criticized?

    A. It is circular.

    *B. It involves an unnecessary assumption.

    C. It makes use of an explanatory comparison.

    D. There is no problem with this explanation.

10. Explanations are designed primarily to provide reasons for believing *that* the thing being explained exists, happened, or is true.

    A. True

    *B. False

Chapter 8

1. The conclusion of one argument sometimes serves as a premise of a second argument.

   *A. True

   B. False

2. What is the conclusion of the following argument? "Blue whales, the largest mammals on earth, may be making a comeback. In August [1988], 11 of the 100-foot long whales were sighted in Norwegian waters by a team of researchers. The coast of Norway has never been safe haven for the blues; hunting by Norway and the Soviet Union eliminated them from these waters decades ago" (*Greenpeace* magazine).

   *A. Blue whales, the largest mammals on earth, may be making a comeback.

   B. In August 1988, a team of researchers sighted eleven of the 100-foot long whales in Norwegian waters.

   C. The coast of Norway has never been safe haven for the blues.

   D. Hunting by Norway and the Soviet Union eliminated the blue whales from Norwegian waters decades ago.

3. What is the conclusion of the following argument? "Gender is not the basis for determining who washes the dishes or mows the lawn because such chores are necessary to the entire family's well-being" (Gayle Kimball, *The 50-50 Marriage*).

   *A. Gender is not the basis for determining who washes the dishes or mows the lawn.

   B. Such chores are necessary to the entire family's well-being.

4. Consider the following argument: "Love is all you need, so don't wait for a good job before you get married. Money just produces hassles. Besides, if you're in love, you don't have to worry about whether you are compatible."

   A. The premises of the argument are dependent.

   *B. The premises of the argument are independent.

5. Consider the following argument: "Chinese green tea is exellent for your health. It contains antioxidants, and, in addition, it neutralizes carcinogens produced by heating meat."

   A. The premises of the argument are dependent.

   *B. The premises of the argument are independent.

6. If you have trouble identifying the conclusion in a passage, the reason could be that the passage is not an argument.

   *A. True

   B. False

7. The word "so" is often used in arguments as a premise indicator.

   A. True

   *B. False

8. All valid arguments are sound arguments.
   A. True
   *B. False

9. If you have trouble identifying the premises in a passage, the reason could be that the passage is nonargumentative persuasion.
   *A. True
   B. False

10. In an argument diagram, an arrow signifies:
   A. The relationship between independent premises.
   *B. The relationship between premises and conclusion.

Chapter 9

1. Translate the following into the appropriate standard-form categorical claim: "Only the gardener is allowed to use the back gate."
   A. Some gardeners are people allowed to use the back gate.
   B. All gardeners are people allowed to use the back gate.
   *C. All people allowed to use the back gate are people identical to the gardener.
   D. All people identical to the gardener are people allowed to use the back gate.

2. Translate the following into the appropriate standard-form categorical claim: "Whales are mammals."
   *A. All whales are mammals.
   B. Some whales are mammals.
   C. Some mammals are whales.

3. Translate the following into the appropriate standard-form categorical claim: "*Do the Right Thing* is the only movie Spike Lee directed."
   A. All movies identical to *Do the Right Thing* are movies directed by Spike Lee.
   *B. All movies directed by Spike Lee are movies identical to *Do the Right Thing*.
   C. Some movies directed by Spike Lee are movies identical to *Do the Right Thing*.

4. Translate the following into the appropriate standard-form categorical claim: "Janis jumps in fright whenever the doorbell rings."
   *A. All times the doorbell rings are times Janis jumps in fright.
   B. All times Janis jumps in fright are times the doorbell rings.
   C. All places the doorbell rings are places Janis jumps in fright.
   D. Some times when the doorbell rings are times Janis jumps in fright.

5. If "Some claims are false claims" is true, what are the truth values of the corresponding claims?

    A. A-claim is true, E-claim is false, O-claim is true.

    *B. A-claim is undetermined, E-claim is false, O-claim is undetermined.

    C. A-claim is false, E-claim is true, O-claim is undetermined.

    D. A-claim is false, E-claim is true, O-claim is false.

6. If "All ravens are black birds" is true, does it logically follow that "Some ravens are not black birds" is false?

    *A. Yes

    B. No

    C. Cannot be determined

7. If "All ravens are black birds" is true, does it logically follow that "All black birds are ravens" is true as well?

    A. Yes

    *B. No

    C. Cannot be determined

8. If "No ravens are black birds" is true, is it also true that "All ravens are non-black birds"?

    *A. Yes

    B. No

    C. Cannot be determined

9. A categorical syllogism may have two or three premises.

    A. True

    *B. False

10. Determine whether the following categorical syllogism is valid: "All mice are mammals. Some mice are not friendly creatures. Therefore, some mammals are not friendly creatures."

    *A. Valid

    B. Invalid

    C. Cannot be determined

Chapter 10

1. In the expression $P \rightarrow Q$, the first term is called the

    *A. Antecedent

    B. Consequent

2. What is the correct symbolization for "Michelle will go to the store, provided her piggy bank has enough cash in it"?

   A. P v M

   B. M → P

  *C. P → M

   D. P & M

3. In truth-functional logic, the word "unless" can be treated exactly as the word "or".

  *A. True

   B. False

4. Consider the following argument: "If Paul goes to the bank, then Queenie the dog will run after him. But Queenie the dog did not run after Paul. Therefore, Paul did not go to the bank."

  *A. Valid

   B. Invalid

   C. Cannot be determined

5. Consider the following argument: "If Paul goes to the bank, then Queenie the dog will run after him. But Paul did not go to the bank. Therefore, Queenie the dog did not run after him."

   A. Valid

  *B. Invalid

   C. Cannot be determined

6. The phrase "only if" introduces the consequent of a conditional.

  *A. True

   B. False

7. Symbolize the correct relationship between "There is fire present" (F) and "There is oxygen present" (O).

   A. O → F

  *B. F → O

   C. F v O

   D. F & O

8. According to DeMorgan's Laws, the expression ~(P & Q) is equivalent to (has the same truth table as) which of the following?

   A. (~P & ~Q)

   B. (~P v Q)

  *C. (~P v ~Q)

9. The antecedent of a conditional claim is also called

   A. The necessary condition

   *B. The sufficient condition

10. After you construct a truth table for an argument, you notice a row in which all the premises have the truth value of T and the conclusion has the truth value of F. What do you know about the argument?

    A. It is valid.

    *B. It is invalid.

    C. Its validity cannot be determined.

Chapter 11

1. An invalid argument can nevertheless offer strong support for its conclusion.

   *A. True

   B. False

2. Consider the following inductive analogical argument: "Over the past twenty years, I've owned three Burberry brand raincoats [nos. 1, 2, and 3], all of which have been warm, comfortable, and stylish. I'm about to buy another Burberry brand raincoat [no. 4]. It too will be warm, comfortable, and stylish." What is the target?

   A. Raincoats 1, 2, and 3

   *B. Raincoat 4

3. In the raincoat argument, what is the sample?

   *A. Raincoats 1, 2, and 3

   B. Raincoat 4

4. In analogical arguments, with regard to a feature that, to our knowledge, the target may or may not have, the greater the diversity within the sample, the _____ the argument.

   *A. stronger

   B. weaker

   C. more valid

   D. less valid

5. "Morker may have won the Teacher of the Year award, but that just means they didn't look very hard for a winner. I know a couple of people who work in Morker's department, and they say he's a real pain to work with. I'd sooner trust my friends than some awards committee." Is there a fallacy here?

   A. Fallacy of biased generalization

   *B. Fallacy of anecdotal evidence

   C. No fallacy

6. "I know I'm a good photographer, but the pictures we got back from our first roll of that new Kodak film were simply superb. The response of the film was fantastic. I'll bet the next roll we use will be good stuff, too." Is there a fallacy here?

   A. Fallacy of hasty generalization

   B. Fallacy of biased generalization

   *C. No fallacy

7. "Did you hear about those three college kids who robbed that old man's liquor store on Main Street? College kids are nothin' but a bunch of punks these days." Is there a fallacy here?

   *A. Fallacy of hasty generalization

   B. Fallacy of biased generalization

   C. No fallacy

8. Zia has taken seven courses at Harvard, and so far she has a grade average of C. All the courses she has taken have been in philosophy and religious studies. She's thinking of enrolling in another course next term, and she expects to make at least a C in whatever subject she takes. Would her analogical argument be stronger, weaker, or unaffected if her previous seven courses had been in four different subjects rather than two?

   *A. Stronger

   B. Weaker

   C. Unaffected

9. Would Zia's argument be stronger, weaker, or unaffected if the new course were in philosophy?

   *A. Stronger

   B. Weaker

   C. Unaffected

10. Suppose that when Zia took the previous courses she had done all her studying alone because she didn't know any of the other students at Harvard, but that now she knows several students and plans to study with them when she takes her next course. Would her argument be stronger, weaker, or unaffected by this new information?

    A. Stronger

    *B. Weaker

    C. Unaffected

Chapter 12

1. Just an hour after she started to fish for the first time, Leia reeled in a twelve-pound bass. When she was asked what her secret was, she pulled a rabbit's foot from her tackle box and said, "I think this had a lot to do with it." What kind of causal pattern is Leia using?

   A. X is the difference

   B. X is the common thread

   *C. Post hoc

   D. No causal relationship claimed

2. Joby tried for an hour to get his computer to run correctly. Finally, in desperation, he grabbed the instruction book and started following along step by step. Step 3 told him to turn on the switch in back of the monitor. He did, and the computer sprang to life. "Eureka! That's it!" he said. What causal pattern was present in this instance?

   *A. X is the difference

   B. X is the common thread

   C. Post hoc

   D. No causal relationship claimed

3. "On Saturday after I bowled, my back ached; it ached again the next Wednesday after another game of bowling. Same story on Friday night. If I want to stop my backache, I may have to give up bowling." What is the causal pattern here?

   A. X is the difference

   *B. X is the common thread

   C. Post hoc

   D. No causal relationship claimed

4. "Did you hear about the old European folk tale that says that if two roosters crow in unison on the morning of August 1, the next winter will be severe, and that if no rooster crows that morning, the winter will be mild?" What causal pattern is in evidence?

   A. X is the difference

   *B. X is the common thread (although it is unknown what X is)

   C. Post hoc

   D. No causal relationship claimed

5. "First my engine goes on the blink, and then the lights in my house go out. There must be a strong magnetic disturbance nearby." What fallacy is indicated here?

   A. Fallacy of reversed causation

   B. Fallacy of ignoring a common cause

   *C. Fallacy of assuming a common cause

   D. Post hoc

6. The claim "Secondary smoke causes cancer in people," if true, implies that the majority of individuals exposed to secondary smoke will contract cancer.

   A. True

   *B. False

7. In an experimental cause-to-effect study, the members of the experimental group are exposed to the suspected causal agent by the investigators.

   *A. True

   B. False

8. In a nonexperimental effect-to-cause study, some of the members of the control group show the effect of the cause being investigated.

   A. True

   *B. False

9. Kretz is hired by a cosmetics company to see whether a new product, Sunscram, will prevent sunburn on fair-skinned people. He runs an ad in the newspaper inviting fair-skinned people to participate and gets fifty respondents, who participate in the sunburn project. Half of the respondents (group A) rub Sunscram on a preselected shoulder area. The other half (group B) applies on the same shoulder area a mixture of lemon juice and water. Both groups are exposed to measured doses of sunshine over a period of two weeks. At the end of the time, Kretz compares the appropriate areas of each volunteer's shoulder and notes the result. What type of argument or pattern of reasoning has Kretz employed?

   *A. Controlled cause-to-effect experiment

   B. Nonexperimental cause-to-effect study

   C. Nonexperimental effect-to-cause study

10. Referring to Kretz's project, which group was the control group?

   A. Group A

   *B. Group B

   C. Neither (the set-up was not an experiment)

Chapter 13

1. The wrong instruction book came with Alyn's new computer.

   *A. Descriptive claim

   B. Prescriptive claim

2. The computer company ought not to have sent Alyn the wrong set of instructions.

   A. Descriptive claim

   *B. Prescriptive claim

3. Alyn used the improper method to hook up the new computer, and as a result the data on several disks were lost.

   *A. Descriptive claim

   B. Prescriptive claim

4. Should Alyn wish to recover lost computer data, an expensive diagnostic program will have to be purchased.

   *A. Descriptive claim

   B. Prescriptive claim

5. Society X passes a law requiring each adult citizen to contribute five dollars each year to the Red Cross. Those who govern Society X justify the new law by saying that the good produced from such mandatory "contributions" far outweighs any good that might be produced if citizens gave on a voluntary—and likely haphazard—basis. What is the moral position taken by Society X called?

   A. Duty theory

   *B. Utilitarianism

   C. Virtue ethics

6. The natural law school of thought says that

   A. It is "natural" for societies to make laws for their citizens.

   *B. Law itself is independent of particular social conventions.

   C. Law itself comes into being through human creation.

   D. Laws ought to conform to the ways human beings "naturally" behave.

7. Under the doctrine of *stare decisis,* precedent is absolutely binding.

   A. True

   *B. False

8. The aesthetic principle that objects are aesthetically valuable if they have the capacity to produce pleasure in those who experience them is compatible with the aesthetic principle that there can be no reasoned argument which concludes that objects are aesthetically valuable.

   A. True

  *B. False

9. Which aesthetic principle below might be called aesthetic hedonism?

   A. Objects are aesthetically valuable if they have the capacity to convey meaning or to teach general truths.

   B. Objects are aesthetically valuable if they have the capacity to help bring about social or political change.

  *C. Objects are aesthetically valuable if they have the capacity to produce pleasure in those who experience or appreciate them.

   D. Objects are aesthetically valuable if they possess a special aesthetic property or exhibit a special aesthetic form.

10. Suppose an art critic adhered to the aesthetic principle that objects are aesthetically valuable if they have the capacity to convey values or belief central to the cultures or traditions in which they originate, or if they are important to the artists who made them. Would John Milton's religious views be relevant to the critic's judgment of *Paradise Lost*?

  *A. Yes

   B. No

   C. Impossible to tell

Chapter 1
What Is Critical Thinking?

Students like to know what they'll be doing in a course, so we tell them our objective straight off: to develop their ability to determine whether or not to accept the assorted assertions, sales pitches, proposals, ideas, theories, pleas, remarks, observations, comments, and other sorts of claims they'll be confronted with throughout their waking lives. Some of these claims come with supporting reasons attached and some don't, but even those that don't, or that come with poor supporting reasons, may still be worth accepting. What's important, we stress, is whether there *are* good reasons for accepting a claim, regardless of whether those reasons are explicitly given.

Students often appear remarkably naive about language. We find it interesting that if we ask, "True or false: Claims can serve many purposes, but only one purpose at a time," a substantial minority of students will answer "true." They'll do this despite their obvious ability to recognize irony, double meanings, and subtle digs in their own conversations as well as the frequent multipurposeful use of language in advertising. Part of the problem may be that these students see an academic classroom as a world different from the one of their everyday lives, so they give the responses they think the former requires rather than the one they know from the latter to be correct. The box on the uses of claims may help reinforce the idea that it *is* their everyday world that this material is about.

We've revised the section on facts and opinions a little. The main thing to be careful about now is probably the distinction between something that is a *matter of fact* (i.e., a factual issue) and something that is simply a *fact* (i.e., simply true). If the phrase "matter of fact" simply refuses to operate independently of the idea of somethings being (in fact) true, then we'll have to change the phrasing a little the next time around.

The distinction between supported claims—that is, arguments—and unsupported claims is easy enough for students to grasp. In practice, though, they sometimes have difficulty telling whether a passage is or contains an argument. A quick reference to the "indicator" boxes in Chapter 8 can be helpful, but these telltale signs so often don't appear in arguments that they can't be depended on.

We continue to think that the concept of an issue is crucial to students; they sometimes have trouble determining what a passage is about. They'll often pick up on the simplest or most concrete notion in a paragraph just because it's the easiest to understand and articulate. Late twentieth-century political rhetoric shows us what speakers think they can get away with in confusing, conflating, and evading issues. We reckon people will have to think a lot more critically than they are now before the politicians stop getting away with it.

Lecture/Discussion Suggestions

Most students come into a critical thinking course with an overly simple view of both factual and theoretical matters. Were they to learn nothing else, they're likely to learn that things are often more complicated than they previously thought. We think this is good, since it can make them more cautious in the future—and, we hope, more thoughtful.

One way to convince students right off that there's more than meets the untutored eye is to bring up a clutch of distinctions and problems surrounding the nature of claims. Although claims are the building blocks for practically everything the text covers, the book does not examine the notion beyond stipulating that claims are the bearers of truth values. The following annotated list provides a skeleton for further discussion of the topic.

• *Types and tokens.* If you write, say, "I don't have any money" on the chalkboard twice and then ask a class how many sentences you've written, students will ordinarily divide about evenly into those who say you've written one and those who say you've written two. Aside from producing some instant controversy, this little exercise enables you to point out the type/token distinction in a natural way: You've written two tokens of the same type; that is, you've produced two entities with physical sizes and shapes (or pitches and volumes, if spoken aloud, although spoken examples can be trickier) and locations in space and time—characteristics that physical objects in general have. The two arrangements of chalk on the board are sentence *tokens.* Both sentence tokens, however, have the same words and arrangements—they both fit a common description. What the two have in common is being of the same *type.* (We might characterize the type in this way: The word "I," followed by the word "don't," followed by the word "have," and so on.) Types are clearly abstract in a way that tokens are not.

Although things are already complicated enough, bright students sometimes ask whether a printed sentence token is of the same type as one written cursively. The answer depends on the description of the tokens of that type. In the long run, we're forced to a hierarchy of types. An example using half dollars illustrates this idea nicely: At the top of the hierarchy is the type *half dollar,* followed by a layer of subtypes: *1989 half dollar, 1962 half dollar,* and so on. A given token, the half dollar in your pocket, is a token of one of these subtypes, and every token of one of these subtypes is a token of each type above it.

It would be nice if we could stop here and say that it is sentence types—or at least types of declarative independent clauses—that bear truth values. But we can't, because many such types are token-reflexive; for example, when I say I'm broke and you utter the same words, we're producing two tokens of the same type, yet what I say might be true while what you say is false. We have to look further to identify just what kind of thing carries truth values.

• *Propositions, sentences, and claims.* Another interesting reaction is nearly automatic if you say, "Je n'ai pas d'argent," "Ich habe kein Geld," "No tengo dinero," and "I don't have any money," then ask the class how many things you've said. They'll generally reply, "You've said the *same thing* in several different ways." Since our sentences are of different languages, they are clearly of different types; noticing that they nevertheless say the same thing is the first step in understanding the difference between a *sentence* (qua a particular group of words) and a *proposition,* which is an abstract and rather mysterious kind of thing invented by philosophers to do a certain job—namely, to bear truth values. If we solve one problem by stipulating that propositions are whatever it is that is true or false in what we say (or "underlying" our words, or "hiding behind" them, or whatever), we invent another problem: We cannot produce a direct example of a proposition. When we attempt to give an example of one, we always produce a sentence instead.

Clearly, in order to avoid more confusion than the problems deserve—especially in a course where there's so much more to do—the text has to run roughshod over these distinctions, or it would never get past them. You'll probably notice that we use the word "claim" sometimes in the way we might use "proposition" and sometimes in the way we might use "sentence" (either type or token). For example, see Chapter 2, in which we say that rewriting the claim is the only way to eliminate syntactical ambiguity.

• *Use/mention.* Finally, we've had success in discussing the use/mention distinction at the beginning of a course.* Most students think that quotation marks are reserved for direct quotations and, occasionally, to express irony (He "borrowed" my car). The paradigmatic use of quotation marks, the one from which the direct quotation usage is derived, is to mark a word or group of words that is being *mentioned* rather than *used.* Consider:

Alexander is twelve years old.

This is a sentence about a person. The name that occurs at the beginning of the sentence is *used* to mention that person. But consider this sentence:

"Alexander" is spelled with seven letters, two of which occur twice.

The sentence begins with a reference not to a person but to a name—to the word "Alexander." Hence it is the *word* that is being mentioned. (The sentence would make no sense if it were construed to be about a person.) In short, we *use* words in combination with quotation marks (sometimes called "quotation names") to *mention* whatever it is that falls between the quotation marks.

If nothing else, learning about the distinction enables students to see that remarks such as

Drink "Coke"

are exhortations to do the impossible—in this case, to drink a word.

To see whether students understand the use/mention distinction, you can ask them to put quotation marks in the proper places in a sentence like this:

Richard's dog is named Cy, but Brooke calls him
Sai, and sometimes Richard refers to Cy as Sigh.

Correct placement of quotation marks should produce this:

Richard's dog is named "Cy," but Brooke calls him
"Sai," and sometimes Richard refers to Cy as "Sigh."

Technically, the commas and periods should be *outside* the quotation marks, since they are not part of the expressions being mentioned. But we are overwhelmed by stylistic convention in this matter. Maybe someday whoever dictates such rules will get it right.

*A concise treatment of the use/mention distinction is found, among other places, in Benson Mates's *Elementary Logic,* 2d ed. (Oxford: Oxford University Press, 1968).

Exercises Unanswered in the Text

Exercise 1-1

2. Rejecting it or suspending judgment about it; we can accept or reject a claim with varying degrees of confidence.

3. Yes, there are many such situations. This is especially true of claims about what we should do.

5. No. There may be reasons for accepting it that have not yet come to light. We should suspend judgment.

6. No; see the answer to question 5.

7. Simply that somebody believes it.

8. That it is true, or that there is very good evidence or justification for it.

10. If Arnold is believed to be knowledgeable on the subject, then yes, Linda has given a reason; otherwise, she has not.

11. False

13. A premise is a claim offered in support of some other claim. Premises are supposed to provide reasons for believing conclusions.

14. An argument is a set of claims, one of which is supposed to be supported by the others.

15. Only people who are mature enough to know when to quit should be allowed to drink alcoholic beverages. Sixteen-year-olds are not that mature. So, they should not be allowed to drink.

17. Yes

18. Influencing somebody's attitude toward something; influencing somebody's behavior.

19. Arguments are designed to settle issues, or at least to contribute to their settlement. The conclusion of an argument answers the question posed by an issue. "Jack is small; therefore, he should not go out for football," for example, is an argument designed to settle the issue of whether Jack should go out for football.

Exercise 1-2

2. c

3. b

4. c

5. b

6. a

7. c

Exercise 1-3

3. Matter of fact

5. Not a matter of fact

6. Not a matter of fact, unless determinations of what is expensive are agreed on

8. Matter of fact

9. Matter of fact

11. Not a matter of fact

12. This is probably about a matter of fact, since actual scores on the same or similar golf courses can be compared to determine who was better.

14. This is controversial in the extreme. Some argue that no claims about what is moral or not moral are about matters of fact; others argue quite the contrary. How one answers this question is really a determination of what kind of theory one accepts about moral claims.

15. Matter of fact

Exercise 1-4

2. Argument

3. Argument

5. Argument

6. No argument

8. Argument

9. Argument

11. No argument

12. No argument

14. Argument

15. No argument

17. No argument

18. Argument

19. Argument, although a fuzzy one

Exercise 1-5

2. Whether we should concentrate our crime-fighting efforts on enforcement

3. Whether there will be different results in the next few years on cases dealing with women's issues

5. Whether Algernon's taking Professor Bubacz's class will get him flunked out

6. This sort of thing can be done two ways: The *real* issue is whether sales taxes hit poor people harder than they hit rich people. But that issue is cast in terms of whether it is dumb to *say* so. As you like it.

8. Whether laws in states that do not allow distribution of sterile needles should be changed

9. Whether it is usually right to suspend judgment unless one is absolutely certain

Exercise 1-6

2. The issue for both Believer and Skeptic is whether the widespread belief in ghosts could be mistaken. The ultimate issue for Believer is whether ghosts exist. It is probable—but less certain—that this is the issue for Skeptic, too. For all we know from this passage, Skeptic might believe in ghosts; what we know for certain is only that Skeptic does not accept the stated argument for ghosts.

3. The issue for both Mr. and Mrs. Sprat is whether they should cut down on their red meat.

4. The issues are very different: Heedless argues one side of the issue, whether isolationists are pathetic (i.e., badly wrong); Cautious is interested in whether protracted, expensive wars abroad are in America's best interests. There's another potential issue that we'd expect these two to disagree about: whether the conflict they presumably have in mind *is* or *would be* a protracted, expensive one.

5. For both speakers, the issue is whether summer is the best season.

6. For both, the issue is whether the explanation for the speedometer's not working is the cable's being broken.

10. These two are discussing the same issue: whether the United States should have troops stationed widely abroad and, it would be reasonable to add, whether the United States should be willing to engage in military adventures abroad.

Exercise 1-7

2. Critic is addressing the issue of whether it's right to sell junk bonds without emphasizing the risks involved. Entrepreneur is missing the point entirely. Entrepreneur is probably doing it just to avoid the issue (or because he is a jerk).

4. One Guy's issue is whether the prices for the machines are too high; Another's issue is whether One Guy can easily afford one of them. Quite different issues.

Chapter 1 Test Question/Exercise Banks

Bank 1-1

For each of the following claims, decide whether it states a matter of fact or a matter of opinion. In cases where it may be difficult to decide, try to identify the source of the problem.

1. Meat grilled over hickory coals tastes better than meat grilled over mesquite.

   Opinion

2. I read in the newspaper that meat grilled over hickory coals tastes better than meat grilled over mesquite.

   Fact (The fact, of course, is only that the person read it in the newspaper—although Parker does insist that hickory beats mesquite hands down.)

3. The air in Cleveland smells better than it did five years ago.

   Opinion

4. There's less hydrocarbon in the air in Cleveland than there was five years ago.

   Fact

5. The air in Cleveland is lower in hydrocarbons because there is less automobile emission than there was five years ago.

   Fact

6. There is less automobile emission in Cleveland than there was five years ago because of the Clean Air Bill passed five years ago.

   Fact (Some will argue about this because of the difficulty of identifying the cause of lowered emissions. Nevertheless, either the change resulted from the Clean Air Bill, or it didn't. Intelligent opinions on this issue may differ, but that doesn't make it just a matter of opinion.)

7. Steven Spielberg's latest movie is his best so far.

   Opinion

8. Siskel and Ebert, the movie critics, gave Steven Spielberg's latest movie two "thumbs up," which is the best rating they give.

   Fact

9. Siskel and Ebert, the movie critics, gave Steven Spielberg's latest movie a rave review.

   Opinion (It seems to us that it's a matter of opinion where you draw the line between a good *review and a* rave *review.)*

10. I could live quite comfortably in this city on forty thousand dollars a year.

    Fact (We think that whether a given mode or standard of living counts as "comfortable" is a matter of opinion, but, we believe, whether the speaker could actually achieve it on forty thousand is a matter of fact.)

11. Theater popcorn contains more than the Recommended Daily Allowance of saturated fat.

    Fact

12. Whether theater popcorn contains more than the Recommended Daily Allowance of saturated fat is a matter of opinion.

    Whether theater popcorn contains more than the Recommended Daily Allowance of saturated fat is a matter of opinion is a matter of fact. You can probably predict the final grade a given student will earn on the basis of whether he or she understands this item.

Bank 1-2

Determine whether each of the following passages is (or contains) an argument.

13. Will a beverage begin to cool more quickly in the freezer or in the regular part of the refrigerator? Well, of *course* it'll cool faster in the freezer! There are lots of people who don't understand anything at all about physics and who think things may begin to cool faster in the fridge. But they're sadly mistaken.

    Clearly, our speaker has an opinion on the subject, but no argument is given.

14. It's true that you can use your television set to tell when a tornado is approaching. The reason is that tornadoes make an electrical disturbance in the 55 megahertz range, which is close to the band assigned to channel 2. If you know how to do it, you can get your set to pick up the current given off by the twister. So your television set can be your warning device that tells you when to dive for the cellar.
    —Adapted from Cecil Adams, *The Straight Dope*

    This passage might be taken as an explanation (see Chapter 7), but it is also an argument, since it is clearly designed to convince us that its main point is correct.

15. Some of these guys that do Elvis Presley imitations actually pay more for their outfits than Elvis paid for his! Anybody who would spend thousands just so he can spend a few minutes not fooling anybody into thinking he's Elvis is nuts.

No argument

16. "The argument advanced at a recent government hearing—that because we will not be dependent on plutonium for more than a few hundred years it 'will not be an important problem indefinitely'—entirely misses the point. Though we may rely on plutonium for only a relatively brief period, the plutonium produced during that period may be with us indefinitely, and it may jeopardize the lives of many times the number of generations that profit from its use."
   —Ronald M. Green, "International Justice and Environmental Responsibility"

Argument

17. You'd better not pet that dog. She looks friendly, but she's been known to bite.

Argument

18. Computers will never be able to converse intelligently through speech. A simple example proves that this is so. The sentences "How do you recognize speech?" and "How do you wreck a nice beach?" sound just the same when they are spoken, but they mean something different. A computer could not distinguish the two.

Argument

19. It is obvious why some men have trouble understanding why women become upset over pornography. Pornography depicts women as servants or slaves, and men cannot conceive of themselves in this role.

Argument

20. I don't care how well Thompson played last week. If he misses practice one more time, he's not going to play in the tournament, and that's that.

No argument

21. Except maybe for finance and business law, schools of business really don't have very much of their own subject matter to teach to students. All the rest is really mathematics, psychology, English, speech, and other standard subjects that business schools call by other names.

Argument

22. Right now there are as many as half a million military-style assault guns in the hands of private citizens in the United States. These small, light, easy to handle weapons are exemplified by the Israeli UZI, the American MAC-10 and AR-15, the KG-99. All of these are sophisticated weapons manufactured for the single purpose of killing human beings in large numbers very quickly.

No argument

23. "Gene splicing is the most awesome and powerful skill acquired by man since the splitting of the atom. If pursued humanistically, its potential to serve humanity is enormous. We will use it to synthesize expensive natural products—interferon, substances such as insulin, and human endorphins that serve as natural painkillers. We will be able to create a second 'green revolution' in agriculture to produce new high-yield, disease-resistant, self-fertilizing crops. Gene splicing has the potential to synthesize new substances we can substitute for oil, coal, and other raw materials—keys to a self-sustaining society."
—John Naisbitt, *Megatrends*

Argument

24. "It is better to be a human being dissatisfied than a pig satisfied; better to be Socrates dissatisfied than a fool satisfied. And if the fool, or the pig, are of a different opinion, it is because they only know their own side of the question."
—John Stuart Mill, *Utilitarianism*

No argument

25. "The personal computer revolution is marked by accidental discoveries. The entire market for these things was a big surprise to all the pioneers who put simple ads in hobbyist magazines and were stunned by an onslaught of eager customers."
—John C. Dvorak

No argument

26. "Recent reports coming out of central and east Africa confirm that approximately ten percent of the population there is now infected with the AIDS virus, and that in time fully one-half will have it. We can expect similar figures in the United States if no more is done than is currently planned. Given the calamitous potential of such an epidemic, the current administration's refusal to recognize the need for massive increases in AIDS research is incredible. That the administration insists on seeing the disease as a problem for small segments of the population—and as something like divine punishment for homosexuals—is an outrage."
—Editorial, the Manchester *Sentinel-Record*

Argument

27. "If American business is to regain an advantageous position in the international marketplace, it must recreate a climate of flexibility and entrepreneurship. Unfortunately, the trend is to seek personal success not through entrepreneurship but through professionalism, as a continued climb in the number of advanced degrees in business and law confirms. If this tendency to seek personal security and prestige by joining the ranks of the professionally comfortable continues, the real winners will be America's overseas competitors."
—Irving Greenberg

Argument

28. Some would prefer to say that every human being is both a body and a mind. Bodies are in space and subject to the mechanical laws that govern all other bodies in space. But minds are not in space, nor are their operations subject to mechanical laws. Bodily processes and states can be inspected by external observers, but the workings of one mind are not witnessable by other observers. And so a person lives through two collateral histories; but the actual transactions between the episodes of the private history and those of the public history remain mysterious, since by definition they can belong to neither series.
   —Adapted from Gilbert Ryle, *The Concept of Mind*

   Argument

29. "[Lionel L.] Lewis discovered that, in recommendations of merit written by administrators and faculty themselves, although they put much emphasis (two-thirds) upon student related activities—teaching, advising, course planning, and popularity—no one argues from any supporting evidence other than, 'Everyone knows.'"
   —David A. Downes, "The Merit Muddle in the University"

   No argument

30. "[Television evangelist Pat] Robertson made a plausible [presidential] candidate. The son of a former senator from Virginia, he graduated Phi Beta Kappa from Washington and Lee, has a law degree from Yale, is a Marine veteran, a former Golden Gloves boxer and a shrewd entrepreneur. His cable-TV network is second only to Ted Turner's, reaching more than 30 million homes."
   —*Newsweek*

   Argument

31. "The main danger of war, even of a war fought with conventional weapons, lies in its unpredictability."
   —Anatoly Gromyko, "Security for All in the Nuclear Age," in *Breakthrough*

   No argument

32. "The recent failure of a Drake University student to halt his former girlfriend's plan for an abortion focuses light on a seldom considered situation: While a woman's right to an abortion should not be weakened, the idea of 'fathers' rights' raised in this case should be discussed."
   —The *Daily Iowan*

   No argument

33. "Today, there is strong evidence—not only in theory but in practice—that families who try to protect dying children from knowing they're dying rarely serve the child's best interests. This conspiracy of silence, however well-meaning, often puts nurses, relatives, and others who spend the most time with the patient, especially in their lonely moments, on the spot."
   —Thomas Scully and Celia Scully, *Playing God: The New World of Medical Choices*

   Argument

34. The president has the morals of an alley cat, his critics say. Shows you what they know. He'll still be reelected.

No argument

35. "The Federal Reserve Board is normally the Stealth bomber of government agencies, zooming in without warning to raise or lower interest rates, and confirming weeks later what action was taken. But last Friday, in an extraordinary pre-emptive strike against a possible surge of inflation, the Federal Reserve Chairman declared that the central bank had raised short-term rates that very day."

No argument

Bank 1-3

Which speakers give arguments for their positions?

36. LARRY: Before we go to Hawaii, let's go to a tanning salon and get a tan. Then we won't look like we just got off the plane, plus we won't get sunburned while we're over there.
    LAURIE: I don't know . . . I read that those places can be dangerous. And did you ever check out how much they cost? Let's let it go.

Larry and Laurie are both giving arguments.

37. SHE: When you think about it, there's every reason why women soldiers shouldn't serve in combat.
    HE: Well, I don't think anyone should have to serve in combat. I wouldn't make anyone serve who doesn't want to.

Neither speaker is giving an argument.

38. STUDENT A: My family is very conservative. I don't think they'd like it if they found out that I was sharing an apartment with two males.
    STUDENT B: But sooner or later you have to start living your own life.

Both A and B are giving arguments. B is arguing for an unstated claim: You should share the apartment with the two males despite what your family would like.

39. INSURANCE EXEC: Insurance costs so much because accident victims hire you lawyers to take us insurers to court and soak us for all we're worth. There should be limits on the amounts insurance companies may be required to pay out on claims.
    ATTORNEY: Limits? Doesn't sound like a good idea to me. What if someone's medical expenses exceed those limits? Do we just say, "Sorry, Charlie"?

Only Attorney is giving an argument.

40. REPUBLICAN: If taxes absolutely must be raised, raise the sales tax. Raising taxes on corporations or income taxes just drives businesses out of state, and that's bad for the economy. The net result is less tax revenue for government.
DEMOCRAT: If you raise the sales tax, people buy less, and that's even worse for the economy. Besides, the sales tax hits poor people the hardest, and they are the ones who least can afford a tax hike.

Both parties are giving arguments.

41. FIRST CITIZEN: There has been a lot of talk in favor of having civilian police-review boards monitor law enforcement activities. That's better than letting internal-affairs units try to do that job.
SECOND CITIZEN: Right. The ethics of law enforcers is as important as the ethics of lawmakers. Letting the police police themselves is like having the foxes guard the henhouse.

Only Second Citizen is giving an argument.

42. MOTHER: If you are looking for a wise investment, try real estate. The price of housing has always risen faster than the rate of inflation.
DAUGHTER: Maybe, but I'm skeptical. What's risen faster than the rate of inflation is the cost of land, not the cost of the structures put on it. Since the population isn't growing and the demand for land is declining, real estate may not be such a great investment any more.

Both parties are giving arguments.

43. FATHER: The governor should reduce government spending before he starts increasing taxes. Taxes just reduce our incomes, and there is plenty of waste in government. For example, a fire department doesn't need a chief, an assistant chief, and a captain. All it needs is one administrator and however many firefighters.
SON: Who takes charge if the administrator is sick or injured?

Both parties are giving arguments. Son is arguing against the claim that a fire department needs only one administrator.

44. TERRY: You don't need to spend a lot of money on a home stereo system. Just buy a good car stereo. They're just as good as home stereos, and they're cheaper. All you need is an AC to DC power converter, and you're in business.
LARRY: Fine, except who says a car stereo is cheaper? Car speakers cost more than home speakers. Also, it isn't exactly cheap to replace your car system if it gets stolen, as often happens.

Both parties are giving arguments.

45. WORRIED ATHLETIC SUPPORTER: I'm particularly concerned with the proposed cuts in the university athletic program. If something has to be cut, let's start with something like dance or basketweaving.
UNWORRIED ATHLETIC SUPPORTER: Oh, don't worry. The university isn't going to kill its cash cow. A strong athletic program is good publicity and brings in lots of contributions. The trustees aren't going to let anything happen to a first-rate program like ours.

Only the second party is giving an argument.

37

46. FIRST MANAGER: I think it is time to change our policy on return items. From now on, let's just give customers their money back, no questions asked.
SECOND MANAGER: Frankly, I don't think that will be such a good policy. Why, just last week you yourself said we should ask people why they want to return things.

Neither party gives an argument.

Bank 1-4

Identify which claims, if any, support has been given for, and state in your own words the reasons that have been offered for these claims. (The same directions may also be applied to the items in the preceding bank.)

47. "For about $200 a ticket you can take a breathtaking flight through the Grand Canyon by helicopter. Fine, unless you are one of the two million people who visit the canyon each year on the ground. For these millions, the pleasures of the canyon's solitude is destroyed by the almost uninterrupted noise from the air. That fact in itself demonstrates that air traffic in the canyon must now be banned—or at least heavily regulated. If the enjoyment of those on the canyon's floor is not enough reason for banning air traffic, then this is: the vibrations may destroy Indian ruins and the noise may drive the peregrine falcon and bighorn sheep out of their normal habitat in the canyon."
—Letter to the editor, *Tri-Counties Observer*

48. "So Rambo has stormed the country and now Coleco Industries, Inc., is trying to capitalize on the fact and has announced that it plans to market an 'action' figure modeled after Rambo in time for the Christmas season. This is an outrage. It glorifies neo-Neanderthal perspectives on war and is a flagrant disregard for the concerns of parents who wish to transmit to their children thoughtful and civilized approaches to conflict-resolution."
—Letter to the editor, *Gulf Coast Social Democrat*

49. "The arrogance of some State Department and U.S. Information Agency employees who took luxury cruises at government expense is shameful.
"Instead of flying by economy class to and from their overseas assignments, some traveled on the *Queen Elizabeth* or other cruise ships. Costs of the ocean voyages averaged $6,084, nearly four times the average airline cost of $1,665.
"One family of four billed the government $21,956 for a 26-day voyage along the eastern coast of South America. A couple were paid $13,761 for a 24-day trip from Bangkok to Honolulu. One official sent in a bill for $12,270 for a Mississippi River cruise on the *Delta Queen.*
"That's not all. The time spent on the cruises was considered by the department to be duty—not vacation.
"General Accounting Office investigators said they were told by foreign service officers that ocean travel was considered 'a fringe benefit.'
"If that is the case, the fringes are due for a good trimming."
—*Omaha World-Herald*

50. "The California State University trustees showed considerable foresight in their recent unanimous decision to strengthen the system's admission standards. . . .

"Public high school curricula deteriorated to such a degree throughout the state during the last two decades that English literature included courses in science-fiction and detective stories.

"That's not all. Social studies courses often were reduced to consciousness-raising sessions complete with rock music and feature films. Foreign-language requirements were abandoned, along with several advanced courses in science and math.

"And students could generally earn credits for working after school. . . ."

"[The new standards are] certain to raise the level of education among would-be college students. And that has to be a good thing."
—Chico (Calif.) *Enterprise-Record*

51. "I don't know whether to be amused or annoyed. The U.S. government spends millions of dollars rounding up herb farmers. Ridiculous! Deaths from alcohol abuse are overwhelming. Surely this is a bigger problem. I doubt even a single death from smoking pot and driving has been reported. And the idea that smoking pot leads to heroin is nonsense. Anyone who is going to become an addict will do so regardless of what they have around."
—Letter to the editor, *Glenn County Today*

52. Trout do feed on mosquito larvae, but they seldom feed on adult mosquitoes. So it is not likely that fish take an imitation mosquito because they are fooled into thinking it is a real one. Most likely they take the mosquito fly for a midge or a gray caddis.
—Adapted from Jack Dennis, *Western Trout Fly Tying Manual*

53. "The breaking of secret codes (cryptoanalysis) provides an example of inductive reasoning closely resembling the inductive reasoning scientists carry out. However, crypto-analysis can be carried out using pen and paper, needing no laboratories. In addition, even simple forms of cryptoanalysis can be quite intriguing. Simple forms of cryptoanalysis can therefore be very useful as classroom examples of inductive reasoning."
—*CT News*

54. "Flamenco and the *Fiesta* (spectacle of bullfighting) are deeply related. This connection is undeniable, and vital for an understanding of either. Both stem basically from the common people, and they stir the same basic emotions and passions. Both are given flashes of erratic genius by gypsies, and a sense of indomitable steadiness and responsibility by the Andalusians. And they have in common another important factor: they are the two most probable ways that the commoner can break out of his social and economic level."
—Donn Pohren, *The Art of Flamenco*

55. "What is the best move to begin a game [of chess]? At one time the masters began automatically with 1 P-K4; then they switched to 1 P-Q4. Paul Morphy, considered by many critics the greatest chess genius that ever lived, *never* played 1 P-Q4. In contrast, Ernest Gruenfeld, one of the greatest living authorities on opening play, ventured on 1 P-K4 only once in his entire tournament career (against Capablanca at Karlsbad 1929). When asked why he avoided 1 P-K4, he answered, 'I never make a mistake in the opening.'"
—Irving Chernev and Fred Reinfeld, *The Fireside Book of Chess*

56. "A pine cut down, a dead pine, is no more a pine than a dead human carcass is a man. Can he who has discovered only some of the values of whalebone and whale oil be said to have discovered the true use of the whale? Can he who slays the elephant for his ivory be said to have 'seen the elephant'? These are petty and accidental uses; just as if a stronger race were to kill us in order to make buttons and flageolets of our bones; for everything may serve a lower as well as a higher use. Every creature is better alive than dead, men and moose and pine trees, and he who understands it aright will rather preserve its life than destroy it."
    —Henry David Thoreau, "Chesuncook"

57. "The evening's 'official' party, thrown by the Samuel Goldwyn Co. to celebrate the premiere of its film *Golden Gate,* was noisy and crowded and located in one of the area's poshest ski lodges. But as usual, the serious action didn't begin until later, at the unofficial afterparties. The hot ticket that night at the Sundance Film Festival in Park City, Utah (pop. 4,468), was a bash thrown in a rented condo by the William Morris talent agency and the 20th Century-Fox. Actually, invitations were hardly needed; anybody who could find a parking spot on the clogged, snow-packed streets and squeeze through the crowd spilling out of the jammed condo could venture into the belly of the Hollywood beast."
    —Richard Zoglin

58. "I am a Korean War veteran, and I just want to say that our commander-in-chief is a lying, cheating, draft-dodging, gay-loving hypocrite who thinks sucking up to the military can make us forget what he did during Vietnam. He can't, as he'll learn when we vote him out of office after one term."
    —Adapted from a newspaper call-in column

Bank 1-5

Identify the passages that contain arguments; in those that do, identify the main issue.

59. "A witty experiment by Philip Goldberg proves what everyone knows, having internalized the disesteem in which they are held, women despise both themselves and each other. This simple test consisted of asking women undergraduates to respond to the scholarship in an essay signed alternately by one John McKay and one Joan McKay. In making their assessments, the students generally agreed that John was a remarkable thinker, Joan an unimpressive mind. Yet the articles were identical; the reaction was dependent on the sex of the supposed author."
    —Kate Millett, *Sexual Politics*

    Issue: whether women "despise both themselves and each other"

60. NBC's coverage of the 1988 Olympics was not very exciting. The anchorman was cool and detached, and, except for basketball, they never zeroed in on a single event long enough for anyone to care. Plus, there was just too much coverage. Anytime you turned on NBC, there was the Olympics. It was like air—always there. And what's so exciting about air?

    Issue: whether NBC's coverage of the Olympics was exciting

61. "When it comes to airborne pollution—chiefly from coal-fired and oil-fired power stations—Britain is again the dirty old man of Europe. In 1985, 21 nations approved of a European Community convention calling for a 30 percent reduction in sulfur emissions by 1993. Britain is the only major North Sea nation that has not signed."
—Brian Jackman, *Sunday Times Magazine*

Issue: whether Britain is the major European contributor to air pollution

62. "My folks, who were Russian immigrants, loved the chance to vote. That's probably why I decided that I was going to vote whenever I got the chance. I'm not sure if I'm going to vote for Dukakis or Bush, but I am going to vote. And I don't understand people who don't."
—Mike Wallace

Answer: no argument

63. It's wise to let states deny AFDC (Aid to Families with Dependent Children) benefits to unmarried kids under eighteen who live away from their parents. This would discourage thousands of these kids from having children of their own in order to get state-subsidized apartments.

Issue: whether states should be allowed to deny AFDC benefits to youths under eighteen

64. A judge's finding that the FBI discriminated against its Hispanic agents is the second time in less than a year that the bureau has been embarrassed by its treatment of minority employees. Last November, black FBI agent Donald Rochon filed a lawsuit in U.S. District Court accusing the bureau of racial harassment when he was an agent in Omaha. The suit is pending.

Increasing the hiring of minorities and treating them equally for promotions must become a matter of greater concern to the FBI. Currently, there are only 423 Hispanic agents and 412 black agents out of a total of about 9,400. The statistics speak for themselves.

Issue: whether the FBI should be more concerned with hiring minorities and with treating minority agents fairly with respect to promotion

65. "Those who accept evolution contend that creation is not scientific; but can it be fairly said that the theory of evolution itself is truly scientific?"
—*Life—How did it get here? By evolution or by creation?*

Answer: No argument

66. "Because real estate is a local investment, I recommend investing within an hour's drive from your home. Personally, I invest within a half-hour drive because then I can properly manage the property and watch it to be sure it is not declining in market value."
—Real estate columnist Bob Bruss

Issue: whether you should invest in real estate located close to where you live

67. "It is indeed said that the Japanese work more than 2,000 hours a year, but this is not so. At Sony—and at Sanyo or Matsushita—the total is somewhere between 1,800 and 1,900 hours."
—Akio Morita, chairman of Sony

Issue: whether the Japanese work more than 2,000 hours a year

68. Obviously the commission should prepare regulations that are consistent with the law. We admit that isn't always easy. But there's no reason for the commission to substitute its judgment for that of the people.

Answer: no argument

69. "And he went from there, and entered their synagogue. And behold, there was a man with a withered hand. And they asked him, 'Is it lawful to heal on the sabbath?' so that they might accuse him. He said to them, 'What man of you, if he has one sheep, and it falls into a pit on the sabbath, will not lay hold of it and lift it out? Of how much more value is a man than a sheep! So it is lawful to do good on the sabbath.'"
—Matthew 12:9–12

Issue: whether it is lawful (or right) to heal on the sabbath

70. That American schools have finally been integrated is a myth. The vast majority of African-American students attend schools whose student bodies are almost entirely African American. And most whites attend schools where only a tiny minority are African American, Latino, or Asian.

Issue: whether American schools have finally been integrated

71. Because men admire muscle and physical force, they assume that women do too.

Answer: No argument

Bank 1-6

The quality of a discussion often depends on how closely the parties attend to the same issue. For the passages below, identify instances in which the speakers are clearly disputing the same issue and in which somebody is missing the point.

72. A: Harriman is a fraud. He didn't even graduate from medical school!
B: Harriman is still the best surgeon at this clinic.

Different issues—Harriman could be a good surgeon and not have proper medical credentials. There have been a few such famous cases. (We ourselves prefer a real diploma on the wall.)

73. A: The legislature should pass a bill banning agricultural burning—when they burn those fields the whole area is covered with a layer of smoke.
B: Forget about agricultural burning—automobile emissions cause the greatest percentage of air pollution in this area.

There is an obvious sense in which these two speakers are addressing the same issue, namely, whether there should be a ban on agricultural burning. But B is clearly dismissing that issue because of another one—whether autos pollute more than burning—which may not be relevant. B may be correct about auto pollution, but it doesn't follow that agricultural burning shouldn't be curtailed.

74. A: Have you seen those advertisements for striptease dancers for private parties? That's exploitative and insulting, if you ask me.
B: Oh, take it easy. They have male strippers for women's parties as well as female strippers for men's parties. So it's not as bad as you thought.

Different issues. Whether stripping is exploitative and insulting is different from whether men and women are equally exploited and insulted.

75. A: I can't believe the student government paid Ramsey Clark over a thousand dollars to come here and give a speech. He's been out of office for years, and he's clearly biased. They should have saved our money.
B: Listen. Ronald Reagan has been out of office for a while now too, and he's clearly as biased as anybody. Nevertheless, people pay *millions* for him to come and speak. So lay off about Ramsey Clark.

Different issues. Presumably the student government is not paying Ronald Reagan millions to come and speak.

76. A: A woman in Tennessee was charged with a felony for not warning rescuers that her fiancé, who had suffered a heart attack, had tested positive for AIDS. That's a good law, since people ought to know when they're stepping into a dangerous situation to help somebody else.
B: Well, I don't think it's such a good law, because the likelihood of catching AIDS from somebody while trying to resuscitate them is very, very small.

These speakers are disputing the same issue—whether the law requiring that one warn others ("reckless endangerment" is the usual charge for failure to do so) is a good law. B is saying, in effect, that it isn't *really that dangerous to help an AIDS-positive victim.*

77. A: I think the oversight laws for police have to be toughened. Right now, it's difficult for society to protect itself against rogue cops.
B: Well, I know you can't be convinced otherwise, but it just isn't true that every officer who's brought up on charges is guilty of those charges.

Different issues. We'd say B is missing A's point—even though what B says may be true.

78. A: Look, it's just good business sense to foreclose on a piece of property when the mortgage defaults. We can't sit around here and carry these loans month after month.
B: The people who owe on these properties are out of work because of the recession, not because of any fault of their own. If we foreclose on them, many will be financially ruined and may never be able to afford a home of their own again.

This is similar to the situation in exercise 73. A and B are disputing the issue of whether to foreclose on the properties, but they are not really addressing each other directly. Since they bring up independent issues in support of their sides and since it isn't clear which argument should be given more weight, the result is often a standoff. In cases like this, one party can benefit not just by supporting its side of the issue but also by attacking the other side's argument.

79. A: About 90 percent of all those colorful kids' books abut dinosaurs contain misinformation and misleading interpretations.
    B: But without those books, cartoons would be children's only source of information about dinosaurs—and they're even *more* inaccurate.

    Different issues.

80. A: The banking industry is going the same direction as the savings and loan industry. If the government deregulates banks the way it did the S&Ls, taxpayers will have another financial disaster on their hands.
    B: The whole regulatory system is archaic, and it oppresses innovation and initiative. If the banks aren't deregulated, they're going to be creating a financial disaster *anyway!*

    B is addressing an entirely separate issue.

81. A: Most cases of date rape happen when the couple have been drinking. That's another good reason for getting booze off the campus.
    B: Yes, well, most of the cases of date rape happen because the girl is encouraging the guy and he just goes with it.

    B is addressing an entirely separate issue.

82. A: Experimentation on animals? Horrid, awful, immoral! No argument would justify experimenting on animals that wouldn't also justify experimenting on humans.
    B: You're overlooking all the medical advances that have resulted from experimenting on animals.

    B is giving an argument for medical experimentation, but is not responding to A's request for a justification for experimenting on animals that wouldn't automatically be a justification for experimenting on people.

Bank 1-7

Identify the main issue in each of the following passages. If two or more issues are present, indicate how they are related—that is, does the settlement of one depend upon the settlement of another?

83. We sometimes make the mistake of thinking that whatever qualifies someone as an expert in one field automatically qualifies that person in other areas. Even if the intelligence and skill required to become an expert in one field *could* enable someone to become an expert in any field—an assumption that is itself doubtful—possessing the ability to become an expert is entirely different from actually *being* an expert. Thus, informational claims put forth by experts about subjects outside their fields are not automatically more acceptable than claims put forth by nonexperts.
    —From Chapter 3 of the text

    Issue: whether informational claims from experts about subjects outside their fields of expertise are automatically more acceptable than claims from nonexperts.

84. The results of a survey conducted by the Public Opinion Laboratory at Northern Illinois University in the fall of 1988 show that on very basic ideas, vast numbers of Americans are scientifically illiterate, laboratory director Jon Miller said. Only about 5 percent of American adults have a minimal knowledge of scientific vocabulary and methodology and an understanding of the impact of science on the world (55 percent did not know that the Earth goes around the Sun once a year; 28 percent didn't know that the Earth goes around the Sun at all.) In an election year when candidates are talking about the Strategic Defense Initiative, acid rain, and the greenhouse effect, this survey shows that many Americans have little idea of what the candidates are talking about.

Issue: whether American adults know enough about basic science to understand discussion of current scientific issues.

85. It's clear, given the recent increases in hate groups and racist violence, that we still need the laws originally crafted to combat the racism of the 1860s. A federal court jury recently ruled that two white-supremacist groups must pay nearly a million dollars in damages to racism protesters. This welcome message tells bigots of all types that if you violate others' rights, you'll be hit where it hurts—in the pocketbook. Ironically, the current Supreme Court has voted to reconsider its 1976 *Runyon v. McCrary* ruling, which permits individuals to seek punitive damages for private acts of discrimination. The irony is compounded by the fact that the Bush campaign made such a strong case for the victims of crime in the 1988 presidential election.

Issue: The first issue is whether bigotry is sufficiently widespread to require repression by the law; the second, less clearly stated issue is whether the commitment of the current Supreme Court (and the Bush administration) to stamp out racism is strong enough.

Bank 1-8

True/False

86. If no reasons have been given for a claim's acceptance, the claim should always be rejected.

False

87. If poor reasons have been given for a claim's acceptance, the claim should always be rejected.

False

88. Sometimes arguments contain only unstated reasons.

False

89. The reasons that appear in arguments may be either good or bad reasons—if they are bad reasons, we still have an argument; it's just a bad argument.

True

90. Claims may serve any of several purposes, but never more than one purpose at a time.

    False

91. Even though the issue that people are fussing over may not be important, there must still be an issue present wherever an argument is present.

    True

Chapter 2
Critical Thinking and Argumentative Writing

This chapter of the text has been evolving since the beginning. The emphasis on ambiguity, vagueness, and clarity has now become an explicit commitment to help students to improve their own writing as well as to read the work of others with a more critical eye.

Our experience is that, in general, students have little trouble with most of the material in this chapter, and they enjoy working with it. Sometimes it even helps relieve frustration: A lot of students know they're being shortchanged in the information they get from our leaders and from those who want to sell us something. And they're often grateful for some critical terminology (even such simple terms as "vagueness" and "ambiguity") and the confidence to use it when they think they're being misled. Confidence plays a *big* role with students, we're convinced. They're so used to getting bad or partial information that accepting it has become a habit. We hope that if they can learn how much they can improve their own writing by holding themselves to higher standards, they'll begin holding others to such standards, too.

Students appreciate the attention that this chapter devotes to vagueness—many have told us that they hadn't realized how much of what they hear is vague to the point of being useless. Incidentally, for students who insist on a more precise explanation of "vagueness," this works in some (but not all) cases: Claim A is more vague than claim B if B implies A but A does not imply B. Thus, "John worked in the garden" is more vague than "John pruned his rose bushes," because the latter implies the former but not vice versa. In short: If the truth conditions of one claim are a subset of the truth conditions of another claim, the latter is more vague than the former. This guideline won't help when the claims' truth conditions are not one a subset of the other.

Ambiguous claims are fun, but they aren't all innocent jokes, of course. They sometimes contribute to serious confusion, and advertising often turns them into misleading weaselers. Professor Donald Henson has pointed out that aside from being fun, discussion of deceptive cases of ambiguity can produce a sense of satisfaction in students early on in a course and help them to appreciate the value of critical-thinking skills long before they've learned to detect pseudoreasoning or analyze arguments.

Lecture/Discussion Suggestions

Textbook material on definitions can be pretty boring for a lot of students—they tend to find it unexciting even if they know it's good for them. Our discussion in the text is brief and to the point, but we thought we'd throw in a suggestion here that has enlivened our classroom more than once.

After describing the three types of definition in the text, we point out a dilemma: Ostensive definition (definition by example) seems necessary on the one hand, but on the other hand, as we'll show, it's almost miraculous that it works at all. That ostensive definition seems necessary can be shown by imagining people in a primitive language-learning situation, for example, children; early *Homo sapiens;* two people thrown together, neither of whom knows a word of the other's language; and so on. Since a language learner in any of those situations knows no words at all, or at least none that those around her know, the first words have to be learned without reference to known words. This limitation eliminates analytic definitions and definition by synonym, as well as other types not discussed in the text. To learn those first words, we're stuck with ostensive definitions. When you question students about how someone in the circumstances described might begin learning, they come up with ostensive definitions pretty quickly.

Then, you point out the difficulty in drawing conclusions from *anything* a person might do to define any particular word ostensively. One way to do this is to imagine you're trying to begin linguistic communication with your students. You point across the room while uttering a nonsense word, say, "fargle," which is a word you mean to teach them. Perhaps you point in the general direction of the door to your classroom. Students are likely to react: " 'Fargle' might mean the same as 'door,' " or "Maybe 'fargle' means the same as 'brown'." Indeed, it might. Or flat, or the color of the door, or exit, or east—who knows? How can you help the students? By pointing to something else that's a fargle and letting them figure out what the two have in common.

You point to a tabletop of a different color from that of the door. This allows students to rule out some of their earlier suggestions, but not all. "Fargle" does not mean the same as "vertical" or "exit," but hosts of candidates for synonyms remain: "flat," "indoors," "material object"; or, to make things interesting, maybe "fargle" refers to the act of pointing. (Thinking that pointing was going to be crucial in your shared enterprise, you decided to start by teaching them how you refer to this crucial notion.)

To further complicate matters, you might explain to them that they weren't even looking in the right direction: In your land, people extend an arm and finger to indicate that the observer should look in the direction of the shoulder (not the finger) to locate the object—that is, your people have a pointing convention that is the reverse of ours.

Matters can continue to be made worse in all manner of ways. "Fargle" could have a disjunctive meaning—it might mean the same as "either flat or brown." Or, it could have a conjunctive meaning—"both flat and brown."

Just as Eskimos have many more words for "snow" than most of us, it could be that your students don't have a single word or handy combination that is synonymous with "fargle." In fact, the same may be true of most of the words in your language.

One way to finish off this little episode is to use Wittgenstein's cube trick. You can tell your students that because words are such trouble, you'll try pictures. Tell them that you're going to draw a picture of a cube. Go to the chalkboard and draw the following figure.

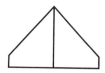

In response to the students' puzzled looks, tell them they probably expected something like this—and draw the usual view of a cube. After insisting that your picture is as good a cube as the one they expected, explain that if they were to go down to the bank building on the corner and lie down on the sidewalk at the corner of the bank and look at the bank, it would look just exactly like your picture. And the bank building is most certainly cube-shaped. You may have to use a savings and loan (if there are any left in your neighborhood), an auditorium, or whatever's handy. Of course your students are probably more used to seeing ice cubes than cubes of this size and from this angle.

It may not be a good idea to go much further than this, unless you want to wind up giving a lecture on symbols, natural signs, nonlinguistic shared experiences, and, finally, a seminar on Wittgenstein. What you *can* accomplish with this little lecture is impressing on your students that the most obvious features of communication are not so simple as they probably thought. This awareness may make it easier later to convince students that careful attention and critical-thinking skills are truly important in avoiding the pitfalls that abound in all but the most superficial communication.

Exercises Unanswered in the Text

Exercise 2-1

2. The most enthusiastic (staunchest, most steadfast, most loyal, and so on) Giants fans live in New Jersey.

3. We heard that he informed you in his letter of what he said.

5. Intentional ambiguity

6. A week ago, they were both exposed to someone who was ill.

8. Scandinavians, as a group, eat tons of cheese every year.

9. Tuxedo Prices Slashed!

11. Everybody knows that giraffes lack the ability to make sounds.

12. This is the greatest disaster to happen during my governorship.

14. Common sense almost certainly rules out an ambiguity here, but, given the instructions for the exercise: "Horatio plays the trumpet by ear; that is, he doesn't read music."

15. Volunteer help requested: Wear construction helmet and work overalls, and be prepared to lift heavy equipment.

17. Intentionally ambiguous?

18. Arm and Hammer laundry detergent, without polluting our waters, gets your wash as clean as can be.

20. No other cleanser gets your bathroom as clean as does Houndstooth cleanser.

21. We're going to look at parcels of unimproved land this afternoon.

23. Two million times a day Americans collectively love to eat . . .

24. . . . with semen samples, frozen in a stainless steel tank, from eighteen men.

26. This book is difficult.

27. Abraham Lincoln wrote the Gettysburg Address on the back of an envelope while traveling from Washington to Gettysburg.

29. In one of Shakespeare's plays, Hamlet gives a long soliloquy.

30. Before the officers' arrival, the two suspects fled the area in a white Ford Mustang driven by a third male.

Exercise 2-2

2. As a group (If this is wrong, we're willing to travel.)

3. As a group

5. As individuals

6. As a group

8. As individuals

9. As a group

11. As individuals

13. As individuals

14. As a group (Although maybe they'd have a better chance as individuals.)

Exercise 2-3

2. In order of decreasing vagueness: (c), (e), (a), (b), (d)

3. (c), (b), (a), (d)

5. (b) and (a) are about the same, then (e), (c), (d)

Exercise 2-4

2. (a)

3. (b)

5. (b)

6. (a)

8. Both are about the same.

9. (b)

Exercise 2-5

2. Not too vague

3. Not too vague. It means, "Hey, don't complain to us if you're offended by this program or if your kids see it."

5. Too vague

6. Too vague

8. Well, maybe too vague, and also potentially ambiguous. Still, you can't expect all details to be stated in the headline of the ad.

9. "Unsafe levels" is not too vague *in this context;* We'd like to see "too high" made a little more precise.

Exercise 2-7

2. The problem here is what "average" means. This could be about the numerical mean musician's and plumber's salaries or it could mean that *most* musicians make less than *most* plumbers.

3. The overall superiority of a current player to one of thirty years ago would be very difficult to measure because of changes in rules, stadiums, length of season, and such.

5. "Mood of the country" could mean a lot of things; so could "more conservative."

6. Better in what way? Is decaffeinated coffee included? Better for *everybody?*

8. Both "tolerate" and "pain" are vague: Tolerate before crying out? Before succumbing? Psychological as well as physical pain?

9. Maybe "harmful effect" is clear enough, but "up to" 50 percent includes as little as a tenth of a percent. And we'd like to know the basis of comparison—cars on which no protection at all is used? On which our old car wax is used?

Exercise 2-8

2. (a) "Blonde" is a term that's vague in several obvious ways. (b) By what standard do you measure how much fun a person has? More *intense* fun? Fun more of the time?

3. (a) How do we know what the "average" chimp and monkey are? (Halfway between a really smart chimp and a really dumb one?) (b) How is smartness being measured here? The standard is not a clear one.

5. (a) The most that can be said is that *reported* crime is up. (b) The claim doesn't spell out a location for the increase. (c) It also doesn't say what kind of crime. Without this information, the 160 percent figure would be meaningless even if some base figure had been given.

6. What counts as a classical musician? As a rock musician? (There are musicians who play both classical music and rock, after all.) And what does "more talented" mean? More *native* talent? Better trained? We're sure something can be made of this claim, but it certainly isn't clear quite what.

8. Suppose you compared December 1–7, 1978, with December 1–7, 1979 (the claim doesn't contain any evidence that the periods discussed were really comparable), with respect to profanity on the networks. What would you count as profane? Individual words or phrases? Where does one profanity end and another begin? How do you compare the incidence of phrases with the incidence of single words? Equally? Were any "profanities" in news reports? If so, their occurrences are due to external events, not a simple choice of the networks. What is the difference between hard and soft profanity? A meaningless statistic.

9. (a) One flaw here is the terms of the comparison. If a married couple is mugged, do we count it as two crimes or one? What if the couple had been two single people—is it counted the same? (b) The statistic could be misleading if one took it to mean that being married all by itself made for some difference in being a victim of crime. It may be that married couples tend to live in more affluent neighborhoods and are better protected against crime and that *that* is what accounts for the difference.

Exercise 2-11

Proper order: 7, 1, 2, 4, 5, 6, 3, 8

Exercise 2-13

2. Students should choose their majors . . .

3. True citizens understand their debt to their country.

5. You should be cautious during the interview.

6. Entrants must indicate that they have read the rules, understand them, and are willing to abide by them. If they have questions, they should bring them to the attention of an official, who will answer them.

8. All who want refunds should apply at the main office and bring along identification.

9. Those who have tried our tea know that it will neither keep them awake nor make them jittery.

11. Not all people have the same beliefs. Some may not wish to put themselves on the line, whereas others may welcome the chance to make their views known to friends.

12. People were created in the image of God.

14. Of all the animals, humans are the most intelligent.

15. The common person prefers peace to war.

18. The pursuit of happiness has led people to prefer leisure to work.

19. When individuals reach adulthood, they are able to make such decisions for themselves.

21. The new city bus has hired several drivers. (If you must specify gender, say "female drivers.")

22. Firefighters, police officers, postal workers, chair.

23. Harold Vasquez worked for City Hospital as a nurse.

25. Mr. and Mrs. Macleod joined a club for married couples.

26. Mrs. Macleod works for the city.

28. Several female students have signed up for this seminar.

29. A judge must be sensitive to the atmosphere in the courtroom.

Chapter 2 Test Question/Exercise Banks

In the previous edition, we moved several exercises out of the text to make room for new stuff. But then we decided we'd miss them, so we're including them here. This is especially true of the first bank: One of us makes sure that words from this exercise crop up from time to time during the semester—students who go to the trouble to look them up find that it pays off.

Bank 2-1

How many words in the list below do you know? For each word that is unfamiliar to you, make a guess about its meaning based on its appearance or sound, and create your own definition. Then look each word up, and find out how close you got. Here's the list (thumbnail meanings given in parentheses):

1. meretricious (gaudy; harlot-like)

2. parvenu (upstart)

3. pursy (short-winded because of corpulence)

4. besotted (stupefied, muddled, as from drunkenness or infatuation)

5. trenchant (incisive, penetrating)

6. mettle (courage)

7. noisome (foul-smelling)

8. ursine (bearlike)

9. pervicacious (extremely obstinate)

10. adjuration (an earnest appeal or a solemn oath)

Bank 2-2

Ask students to give definitions by example of as many of these as they can. They can use names or descriptions of items that they can't point to. They'll have trouble with lots of these, of course. Have them try to identify the source of the trouble in such cases. Each item is followed by our suggestion for an answer or by a comment.

11. planet: Mars

12. dictator: Hitler

13. tall item: the World Trade Center

14. thing: Any object you point to and name. But notice that no matter what you point to, it will not be clear to an observer what qualifies that object as a thing. This word is much too general (that is, vague) to be easily defined by example. (If you used the lecture/discussion suggestions at the beginning of this *LA* chapter, at least some of your students were ready for this.)

15. abstraction: the square root of 2

16. genius: Albert Einstein

17. World Series winner: Oakland Athletics

18. expensive gift: a Rolls-Royce

19. unicorn: Can't do it; a drawing of a unicorn is only an example of a drawing of a unicorn.

20. charity: the Red Cross. As an abstract noun (as in "Charity begins at home"), this word is more difficult to define by example. You must point to an act or describe an act of generosity, sacrifice, and so on.

21. ambiguous claim: "He wiped his moustache off."

22. education: We think this word is too vague to be defined by example.

23. immoral act: torturing puppies just for amusement

24. toothache: We don't think you can get much closer than indicating someone who's having a toothache, although even then it won't be clear that it is the toothache and not the person's behavior you are exemplifying. Like other sensations, pains are not the sorts of things we can point to, although we can point to the places where we're *having* them.

25. the color red: This is more difficult than it appears. A drop of blood is an example of a red thing, but is it an example of *the color red?*

26. classification system: class rankings of seniors, juniors, and so on.

27. industrial hazard: sulfur dioxide

28. reasoning: A proof in geometry; any of the examples in Chapter 8.

29. concept: number. What we said about "thing" goes for this one, too.

30. problem: this very item

Bank 2-3

For each of the following, indicate what kind of meaning is given: extension, intension, or neither one. Our answers/comments follow.

31. "Free country" means a place like the United States, Canada, or France.

    Extension, although it's arguable that the inclusion of "place like . . ." actually specifies a rudimentary intension

32. "Epistemologist" means someone who studies the nature of knowledge.

    Intension

33. "Widow" refers to a woman whose husband has died.

    Intension

34. What I mean by setting a good example is not putting your feet on the table.

    Extension

35. "Poltroonery" means the same thing as "cowardice."

   Intension

36. Honor means being willing to lay down your life for a just cause.

   Intension (Had a specific example of the laying down of a life been mentioned, the proper answer would have been extension.)

37. Towering clouds mean that it's going to rain.

   Neither extension nor intension

38. Happiness means having your own VCR.

   Extension

39. Being a soldier means being able to tolerate the sight of blood.

   Intension, if it's either

40. A word means anything you want it to.

   Neither

Bank 2-4

Define each of the following by synonyms, using one synonym that carries a complimentary meaning and one that carries a derogatory emotive meaning.

41. thin person: *slender person; skinny person*

42. thrifty: *frugal; tight*

43. farmer: *agriculturalist; hick*

44. proud: *self-esteemed; haughty*

45. display: *showcase; show off*

46. government worker: *public servant; bureaucrat*

47. drinker: *imbiber; drunk*

48. humble: *docile; wimpy*

49. decayed: *aged; rotted*

50. intellectual (noun): *thinker; egghead*

Bank 2-5

For each of the following, give an analytical definition that is flattering. (We've added our own suggestions.)

51. conservative (noun): a person whose political views are guided by the wisdom embodied in traditional institutions

52. politician: one dedicated to public benefit through governmental service

53. feminist: a person devoted to the cause of righting the wrongs of economic and political inequality and social injustice for women

54. liberal: a person whose political philosophy is guided by ideas of democracy, reform, and progress

55. educator: one who preserves and transmits knowledge and culture to succeeding generations

For each of the following, give an analytical definition that is *un*flattering.

56. playboy: a man who treats women as though they were merely objects for his amusement rather than real people

57. hunter: a person who murders animals

58. teenager: an ignorant youth between thirteen and twenty, known for poor judgment, bad manners, and a short attention span

59. educators: people who teach a subject because they can't make a living actually doing it

60. physicians: people who prescribe medicines of which they know little, to cure diseases of which they know less, in human beings of whom they know nothing (attributed to Voltaire)

Bank 2-6

Which of these informal definitions are by example, which by synonym, and which analytical?

61. "Congenial" means companionable.

By synonym

62. Mayonnaise is a thick sauce of egg yolk beaten together with vegetable oil and seasonings.

Analytical

57

63. Meat that contains larval worms is said to be measly.

   Analytical

64. "Hit me" means the same as "Give me another card."

   By synonym

65. A diode is a solid-state electronic device that allows the passage of an electric current in only one direction.

   Analytical

66. "Either" is a disjunctive correlative used before two or more words, phrases, or clauses that are joined by "or."

   Analytical

67. A professional bureaucrat is anyone like our present governor.

   The answer we prefer is definition by example, but one might easily argue that the definition is analytical because of the "anyone like" phrasing. We take the force of such claims to be something like, "Now that's what I call a professional bureaucrat!"

68. Interest is an amount paid for the use of borrowed money.

   Analytical

69. Real property? Why, your house and land are real property.

   By example

70. A slice occurs when the ball flies in a curve because of lateral spin; the slice curves to the right if the golfer is right-handed and to the left if the golfer is left-handed.

   Analytical

Bank 2-7

Determine which of these claims are best classified as semantically ambiguous (and which of those contain grouping ambiguities), which are syntactically ambiguous, and which are free from ambiguity.

71. People who go shopping often go broke.

   Semantically ambiguous: "go broke," and syntactically ambiguous: does "often" go with "shopping" or with "go broke"? (Because of their distant relationship with grammar, many students read "broke" as "broken" and thus get a second version of a semantical ambiguity.)

72. All snakes are not poisonous.

Syntactically ambiguous

73. The wizard made a pig of himself.

Semantically ambiguous (on both "made" and "pig")

74. John plays with toys more than Linda.

Syntactically ambiguous

75. He went to the store but was held up in the process.

Semantically ambiguous

76. The team was upset.

Semantical ambiguity on "upset" and grouping ambiguity on "team"

77. He passed out and was later found by a group of stray sheep.

Semantically ambiguous

78. She watched him dance with intensity.

Syntactically ambiguous

79. Carlton harassed the man on the motorcycle.

Syntactically ambiguous

80. When the head waiter asked whether she had reservations, she said, "Yes, but I'm going to eat here anyway."

Semantically ambiguous

81. If properly frosted, a person shouldn't notice lumps in a cake.

Syntactically ambiguous

82. San Francisco (AP) December 13, 1985—"A group of citizens angry about the lack of public restrooms downtown is planning a sit-in at City Hall, leaving employees no place to go."

Semantically and syntactically ambiguous; they work together in this one.

83. She looks more like her mother than her father.

Syntactically ambiguous

84. He dislikes her smoking.

Semantically ambiguous

85. Residents of the continental United States have more pets than those of Alaska.

Grouping ambiguity; semantically ambiguous

86. Susan got in trouble for messing up the house with her younger sister.

Syntactically ambiguous

87. Sign in a hotel: NO SMOKING ROOMS AVAILABLE

Syntactically ambiguous

88. Eighteen people have slept in the new hotel's most expensive suite.

Grouping ambiguity

89. After finishing his term paper, he went out for a beer and left it in his instructor's mailbox.

Syntactically ambiguous

90. There is a job for everyone.

Grouping ambiguity

91. "Police said Sunday that a Lebanese woman arrested in Milan planned to deliver photographs of American hostages to an Italian man who has been linked to arms scandals. . . . The man . . . was questioned by police after they found the photos and a letter from a hostage hidden in a false bottom of the woman's suitcase Thursday."
—From an Associated Press dispatch, *Sacramento Bee*

Syntactically ambiguous: Was the hostage hidden in the suitcase?

92. "My husband got his project cut off two weeks ago, and I haven't had any relief since then."
—From a letter requesting public assistance, as quoted in Ann Landers, *Chicago Tribune*

Semantically ambiguous

93. "A lot of people are living to 100 who never used to."
—Herb Caen, *San Francisco Chronicle*

Syntactically ambiguous, or worse

94. "I want Michael Dukakis to be the next president of the United States in the worst way."
—Senator Joseph Biden, D-Del., campaigning for Dukakis, quoted in the *San Francisco Chronicle*

Syntactically ambiguous

Bank 2-8

Our students generally have a good time with these.

95. Invent three examples of semantically ambiguous claims.

96. Invent three examples of syntactically ambiguous claims.

97. Invent three examples of claims containing grouping ambiguities.

Bank 2-9

98. Find an example of an ambiguous claim in a paper you have written for another class.

99. Find an example of an ambiguous claim in a newspaper or magazine. (Hint: Headlines are sometimes great sources of such claims.)

Bank 2-10

Rank the claims in these sets from most vague to least vague.

100. Joanna
    a. Is left of center in her political views.
    b. Has voted for the socialist candidate for president in the last four elections.
    c. Usually doesn't vote for Republicans.
    d. Is a liberal.

Decreasingly vague: (a) and (d) are about equal, (c) somewhat less vague, then (b).

101. When Louis returned from his trip, he told me
    a. That the airline had lost his bags twice.
    b. That it had been a nightmare.
    c. That all the clothes except those on his back spent the weekend in Miami and Cleveland while he was in New Orleans and Detroit.
    d. That he had to wear the same clothes for three straight days because of airline foul-ups with his luggage.

Decreasingly vague: (b), (a), (d), (c).

102. a. I hear a funny noise in my engine.
    b. I have an engine problem.
    c. When I give it gas, I hear this funny sound in my engine.
    d. My engine makes a strange noise sometimes but not at other times.
    e. There is an unusual ticking sound in my engine when I accelerate from zero to around thirty.

Decreasingly vague: (b), (a), (d), (c), (e).

103. a. The students with the most points at the end of the semester will get the best grades.
    b. The top 10 percent of the class will receive As.
    c. Everybody whose average is 90 or above will get an A.
    d. The class will be graded on a curve.
    e. Grading will be relatively tough in this course.

    Decreasingly vague: (a), (e), (d); (b) and (c) about equal.

104. The administration has indicated it would
    a. Not be satisfied until the problem was solved.
    b. Propose new legislation to combat the problem.
    c. Send a bill to the Congress during the next session.
    d. Take the problem under advisement.

    Decreasingly vague: (d), (a), (b), (c).

105. a. Smoking is hazardous to your health.
    b. Smoking is linked with lung disease.
    c. Smoking has been demonstrated to cause lung cancer and emphysema.
    d. Smoking is not good for you.
    e. Smoking is linked with lung cancer and emphysema.

    Decreasingly vague: (d), (a), (b), (e), (c).

106. a. Dennis was a monster all evening.
    b. Dennis was well-behaved while the guests were here.
    c. Dennis was ill-mannered toward the guests.
    d. Dennis threw a tantrum in front of everybody.

    Decreasingly vague: (a) (and ambiguous, too), (d); (b) and (c) about equal.

107. a. Whitney was hungry, so she helped herself to more potatoes.
    b. "I'm drowning!" she screamed. "Someone help me!"
    c. Morgan helped her mother at every opportunity.
    d. Derrick discovered he could not lift the box unless someone helped him by lifting one end.
    e. The word "help" has four letters in it.

    These are all about equally precise with the exception of (c), which is more vague.

108. a. His were the most awful, despicable, outrageous crimes that have been committed in this county in the entire century.
    b. He murdered seven innocent people.
    c. He shocked the sensibilities of the whole region with his horrible crimes.
    d. He was guilty of seven felonies and about nine misdemeanors, including murder and abuse of the mails.
    e. He chopped up seven people and sent their parts to the governor's office.

    Decreasingly vague: (c), (a) (a close second), (d), (b), (e).

Bank 2-11

Determine whether these claims are too vague in the contexts that are stated or implied.

109. During his first news conference of the year, the president said today that his administration was going to crack down even harder on international terrorism.

     Too vague to be very informative; this speaks as much of an attitude as it does of plans to combat terrorism.

110. Said at a party: "What did I think of *The Flintstones?* I thought it was pretty good. You ought to go see it."

     Too vague to be much of a recommendation unless the listener knows her taste in movies is similar to the speaker's.

111. My aunt lost most of her possessions when her house burned down last month.

     Sufficiently precise for most contexts; too vague, of course, if the remark is directed to an insurance claims agent.

112. Well, let's see. To get to the Woodward Mall, go down this street a couple of blocks, and turn right. Go through several stop lights, turn left, and go just a short way. You can't miss it.

     Hopelessly vague.

113. Your chances of winning the grand prize in the lottery by purchasing a single ticket are approximately 1 in 16,000,000.

     Precise enough.

114. I can't tell you how much I love you. You make me very happy.

     Vagueness is not inappropriate here.

115. The 50k of memory that remains in the computer after the program is loaded is enough to produce short documents but not long ones.

     Too vague to be of much use—how short is short?

116. How many miles to a gallon does it get? Oh, you'll be quite satisfied if you buy this little beauty. It gets really impressive mileage.

     Too vague for a potential buyer. But the vagueness is supportive of the speaker's purpose, which is to evade the question.

117. Advertisement: "The Aquaclear water filter—it really will improve the taste and odor of your water."

     Too vague to be useful.

118. From the label of a can of spaghetti sauce: "Made with real meat."

   Too vague, if you care what kind of meat goes into your spaghetti.

119. Teacher to student: "How long should your term paper be? As long as it takes to do justice to your subject."

   Too vague (How does your standard answer to this question compare?)

120. Instructions for a lawn mower: "For best service, crankcase oil should be replaced at least once each season."

   Too vague—"best service" means what? Replace at least once each growing season?

121. Renaissance music simply lulls me to sleep.

   Precise enough. The remark is not designed to describe the music, just the speaker's reaction to it.

122. Property owner, showing his property to guests: "The lot extends back to about where that large oak tree stands."

   Precise enough.

123. Same property owner, showing his property to a potential buyer: "The lot extends back to about where that large oak tree stands."

   Too vague.

124. One father, speaking to another: "I read recently that young children who are required to do chores around the house tend to grow up to be happier, more secure adults than children who have everything done for them."

   While this remark is not too vague for a casual conversation, the listener should be very careful not to take it as advice. It does not lend itself to implementation unless much more detail were to be spelled out, never mind confirmation of the general claim itself.

125. From a gardening book: "Horse manure is many times more beneficial to your garden than that from cows."

   Sufficiently precise to count as good advice.

126. It seems clear that by the end of this decade they'll have produced a machine that can really think.

   Too vague in any context.

127. From a rebate offer sticker for Johnson's vinegar: "Mail this form, along with a proof of purchase from a one-quart bottle of Johnson's Vinegar to the address below. You'll receive your $1.00 rebate check in about four weeks."

   "Proof of purchase" is too vague (given that there's nothing identified as such on the bottle). A label might be considered proof of purchase by some people, though others would claim that at best it shows possession, not purchase.

128. Advertisement: "If your house is properly insulated, the Agwar console humidifier should enhance your comfort when the weather turns cold."

Too vague to help determine whether to purchase a humidifier or whether to purchase this brand. The vagueness does help protect the manufacturer from charges of false advertising, however.

129. Overheard at a wine-tasting: "This chablis is just a bit too ambitious for my taste."

Too vague, unless "ambition" is an addition to the enologist's vocabulary that the authors have not heard about.

130. Take two of these pills three times daily before meals.

The meaning of "before meals" is standard enough for us to say that this claim is precise.

131. The president has determined that tax reform will be his first priority during his second term in office.

Vague enough that we wouldn't make any predictions about taxes based on it.

132. From a consumer advice publication: "Electric heaters cost more to run than kerosene heaters, but they are safer."

Unless the publication goes on to elaborate more specifically on the cost disadvantages and safety advantages of electric as opposed to kerosene heaters, this claim is too vague to be of much help to a consumer wishing to make a wise decision.

Bank 2-12

Would you say that the following claims are ambiguous, too vague, or neither in the contexts in which they were most likely uttered?

133. "Now, how would you like your hair cut, Madam?"
"Oh, just make it a little shorter."

Too vague

134. "In Los Angeles, a 'humor wagon' makes weekly visits to hospitals to entertain children with cancer."
—UPI article

Ambiguous

135. According to the USDA guidelines, you should eat "two to three servings of vegetables each day."

Maybe you know what counts as a serving, but we don't. Too vague.

136. Doctor: "The arrhythmia you are experiencing indicates that you should lay off jogging for a while."

   Too vague. How long is "a while"?

137. "Your satisfaction is guaranteed with our two-year limited guarantee."

   "Limited"? Too vague.

138. 'PRIESTESS' WAS HOOKER TO JURY
   —AP headline

   Ambiguous

139. DEATH HAMPERS BREEDING
   —*Enterprise Record* (Chico, Calif.)

   Yup—it would do that. Ambiguous.

140. FROZEN EMBRYOS RULED CHILDREN
   —*Daily News-Record* (Harrisonburg, Va.)

   Ambiguous

141. The snacks are delicious. But remember to wash the spoons before you eat them.

   Ambiguous

142. Why You Want Sex Changes as You Age
   —*American Health/Psychology Today*

   Ambiguous

143. The girls played with the boys.

   Ambiguous

144. POLICE NAB STUDENTS WITH PAIR OF PLIERS
   —*Journal and Courier* (Lafayette, Ind.)

   Ambiguous

145. There will be over one hundred consolation prizes worth over $10,000.

   Ambiguous

146. "Men burn off 438 calories per hour gardening."
   —Breakthroughs

   Gardening? Vague.

147. The instructions for the previous set of exercises: "Determine whether these claims are too vague given the contexts that are stated or implied."

What it is to be too vague is sometimes, unfortunately, pretty vague itself—but, we trust, not too vague for a set of exercises intended to foster discussion and illustrate that the vagueness of claims is a matter of degree and not something that has to be avoided in every context.

Bank 2-13

Discuss whether the vagueness of the following passages is appropriate to the contexts that are stated or implied. Pay particular attention to any underlined expressions. (These are a bit more difficult than the previous ones.)

148. According to estimates from the New York Medical College in Valhalla that were reported in the November 21 *New England Journal of Medicine,* more than two million people in the United States have been infected by the AIDS virus. Steven L. Sivak and Gary P. Wormser concluded that for every living adult with AIDS (7,152 as of early November), there are 300 infected individuals.
    This figure is much higher than those published by the Centers for Disease Control in Atlanta, which estimates that for each of the 14,653 cases of adult AIDS that have been diagnosed in the United States, there are only a few hundred infected individuals.
    —Adapted from a report in a weekly science news magazine

"More than two million" is not vague in this context, since the exact estimate can be derived by multiplying 7,152 by 300. "Much higher" and "a few hundred" are much too vague for a report in a science news publication, since neither expression makes it at all clear just how different the CDC estimate was from the NYMC estimate.

149. One demographer thinks that more than 20 percent of the women born in the mid-1950s may never have a child, a rate of childlessness that is almost triple the rate of the previous generation.
    You will hear this ascribed to a breakdown of traditional values or to rampant selfishness. But this glib explanation misses the deeper truth, which is more subtle and less personal. People haven't suddenly become more selfish. Changing economic and social realities have simply made children less economically essential and, therefore, more a matter of choice. When people urge a return to traditional values, they're talking about the impossible: reversing centuries of economic and technological change that have altered women's roles. Women's liberation is less an idea than the result of changes that, by reducing pressures for childbearing, inevitably led to more educational and job opportunities.
    —adapted from a news magazine essay

The first occurrence of "traditional values" is quite vague. Does a simple interest in having children count as such a value, or do the values referred to produce the interest in having children? "Rampant selfishness" presumably includes not wanting to share one's time, treasure, or energy with children; beyond that, it isn't clear what is intended. "Changing economic and social realities" and the succeeding underlined expressions are quite vague, but we can easily guess at what the author has in mind for them. The same goes for the last of the underlined expressions.

The main point of this paragraph—that having children is no longer an economic necessity—is somewhat more difficult to find than it might have been had there not been so many very general (and vague) ideas present in the passage.

150. "The right of the people to be <u>secure in their persons</u>, houses, papers, and effects, against <u>unreasonable</u> searches and seizures, shall not be violated, and no Warrants shall issue, but upon <u>probable cause</u>, supported by Oath or affirmation, and particularly describing the place to be searched, and the persons or things to be seized."
—United States Constitution, Fourth Amendment

A discussion of this passage should highlight the notorious vagueness of "unreasonable" and "probable," as well as the fact that such vagueness is inescapable and (probably) desirable in a "living" constitution—that is, one flexible enough to adapt to changing circumstances. "Secure" is another term that students seize upon as too vague. It should be noted that the first claim of the passage, through the word "violated," means simply that people shall not be subject to such searches and seizures.

151. "Comprehensive Coverage. The insurer will <u>pay</u> for <u>direct and accidental damage</u> to the insured's automobile and its <u>equipment</u> not caused by <u>collision or upset</u>."
—From an automobile insurance policy

In this context vagueness is inappropriate, from the standpoint of both the insured and the insurer, though even here it is probably impossible to eliminate it completely. "Pay"—in whole or in part? Who determines the expense of repairing the damage? "Direct and accidental damage"—what all is included by this phrase? Rust damage? Oxidation of the paint? Mechanical damage caused by accident, such as using the wrong type of gasoline? "Equipment"—is equipment added by you since purchasing the car covered? "Collision or upset"—are collisions with animals covered? With falling objects? (Students seem to enjoy discussing this item.)

152. "I believe the worth of any economic policy must be measured by the <u>strength of its commitment</u> to American families, <u>the bedrock of our society</u>. <u>There is no instrument of hard work, savings, and job creation as effective as the family.</u> There is no cultural institution <u>as ennobling as family life</u>, and there is no superior— indeed, no equal—means to rear the young, protect the weak, or attend the elderly—none. Yet <u>past government policies</u> betrayed families and <u>family values</u>. They permitted inflation to push families relentlessly into higher and higher tax brackets. And not only did the personal exemption fail to keep pace with inflation, in real dollars its actual value <u>dropped dramatically</u> over the last thirty years."
—Radio address given by Ronald Reagan in December 1985

The first portion of this passage strikes us as containing much that is vague, although the passage improves somewhat toward the end. "Strength of its commitment" must mean simply the fairness of the amount families are taxed, although it sounds like it might mean more; "the bedrock of our society" is a powerfully emotive phrase, but its meaning is especially vague. Perhaps the following sentence is designed to spell out that meaning, but it is not at all clear what it means either. Families may save (e.g., for the children's education), but it is not clear how families contribute to hard work or job creation. These phrases and claims, like "as ennobling as family life" in the next claim, are principally homilies and emotively charged expressions designed to produce a positive attitude about the president's view of families.

"Past government policies" is spelled out more or less clearly in the following remarks— at least one such past policy is identified; "family values" is not too vague; we are probably safe in guessing that these are simply whatever values contribute to keeping families together. (Is the president saying that past government policies have contributed to break-ups of families? If not, what would follow from this claim?)

The last portion of the passage is much more precise and understandable, although "dropped dramatically" could mean nearly any decrease—one politician's dramatic drop is not necessarily another's.

As part of a political speech, this passage is probably typical in its overall degree of vagueness. Politicians—Democrats, Republicans, and others alike—would probably have a lot less to say if we held them to any high standard of precision.

Bank 2-14

Ask students to do the following. (It's their turn.)

153. Make up a claim and a couple of contexts for it so that the claim is too vague in one context but sufficiently precise in the other.

154. In a paper written for another class, find a sentence or passage that is too vague for its context.

155. Find an example in a newspaper or news magazine of a sentence or passage that is too vague for its context.

156. Write another version of the example you gave for item 155 so that it is no longer too vague.

157. Find an example in a radio or television advertisement of a claim that is vague enough to add nothing new to a potential buyer's information. (These are *easy* to find—it's safe to require a handful of them.)

Bank 2-15

Determine what kind of meaning is probably intended for the following: extension, intension, or neither. (As listed below, the first ten are extension, the second ten are intension, and the last couple are neither. We leave it to you to mix them up as you like.)

Extension

158. A superstar is someone like Bruce Springsteen.

159. What do I mean by liberals? I mean the Kennedys, the Mondales, the Clintons—people like that.

160. The West Indies includes Barbados, Cuba, Haiti—all those islands out there in the Caribbean.

161. The tournament winner is that guy standing over near the scorer's table with the big smile on his face.

162. "Flower" refers to pansies, peonies, daisies, and so on.

163. Spirits? That's like brandy, whiskey, vodka, right?

164. The ex officio members of this committee are Forbes and Lopez.

165. All the words in the world—that's what the word "word" means.

166. See that guy over there? He's a perfect example of what I have in mind when I say the people around here are weird.

167. Lady, as applied to this orchestra, "musician" means just one person, and he's talking to you.

Intension:

168. A mob is any group of Democrats.

169. A levee is an embankment designed to prevent flooding.

170. "Levi's" is a trademark that used to apply only to heavy denim jeans made by Levi Strauss.

171. When they say, "Terminate with extreme prejudice," I think they mean "kill."

172. A celebration is a sesquicentennial only if it happens on something's 150th anniversary.

173. Streaking was a fad in which a person wearing no clothes ran through a public place.

174. The matador is the main bullfighter, the guy who kills the bull if all goes well; the picador is the guy who sits on a horse and carries a bunch of spears with ribbons on them.

175. Anything that resembles a human can be called a hominoid.

176. Budgerigars are the kinds of parakeets that people keep as pets.

177. No, a brahman is not a kind of bull; it's a Hindu of the highest caste.

Neither Extension nor Intension.

178. "Obbligato" is a very difficult word to spell correctly.

179. Ninety percent means you will get an A for the course.

Which item in each of the following sets of claims has the most negative emotive force? (These are easy to answer; the point is to impress on students how many positive and negative ways there are to say essentially the same thing. It's then hoped that they will learn to control the emotive force of their own remarks. Besides, these can be fun.)

180. Mr. Gardner
     a. is a social drinker.
     b. is alcohol-dependent.
     c. is a heavy imbiber.
     d. enjoys tippling.
     e. is a drunk.

181. Shirley always had trouble finding clothes that fit because she was
     a. so petite.
     b. quite small.
     c. a runt.
     d. diminutive.
     e. tiny.

182. a. He had done some unfortunate deeds in his day.
     b. He had the moral sensibility of a reptile.

183. a. She occasionally lapsed in her duty toward others.
     b. She was vicious toward others.

184. a. He was a cautious sort.
     b. He was spineless.

185. She was
     a. well-traveled.
     b. shopworn.

186. When he told others what he thought of them, he was
     a. honest.
     b. blunt.
     c. ruthless.
     d. rude.

187. Luigi is
     a. clumsy.
     b. like a bull in a china shop.
     c. a klutz.
     d. not very well coordinated.

188. My new roommate
     a. talks all the time.
     b. loves to talk.
     c. is loquacious.
     d. hardly ever gives his larynx a rest.

189. a. The Raiders gave the ball game away.
    b. All the breaks went against the Raiders.
    c. The Raiders couldn't buy a piece of good luck.

190. That novel you gave me to read
    a. put me to sleep.
    b. was dull.
    c. wasn't as interesting as most things I've read lately.

191. a. I've never been fond of bowling.
    b. Bowling bores me to death.
    c. I'd rather read the phone book than bowl.

    Students should be asked why (c) seems meaner than (a) and (b)—it's ironic that a touch of humor (ridicule, really) can make a remark more vicious.

192. Professor Henderson's class
    a. doesn't require much studying.
    b. is a gut.
    c. is easy.

193. He'll never make a good wide receiver because
    a. he has trouble holding onto the ball.
    b. he has bricks for hands.
    c. he can't catch.

194. a. Conversation is not Daryll's forte.
    b. Daryll is not very clever.
    c. Daryll would lose a duel of wits with a gum ball machine.

Bank 2-17

Arrange the lettered items in order of increasingly favorable emotive force. You or your students may want to fuss about some of our rankings. We've said (a)=(b) when (a) and (b) seem equally favorable to us.

195. What a thing to wake up to each morning! All you hear are birds
    a. chirping.
    b. cheeping.
    c. chattering.
    d. screeching.
    e. making a racket.
    f. singing.

    (d)=(e), (c), (a)=(b), (f)

196. Karl's diet really took the pounds off; he looks really
    a. slender.
    b. thin.
    c. svelte.
    d. trim.

    (b), (a), (c)=(d)

72

197. a. Danielle sings beautifully.
    b. Danielle has an excellent ear for pitch, a wide range, perfect timbre, and fine phrasing.
    c. Danielle sings like an angel.

(b), (a), (c). A flattering comparison or metaphor (or an unflattering one, for that matter) is often a stronger way of saying something than the simple use of adjectives.

198. Personally, I find Harold very
    a. agreeable.
    b. congenial.
    c. manageable.
    d. submissive.
    e. flexible.
    f. yielding.

(d), (c), (f), (a)=(e), (b)

199. In my view, Mrs. Tuttle might be described as
    a. innocent.
    b. childlike.
    c. guileless.
    d. simple.
    e. artless.
    f. naive.

(d), (e), (f), (b), (a), (c)

200. The house the new architect designed for the Washingtons is
    a. unique.
    b. like nothing I've ever seen.
    c. innovative.
    d. different.

(d)=(b), (a), (c)

201. Kim
    a. reads all the time.
    b. is a voracious reader.
    c. is extremely well-read.
    d. is a bookworm.

(d), (a), (b), (c)

202. Lytton is quite rich, but then he is
    a. frugal.
    b. stingy.
    c. thrifty.
    d. miserly.
    e. greedy.
    f. a skinflint.

(f), (b)=(d)=(e), (a)=(c)

203. I've known Hawthorne for twenty years, and you're right, he's
    a. domineering.
    b. masterful.
    c. lordly.
    d. overbearing.
    e. dictatorial.
    f. bossy.

    (e), (d)=(f), (a), (c), (b)

204. The paper you turned in last week was
    a. mediocre.
    b. fine.
    c. competent.
    d. adequate.
    e. quite good.

    (a), (d), (c), (e), (b). The last two are so close that one's tone of voice makes more difference than the choice of word.

Bank 2-18

205. Ask your students to write two letters of general recommendation, one positive and one not so positive, for the same individual. Both letters are to describe the same facts—for example, that the individual graduated with a B average, played varsity tennis, seems well liked by others, has a sense of humor.

206. Have students read a commentary or editorial in a newspaper and identify as many emotively charged words and phrases as they can. Have them come up with neutral equivalents for the words on their lists.

Bank 2-19

Identify any unnecessary and potentially offensive references to gender, race, or other features. Rewrite the passages in neutral language. (Note: There are a couple that are perfectly acceptable as they are—it's a good idea to include such items from time to time.)

207. Mrs. Karla Ashcroft won the award for best student in the sciences.

    Karla Ashcroft won the award. . . .

208. Mike O'Neill and his wife, Karen, arrived at the party at eight o'clock.

    Mike and Karen O'Neill arrived at the party at eight o'clock.

209. The job of lineman is the hardest job in the telephone company. Those guys get called out in all kinds of weather.

    People who work out on the lines have the hardest jobs in the telephone company. They get called out in all kinds of weather.

210. The Speaker of the House gave a pretty good speech, but he did not answer any questions afterward.

    No changes required.

211. Congressmen George Thurlow and Shirley Chisolm first ran for public office during the same year.

    Congressman George Thurlow and Congresswoman Shirley Chisolm first ran for public office during the same year.

212. General Colin Powell is the first black army officer to have achieved the chairmanship of the Joint Chiefs of Staff.

    General Colin Powell is the first black army officer to become the chair of the Joint Chiefs of Staff. (This is a bit tricky, of course, since many students will think the reference to Powell's being black is what's objectionable in the original. But that reference is crucial to the meaning of the claim; "chairmanship" is neither necessary nor acceptable where "chair" will do.)

213. Crime report on television (or in the newspaper): "Police are looking for a white man about thirty years old, with brown hair and brown eyes, about five feet ten inches tall. He has tattoos on both forearms—a picture of a snake on the right and the word "mother" on the left."

    No change necessary; the reference to race is part of the description.

214. Another crime news item: "Authorities who were investigating the Eastgate Mall burglaries last night arrested Lewis Thompkins, a black man about twenty-five years old."

    Unless it is a standard practice to identify the races of all people arrested by the authorities, it is discriminatory to do so for any people arrested. (We've heard some pretty good arguments in favor of the policy of never identifying an arrested person's race.)

215. The one hundred most highly paid chief executives in America are paid from one million to twenty-seven million dollars a year. The men in those jobs cannot possibly be worth that kind of money.

    The people in those jobs . . .

216. "That's one small step for a man, and one giant leap for mankind."
    —Neil Armstrong, upon first setting foot on the moon

    There. We finally made it.

Bank 2-20

Below are descriptions of three characters from Anthony Trollope's *Barchester Towers*. Trollope's words produce some vivid images. An interesting and useful exercise is to ask students to write a brief (e.g., one-page) essay explaining what images are evoked and analyzing why and how Trollope's words succeed in creating these images. Alternatively, ask students simply to list the charged words in the descriptions. (This is as close to literary analysis as we'll get—we promise.) The selections are from the 1963 Signet Classics edition.

217. "Mr. Slope is tall and not ill-made. . . . His countenance, however, is not especially prepossessing. His hair is lank and of a dull pale reddish hue. It is always formed into three straight, lumpy masses, each brushed with admirable precision and cemented with much grease. . . . His face is nearly of the same colour as his hair, though perhaps a little redder: it is not unlike beef—beef, however, one would say, of a bad quality. . . . His nose, however, is his redeeming feature: it is pronounced, straight and well-formed; though I myself should have liked it better did it not possess a somewhat spongy, porous appearance, as though it had been cleverly formed out of a red-coloured cork."

218. In person Dr. Proudie is a good-looking man, spruce and dapper and very tidy. He is somewhat below middle height, being about five feet four, but he makes up for the inches which he wants by the dignity with which he carries those which he has. It is no fault of his own if he has not a commanding eye, for he studies hard to assume it. His features are well-formed, though perhaps the sharpness of his nose may give to his face in the eyes of some people an air of insignificance. If so, it is greatly redeemed by his mouth and chin, of which he is justly proud.

219. Exteriorly, Mr. Arabin was not a remarkable person. He was above the middle height, well-made, and very active. His hair, which had been jet black, was now tinged with gray, but his face bore no sign of years. It would perhaps be wrong to say that he was handsome, but his face was nevertheless pleasant to look upon. The cheek-bones were rather too high for beauty, and the formation of the forehead too massive and heavy: but the eyes, nose, and mouth were perfect. There was a continual play of lambent fire about his eyes, which gave promise of either pathos or humor whenever he essayed to speak, and that promise was rarely broken. There was a gentle play about his mouth which declared that his wit never descended to sarcasm.

Of course, there is no one right set of remarks to make about these passages. At the very minimum, students should see (and, believe it or not, some don't) that Trollope describes Mr. Slope in a most unflattering way; that he is almost equally unflattering toward Dr. Proudie, but in a much more subtle way; and that, despite honestly detailing certain physical shortcomings of Mr. Arabin, Trollope manages to convey a very positive impression of this individual. The TV generation seems to have a surprising amount of trouble with this exercise; all the more reason to take the time to do it.

Bank 2-21

True/False

220. Definitions are used only to clarify the meaning of expressions that are not understood.

False

221. Definitions by synonym or definitions by example might serve to reduce the vagueness of an expression.

False

222. It is possible to explain the meaning of the word "thing" by using a definition by example.

False

223. A definition by example could be used to differentiate the meanings of "creature with a heart" and "creature with a kidney."

False

224. The intension of an expression can be stated only in an analytical definition or in a definition by synonym.

True

225. The word "centaur" could be defined by example.

False

226. The extension of at least some expressions can be stated in a definition by example.

True

227. It is possible for two synonyms to have approximately the same emotive force.

True

228. Definitions by example, definitions by synonym, and analytical definitions can all be used to evoke an attitude about the thing defined.

True

229. A definition used to reduce the vagueness of an expression is called a precising definition.

True

Bank 2-22

With the help of a dictionary, explain the differences between the expressions paired below. (If critical thinking shades into improvement of vocabulary and word usage, so much the better.)

230. Childish, childlike

231. Continual, continuing

232. Oral, verbal

233. Flammable, inflammable

234. Famous, notorious

235. Imply, infer

236. Egoist, egotist

237. Valid, true

238. Agnostic, atheist

239. Uninterested, disinterested

240. Decayed, decadent

241. Precedent, precedence

242. Less, fewer

243. Original, aboriginal

244. Unnatural, supernatural

Bank 2-23

Classify each of the following as either definition by example, definition by synonym, or analytical definition. (Items 245–254 are by example; 255–264 are by synonym, and 265–274 are analytical. Mix them up as it pleases you.)

Definitions by example

245. My idea of a successful philosophy major is Steve Martin.

246. When I saw my old crowd at my high school reunion, I suddenly realized what the phrase "motley crew" really meant.

247. The *New York Times* is what I mean by a real newspaper.

248. What Lani just did from the high board is called a full gainer.

249. The simple tools are the pulley, lever, inclined plane, wheel and axle, screw, and wedge.

250. The inscription over the door of the administration building is a sample of a gothic script called Fraktur.

251. "Tenor" applies to vocal ranges like Pavarotti's.

252. Four spades and a heart make a four-flush.

253. I may not be able to explain what pornography is, but the magazines on that rack are cases in point.

254. "It was a dark and stormy night" is what I mean by "cliché."

Definitions by Synonym

255. A foible is a weakness.

256. The public press is sometimes known as the fourth estate.

257. Originally, the word "quarantine" meant forty days.

258. You can use "recreant" nearly anywhere you can use "cowardly," but nobody does anymore.

259. To fledge an arrow is to fletch or feather it.

260. "Shirker" means the same as "slacker."

261. Drywall and Sheetrock are the same thing.

262. You can say either "oscillation" or "vibration"; they're both appropriate, and they amount to the same thing.

263. I can never understand sports announcers' talk of "momentum." It seems to mean nothing more than "doing well."

264. "Pferd" is German for "horse."

Analytical Definitions

265. To philosophers, a realist is a person who believes in the existence of a world outside the mind.

266. The Ojibwa are a tribe of Algonquian Indians of the Lake Superior region.

267. "Bored person" is anyone over twenty-five who lives in Oklahoma, according to my cousin, who lives there.

268. An ogre is a monster who dines on humans.

269. "A miracle: an event described by those to whom it was told by men who did not see it."
    —Elbert Hubbard

270. "Fork, n. An instrument used chiefly for the purpose of putting dead animals into the mouth."
    —Ambrose Bierce

271. "Military intelligence. A contradiction in terms."
     —Groucho Marx

272. "Conservative, *n*. A statesman who is enamored of existing evils, as distinguished from a liberal, who wishes to replace them with others."
     —Ambrose Bierce

273. "Conversation—the enemy of good wine and food."
     —Alfred Hitchcock

274. "A metaphysician is a man who goes into a dark alley at midnight without a light looking for a cat that isn't there."
     —Charles Bowen

Bank 2-24

Classify the following definitions according to their use: to reduce vagueness, to introduce or explain a new or unusual word, to evoke an attitude about something, or to accomplish some other purpose.

275. Energy-efficient house: A house that, at a minimum, has no teenagers.

     To amuse

276. When we use the word "argument" in this class, we'll mean a set of claims, one of which is supported by the others.

     To make precise; to reduce vagueness and ambiguity

277. A barrister is a lawyer in Britain who actually argues the case in court.

     To define an unfamiliar word

278. " 'Best-seller' just means 'not written for anyone with an I.Q. of over a hundred and one.' "
     —George L. Farris, author of several non-best-sellers

     Persuasive definition; sour grapes in abundance

279. The "HO" in "HO gauge" stands for "half-O," which refers to an older scale for model trains. HO gauge is one-half the scale of O-gauge, or one-sixty-fourth of full size.

     To define an unfamiliar phrase

280. No, as far as the bus company is concerned, you count as a senior citizen only after you've reached sixty-five. You won't be able to get the discount fare for three more years.

     Precising definition

281. A floppy disk can come in 5¼-inch or 8-inch size or in 3½-inch size, but a 3½-inch disk is called a microdisk.

   To define an unfamiliar word ("microdisk")

282. "Tombstone: an ugly reminder of one who has been forgotten."
   —H.L. Mencken

   An analytical definition with a darkly humorous purpose, to underscore how short-lived will be others' memories of us after our demise

283. Beard: a bettor who places bets for a friend with a bookie who has cut off the friend for not paying, for snitching to the police, or for having won too much.
   —the Los Angeles Police Department

   To explain a word that may be unfamiliar to the listener

284. "Conservatism is realism about mankind's limitations."
   —George Will

   A persuasive definition favorable to conservatism

285. "Marriage is not only a divine institution, but is the only one instituted in the Garden of Eden which has come down with its continuous line of blessings to the present time."
   —Sylvanus Stall, *What Every Young Man Should Know* (1904)

   To produce an attitude about marriage

286. "Now if we set about to find out what . . . [a] statement means and to determine whether to accept or reject it, we would be engaged in thinking which, for lack of a better term, we shall call critical thinking."
   —B. Othanel Smith

   To reduce vagueness

287. "The cliché is prefabricated language; it is packaged and ready for immediate delivery."
   —William F. Irmscher and Harryette Stover, *The Holt Guide to English*

   Persuasive definition of a negative sort; of course a cliché is by definition trite and hackneyed.

288. "In the category of *economically privileged,* we shall include families with total annual incomes of $75,000 or more."
   —Sarah Hartford and Samuel Cohen, *Trends in College Admissions*

   Precising (stipulative) definition

289. "All the perceptions of the human mind resolve themselves into two distinct kinds, which I shall call Impressions and Ideas."
—David Hume, *Treatise on Human Nature*

To introduce two words

290. "Subduction zone: In interpretations of plate tectonic theory, a belt along the under-margin of a continental plate, where the colliding oceanic plate descends toward or into the mantle."
—Robert M. Norris and Robert W. Webb, *Geology of California*

To explain a new word

291. "When we talk about formatting we are referring to the ways in which Multiplan [a microcomputer-based spreadsheet program] allows us to specify the appearance of our information on the screen and on the printer."
—Erwin Schneider, *Multiplan User's Guide*

To introduce a new use for a word

292. "In this book we use the word *universe* to denote a 'model of the Universe' and avoid making pretentious claims to a true knowledge of the Universe."
—Edward R. Harrison, *Cosmology*

This definition seems to be some sort of vague statement of humility; the author is cautioning his reader not to expect the ultimate truth.

293. ". . . what we call temperature is nothing else but a measurement of the degree of molecular agitation [in a substance]."
—George Gamow, *One, Two, Three . . . Infinity*

This analytic definition is a precising one. If you and some bright students push on this one hard enough, some interesting discussions can happen.

294. "Rock journalism is people who can't write interviewing people who can't talk for people who can't read."
—Frank Zappa

A denigrating persuasive definition

Bank 2-25

The following terms should be easy to invent persuasive definitions—either positive or negative—for. It's a good idea to remind students that persuasive definitions can be analytical definitions, definitions by example, or definitions by synonym; it will help them keep straight the difference between *kinds* of definitions and *uses* of definitions.

295. Attorney

296. Psychiatrist

297. Hippie

298. Republican

299. Poet

300. Banker

301. Education

302. Marxism

303. Ballet

304. Weight lifting

Bank 2-26

305. Find an example of a persuasive definition.

306. Find an example of a precising definition.

Bank 2-27

Criticize the following claims based on the material from Chapter 2 of the text.

307. "A requirement for this course is a term paper on some topic."
     —Statement on course syllabus

     Too vague

308. CHILD'S STOOL GREAT FOR USE IN GARDEN
     —Headline in Buffalo *Courier-Express*

     Ambiguous

309. LOUISIANA GOVERNOR DEFENDS HIS WIFE, GIFT FROM KOREAN
     —Headline in *Milwaukee Journal*

     Ambiguous

310. Cash customers this line only.

     Ambiguous

311. "Who won?"
     —ABC poll question, after the Clinton-Bush presidential debate

     Ambiguous and exceedingly vague

312. "5 times 3 plus 2"

     Ambiguous

313.   SLOW
        CHILDREN AT PLAY
        —An old joke.

The signs aren't really ambiguous.

314. "Is evolution a fact?"

Vague and ambiguous

315. Place the box next to the refrigerator before you open it.

Ambiguous

316. "The enormity of what's taken place is sinking in now."
     —George Bush, just after his election

We don't think Bush knew what "enormity" means. Have students check their dictionary.

317. "The instructor will not inform a student that he or she will be charged with cheating during an examination."
     —Statement on course syllabus

Ambiguous

318. "Alcohol is present in about 50 percent of fatal traffic accidents among teenagers."

"Alcohol is present" is pretty vague for almost any context; so is "about 50 percent," but in many contexts it would not be too vague.

319. "All of you are not thinking."

Ambiguous

320. Computer salesman to customer who does not know what kind of computer he needs: "You really need a model with a 100 meg hard disk and tape backup; those use 1-meg SIMMS for a total of 4 megs of RAM."

Use of unfamiliar words, obviously intended more to impress the customer than to inform

321. "We can't and we won't lower the quality of faculty in the California state universities, but it may be time to redefine what we mean by 'quality.' "
     —California State University System Chancellor Barry Munitz

This is almost gobbledygook. What it might be to "redefine" quality is pretty vague; it sounds as if he plans to lower standards and disguise the fact with redefinitions.

322. "I am a fuzzy bunny lover."
     —From a student paper

Ambiguous

323. "Life its own self, as Dan Jenkins said. Life its own self. Figure that one out, Norm. But what it means is, I have a lot more to learn from President Reagan."
—George Bush, when asked, upon first becoming president, whether his predecessor, Ronald Reagan, was advising him (quoted in Ross and Petras, *The 776 Stupidest Things ever Said*)

In other words, "yes."

324. "Bruce Sutter has been around for a while and he's pretty old. He's thirty-five years old. That will give you some idea of how old he is."
—Ron Fairly, San Francisco Giants broadcaster (quoted in Ross and Petras, *The 776 Stupidest Things Ever Said*)

We don't cover it in the text, but although stating the obvious doesn't necessarily impede clarity, it can make you look silly. The following headlines, sent from Bangs Tapscott, suffer the same problem.

325. MAN IS FATALLY SLAIN

326. WAR DIMS HOPE FOR PEACE

327. "My position on Vietnam is very simple. And I feel this way. I haven't spoken on it because I haven't felt there was any major contribution that I had to make at the time. I think that our concepts as a nation and that our actions have not kept pace with the changing conditions, and therefore our actions are not completely relevant today to the realities of the magnitude and the complexity of the problems that we face in this conflict."
—New York governor Nelson Rockefeller, when asked by a reporter about his position on the Vietnam war

Gobbledygook

328. He may have trouble with the long putts, but nobody is better at dropping his shorts.

Ambiguous

329. "In terms of arting, where the reference condition is not fixed or even known conceptually but rather something coming to being, what can we hope through our formative hermeneutic movement? To make the 'otherness' of the arting process more other, more 'objective' in a newer sense and less 'subjective' in the older sense, so that the arting process itself speaks more purely?"
—Kenneth R. Beittel, Penn State University (quoted in Edwin Newman, *Strictly Speaking*)

Vague, unnecessarily complicated, and silly

330. "To make tea, make water not too hot. Too hot water is not for best flavor."
—Instructions to an imported tea

Too vague for us

331. The sink did not drain because the trap was clogged.

Ambiguous

332. "If the lights burn dimly or not at all when you first turn them on, the battery is probably run down. Test the battery. If it is run down, you should try to find out what caused it."
—Crouse and Anglin, *The Auto Book*

"Burn dimly" probably isn't too vague for most readers of a car-repair manual.

Bank 2-28

True/False

333. It is rarely, if ever, appropriate to insist that a claim be totally free from vagueness.

True

334. Vague claims are more difficult to prove false than precise claims.

True

335. Any definition by example of the word "terrier" would also qualify as a definition by example of the word "canine."

True

336. If you want to make a word's meaning more precise, a definition by synonym will work better than an analytical definition.

False

Bank 2-29

Evaluate the following quotations from a local newspaper.

337. "Sexual offenses are becoming native to our culture."

338. "Dangerous offenders incorporate pornography into their preparatory stimulation before seeking a victim."

339. "Pornography interferes with interpersonal relationships in everyone who uses it."

We would like to see discussion emphasize the obscurity of item 337, the vagueness of item 338, and the question of the knowability of both items 338 and 339.

Bank 2-30

Comparative general claims for criticism:

340. A new antilock rear brake system has reduced the distance required to stop from fifty miles per hour by 11 percent.

We presume that the car stops 11 percent more quickly than the same car did without the new brake system. It is possible that there's some weaseling going on here if the context leads one to believe that the car stops 11 percent faster than the competition.

341. Reagan was a better president than Nixon was.

How so? In what way?

342. The county unemployment rate went up 40 percent during our opponent's administration, but since we took the reins it has risen only 35 percent in the same length of time. Clearly, we have done the better job.

Probably not, as a matter of fact. It's wise to remember that events at the national level affect the rate of unemployment at least as much as county administration. More to the immediate point: If the number of unemployed at the beginning of the speaker's administration was the same as it was at the end of the opponent's, the latter did the better job. (Say that the number of jobless in the county was 5,000 at the beginning of the opponent's administration and 7,000 at the end of it—an increase of 40 percent. If the number of jobless increased by 35 percent during the speaker's administration, a total of 2,450 were added to the unemployment rolls during that time, whereas only 2,000 were added during the opponent's.)

343. "The pride is back."

As compared to the past, presumably. This Chrysler advertising slogan, taken from a popular song, "Born in America," strives to stir patriotic sentiment for Chrysler products (note pseudoreasoning). There is no definitive way to measure national pride, of course.

344. The office has become more productive since we changed from typewriters to word processors, although it took about half a year for the staff to learn how to use them well enough to produce the gain.

"Productive" is somewhat vague, although it can be made quite clear.

345. The increase in the number and support of conservative think tanks has been substantial since the mid-1970s. The American Enterprise had twelve resident thinkers when Jimmy Carter was elected; today it has forty-five. The Heritage Foundation has sprung from nothing to command an annual budget of $11 million. The budget of the Center for Strategic and International Studies has grown from $975,000 ten years ago to $8.6 million today. Over a somewhat longer period the endowment of the Hoover Institution has increased from $2 million to $70 million.
—Adapted from Gregg Easterbrook, "Ideas Move Nations"

Although some of the language may sound vague—for example, "sprung from nothing"—these are all straightforward comparisons with relatively well identified times in the past.

346. You'd be better off if you got more sleep.

Unclear terms of comparison: better off than what? Also, the comparison itself is obscure: In what way better off—looks, health, attitude, or what? The terms of the second comparison are clearer, but it's still pretty unclear how much additional sleep counts as more.

347. Reading novels is a more productive use of one's time than going to movies.

Just any old novel? More productive of what? Just any old movie?

348. I'd much rather stay home and read a novel than go to a movie.

This kind of remark is different from item 347. The speaker is describing a preference that is clear enough for nearly any context in which the claim might be made.

349. Doctor Mohanty is younger than I.

Clear comparison unless the context is unusual.

350. The best American film of the 1980s was *Out of Africa*.

Best in what way?

351. In 1985, more people were killed by handguns in the United States than in Great Britain.

Clear comparison (The score, for the record: Us, 10,728; Them, 8.)

352. Beer drinkers are 23.2 times more likely than teetotalers to have unhappy marriages.

What's a beer drinker? Anybody who ever drinks a beer? How are unhappy marriages distinguished from happy ones (or so-so ones)? Could such a comparison really be accurate to a decimal place? This isn't a very helpful statistic.

353. "The answer to the question, 'How are blacks doing in America?' is 'Better than ever before.'"
—Ronald Reagan, on the first national observation of the birthday of Martin Luther King, Jr.

In what way better? Income? (The median family income for black families was higher when Reagan made his comment than it was in 1968, the year Martin Luther King, Jr., was killed. It was also further behind the median family income for whites than in 1968.)

354. George Bush ran a more negative campaign in 1988 than did Michael Dukakis.

"Negative campaign" is vague. And it may be that the speaker means that Bush was negative for more of the campaign than was Dukakis, since the latter, it is generally thought, slung mud only near the end.

355. NCAA rules for recruiting athletes are broken more frequently by Division 1 schools than by Division 2 schools.

This could mean either that the typical Division 1 school breaks rules more frequently than the typical Division 2 school or that the aggregate of Division 1 violations is greater than the aggregate of Division 2 violations.

356. Chrysanthemums that have been pinched back produce bigger blooms than those that have not.

This seems clear and reasonable. Most people who would be interested in the claim would know what "pinched back" means.

357. The North Koreans still have a stronger military force than the South Koreans.

"Stronger" could mean either bigger in terms of more troops, or better armed, or both, or maybe something else yet.

358. Compact discs produce a clearer sound than do vinyl records.

We don't have any trouble with this, although what counts as a "clearer sound" may be different for different listeners. (Some music critics find vinyl records "warmer" than CDs. We don't know what that means either.)

359. [Background: *Aspartame* is the generic term for the sweetener known as NutraSweet and manufactured by G. D. Searle & Co. Ellen Ruppell Shell wrote an article for the *Atlantic* ("Sweetness and Health," August 1985) in which she stated that claims made by Searle & Co. that aspartame's component amino acids (aspartic acid and phenylalanine) occur naturally in many foods are "somewhat misleading." The following are brief excerpts from a letter and reply in the January 1986 edition of the magazine.]

"Shell alleges that aspartame 'delivers . . . amino acids in a much more concentrated form than a person would normally consume.' Aspartic acid and phenylalanine occur naturally in protein-containing foods, and the normal diet provides quantities far exceeding those derived from aspartame in aspartame-sweetened foods. . . ."
—John P. Heybach, Director, Scientific Affairs, NutraSweet Group, G. D. Searle & Co.

"As a scientist, Dr. Heybach surely understands that concentration and quantity are two very different things. Aspartame delivers aspartic acid and phenylalanine in a much more concentrated form than do normal proteins, which contain up to eighteen other amino acids to balance the load."
—Ellen Ruppell Shell

These brief excerpts are not intended to settle the aspartame issue, of course, but to give students an opportunity to sort out just what issue the two writers differ on: what is being compared to what?

Evaluate these claims, paying particular attention to problems of clarity. Some of the claims present problems of knowability, though we don't address knowability per se in this chapter.

360. Professional sports? Never watch 'em. They're all fixed.

It's theoretically possible but very unlikely. Even if the claim were true, how would anybody go about establishing it? We'd like to hear the proof.

361. My liberal colleagues in Congress are all big spenders.

How do you identify "liberals" (or "conservatives," for that matter)? The class is too vaguely defined, as is that of "big spenders." Note: If the speaker defines "liberals" as those who vote to spend the most money, he has begged the question—he has, possibly surreptitiously, turned it into an analytic claim.

362. The world and everything in it was created fifteen minutes ago, complete with fictitious memories and false records.

As Bertrand Russell noted, there's no way to disprove *this claim.*

363. I'm not very photogenic—no photograph anybody has ever made of me really looks like me.

"Photogenic" is not a clearly defined notion, but there probably isn't anything that can be done about it. We doubt that no photograph resembles the speaker; it's more likely that he just doesn't like the way he looks in the photographs. Maybe he just doesn't like the way he looks.

364. Bomb threats on abortion clinics are called in by the clinics themselves to gain sympathy and support from the public and news media.

The general claim would be very difficult to establish, though one might know of a particular instance in which this event happened.

365. Digital recordings may be all the rage these days, but every serious audiophile knows that a good analog disc played on a music system of high quality is better than even the best digital version.

"Serious audiophile" isn't clear—could the speaker mean those people who prefer analog recordings and hence be begging the question? Some of the other phrases are vague too—"good analog disc," "system of high quality"—it may or may not be possible to specify more clearly what's intended by such terms.

366. The universe and everything in it doubled in size last night.

Unknowable claim—although this is controversial among philosophers.

367. Every account that Delwood has worked on has come back with computational errors in it.

We don't find anything wrong with this one. "Computational errors" could be spelled out precisely, but the context probably does not require such precision.

368. From a letter to the editor: "It appears that the administration's foreign policy is increasingly far out."

What's being said about the administration's foreign policy? Who knows?

369. "In no previous epoch were adversaries so continuously and totally mobilized for instant war. It is a statistical certainty that hair-trigger readiness cannot endure as a permanent condition."
—Nobel Peace Prize winner Dr. Bernard Lown, cofounder of International Physicians for the Prevention of Nuclear War

"Continuously and totally mobilized for instant war" is not too vague; everyone understands what Lown means. "A statistical certainty" is apt to be less clear to many listeners. These claims would pass muster in many contexts, however. Note that only the first one is a general claim.

370. Conservative Christians are a politically sophisticated voting bloc.

This may be an expression of praise; then again, it may not. The claim does not make clear exactly what is being said about conservative Christians. It's not even totally clear who conservative Christians are.

371. Of the over 100,000 aliens who married U.S. citizens last year, 40 percent did so only to bypass immigration laws.

We're skeptical whether such a precise percentage could be known in such a matter.

372. "It is prudent to assume that all nations attempt to spy on other nations to the extent that their capacities and interests dictate."
—Baltimore Sun

It is known that many nations employ spies, and it is a reasonable inference from what is known about history and human nature to believe that most do. Further, the assumption is prudent.

373. Every Communist country in the world has been a violator of the fundamental human rights of individuals.

We recognize clear-cut cases of Communist countries and violations of fundamental human rights, but both terms have very fuzzy edges indeed; general claims like this one require more precision if they're to be acceptable.

374. "Caution: Cigarette smoking is hazardous to your health."

Vague, but knowable. And known.

375. Most voters in the 1988 presidential election believed that the Republican candidate better represented traditional values than did the Democratic candidate.

It would be hard to know whether this was true even if we could identify just what "traditional values" meant. There may be something to this claim, but it would take someone more willing to go out on a limb than we to say exactly what it is.

376. All of the last three years have been extremely dry.

"Extremely dry" is pretty vague, but it isn't that bad; this could still be a useful claim.

377. Obscene movies available at movie rental outlets are harmful to children who watch them.

Defining "obscene" is notoriously difficult, but there surely are items most people would agree fit the term. What counts as harmful to children may be just as difficult to determine. This is a pretty vague claim.

378. Nobody under seventeen is permitted unless accompanied by an adult.

This is clear enough, provided we know what counts as an adult.

379. Most of the science books in the high school library were published before 1960.

What's a science book? This probably isn't as important as whatever inference is likely to be drawn from it. We presume that this means an awful lot of the library's science books are seriously out of date.

Chapter 3
Evaluating Informative Claims

This chapter occupies an important niche in the overall scheme of the text. Our position is that critical thinking includes determining whether a claim is worth accepting even when only bad reasons or no reasons (including pseudoreasons) have been given for it; for this reason we need to say something about how to determine when such unsupported claims can reasonably be accepted. This chapter carries much of that burden.

Students find most of the material in this chapter familiar, but not many of them have had occasion to contemplate its importance. Background knowledge, for example, is vitally important to each of them, but an appreciation of its importance runs contrary to the standard "is it going to be on the exam?" attitude. Similarly, students are vaguely aware that all the knowledge they have that isn't based on personal observation is based on somebody else's word. But something so crucial as knowing why somebody else's word is worth taking is a matter they are unlikely to have contemplated very carefully, even though they often have strong opinions about a source's credibility. Typically, they will distrust the sources of claims they find disagreeable and blindly trust the authors of the remainder. Sometimes, students (like the rest of us) would like to believe in a source just because he or she is charming or unusual—Harry Truman, who's quoted in the "Authority of Experience" box, for example. We'd like to think that such a colorful curmudgeon knew what he was talking about. Harry would have been better off if he'd read the chapter.

You can expect a number of the exercises in the chapter to stimulate some discussion. So even though there are fewer exercises in this chapter than in some of the others, you can expect at least some of them to eat up a good bit of class time.

In some of the exercises, we ask the student to rank various sources in terms of their credibility about some subject. We predicate the task on the assumption that nothing is known about the sources beyond what is given in the exercise. Thus, if the request is to rank, say, the credibility of a professor of sociology against a state senator with regard to some sociological question, we would expect the professor to be ranked above the senator even though in fact a given senator may be more of an expert about the issue than some particular sociologist. Your students—and quite likely you, too— may disagree with some of the rankings we give in the answers. But we've found that the discussion that results from the disagreement is useful to our objectives in trying to give guidance in the difficult task of ascertaining credibility.

The sensational tabloid headlines are amusing (but the realization that millions of people buy those tabloids is less amusing), and students get a kick out of the "Fearless Forecasts" box. None of this should undercut our trust in the general reliability of expert opinion, however.

Exercises Unanswered in the Text

Exercise 3-2

1. Poor lighting; noisy surroundings; distractions; fog, haze, or other bad weather

2. When we are emotionally upset, preoccupied with other matters, or fatigued

3. a. Our own observations
   b. Our background knowledge
   c. Other credible claims
   d. Credible
   e. Biased

4. Our own firsthand observations

5. Our memory

Exercise 3-4

2. If the friend's interests and needs are similar to ours and we trust her judgement, then we like (b) best. Source (c) will certainly be biased, and (a) might be. Expertise among writers of newspaper columns varies a lot, as does level of bias; at best they're writing for a *mass* audience. Source (e) brings up many of the same problems, plus the possibility of advertising pressure. Magazine reviews, however, usually go into more detail and are more sophisticated than those generally found in newspapers; they are therefore probably more valuable sources for people who are moderately knowledgeable.

4. We'd expect the former owner's mechanic to know the car best. We'd expect the salesperson to be the least reliable, mainly because of bias. The independent mechanic is probably unbiased and knowledgeable but isn't likely to be able to learn as much about the former mechanic in a short time. We would not trust ourselves to be unbiased, especially if the car is a sporty red convertible.

5. Our first choice is the magician. We think most of the rest are about equally credible, except for the psychic, whom we presume would be biased.

Exercise 3-5

4. We think that the *New England Journal of Medicine* and the National Institutes of Health are the most credible sources for this and most matters relating to health. Your physician, *Runner's World,* and *Time* are about equally credible, but all three of them must rely on other sources for their information about the subject, and all three have access to about the same sources (of which the *New England Journal of Medicine* is a prime example).

5. A physician would be a credible source of information about the physiological and biological processes involved in the development of a human being from conception to birth. A lawyer would be credible on the various legal issues surrounding abortion. A minister would be a credible spokesperson for a particular religion's position on the question asked. Because philosophers receive special training in detecting tacit assumptions, recognizing subtle distinctions, and evaluating reasoning, it would be reasonable to expect a philosopher to offer the most careful and comprehensive treatment of the question. If you thought that *you* are the most credible source, then you probably assume that the question is purely subjective. Such is not necessarily the case; it is another assumption that bears some examination, and for guidance in that examination it would again be reasonable to turn to a philosopher.

Exercise 3-6

2. a. Since he spent two years in the Peace Corps in Venezuela, Calhoun would be a credible source of information on this question. Note, however, that his experience in Latin America may have been limited to Venezuela and may be somewhat out of date, though the fact that he is a consultant in "numerous developing countries" leaves open the possibility of more recent and more widespread experience.
   b. The assessment of Calhoun's credibility on this subject parallels the previous answer, for the most part. Calhoun was in Latin America very soon after the Cuban revolution, and so his views on its *immediate* effects, at least in Venezuela, should be very credible indeed. It is not clear how much this part of his experience would translate into credibility on the revolution's long-range effects, however.
   c. We would expect Calhoun to be a real expert on the physical principles involved in water pumping and transportation (which would ultimately account for a faucet's leaking), and we would expect him to have had extensive hands-on experience with pipes, tools, washers, and so on. But he is not a plumber, and so we should not assume he's as much of an expert on leaky faucets as is someone who spends each day dealing with these items and who knows the tricks of the trade.
   d. We would expect Calhoun to be a well-qualified expert on *some* aspects of technology in Third World countries, but whether he would be similarly qualified about *every* aspect—for example, the use of computers—is something the biography does not tell us. We would put his credibility ahead of that of most people on such subjects as computers in developing countries, but not ahead of someone whose expertise is in that very field.
   e. We would expect Calhoun to have some knowledge concerning this matter, but his company's involvement in the pipeline is likely to produce some bias in his opinions. Unless we had reason to think Calhoun was unbiased, we would prefer a neutral party's opinion, all things considered.
   f. Calhoun doubtless has some considerable expertise in matters like this, since he has had such substantial success in them. We would rate him a very credible source.
   g. There is no reason to think Calhoun especially qualified in this matter.

Exercise 3-7

We don't presume to give a "right" answer for each of these, but we'll try to provide a few notes that may be worthwhile.

1. Expecte huge bias from the National Rifle Association on one side, of course, and, *maybe,* similar bias on the other side from groups like Handgun Control. Police chiefs, lately willing to speak on this issue, may be more believable. The most interesting—and reasonable—stuff we've heard about lately has come from James Wilson, a professor at UCLA. At this writing, we know of the work only at second hand.

2. There are quite a few, on quite a few topics, of course. Students should be reminded that being an expert in a field does *not* guarantee that one will make wise decisions; technical expertise does not necessarily translate into good judgment about public policy. (For example, Sam Nunn may know all there is to know about military hardware, budget, and even tactics, but this does not mean he knows whether it is best for us to go to war.)

3. Polished speech, a nice sense of humor, good looks, a personal connection to the listener (e.g., a relative or someone from the same town), agreement with the *listener's* views.

Exercise 3-9

2. We think it's probably false that Ms. Haskew actually taught paganism and devil worship in her fourth-grade classroom. Whether she even mentioned it is probably arguable, at least from what little is provided here (there was little more on that particular issue in the article we saw). Given the quotation from one of the parents who opposed Haskew, we expect the problem was that she tried to teach her students *anything at all.*

3. Almost certainly true—we'd expect Mr. May to have done his homework.

4. Further information necessary (and probably not forthcoming). We hope reasonable people can take different positions on this issue, because the authors of this book do. One thinks the claim is more likely to be true than not; the other thinks there's no more evidence to believe it true than to believe it false.

5. We think this is probably true. Notice the difference between the issue here—which has to do with the purpose of the commission—and the one mentioned in item 4.

6. Probably false, at least as it's written here

7. Probably false

9. Probably true

10. Probably true

11. That the British manufacturer of Monopoly made the claim about the items being smuggled in Monopoly sets is very likely true.

13. We find this incredible—that is, we don't believe it. That is, what we understand of it we don't believe. The "foundation" referred to is, we expect, something short of a reputable scientific institution, and the fact that the manuscript (which one of the authors received in the mail) is not published by a known publisher hardly lends credibility. Mainly, however, the observations expressed in this passage conflict directly with our background knowledge.

14. Since these claims are made by an individual who, as a staff writer for a reputable nontechnical science magazine, is probably well informed; and since they are printed in *Esquire,* a magazine that is not in general a suspicious source of information; and also since they coincide with our own observations that a person's features seem to become more pronounced with age, we'd be inclined to accept them. The claims are not, of course, particularly precise, and they are general statements not intended to apply to each individual person to the same degree. (Incidentally, we would be pleased to see a more authoritative source—for example, a professor of physiology writing in a science journal—pronounce them false.)

15. Probably true

16. This comes from a credible source. Without hearing conflicting claims from other equally credible sources, we'd accept it as a reliable assessment of the evidence as of that date.

Chapter 3 Test Question/Exercise Banks

Bank 3-1

Assess each of the following claims as probably true, probably false, as requiring further documentation before judgment, or as a claim that cannot properly be evaluated. Consider both the nature of the claim and the source.

1. "In the early 1800's, bears were a nuisance to settlers in upstate New York."
   —Smithsonian

   Probably true

2. NO CHOLESTEROL!
   —Label on Crisco Corn Oil

   Probably true. Vegetable oils do not contain cholesterol, and even if you didn't know that, such claims made by national brands are usually true (despite several famous exceptions).

3. "Mezzo-soprano Frederica von Stade's two little girls always tried to keep her from singing in church because, they said, every time she did, everyone would turn around and stare at her."
   —Joseph McLellan, in the *Washington Post*

   Probably true

4. "By age 30, roughly a quarter of men and women have discernibly graying hair. Even so, only 28 percent of us ever become completely white haired."
—Lowell Ponte, *Reader's Digest*

Probably true

5. "Enough is enough! A national survey finds a majority of American adults do not support more restrictive or tougher anti-smoking measures."
—The Tobacco Institute

Probably true, but you'd want to know more about the poll and the questions it asked before drawing any conclusions from it.

6. "In the near future look for floods in Britain which will culminate in the flooding of Parliament."
—A prediction made by Maitreya Swami, "The World Teacher," in the *News Release of the Tara Center,* N. Hollywood, Calif.

Probably false. We won't get into the philosophical difficulties involved in attaching truth values to future contingent events.

7. "Smoking more than triples the likelihood of premature facial wrinkling."
—Dr. Donald Kadunce, lead author of a group of University of Utah scientists, reporting in *Annals of Internal Medicine*

Probably true, but you'd probably want to have a look at the study to see, among other things, how the degree of wrinkling is ascertained.

8. "With due regard to the recent experience by certain individuals in the Russian city of Voronezh, the Space Brothers who landed and exited from their craft were on a peace mission. . . . What was thought to be and reported mistakenly as a knife held in the hand of one of the Space Brothers was a thought, only in the mind of the reporter. . . . What was being held was a communication device. . . . this device was translating the thoughts of the Space voyager into the language that could be understood in that particular part of the world."
—Press release, Unarius Academy of Science

Probably false. So why was Space Brother even thinking of a knife?

9. University student to prof.: "I'm sorry I missed the test on Thursday, Dr. Aarsack. My grandmother unexpectedly died, and I had to go home."

This is a good discussion item, though the straightforward answer is that more documentation is needed.

10. "A few years ago AT&T did two surveys showing that technically trained persons did not achieve as many top managerial jobs in the company as liberal arts graduates did."
—*New York Times*

It is often risky to accept what secondhand reports say about what surveys "show," but the New York Times *is a very credible source. This claim is probably true. Note, however, the vagueness of "did not achieve" and "top managerial jobs."*

11. According to Funk & Wagnalls *Hammond World Atlas,* the three longest rivers in the world are the Nile, the Amazon, and the Yangtze.

    Probably true; if you can't trust your Funk & Wagnalls in a matter like this, who can you trust?

12. Letter to the editor: "Your editorial page of October 15 contained a cartoon that was highly offensive. . . ."
    —*Midfield Sentinel*

    Probably true; the individual is the best authority on what he or she finds offensive.

13. "Driven by the Gramm-Rudman mandate to cut $46 billion from the budget for fiscal 1987, OMB director James Miller is proposing to sell off whole programs and agencies from the federal establishment. Miller's hit list is mostly secret for the time being, but administration sources say it includes some large, costly and much-venerated legacies of the Democratic past. One example: the Bonneville Power Administration, which provides low-cost electricity to the Pacific Northwest from a far-flung system of hydroelectric dams and substations, including the Grand Coulee Dam."
    —*Newsweek*

    This is probably true, since we would expect Newsweek *to have good Washington sources in such matters. But notice: What is it that's probably true? The claim itself is quite vague. What does "proposing" mean, for example?*

14. "Q: Did Marilyn Monroe keep a diary about her relationships with John and Robert Kennedy?"
    "A: No."
    —Walter Scott's Personality Parade, *Parade*

    Scott's question-and-answer column is probably a reasonably reliable source of information about the questions asked. Secret diaries are always a possibility, of course.

15. Remark heard in a coffee shop: "There is a disproportionate percentage of left-handed people in politics."

    This claim would take much more authority before we'd believe it. Much of this sort of casual conversation is based on anecdotal evidence (see Chapter 12). The claim is also vague: What does the speaker mean by "politics"?

16. Comment from an acquaintance: "I saw Bigfoot with my own eyes! It was huge!"

    Probably false; observational error is more likely than incorrect background knowledge.

17. "Every day 5,000 Americans try cocaine for the first time—a total of 22 million so far—according to estimates by the National Institute on Drug Abuse. About five million people are believed to be using the drug at least once a month, and they are administering it to themselves in increasingly destructive ways."
    —James Lieber, in the *Atlantic*

We don't know much about the National Institute on Drug Abuse, but we have found the Atlantic *to be pretty reliable in factual matters. Notice that no exact figures are claimed; the first is explicitly said to be an estimate, and the phrases "about" and "believed to be" qualify the second. We would expect these claims to be close to the truth.*

18. "General Motors is on a journey to a far-off place just around the corner, the 21st Century. With the help of its thousands of scientists, designers, and engineers, GM is embarking on an odyssey into the unknown. Roads paved with scientific and techno-logical wonders that might seem like science fictions. But at GM, they're reality. . . ."
—From a General Motors magazine advertisement

This is too vague to make a judgment about. (In fairness to the ad, we might note that a couple of later passages in it were less vague. But not much.)

19. You've taken your car in to the local branch of a nationwide chain of brake and muffler shops for an advertised "free brake inspection." After the inspection, the service manager tells you: "I'm afraid your linings are almost completely gone and the drums need turning. You need a complete brake overhaul."

Probably true. The fact that the brake shop is part of a nationwide chain gives a measure of credibility to the service report, even if the shop is independently owned; there would be someone beyond the service manager to complain to if you discovered the service report was dishonest. However, unless you've been having problems with your brakes or have verified the service report by your own visual inspection, you should get a second opinion in a case like this. Brake inspections are widely offered free or for a small charge.

20. From a short glossary at the end of an article on hard disk storage systems in a computer magazine: "*Transfer rate:* The rate at which stored data travels from the hard disk to the Macintosh bus. Mac serial ports clock at 920 kbits/sec, unless the hard disk is configured to run AppleTalk Transfer Protocols."

Probably true. Most reputable specialty magazines get their facts right most of the time. There are many such areas, however, from automobiles to computers to fitness, in which magazines devoted to the subject print controversial opinions. A person familiar with the field usually knows which areas are controversial; if you're a neophyte, ask the opinion of a more knowledgeable friend.

21. "Do you feel insecure? Or are you confident about your position in life? According to Dr. Ian Cameron, how and where you stand in an elevator will reveal the answers to these questions."
—Reported in the *National Examiner.* Dr. Cameron is described in the article as "a noted scientist and researcher."

Is this remark the conclusion of a study? A speculation on the part of Dr. Cameron? Who is Dr. Cameron, anyway? We are suspicious because so little information is given about him. More importantly, the claim runs counter to our background knowledge. Our experience indicates that when we are free to choose where we stand in an elevator, our choice is affected by whether we must push the elevator buttons, how many other people are in the elevator, how close our destination floor is, and so on. We don't think very much can be determined about one's personality by observing how and where he or she stands in an elevator.

22. "[Atmospheric nuclear] tests do not seriously endanger either present or future generations."
—Edward Teller, physicist, one of the "fathers" of the atomic bomb, 1958

We'd expect this kind of claim, coming from such a source, to be trustworthy. That it turned out to be false probably shows either that Teller was biased or that there was not enough information on the effects of atmospheric tests in 1958.

23. From a letter to the editor by a person we've never heard of: "Eighty-five percent of the jail population smokes."

What's meant by "jail population" is a bit vague; we presume the letter is talking about inmates. We find the claim plausible—at least we would not be surprised if it were true. This plausibility is inherent in the claim; it is not due to the fact that any particular person made it, especially since no source information is provided.

24. "Warning: St. John [in the Virgin Islands] is very much a 'cash only' island. Most restaurants and car rental agencies accept cash or travelers checks only."
—Janet Fullwood, travel writer for the *Dallas Times Herald*

Probably true

25. "In the history books, the personal-computer slump of 1985 will be a footnote compared to the Japanese assault on the American semiconductor industry."
—*Newsweek*

Probably true, but with reservations: this claim is phrased vaguely (what does it mean to be a footnote?).

26. "The West German Cabinet has conditionally agreed to let private companies enroll in the research [on the Strategic Defense Initiative]."
—From an editorial in the *Los Angeles Times*

Probably true

27. "The yearly cancer rate for men in Glasgow, Scotland, is 130 cases per 100,000."
—"Atlas of Cancer in Scotland," World Health Organization (an agency of the United Nations)

Probably true

28. "My cat has fewer brains than a hubcap!"
—Spoken by one of the authors of the text after his cat had spent three days on his housetop

Probably false

29. "The American word 'yup' means 'sex' in Russia."
—Comedian Yakov Smirnoff (who was born and lived in Russia for sixteen years before emigrating to America in 1977). Smirnoff uses the claim in question as a basis for "yuppie" jokes.

Probably true

30. According to a Baron Gottfried von Swieten, King Frederick of Prussia claimed that he had once given a chromatic theme to Johann Sebastian Bach, who had immediately made of it a fugue in four parts, then in five parts, and finally in eight parts.
—From H. T. David and A. Mendel, *The Bach Reader*, reported in *Gödel, Escher, and Bach,* by Douglas R. Hofstadter

One needs to know something of music to realize how incredible this remark is. To improvise a six-part fugue is nearly beyond imagination (Hofstadter likens it to playing sixty games of chess simultaneously while blindfolded and winning them all). Even Bach, whose genius strains credibility on many counts, is unlikely to have been able to improvise an eight-part fugue. Presumably either King Frederick or the good Baron was doing some exaggerating.

31. Hudie Ledbetter ("Leadbelly") was not only a writer and performer of songs but also an unusually powerful man. Alan Lomax, the historian of American folk music, wrote that "in the Texas Penitentiary he was the number one man in the number one gang on the number one farm in the state—the man who could carry the lead row in the field for 12 or 14 hours a day under the broiling July and August sun." He could pick a bale of cotton in a day—that's 500 pounds!
—Adapted from liner notes to the record *Leadbelly* (Everest recording FS-202)

We find this more likely to be true than the previous item, but one should be warned that claims like this are subject to exaggeration, especially over time. (Legends tend to grow after their subjects are gone.) No source is given for the last claim in the passage, but Lomax knew Ledbetter and probably had at least some firsthand information about his physical prowess.

32. "1985 was a turbulent year. It was a year that began with record profits and sales. It was also a year in which we reported the first quarterly loss in Apple's history. We had to take swift action. We did. And it's working."
—Apple Computer, Inc., *1985 Annual Report*

The remarks about profits, sales, and a quarterly loss are probably true; they are easily investigated. The remarks about taking swift action and that the actions taken are "working" are vague enough to be difficult to evaluate.

33. "Of all species, only pigs and humans like liquor."
—Charles Halsted, Professor of Internal Medicine, University of California, Davis

We'd ordinarily accept this claim as probably true, if it were not for the fact that one of us once had a dog that loved to lick wine jugs.

34. "Lottery director Mark Michalko said Thursday that allegations that Californians are squandering money they once used for food to buy lottery tickets 'are just not correct.' . . . California Grocers Association president Don Beaver raised the issue earlier in the week, saying five supermarket chains had complained that grocery sales dropped about 5 percent after lottery tickets went on sale October 3."
—*Sacramento Bee*

Based just on information contained in this news item, we'd suspend judgment on the question of whether lottery sales have diminished food sales.

35. "Contrary to popular belief, 'The Star-Spangled Banner' has been the nation's official song only since 1931."
—James Kilpatrick, syndicated columnist

We'd be very surprised if Kilpatrick were mistaken about a fact like this.

36. "[Bybon, a Greek of the sixth century B.C.] threw a 315-pound block of red sandstone over his head. The feat was reported after archeologists found a description of Bybon's act inscribed on the rock itself."
—*The Book of Lists*

We think this may be true; there are people around now who could perform this feat. (It isn't said how far *Bybon threw the rock.) Notice, however, that the documentation of Bybon's act would be a little difficult to corroborate at this point.*

Bank 3-2

Keeping in mind the sources cited, discuss the credibility of the claims made in the passages.

37. "The UFOnauts are usually clothed in shiny, tight fitting, one piece suits, and in most reports seem able to breathe our air without difficulty. Telepathy seems involved in most contacts. . . . If you are tired of the same old pseudoexplanations, official debunkings, and lame duck logic from quacks suffering megalomania, then you are invited to join the concerted efforts of the UFO Contact Center. . . ."
—From a pamphlet, undated, issued in the 1980s by Aileen E. Edwards, director of UFO Contact Center International in Seattle, Washington.

The "center" is a clearinghouse for those who have had contact with extraterrestrials to share their fears and insights without condemnation. Edwards herself has had such an experience, says the pamphlet, and now is reaching out to help people with similar stories. The language has a typical "us vs. them" flavor, with those who would offer a more coherent explanation labeled as "quacks"; the assumption is that those who have certain experiences are best able to determine "what really happened."

38. "'You hear in the folklore about miracles happening, but I have never seen one thing yet that could be called an actual medical cure,' says Douglas Sharon, a University of California, Los Angeles, anthropologist who has studied curandrismo [Peruvian folk medicine] on the north coast of Peru for 18 years."
—From a *National Geographic Magazine* news feature

This seems a clear-cut case of good credibility; yet the feature goes on to point out that several other anthropologists, conducting a study for the National Institute of Mental Health, have found that in thirty-eight cases of nervousness, faintness or dizziness, poor appetite, nausea, and the like, the curanderos (the folk healers) were effective in thirty-five of the cases in alleviating all symptoms. Researchers tentatively suggest the curanderos use psychotherapeutic methods to eliminate psychosomatic symptoms in their patients. So part of the credibility rests on what one calls "an actual medical cure."

39. "Based on a survey of more than 100,000 people, Toshitaka Nomi and Alexander Besher have drawn up some startling conclusions about blood type and personality. If you are type O, you are probably aggressive and realistic. Type A? You are

naturally industrious, detail-oriented, and peace-loving. Type B's are creative and individualistic. AB's tend to be rational, but moody. YOU ARE YOUR BLOOD TYPE presents detailed analysis of the different blood types and explores the compatibility between the different types."

—From a news release from Pocket Books about the first Western account "of the Japanese pop-phenomenon of blood-type analysis."

According to the release, the principal author, T. Nomi, is carrying on his father's work in blood-typing theory; Nomi's qualifications are that he has written many articles on the theory, has made many TV appearances, and has sold five million copies of twenty-two different books. Besher publishes translations of modern Japanese literature and contributes to the personal computer newsweekly InfoWorld. *Given these qualifications of the authors and the nature of the reported results, we remain skeptical.*

40. The mail order company Hammacher Schlemmer & Co. says in its consumer catalogs that it sells nothing but the best. The company supports its claims by what it calls independent testing. But Bruce Nash and Allan Zullo, in a book called *The Mis-Fortune 500* (New York: Pocket Books, 1988), say that while a 1986 letter to potential customers claimed that a "completely separate" "consumer" organization tested and compared the products offered by Hammacher Schlemmer, in reality:

"The testing organization is called the Hammacher Schlemmer Institute.

"The institute is funded by Hammacher Schlemmer & Co.

"The institute's board of directors is composed of Hammacher Schlemmer officials.

"The institute is located at Hammacher Schlemmer company headquarters in Chicago."

The company maintains that the Institute is separate from its other divisions; yet it strains credibility when the implied comparison is between the Institute and say, Consumers Union. Presumably the authors of The Mis-Fortune 500 *have presented the whole story in their book, but their claim to fame is to have been the coauthors of several baseball "hall of shame" books and to have appeared on "Late Night with David Letterman." The point is that the examples culled from press reports are intended to show business at its worst—without including mitigating circumstances. We tend to swallow negative claims more easily, especially if they are embarrassing to Big Business or Big Government.*

Bank 3-3

Each of these items consists of a brief biography of a real or imagined person followed by a list of topics. Discussion of the credibility and authority of the person described on each listed topic should be based just on the information given in the biography.

41. Robert A. Weinberg is a professor of biology at the Center for Cancer Research of the Massachusetts Institute of Technology and a member of the Whitehead Institute for Biomedical Research. His B.A. (1964) and Ph.D. (1969) are both from MIT. He did postdoctoral research at the Weizmann Institute of Science in Israel and at the Salk Institute for Biological Studies. In 1962, he returned to MIT, and

the following year he was made a member of the faculty at the Center for Cancer Research. He joined the Whitehead Institute in 1982.

a. Whether your sore throat is "strep throat"
b. Whether there should be a constitutional amendment prohibiting abortion
c. Current investigative techniques in biology
d. The effectiveness of laetrile as a cancer therapy
e. The composition of red blood cells
f. The rate of heart disease among Eskimos
g. The effect of calcium supplements to the diet on high blood pressure

We'd expect Dr. Weinberg to be an expert in topics (c) and (e), and we'd expect him to be well informed about (d) as well. He'd be slightly less an authority on (f) and (g), but anything he might say about these subjects would carry more weight than the views of a lay person. We would not expect him to be an authority on (a), and his views on (b) would have to speak for themselves—that is, his scientific background would not lend any special credibility to his views on (b).

42. Robert Kuttner is the economics correspondent of *The New Republic,* a columnist for *Business Week* and the *Boston Globe,* and a contributor to the *Atlantic.* After graduating from Oberlin College in 1965, he studied at the London School of Economics and took a master's degree in political science at the University of California, Berkeley. In addition to his writing, Kuttner served in Washington from 1975 to 1978 as the chief investigator for the Senate Banking Committee. In 1979 he was a fellow at Harvard's John F. Kennedy School of Government. He subsequently edited the journal *Working Papers.* Kuttner is the author of *Revolt of the Haves* (1980) and, most recently, *The Economic Illusion* (1984), which was nominated for a National Book Critics Circle Award.

a. The effects of inflation on the stock market
b. The Federal Deposit Insurance Corporation (FDIC), which insures deposits at banks and savings and loan institutions
c. Restaurants in London
d. Politics and upper income groups in America
e. Poverty among Native Americans

We would expect substantial expertise from Mr. Kuttner on topics (b) and (d)—the latter because of his 1980 book—and more than lay knowledge about (a). We'd sooner trust him than someone who hasn't lived there on (c), and we would expect no more expertise about (e) than we'd expect from other well-informed nonspecialists.

43. James A. Van Allen received a Ph.D. in physics from the University of Iowa in 1939. During World War II, he was a gunnery officer with the Pacific Fleet. After the war, he returned to the University of Iowa, where he became professor of physics and chairman of the Department of Physics and Astronomy. In 1958, during the mission of Explorer 1, the first successful U.S. earth satellite, he discovered the radiation belts surrounding the earth that are named for him. He was the principal investigator for the space probe of Jupiter's radiation belts and one of the discoverers of the radiation belts of Saturn. He was chairman of the group that developed the Voyager and Galileo space missions and is currently principal investigator for the Pioneer 10 and Pioneer 11 projects.

a. The number of women employed by the National Aeronautics and Space Administration
b. The uses of satellites for national security purposes
c. The biological effects of ultraviolet radiation
d. The structure of comet tails
e. Recent geological activity along faults in southern California
f. The impact of a manned space station on science and technology

We assume Van Allen's opinions on (f) would be very informed. He would also have great credibility on (d) and only slightly less on (c). His remarks on (b) would carry more weight than those of a lay person, but we would need further information about him before regarding him as an authority on (a) or (e).

44. David A. Kilbourne taught himself to program in three different computer languages by the time he was sixteen. At seventeen, he was a member of a loose-knit southern California group of computer "hackers" that specialized in tapping the data bases of large corporations, including the telephone company and several banks. In 1984, Kilbourne was charged with using his home computer and a telephone communications device to manipulate data in the Pacific Bell Telephone data base to avoid telephone bills for his household and those of several friends for almost two years. It was also discovered that he had savings accounts at two Bank of America branches, with balances totaling over seventy thousand dollars, despite never having made a deposit or even "officially" opening the account. Kilbourne was found guilty on several counts of defrauding the two companies and was put on three years' probation. During his probation, Bank of America hired him as a consultant to assess the security of its computer files, a job at which he worked for nearly a year. He now works for a legitimate software house in the Silicon Valley. (Asked which side of the law he preferred working on, Kilbourne replied, "Everything considered, being an outlaw was more fun.")

a. The morality of software piracy
b. Corporate data banks
c. Telecommunications
d. Purchasing a computer for a small business
e. Electronic games
f. Computer programming

We'd listen to Kilbourne with attention on topics (b), (c), and (f), and we'd give his opinions more weight than our own on (d) and (e). We think we could get better authority on (a).

45. Dave Vink Quigg is a scientist at the U.S. Department of Agriculture Forest Service's Northeastern Forest Experimental Station in Durham, New Hampshire. He graduated from Humboldt State University in California with a degree in biology (1958) and earned a Ph.D. in plant pathology from the University of West Virginia (1965). After serving for seven years as a consultant to the Pennsylvania state park system, he was employed by the U.S. Forest Service as a specialist in tree diseases. His major area of research has been in the resistance mechanisms of trees to injury and infection.

a. The effects of improper pruning techniques on fruit trees
b. The kind of fertilizer to use on ornamental shrubs
c. Resistance mechanisms of mammals to disease and infection
d. The characteristics of various types of softwoods relative to their use in the building industry
e. How to transplant a small tree
f. Use rates of campground facilities in Pennsylvania state parks
g. Methods of controlling garden pests

Quigg would have more credibility on each of these subjects than a lay person, though we would regard him as most qualified on (a) and (e) and least qualified on (b), (c), and (g).

Bank 3-4

Discuss the credibility and authority of each individual or group listed with regard to the questions or issues posed. Whom would you trust as most reliable on each subject?

46. You are thinking of insulating your attic and need advice relative to how much insulation you should install.

    a. A company that sells insulation but does not install it
    b. A company that sells and installs insulation
    c. An energy consultant from your local gas and electric company
    d. *Consumer Reports*
    e. A friend who has recently had his attic insulated

    We think you are most likely to get the best information from (d), with (c) a close second; (a) and (b) are about equal in credibility, and (e)'s ranking depends on where he got his information.

47. You've purchased a wood-burning stove. You are uncertain, however, what kind of wood to burn in it. You've heard that some produce more smoke, some are more likely to contribute to chimney fires, some burn hotter than others, and so forth.

    a. The dealer from whom you purchased the stove
    b. A friend of yours who has used a wood-burning stove for years
    c. Another friend who sells firewood
    d. A U.S. Department of Agriculture publication, "Comparative Properties of Fuelwood"
    e. A professor of environmental horticulture at a state university

    All these sources are credible, but (d) should rank first, and, most likely, (a) should rank last.

48. You have saved up for a vacation and are considering taking a cruise on a cruise ship. You are unsure whether this would be the right kind of vacation for you and, if it is, what kind of cruise would be best for you and your budget.

a. A travel agent
b. A cruise line representative
c. A friend who has been on a cruise
d. A newspaper travel writer

Notice that there are two issues at stake, not just one: whether to take a cruise and which cruise. We'd trust (d) first on both issues if you are fortunate enough to talk with him or her personally (and not just by letter to the paper). After that, we'd trust (c) and (a) more or less equally on the first question (one knows you, and one knows cruises) and (a) on the second question; (b) could be expected to be biased in favor of a particular line, we'd think.

49. A number of your friends have taken up jogging, and you wonder whether your taking it up might have genuine health benefits for you.

    a. Your family physician
    b. A magazine for runners
    c. A friend who teaches physical education in high school
    d. The author of a best-selling book on sports medicine
    e. A friend who is president of a local runners club

(b), (c), and (e) might tend to be promoters of jogging, so we'd be mildly skeptical of any pro-jogging claims they might make (but less skeptical of any liabilities of jogging that they might mention). We'd find (a) a more credible source, although many general practitioners may not have the time to keep up on such specialized areas. The best potential source is probably (d), although we'd be cautious unless we knew something about the author; he or she might also tend to exaggerate either the benefits—or the risks—of jogging.

50. Spring has come, and it's about time to plant some tomatoes. Or is there still a danger of frost?

    a. The owner of your local nursery
    b. Aunt Maude, whose garden has kept her friends and family in tomatoes for years
    c. A friend who grows tomatoes commercially
    d. A friend who gives the weather report on Channel 8 News each evening
    e. "Outdoor Planting Table" in *The Old Farmer's Almanac*

Notice that this question is about weather, not tomatoes. We'd trust (c), though (a), (b), and (d) are also credible sources on this subject. As amazing as (e) sometimes is in the accuracy of its predictions, it may not be sufficiently fine-tuned to your locality.

51. You are looking at a sailboat that you're considering buying, but you've never owned one before and don't know whether you should buy this one.

    a. The boat salesman at the marina that owns the boat
    b. A boat salesman from another marina
    c. A friend who has owned several similar boats
    d. A buyer's guide published by a sailing magazine
    e. Your own appraisal

Of course you must consider (e), since if you have doubts from the beginning you're likely to be unhappy with the purchase. We think (c) can be either the best source on the list or the worst, depending on his or her judgment and experience. (What do you know about the friend's sailing experience?) Source (d) can be good with regard to the boat, but remember that the writers of the guide don't know you or your situation; (a) can be depended on to be more upbeat about the boat than a neutral party; (b) may want to sell you one of his boats.

52. Even though your wisdom teeth are not bothering you, your dentist tells you they should be extracted because they may give you trouble later. Should you have them pulled or wait until they cause problems?

   a. Your dentist
   b. Your physician
   c. A friend who is studying to become an orthodontist
   d. Your sister, who is a dental hygienist
   e. Your brother, who is six years older than you, who still has his wisdom teeth and has had no problems with them

   Assuming your dentist specifies more clearly the risks you take by not having the teeth extracted now, we'd go with his or her opinion rather than any of the outside sources.

53. Jones wants to quit smoking. He has heard of a kind of chewing gum that contains nicotine and is said to relieve some of the physiological symptoms of withdrawal. But the gum requires a prescription and is quite expensive, and he knows nothing of how well it works or any side effects it may have. Should he consider using it?

   a. Jones's physician
   b. An advertisement published by the manufacturer of the gum
   c. A report in a news magazine of a study done on the use of the gum
   d. A friend of Jones who has used the gum in an attempt to quit smoking

   Clearly, opinion (a) is worth having and required anyway for the prescription. We think that (c) is likely to be the next best source of information, since (b) may be one-sided and Jones may not have the same experience as (d).

54. It's quite important that you travel to another town about four hours away by car, but you are concerned about whether you should drive because of adverse weather conditions.

   a. The local television news
   b. The local newspaper
   c. A friend who has made the trip in all kinds of weather
   d. The state police telephone service
   e. The local police department

   In descending order, we'd trust (d), (a), (e), (b), and (c). The local police probably know more about local conditions but less about conditions some distance away; the local newspaper's information may be too old to be useful; and we don't trust a friend who will drive in just any weather conditions.

For the following, discuss which source you'd trust more, and give at least one reason why.

55. In the 1988 presidential campaign, several Republican leaders expressed concern about the qualifications of Indiana Republican senator Dan Quayle to become vice president. Discuss whether such concerns should carry more weight with voters when expressed by Republican leaders than when stated by Democratic leaders.

56. Discuss whose opinion on the foreign policy of the current administration is more credible.
   a. A former U.S. president of the same political party as the current president
   b. A former U.S. president not of the same political party as the current president

57. Discuss whose opinion on the foreign policy of the current administration is more credible.
   a. A Ph.D. in political science whose speciality is U.S. foreign policy
   b. The chairman of the U.S. Senate Foreign Relations Committee

58. Discuss whose opinion on the condition of the tires on your car is more credible.
   a. A salesperson at Goodyear
   b. A mechanic at a garage certified by the American Automobile Association

59. Issue: A proposal for legislation regarding automobile insurance rates is on the ballot. Discuss whose opinion on the benefits for consumers is more credible.
   a. A spokesperson for the insurance industry
   b. Ralph Nader

60. Is the pitcher tiring? Discuss whose opinion is the more credible.
   a. A minor league pitching coach
   b. Reggie Jackson

61. Did life evolve, or was it created? Discuss whose opinion is the more credible.
   a. A biologist
   b. A minister

62. Can you get a manzanita tree to grow in Pennsylvania?
   a. A Pennsylvania (where manzanita doesn't grow naturally) nursery worker
   b. A California (where Manzanita does grow naturally) nursery worker

63. What percentage of American high school students have smoked marijuana?
   a. *USA Today*
   b. Americans for Legalized Marijuana (ALM)

64. How many homicides involve the use of a stolen firearm?
   a. A Democratic U.S. Senator
   b. A Republican U.S. Senator

65. Which of two current movies you would be more apt to like?
   a. A movie critic whose opinions you enjoy listening to
   b. A friend

66. The best weight-lifting regimen to follow
   a. Arnold Schwarzenegger
   b. Roseanne

Bank 3-5

These are similar to the previous group, but the issues are somewhat more general. You may want to add to or otherwise modify our lists of sources. And do keep in mind that we are glad our livelihoods do not depend on a general consensus on *our* rankings.

67. Issue: Should lawyers allow their clients to lie?

   a. The U.S. Supreme Court
   b. A law school professor
   c. A political science professor
   d. The American Bar Association
   e. A practicing defense attorney

   This question is not so straightforward and simple as it might seem. For instance, has a client who is forced to tell the truth in effect been denied an effective defense? Can one even know that one's client has lied? In forming our opinion on the subject, we'd be most influenced by the reasoning of the person who seemed to have the best grasp of the various subsidiary issues involved. In other words, in this case it's the reasoning rather than the credentials of the reasoner that will carry the most weight. (We would not anticipate that any of the sources listed would be deficient in powers of reasoning.)

68. Issue: In the O.J. Simpson murder case, did the judge rule correctly in admitting evidence that was obtained at Simpson's house before a search warrant was issued?

   a. A well-known defense attorney who heads the American Trial Lawyers Association
   b. The former district attorney for Los Angeles County
   c. A retired judge on the U.S. Court of Appeals

   We put (c) way out in front, and the other two equally biased on opposite sides of the issue.

69. Issue: Does violence on television contribute to violent behavior on the part of young viewers?

   a. The president of the National Association of Broadcasters
   b. The president of an organization called "Parents Against TV Violence"
   c. A university sociologist
   d. Regular panel members of a program such as "Crossfire" or "The McLaughlin Group"

   We rank (c) first, followed by (b), who would be ahead of (a). We do know what side (b) is on from the outset, of course, but that's somewhat different from having a vested interest in one side of the issue in the way that (a) does. We find most of the people like those mentioned in (d) to be full of hot air on most subjects.

70. Issue: Do mountain bicycles cause ecological damage when ridden on hiking trails?

    a. An environmental scientist at the Harvard School of Public Health
    b. The chair of the Sierra Club task force for determining club policy on the wilderness use of mountain bicycles
    c. A spokesperson for a bicycle manufacturer
    d. A park ranger from a state park where mountain bicycles have been permitted on hiking trails
    e. A representative of the Washington Mountain Bike Riders' Association

    Our ranking: (d)=(b) first, then (e)=(c)=(a)

71. Issue: How did the economic policies of the Sandinista government affect the standard of living of most Nicaraguans?

    a. The editor of a daily newspaper in a small town
    b. A friend who just returned from a trip to Nicaragua "to see what was going on"
    c. A professor of Latin American studies at Ohio State University
    d. A Republican state senator in Arizona
    e. A politically radical councilwoman for a middle-sized New York city

    Our ranking: (c), (a), (b)=(d)=(e). You might point out that it is difficult to use standard measurements of the effects of economic policies in places where there has been war in the not-so-distant past.

72. Issue: Are schools of business turning out too many ill-prepared M.B.A. graduates?

    a. The dean of the school of business at the University of Chicago
    b. The president of the Hewlett-Packard Corporation
    c. An editorial in the *Wall Street Journal*
    d. A recent graduate with an M.B.A.

    Our ranking: (c), (b), (a), (d)

73. Issue: What levels of mercury and other metals in fish are high enough to make their consumption hazardous to humans?

    a. An article in a journal called *Diet and Health,* published for vegetarians
    b. A commercial fisherman
    c. A family medical doctor
    d. A spokeswoman for the National Institutes of Health
    e. A toxicologist who works for the Los Angeles coroner's office

    Our ranking: (d), then a substantial gap, then (e) and (c), another gap, then (a), (b)

74. Issue: Whether a recently completed nuclear power plant is safe.

    a. The power company that owns the plant
    b. The contractor in charge of the plant's construction
    c. A spokesman for the Nuclear Regulatory Agency
    d. The president of the Sierra Club

112

e. A contractor hired by a nearby city who has seen the blueprints of the plant but has not made an on-site inspection

f. The author of a statistical study on safety, malfunctions, and accidents at power plants of the same type

Our ranking: (f), a gap, then (c), (e), then (a)=(b)=(d). We would not put too much confidence in any of the sources listed, as a matter of fact. The last alternative, (f), is hypothetical; there are relatively few nuclear power plants of any one type; their construction has so far been "custom"—that is, idiosyncratic.

75. Issue: Whether it's possible for a person to have an "out of body" experience.

a. A psychic
b. A physicist
c. A person who claims to have had such an experience
d. A physician
e. A philosopher
f. A magician
g. A psychologist

Our ranking: (e), then everybody else. None of the other sources has had experience or training in what is possible. Were we evaluating the question of whether a given individual had actually had such an experience, we'd have required a different ranking.

76. Issue: Whether Viking explorers actually landed in the New World before Columbus.

a. A historian
b. The publisher of a Norwegian-language newspaper in Willmar, Minnesota
c. A Norwegian archaeologist
d. An Italian archaeologist
e. An archaeologist of French ancestry who grew up in Texas

We take this one, including our ranking, lightly (although some Italians and some Norwegians don't): (e), (a), (c)=(d), (b).

77. Issue: Were there unjustifiable cost overruns in the construction of ships made for the U.S. Navy by Lytton Industries?

a. The chair of the Senate Armed Services Committee
b. The accounting director for Lytton
c. The Navy Chief of Staff
d. The OMB (Office of Management and Budget)
e. An article in *The Progressive* (a left-of-center political journal)

Our ranking: (d), (a), depending on the individual's politics, then (c)=(e), (b)

Bank 3-6

Topics for brief essays.

78. What factors help establish someone as an expert?

79. Discuss three ways a person can increase his or her background knowledge.

80. Are there conditions in which your own observations may not be totally reliable? Explain.

81. List several topics on which you may not trust yourself to give a totally unbiased judgment.

82. Discuss the conditions under which it is reasonable to regard an eyewitness account as credible.

83. Discuss the news media as a source of information about current events.

84. If the claims of an expert turn out to be in error, were you unreasonable in having accepted them in the first place? Why, or why not?

85. How do you handle a conflict between the opinions of experts who do not agree?

86. Why do you suppose sensationalism (as found in supermarket tabloids, for example) has such a wide audience despite its frequent conflicts with our background knowledge?

87. Make up an issue and a list of sources like those in Bank 3-3, and give your own ranking of the credibility of the sources you listed.

Bank 3-7

88. List fifteen items that you believe to be true about current popular music. When you are finished, trade your list for that of a classmate. Place each item from your classmate's list into one of three categories: (1) those you believe to be true, (2) those you believe to be false, and (3) those you are uncertain about. Next, explain to each other why you assigned the items as you did. Finally, based on this discussion, compile a third list that contains only those items from the original lists that both of you know to be true. Submit this list to your instructor for any comments he or she might have.

89. To the instructor: Have a colleague come to your class and speak for four or five minutes about an unannounced topic. Afterward, ask the class some pointed questions about the speaker's appearance, presentation, and topic.

90. If there is a palm reader (or someone similar) nearby, send a couple of members of the class for a reading, and have them make a report. Other members of the class should press for a full accounting.

Bank 3-8

True/False

91. You should assume that the claims made by others are false unless you have some specific reason to believe otherwise.

False

92. If you have reason to believe that an expert is biased, you should reject that expert's claim as false.

   False (The possibility of bias is occasion to question his or her claims, to suspend judgment on them, to give more weight to alternative claims from unbiased experts, and so on—this is different from rejecting the original expert's claims as false.)

93. Except when we have the means to record our observations immediately, they are no better than our memories happen to be.

   True

94. Fallible or not, our firsthand observations are still the best source of information we have.

   True

95. Reference works such as dictionaries are utterly reliable sources of information— otherwise they wouldn't be reference works.

   False

96. Factual claims that conflict with what we think we know ought to be rejected, but only if we can disprove them through direct observation.

   False

97. A surprising claim, one that seems to conflict with our background knowledge, requires a more credible source than one that is not surprising in this way.

   True

98. Factual claims put forth by experts about subjects outside their fields are not automatically more acceptable than claims put forth by nonexperts.

   True

99. You are rationally justified in accepting the view of the majority of experts in a given subject even if this view turns out later to have been incorrect.

   True

Chapter 4
Nonargumentative Persuasion

There isn't a lot to say about the material in the first part of Chapter 4, except that most of us run across it more than any other kind of material found in the book. We note in the text that our list of nonargumentative persuasive devices does not presume to be exhaustive. Since many attempts to win acceptance for claims by slanting will not fall under our list of techniques, we encourage our students to *explain* how and in what way a given passage is slanted, rather than to try simply to classify.

Maybe we're insinuating something ourselves by putting the section on the news media in this chapter, but this is where it seems to fit best. We have no such second thoughts about the section on advertising.

Exercises Unanswered in the Text

Exercise 4-1

1. Hyperbole (in Chapter 6, we'd call this "straw man")

2. Dysphemism

3. Not a slanter

4. Dysphemism

5. Not a slanter

6. Dysphemism

Exercise 4-3

2. Innuendo

3. Persuasive comparisons

5. Euphemism

7. Euphemism

9. We don't think this is a slanter. But it *is* an interesting use of ambiguity (see Chapter 2). It's true that Morgan is trying to become a politician in the sense of running for public office; but the speaker is using "politician" in another sense, one in which it has negative associations. The fact that Morgan wants to be a politician in the first sense does not mean he must be one in the second.

10. Persuasive definition

Exercise 4-4

2. Quotation marks are downplayers (or a subtle variety of ridicule); the rest is a series of loaded questions.

3. Innuendo in the last remark

5. No slanters here, as far as we can tell (the *Journal* is ordinarily rather fond of Gingrich).

6. There are clear opinions being expressed in this passage, but we don't see them as being expressed in slanted language.

8. The word "clarified" is our nominee for Euphemism of the Year—it's clear the two memoranda were in direct conflict with one another.

9. "So-called" is a downplayer; "fat-cat" is a derogatory adjective; the idea of district attorneys getting rich is distortion (they don't get the money personally), although this is not strictly speaking a use of slanted language; "without ever getting around to" is a dysphemism for "without having to."

Exercise 4-16

We realize we could get in some trouble here, but we thought we'd try to give a hand to anybody out there who has to deal with this stuff without having made a career of reading political journals and reading between the lines of nonpolitical journals. Here's our best shot at ranking the listed publications on a scale of 1 through 9, with 1 being the most left-leaning and 9 the most right-leaning. Bear in mind, as must students, that a given ranking does not mean that we think *every* story in a paper or magazine has the slant we're assigning the publication. In fact, we believe that the *New York Times,* which we're giving a neutral 5 for a score, is very heavily biased on some issues; it's just that it's likely to biased in one direction on one issue and in another direction on another issue. (As of this writing, it seems to be extraordinarily politically correct, and it has been remarkably critical of the Clinton administration during its first two years. These, notice, are our evaluations; we have colleagues who would question our views!)

New York Times: 5
Washington Post: 4½
Wall Street Journal: 7
USA Today: 4½
Newsweek: 4½
Time: 4½

U.S. News and World Report: 5½
The New Republic: 4
National Review: 9
The Progressive: 1
The Nation: 2

Chapter 4 Test Question/Exercise Banks

Bank 4-1

Isolate and discuss slanting devices that appear in these passages.

1. Not everyone thinks that Senator Jesse Helms is the least admired American public figure (as opinion polls show). Even now, one or two southern Republicans lust after a Helms endorsement.

   "Not everyone" implies that most do—innuendo. The parenthetical remark is a proof surrogate. "Even now" insinuates (innuendo) that by this time hardly anyone has regard for Helms or for a Helms endorsement. "One or two" is a weaseler. "Lust after" belittles the desire for a Helms endorsement: It cheapens both Helms and those who want his support.

2. From a letter to the editor: "In Sacramento, money talks, which is why our politicians kowtow to the local developers. So much for voting for honest people whose primary concern should be people, not money."
   —Sacramento Bee

   "Money talks" is a cliché; "kowtow," though its original touch-the-forehead-to-the-ground meaning is fading among all except those who read novels about the nineteenth century, still carries the sense of obsequious deference that brings it close to hyperbole here. The whole tone of the last sentence is slanted—it insinuates both that politicians are dishonest and that their primary concern is money (innuendo, and not very subtle).

3. Perhaps the "religious leaders" who testified at the state board of education's public hearing on textbooks think they speak for all Christians, but they do not.

   Note especially how quotation marks around "religious leaders" serves to question the credentials of those individuals.

4. The United States will not have an effective antiterrorist force until the army and the air force quit bickering about equipment and responsibilities.

   "Bickering" belittles the nature of the controversy.

5. Maybe it's possible, after all, to sympathize with the Internal Revenue Service. The woes that have piled up in its Philadelphia office make the IRS look almost human.

   "After all" suggests that the IRS usually deserves no sympathy; "almost human" implies that the IRS is actually inhuman.

6. We clearly can't trust the television networks, not when they've just spent two days interviewing young children on their feelings about the deaths of the astronauts. This attempt to wring every drop of human interest from the tragedy is either frighteningly cynical or criminally thoughtless regarding the damage that can be done both to the children interviewed and to children who see the interviews.

   "Wring every drop" is a cliché and an exaggeration; the adverbs "frighteningly" and "criminally" approach hyperbole, especially the latter.

7. The antigun people think that just as soon as guns are outlawed, crime will disappear, and we'll all live together as one big, happy family.

   This trades on a stereotype; it's an excellent opening for a straw man.

8. "Sam Goldwyn once said that an oral agreement isn't worth the paper it's written on. We wonder what he would have said about the Pennzoil-Texaco case."
   —The Worcester, Mass., *Evening Gazette*

   (Background: In 1985, Pennzoil offered to buy out Getty Oil Co. for $5.3 billion. Although both parties agreed to the deal and press announcements were issued, Getty abruptly backed out when Texaco offered $10 billion for Getty. Getty accepted the Texaco offer, and Pennzoil sued for $14 billion in damages.) This is a persuasive comparison, of course.

9. "Would you want to appoint my opponent as president of your company?"
   —President Ferdinand Marcos of the Philippines, speaking to a group of Philippine businessmen about his 1986 election opponent, Corazon Aquino

   Innuendo based on a form of persuasive comparison

10. "Early in the third phase of the Vietnam War the U.S. command recognized that the term 'search and destroy' had unfortunately become associated with 'aimless searches in the jungle and the destruction of property.' In April 1968 General Westmoreland therefore directed that the use of the term be discontinued. Operations thereafter were defined and discussed in basic military terms which described the type of operation, for example, reconnaissance in force."
    —Lieutenant General John H. Hay, Jr., *Vietnam Studies*

    Euphemism

11. Robert may be a pretty good gardener, all right, but you'll notice he lost nearly everything to the bugs this year.

    Innuendo, downplayer ("but")

12. "The Soviet regime [once] promulgated a law providing fines for motorists who alter their lights or grills or otherwise make their cars distinguishable. A regime that makes it a crime to personalize a car is apt to make it a crime to transmit a cultural heritage."
    —George Will

    A persuasive comparison.

13. "TO CHICO'S WHOLESALERS AND RETAILERS OF PORNOGRAPHY: DO YOU HONESTLY BELIEVE THAT PORNOGRAPHY HAS NO EFFECT ON THE BEHAVIOR OF PEOPLE?"
    —From an ad in the *Chico Enterprise-Record*

    The phrase "do you honestly believe" is almost always used to refute without argument the claim that follows it. It isn't a type of slanter discussed in the text, though you might get away with calling it a proof surrogate.

14. Rodney Dangerfield? Yeah, he's about as funny as a terminal illness.

    Persuasive comparison

15. "Within the context of total ignorance, you are absolutely correct."
    —Caption in a *National Review* cartoon

    The height of downplaying, as it were, although the remark is clearly designed more to amuse than to persuade

16. Handguns are made only for the purpose of killing people.

    This could be called stereotyping—in this case, an oversimplified generalization about a class of things instead of people.

17. "If we stop the shuttle program now, there are seven astronauts who will have died for nothing."
    —An unidentified U.S. congressman, after the space shuttle disaster of January 1986

    You'll recognize this as primarily a piece of pseudoreasoning (false dilemma), but the phrase "will have died for nothing [or in vain]" is a highly charged cliché.

18. It is, of course, *conceivable* that the Qaddafi regime has nothing to do with terrorist attacks on Israeli airports, but . . .

    The downplaying "but" makes it almost certain that "conceivable" is functioning here as a weaseler.

19. If the governor is so dedicated to civil rights, why is it that the black citizens of this state are worse off now than when he took office?

    Loaded question

20. Chewing tobacco is not only messy, but also unhealthy (just check the latest statistics).

    The parenthetical addition is a proof surrogate.

21. Once you've made our Day Planner a part of your business life, there's a good chance you'll never miss or be late for another appointment.

    "There's a good chance" is a weaseler.

22. ". . . despite the idealist yearnings in the body politic that this [the baby boom] generation supposedly epitomizes, the darker side of the lust for power is still present. Just witness the saga of the collapse of the once-promising career of Mayor Roger Hedgecock [former mayor of San Diego]."
    —Larry Remer and Gregory Dennis

    The passage insinuates an almost obsessive desire for power on the part of Hedgecock.

23. "If it ain't country, it ain't music."
    —Bumper sticker

    Another hyperbolic false dilemma

24. Professor Jones, who normally confines his remarks to his own subject, ventured out on a high-wire to comment on the commission's findings.

Jones' credentials regarding evaluation of the commission's findings are impugned (innuendo), and the significance of his comments is downplayed.

25. I simply won't go into those cowboy bars; they're full of guys who disguise their insecurities with cowboy boots and hats.

Stereotyping

26. "Can [former Representative Jack] Kemp or anyone believe that $27 million in 'humanitarian' aid would replace all that South Africa has done [to support Angolan rebels]?"
—Anthony Lewis, *New York Times*

(Kemp sponsored a bill that gave $27 million in humanitarian aid to Jonas Savimbi's UNITA rebels for their fight against the government of Angola.) "Can anyone believe" suggests that the Kemp proposal is not to be taken seriously and is perhaps not taken seriously even by Kemp himself. The quotation marks around "humanitarian" serve to question whether the aid would be genuinely humanitarian.

27. "Notre Dame people like to point out that, unlike other [college football] powerhouses, their players must face tough admissions standards, shoulder the regular course load and forget about being red-shirted to gain additional playing years. And, of course, it's a lot more fun to point out those things if your guys are out there stomping on 24-year-old golf-course management majors every Saturday, the way they used to."
—*Newsweek*

Hyperbole; we expect there are football players for other teams who don't major in golf-course management and are under twenty-four.

28. "Trivial pursuit" is the name of a game played by the California Supreme Court, which will seek any nit-picking excuse preventing murderers from receiving justice.

Persuasive definition. Notice the switch in this one: Usually the slant is against the word or idea being defined; here the object of the attack occurs in the definition.

29. "Any person who thinks that Libya is not involved in terrorism has the same kind of mentality as people who think that Hitler was not involved in persecuting Jews."
—Robert Oakley, U.S. Ambassador-at-Large for Counterterrorism, in a 1991 interview on National Public Radio's *All Things Considered*

Persuasive comparison

30. "Although you were not selected to receive the award, I congratulate you for your achievements at California State University, Chico."
—Excerpt from a letter written by a university president and sent to an unsuccessful contender for a campus award.

Downplayer: "although"

31. "Nazi propaganda chief Joseph Goebbels . . . justified the attack on thousands of Jews as a step toward removing an 'infection' contaminating Germany. 'It is impossible that, in a National Socialist state, which is anti-Jewish in its outlook, those streets should continue to be occupied by Jewish shops.'"
—Reuters report in the *Sacramento Bee*

Stereotype

32. Voting is the method for obtaining legal power to coerce others.
—From a commentary on a grocery bag urging citizens not to vote and thus not to encourage the majority to take away the life, liberty, and pursuit of happiness of the minority.

Persuasive definition

33. "To those who say that the analogy of Hitler is extremist and inflammatory in reference to abortion, I would contend that the comparison is legitimate. . . . The Supreme Court, by refusing to acknowledge their personhood, has relegated the entire class of unborn children to a subhuman legal status without protection under the law—the same accorded Jews under the Third Reich."
—Jerry Nims, writing in the *Moral Majority's Liberty Report*

Persuasive comparison

34. "The beginning of the end of moral relativism was of course the landslide election of Ronald Reagan. He promised to bring the country back from its malaise, and in many ways he has succeeded, largely by speaking of and pursuing values the elite considers 'simple.' This is why symbolic issues ring with so many voters; whatever their narrow interests, they want to vote against relativism and for the values they share."
—Editorial, *Wall Street Journal*

Dysphemism—opposite of euphemism—branding criticism of Reagan as well as public soul-searching as "moral relativism" without examining its content

35. To study the epidemiology of deaths involving firearms kept in the home, we reviewed all the gunshot deaths that occurred in King County, Washington (population 1,270,000), from 1978 through 1983. . . . A total of 743 firearm-related deaths occurred during this six-year period, 398 of which (54%) occurred in the residence where the firearm was kept. Only 2 of these 398 deaths (.5%) involved an intruder shot during attempted entry. Seven persons (1.8%) were killed in self-defense. For every case of self-protection homicide involving a firearm kept in the home, there were 1.3 accidental deaths, 4.6 criminal homicides. . . . Handguns were used in 70.5% of these deaths.

We find this almost entirely free of slanters. "Only," in the fourth sentence from the end, downplays the number of intruders shot, but then it is a small number that's being downplayed.

36. Libya's strongman, Colonel Muammar Qaddafi, is the kingpin of Mideast terrorism, as Israeli and Western intelligence sources assert. Qaddafi's 'who, me?' denials are as believable as would be his announcing conversion to Judaism.

Both "strongman" and "kingpin" are slanters, and the second sentence is a persuasive comparison.

122

37. A political endorsement by the Reverend Jerry Falwell, the high-priest of holier-than-thou and "let's hear it for apartheid," would help a political candidate as much as an endorsement from the Ayatollah Khomeini.

   "Holier-than-thou" is a clichéd slanter; and the "let's hear it for apartheid" epithet is a jeer, regardless of the fact that Falwell supported apartheid in South Africa. The whole is, of course, a persuasive comparison.

38. As if they alone were concerned with clean air and pure water, these self-anointed environmentalists question whether there will be nitrate pollution from the new subdivision and whether Madrone Creek can accommodate storm runoff from the development. Their no-growth ideas are familiar to everyone in the community.

   "As if they alone were concerned" insinuates both that others are concerned and a smugness on the part of the people in question. "Self-anointed" is a standard slanter; nearly anybody who takes up a cause is self-anointed, in a manner of speaking. "No-growth ideas" is probably exaggeration, although probably not hyperbole. If this entire passage were rewritten in neutral language, you couldn't tell which side of the issue the author was on.

39. "The people who [fought] the Soviet-backed government in Nicaragua [were] freedom fighters just as George Washington was in our country."
   —Ronald Reagan

   Persuasive comparison

40. Surely you can't say that the American people have ever been behind Bill Clinton. After all, he got a mere 43 million votes in 1992, which is five million fewer than George Bush got when he beat Dukakis in 1988.

   "Mere" is a downplayer

41. Whether a policy will help the people of the United States is a question Bob Dole and Newt Gingrich don't even think about until they've answered the one that's more important to them: Will this policy do damage to the Democratic Party?

   Although this is a pretty nasty thing to accuse a politician of, the accusation itself is not made in particularly slanted language. (We refer students to the passage on negative facts near the beginning of the section on slanters.)

42. "Who is to blame for this lackluster campaign?"
   —NBC's John Chancellor

   Loaded question

43. All that effort spent giving Kuwait back to the Kuwaitis was like taking a crime syndicate away from one Mafia boss and handing it to another. The Kuwaitis already own half the civilized world, and we've put them back in the driver's seat. Their so-called justice system is handing out cruel punishments to alleged collaborators, many of whom were simply trying to stay alive during the Iraqi occupation.

   In our view: The first sentence is a persuasive comparison; the remark about owning half the civilized world is hyperbole; "so-called" is a downplayer of sorts—the quotation marks around "justice" serve the same purpose of letting the reader know the word is not intended to be taken literally. The last part of that sentence is interesting: One way of staying alive, of course, was collaboration; shouldn't the real question be whether it was coerced or volunteered?

44. With her keen instinct for political survival on full alert, Governor Richards suddenly saw the wisdom of the proposal that she had opposed for so many years.

   Innuendo—insinuates that her changed mind on the proposal was politically motivated and unprincipled

45. The Best Way to Clean Up Congress
   —Title of article by Rowland Evans and Robert Novak

   Innuendo

46. "[The CIA] instructed security forces in Uruguay, demonstrating torture techniques on beggars taken off the street. These activities, and many hundreds more like them, have been thoroughly documented by government investigations, by the press, and by the testimony of former CIA employees."
   —Progressive Student Union

   Proof surrogate

47. "HOUSTON (AP)—Houston Oilers owner Bud Adams met with the controversial coach of the Oilers, Jerry Glanville, for more than two hours Saturday afternoon. 'At that meeting we mutually decided that Jerry would not return as our head coach,' Adams said."

   Euphemism

48. "Smokers unite! The reason the antismoking crowd doesn't want you to smoke can be summed up in a single word: dictatorship."
   —From a newspaper call-in column

   Persuasive explanation

49. Miracle X-K3 battery additive extends the life of your battery up to five years.

   Weaseler

50. Orlando is a little town with friendly and helpful residents. Still, you might not want to live there. In the summer it's hotter than the Sahara Desert.

   Downplayer and a persuasive comparison that borders on hyperbole

51. The statistics Dr. Swain trotted out to prove that bicycle helmets save lives miss the point that a helmet law for bicyclists infringes on individual rights.

   "Trotted out" dismisses the statistics without argument and insinuates that they do not deserve serious consideration. Innuendo.

52. "All men are rapists."
   —Marilyn French

   Hyperbole

53. "I was amazed when I read that frog licking has become a major preoccupation in Colorado. How could this possibly get started? It had to be this way. An environmentalist is out in the woods communing with nature. Probably some overgrown Boy Scout in little green shorts, a backpack filled with wheat nut mix. He's wearing his Walkman, skipping along some nature trail . . . maybe even humming. Ommmmm-Ommmmm-Ommmmm. He looks at a tree and maybe he says, 'Hi Greg.' Maybe he hugs the tree. 'Oh, I am at one with this tree.' Then he spies a frog and suddenly stops. 'Oh, look at that frog. Maybe I should pick it up and lick it.' And gets high as a result. You see, the Colorado spotted toad secretes a hallucinogenic substance that can get you high if you lick it near the back of its head."
   —Rush Limbaugh

   Persuasive explanation/stereotype

54. A "provost' 'is the head academic officer in a university, whose chief function is to dream up work for faculty committees to do.

   Persuasive definition

55. ". . . the basic right to life of an animal—which is the source of energy for many animal rights wackos—must be inferred from the anticruelty laws humans have written."
   —Rush Limbaugh

   "Wackos" is a dysphemism.

56. Perhaps we shouldn't serve this cheese to the guests, dear. It seems to be a bit, uh, mature.

   Euphemism. "Perhaps" may be a weaseler in this context.

57. "Some feminists edge nervously away from Andrea Dworkin and Catharine MacKinnon, who are the Al Sharpton and Louis Farrakhan of feminism. . . ."
   —Time

   Persuasive comparison

58. Yes, well, in a way I agree with you.

   Weaseler

59. Moore and Parker are both getting a little thin on top.

   Euphemism

60. Yes, of course, we must protect the rights of innocent people—up to a point. The main thing is to make the streets safe again. Something must be done to reduce crime.

   "Up to a point" is a downplayer.

61. What explains the mad dash to distribute free condoms in our public schools? The misguided and ridiculous notion that kids are going to have sex no matter what.

Loaded question

62. I'm not among those who wonder why the senator hasn't made a full disclosure of his financial dealings prior to taking office.

Innuendo

63. That the proposal before us is a good one is, surely, obvious

Proof surrogate

64. The conservative mind is rigid and inflexible, like an orange peel that's dried out in the sun.

Stereotype/persuasive comparison

65. "A feminazi is a woman to whom the most important thing in life is seeing to it that as many abortions as possible are performed."
—Rush Limbaugh

Persuasive definition

Bank 4-2

Note to the instructor: These exercises are longer or more difficult. We'd ask students to discuss any instances of nonargumentative persuasion or pseudoreasoning and to explain any slanting techniques. As a further exercise, they can be asked to rewrite the passage in language that is as emotively neutral as possible but still retains the same informational content.

The following are filled with slanters, and explaining them all would take up a great deal of space; so, we'll comment only on the ones we find obscure, unusual, or tricky.

66. "Citizens for a Clean Community caused quite a commotion the other day when it announced its campaign to end the sale or rent of so-called adult and X-rated videos and movies.

"There immediately came the usual charges of censorship and free speech violations—as could have been predicted.

"We certainly would be the first to defend someone's right to read or view whatever they please. But make no mistake, those who are offended by this smut have every right to express their frustration by protesting its distribution. . . . And this kind of material is completely debasing and has no redeeming value whatsoever. . . ."
—*Cascade News*

Don't forget the downplaying role of "the usual charges . . . as could have been predicted."

67. "What kind of crazy political system is it where a man who wants to run for president must begin by withdrawing from public life? It's become an American tradition, dating perhaps back to Richard Nixon in 1962. Gary Hart followed the pattern when he 'declared his "interest" in the presidency' (as the *Washington Post* chastely put it) by announcing that he won't run for reelection to the Senate this year. Good luck to Hart. I voted for him once before, and wouldn't mind voting for him again. But really. Is this necessary?"

   —"TRB from Washington," in *The New Republic*

   There is a weak argument for withdrawal's having become a tradition, with Nixon the only example offered in evidence. What do you make of the reference to Hart's " 'interest' in the presidency"?

68. "The disbarment proceedings currently being conducted against New York Attorney Roy M. Cohn are the sickest example in recent memory of the sheer pettiness and vindictiveness of many liberals. Soundly and repeatedly trounced at the polls, they have retreated into their few remaining bastions and pulled up the drawbridges. Nationwide, their principal fortresses are the media and the academic faculties; in the case of New York, they also control the bar. It is this latter they are manipulating to wreak vengeance on Roy Cohn."

   —William Rusher, in *National Review*

69. Members of the baby-boom generation, the generation that is now becoming yuppies instead of growing up, refuse to see the light. After being the center of the universe during the sixties and seventies, they expected to own it by the mid-eighties. They grew up believing they would have tremendous jobs, wonderful houses, exotic travel, great marriages, and beautiful children as well as European "personal" cars, fancy music systems, high-tech kitchens, and wine in the cellar. But it isn't turning out that way for most of them. Having glutted the professional marketplace, they live on depressed salaries; their dependence on immediate gratification causes them to spend like sailors—on the right stuff—driving prices of their playthings through the roof.

   But they are addicted to their ways. Those who moved to Manhattan can't bear the thought of living anywhere else but can't afford to live there. According to the *New York Times,* single-room-occupancy hotels that used to house the poor now contain tenants who cart in their stereos and tape decks, their button-down shirts, and their Adidas running shoes. One young woman says her bathroom is so filthy she showers with shoes on.

   This insistence on doing it *right* bespeaks a refusal to grow up disguised as a commitment to—what?—"quality of life"? One no-longer-really-young professional says, "It used to be you moved to the suburbs for the children. But on some level we still think of ourselves as children." Peter Pan, call your office.

   —*Very* freely adapted from George Will, "Reality Says You Can't Have It All," *Newsweek*

   This piece is very difficult to analyze on a part-by-part basis. Here and there you can identify a device (the last sentence reminds us of a horse laugh of sorts), but the entire piece is written with tongue at least in the direction of cheek. Exaggeration plays a role, with the activities of some baby boomers taken to represent those of an entire generation, but this is really an inductive argument. The choice of examples is prejudicial. You almost have to talk about the tone of the whole piece to do it justice.

70. "The arms buildup that President Reagan gave us is an albatross around our necks. We spent a trillion dollars on it. Do you realize how much a trillion dollars is? That's a one with twelve zeros after it. That's $4,000 for (or rather *from*) every man, woman, and child in the United States. And what was it all for? Are we any safer now for having spent all this treasure? Do you *feel* any safer now than you did before? Our children, who will eventually have to pay for all this because of the national debt, will look back on us as a generation of lunatics."
—Letter to the editor of the Bellevue (Ind.) *Star-Reporter*

71. "Britain has done all it can to sabotage the development of the European Community. For a while it was Margaret Thatcher, and after that her equally right-wing successor, John Major, who served as mouthpiece for the isolationist camp in Britain. It's clear to any intelligent listener that the people they're really speaking for are not the average people in the street, who would benefit from joining the rest of Europe, but a small number of the English super-rich who don't want to rock the boat. As long as Britain remains independent, they get to pull the strings—and make the profits. These money types are joined by a few nineteenth-century throwbacks who are arrogant enough to think that England has an empire to protect and exploit."
—Editorial, *Athens Courier*

72. Well, it looks like the wimps are coming out of the woodwork all over the place. If you're a man, the fashionable thing to be these days is "sensitive." Articles with titles like "Babies and Men," "The Divorced Father," and—can you believe it?—"Men Cry Too" are cropping up all over the place. You'd think today's males were unleashing the bottled up agonies of a couple of thousand generations from the way they like to step into the spotlight and bare their sensitive souls to anybody who'll listen. They say there are more divorces today, and maybe because of the safety of numbers, a divorce is an excuse for a guy to become a softhead; the summons server may as well deliver a license to cry in public.

   If a kid wants his modern daddy to come out and toss a ball around, he'll have to drag him out of the kitchen first. After making him take off the apron, of course, so he won't embarrass his kid in front of his buddies.

   It's a good thing the women are getting out there and learning to run the world. Today's men are busily forgetting how to do it.

   This diatribe actually contains a rudimentary argument. (The existence of the articles cited is offered as evidence for increased sensitivity among men.)

73. "It [the feminist movement] was crazy. The lunacy, unfortunately, wasn't confined to sex. Male reviewers abased themselves before Miss [Susan] Brownmiller's book, *Against Our Will,* and the male editors of *Time* magazine, in a spasm of liberal gallantry, named her as one of its 12 Women of the Year, thereby atoning for five decades of Men of the Year."
—Joseph Sobran, "The End of Feminism"

   Not as "macho" as the previous one, but not without its slanters

74. "The environmental lobby used to be the watchdogs of government and industry, barking at their heels and snapping at them when they tried to grab at the country's virgin resources. In the nineties, the environmentalists have begun to look just like the people they're supposed to be watching. Representatives of the Audubon Society,

the Sierra Club, the Wilderness Society, and the National Wildlife Federation look just like other Washington, D.C. bureaucrats, lined up with their folded lap-top computers inside their attaché cases, all of them desperate to become the next assistant secretary of the interior."
—Paraphrase of an anonymous environmentalist's remarks on a radio program

75. "The executives responsible for the recent corporate catastrophes popularly known as Agent Orange, asbestos, and the Dalkon Shield are not in jail and will not go to jail. With the exception of informed victims, few of us describe these cases in the language of crime, even though in each case there is a wealth of evidence that victims were put at unacceptably high levels of risk of severe injury and death and that corporate executives knew of the risks, yet failed to take appropriate preventive action. Even Morton Mintz, the award-winning *Washington Post* investigative reporter and author of *At Any Cost: Corporate Greed, Women, and the Dalkon Shield,* a powerful indictment of the A.H. Robins pharmaceutical company, does not use the word 'crime' in telling the sordid tale of the Dalkon Shield."
—From Russell Mokhiber's "Criminals By Any Other Name," *The Washington Monthly*

"Catastrophe," "powerful indictment," and "sordid" are obviously emotive; the rest is more subtle.

76. "Some of the ill will [at Dartmouth College] has been provoked by a student-run newspaper called *The Dartmouth Review.* Ten of the dirty dozen who destroyed the shanties [built on the Dartmouth campus as an antiapartheid protest] reportedly work for the six-year-old weekly, a New Right mouthpiece that is run independently of the college and has the support of such leading off-campus conservatives as William F. Buckley, Jr. Considered troublemakers by the administration and many faculty members, and disowned by former supporters such as Rep. Jack Kemp, the Review's editors traffic in outrage and offense."
—*Newsweek*

77. An advertisement for Steven Spielberg's movie *The Color Purple* showed a silhouette of a woman sitting on a rocking chair, reading a book. Marlette, the political cartoonist for the *Charlotte Observer,* drew a cartoon take-off on this motif. In the "advertisement" for Marlette's "movie," which is entitled *The Colored People,* Ronald Reagan is shown in silhouette on a rocking chair, reading a book entitled *Civil Rights Reversals.* Beneath the picture is listed the "cast of characters": "Starring RONALD REAGAN as Whitey, EDWIN MEESE [who was Reagan's attorney general] as Affirmative Action, and Introducing APARTHEID as The Good Old Days."

78. "Must the NFL—fat, sassy, the General Motors of professional sports—meet a similar crisis [to the one the National Basketball Association went through in 1983–1984] before it tries to solve its own plague of drugs?
    "For years, since Don Reese's personal revelation and charges of league-wide drug involvement, the NFL has lived under a cloud of suspicion. Initially, it seemed the front offices, deeply concerned that their image remain pristine, chose to look the other way. Now they've acknowledged the problem, and have chosen to push for testing; this year, eight franchises asked their players to undergo post-season analysis, but each was refused."
—Tom Jackson, *Sacramento Bee*

79. "It's past time that you and I and every other American asked some cold, hard questions.

"Who lost Iran?

"Who lost Afghanistan?

"Who lost Vietnam, Laos and Cambodia?

"Who crippled the FBI and the CIA?

"Who sold the Russians computers and other sophisticated equipment which have been used to stamp out freedom?

"Who is keeping our kids from praying in school?

"Who lets hardened criminals out on the street to kill, rape and rob again before their victims are buried or out of the hospital?

"Who says that America should do little if anything to help human beings who are daily being killed and beaten up by Marxist dictators?

"The answer in every case is LIBERALS.

"But America is waking up to what the liberals have been doing to it.

"To quote Michigan professor Stephen Tonsor, 'New Deal liberals are as dead as a dodo. The only problem is they don't know it.'"

—Richard Viguerie, *The New Right*

Bank 4-3

Writing assignments: Construct seven sentences, each illustrating a use of the slanter indicated.

80. Dysphemism

81. Loaded question

82. Proof surrogate

83. Stereotype

84. Euphemism

85. Innuendo

86. Hyperbole

Chapters 5 & 6
Pseudoreasoning I & II

Our notion of pseudoreasoning is, more or less, the old notion of "informal fallacy." If you prefer that term, nothing we say about the subject in the text will cause any substantial difficulty. We prefer the pseudoreasoning label for a couple of reasons—it connects nicely with "pseudoreason" and other "pseudo-" terminology, and it doesn't require distinguishing an *informal* fallacy from a *formal* fallacy. To appreciate this distinction, students would already need to understand the distinction between valid and invalid arguments. We do introduce the term "fallacy" right off in Chapter 5, in case you decide you need it.

Chapter 5 deals primarily with pseudoreasoning that appeals to our feelings, emotions, urges, drives, instincts, and so on; Chapter 6 covers much of what's left over. Together, they do not by any means exhaust the possibilities. As the text points out, many cases of pseudoreasoning simply have no standard names, and the number that do have names make up a list too long to deal with in a class. So, we point out to students that a case of pseudoreasoning does not have to fit one of our patterns.

However, there are cases of *legitimate* reasoning that bear at least superficial likenesses to our patterns of pseudoreasoning, and students are often too quick to label these as pseudoreasoning. They tend to get tunnel vision and to be more afraid of *missing* a case of pseudoreasoning than of making a bad call the other way. One of these errors is not necessarily more important than the other—another thing we keep having to point out.

We tell students to think of the labeled patterns as "pseudoreasoning alert signals"— when readers or listeners encounter something that reminds them of one of these patterns, they should look at it very closely to make sure it is not pseudoreasoning rather than immediately assuming it is.

We've noticed that students tend to confuse appeals to common practice (and, sometimes, "two wrongs make a right" pseudoreasoning) with legitimate appeals to fair treatment. An instance of the former occurs when A thinks he can justify X because some or lots of other people do X. But we get the latter when A says that if *he* deserves criticism for doing X, so do all the other people who do it. In the latter case, of course, A is right, but students will often see this legitimate appeal as more pseudoreasoning. Tunnel vision.

Again, we emphasize that it is more important to be able to determine whether a given appeal or consideration is relevant to the issue at hand than to be able to determine which emotion the appeal is based on or which formula the consideration is an instance of.

Burden of proof and begging the question both get more extensive treatments than in the third edition. We are more and more struck by the important role played by the former in faulty reasoning; unfair burdens of proof ruin debates before they get started.

You'll surely notice that the pattern we give in the text for false dilemma is also the pattern of the disjunctive argument, a valid form. So we include examples of the pattern that amount to pseudoreasoning and those that do not—that is, we point out when it is not reasonable to believe that the disjunctive premise is true and when it is reasonable to believe that it's true. It's wise to stress this point in class as well; one thing to say is that it points up the difference between logic (where we're concerned about the validity of the argument, and disjunctive argument is obviously valid) and critical thinking, where the soundness of the argument is what counts, including the truth of the premises. In cases of false dilemma, *we never get to the question of the argument's validity,* because, if we're familiar with false dilemma pseudoreasoning, we realize that the disjunctive premise has already tried to sell us a bill of goods. Unless we're considering an argument hypothetically (what would happen *if . . .?*), we as critical thinkers are not ordinarily concerned about what follows from false premises.

We should remind you again that some of the letters to editors and the "newspapers" they are alleged to have appeared in—those not credited in the acknowledgments section of the text—are fictitious. Any resemblance of such letters to those penned by actual people or of the publications to any that actually exist is (more or less) coincidental.

(Incidentally, you'll find that there is a total of exactly one problem bank for these two chapters. But it's big enough to satisfy the needs of all but the most voracious of exercise consumers.)

Exercises Unanswered in the Text

Exercise 5-1

2. Two wrongs make a right

3. Wishful thinking

5. Scare tactics

6. Appeal to belief

8. Horse laugh/ridicule

9. This looks like an appeal to pity, and it is. But it isn't pseudoreasoning. This is the sort of case that often gets tossed automatically into the pseudoreasoning category but that doesn't belong there. He has given a perfectly good reason for patronizing the store; it just doesn't have anything to do with ice cream (although he does mention, in a separate claim, that the place "has the best"). This example illustrates the point that evaluation has less to do with classifying the emotion to which one appeals than with determining the relevance of the appeal.

Exercise 5-2

2. Yes, unless it is known that the brand is a best-seller because of promotion or other facts that do not reflect on its quality

4. Yes

5. No

6. Yes

8. Yes. It would be relevant if you want to avoid disagreement, or if you want to argue against their opinions.

9. Yes

Exercise 5-3

"Decided" has indeed brought in a red herring, one that is getting to be standard equipment in this debate. He speaks as if the issue of nondiscrimination laws were whether gays and lesbians should get special rights that others do not have. But this issue is whether they should be free from discrimination in the way that others are free from it. Nondiscrimination laws require that people be treated equally with regard to whatever features they mention; they do not provide "special rights that everybody else doesn't have."

Exercise 5-4

2. The appeal to pity may be relevant to whether or not the boy should be *given* an increase in his allowance, but it is not relevant to whether or not he has *earned* such an increase.

3. No pseudoreasoning

5. Horse laugh/ridicule pseudoreasoning

6. Common practice pseudoreasoning

8. Scare tactics: relevant to whether one should buy a radio; not relevant to whether that radio should be a Cobra

9. Bandwagon pseudoreasoning

Exercise 5-5

2. a. Whether voting for Tomley will affect street crime
   b. Combination of fear and indignation
   c. The presence of widespread street crime may be relevant, but one person's fears are not much evidence. Further, it's worth noting that the person occupying the mayor's office is hardly in a position to make substantial reductions in street crime single-handedly. The sentiment is relevant only to the extent that such a person *can* have such effects.
   d. Scare tactics, appeal to indignation

3. a. Whether the student deserves a better grade
   b. This is not really an appeal to feelings or emotions but to subjectivity
   c. Not relevant
   d. Subjectivist fallacy

5. a. Whether Richard should be allowed to top off his tank
   b. Not especially an appeal to feelings or emotions
   c. Whatever we call it, Richard's claim is not relevant.
   d. Your choice: Appeal to belief or common practice; some kind of case can be made for each.

6. No pseudoreasoning

8. a. Whether the Army Reserves disturb the solitude of the park
   b. Pride, patriotism carried a bit too far and in a silly context
   c. Irrelevant
   d. Not on our list, but we might call it "wrapping oneself in the flag."

9. Appeal to spite

Exercise 5-6

2. a. Whether one ought to buy Sunquist grapefruit; whether Sunquist tastes better than others
   b. Greed
   c. Relevant to the claim that Sunquist should continue to be successful, but clearly irrelevant to any claim about the quality of the fruit
   d. Not on our list; greed, avarice, covetousness, lust for power, and so on, all operate similarly in cases like this.

3. a. Whether the military budget should be cut
   b. Fear
   c. The considerations are relevant to whether there should be a military budget. They are not relevant to the size of that budget or to whether it should be cut.
   d. Scare tactics

5. a. Whether Glen Haven Scotch will enhance your image (show that you've "made your mark")
   b. Vanity, pride
   c. Irrelevant. We figure that about the only thing one can infer from the brand of liquor people drink is how much they spent for it, and this doesn't even tell you much about their financial status.
   d. Apple polishing

6. a. Whether prison guards' salaries should be increased
   b. Sympathy; a sense of fair play
   c. We find this perfectly relevant. Every consideration mentioned supports the main thesis.

8. a. Whether the word "manpower" should have been replaced
   b. Ridicule
   c. Irrelevant. Whether there are other words that *could* be replaced for roughly similar reasons is irrelevant to the issue of whether *this* word should be replaced in this context. (Some words with apparent gender-specific parts may be more offensive than others to some people.)
   d. Horse laugh

9. a. Whether the death penalty is a good thing.
   b. The sentence begining "Third . . ." and the one following it appeal to the opinions of others who, as laypersons, have no special knowledge of the subject.
   c. We think this appeal is irrelevant.
   d. Appeal to the belief. (The first two arguments are not pseudoreasoning, however.)

11. a. Whether the mentioned charities will put the speaker's estate to better use than would the relatives
    b. No real appeal to an emotion is present
    c. The considerations mentioned are relevant
    d. No pseudoreasoning

12. a. Whether the jobs bill is an excellent idea
    b. We're not sure what to call it. Enthusiasm? Impatience?
    c. It is irrelevant; it may be important to do something, but that doesn't mean it's important to do *this* thing!
    d. Smokescreen/red herring

13. a. Whether the teacher should make an exception to the no-make-up policy (at least we presume that's the issue; this could simply be an explanation)
    b. Pity, or something close
    c. Relevant; not necessarily sufficient, of course, but at least relevant
    d. No pseudoreasoning

15. a. Whether Alexander did a good job for American education
    b. Indignation
    c. Not relevant; it may be important to know these facts about Alexander for some other reason, but it is not relevant to an assessment of his job as secretary of education
    d. Appeal to indignation

16. a. Whether creationism is preferable to evolution theory
    b. A combination of flattery ("the image of God," and so on) and humor (the monkey and zoo business) with a little indignation thrown in for good measure
    c. Not relevant to the truth of the two views; may be relevant to which view a person would *like* to be true
    d. Apple polishing, of a sort; horse laugh/ridicule

18. a. Whether baby boomers should have an aggressive savings plan
    b. Fear
    c. Relevant
    d. No pseudoreasoning

19. a. Whether Tonya Harding should resign from the Olympic Team
    b. Pity
    c. Irrelevant to the stated issue; relevant to the issue of whether people should "pile it on like this."
    d. Appeal to pity

Exercise 5-7

This exercise, while a bit more complex, provides excellent practice in sorting out related issues and determining which considerations are relevant to which. There may be other ways to analyze the passages; we invite you and your students to come up with alternatives.

Letter 2

Issue: Whether the magazine should run the ad

Sentiment: There are several appeals in this letter. The first is an attempt to arouse indignation toward people who have anything to do with or stand to gain by the promotion of tobacco use. Any such people, the letter claims, "have the blood of cancer victims" on their hands. The second appeal, less powerful perhaps than the first, is to one's sense of resentment at the power of the tobacco industry and its supporters. Finally, the comparison of tobacco workers with those who traffic in other drugs—marijuana, cocaine, and heroin—is designed to appeal to one's sense of proportion ("justice" may be too strong a word) in that, given the harm that tobacco causes, tobacco workers have no more claim to their jobs than those who deal in the other drugs.

Relevance: This letter brings at least one relevant consideration to bear on the issue. The claim is that every activity that promotes the use of tobacco (including running the ad) contributes to the serious detriment of people's health. This claim, if true, furnishes a reason for not running the ad, although it is not clear how much weight it should be given. The extent of the relevance of the consideration would be very difficult to determine, since it would be very nearly impossible to assess the effects of running the ad in *The Progressive.*

Letter 3

Issue: Same as preceding letter

Sentiment: The last sentence of the first paragraph and the final paragraph both make the same appeal as letter 1 made, although it is done here with somewhat less vigorous language.

Relevance: Notice that the second paragraph and the first half of the first paragraph describe the ad but say nothing about whether it should be run—that the ad shows shrewdness on the part of the tobacco industry is not relevant to the issue. (Were the claim that the ad is fraudulent, however, it would be relevant.) The remainder of the letter can be treated much like the first letter.

Letter 4

Issue: This letter addresses a different issue, namely, what would be an intelligent way to deal with the tobacco industry and similar industries that have hazardous effects.

Sentiment: There is much less emotional appeal in this letter. The first sentence begins such an appeal but then drops, and an entirely different approach is taken. The expression "kills people in wholesale lots" is emotively powerful, but appears almost in isolation.

Relevance: We find this letter rather carefully conceived; it does not strike us as pseudoreasoning. You may find problems with it that we don't.

Exercise 6-1

2. Begging the question

3. Ad hominem (circumstantial)

5. Slippery slope

6. No pseudoreasoning, it seems true

8. Ad hominem (pseudorefutation)

9. Straw man (in the second sentence; the first sentence may be false, but it isn't pseudoreasoning)

11. Ad hominem (pseudorefutation)

12. Straw man

14. Begging the question

15. Ad hominem (pseudorefutation)

Exercise 6-2

2. False dilemma (and some straw man, too)

3. Begging the question

5. Straw man

6. Straw man, potential false dilemma

8. False dilemma (sneaked into the next-to-last sentence). There are other things going on in this one, too: probably a loaded question near the beginning and another at the end.

9. Begging the question

Exercise 6-3

2. Ad hominem (pseudorefutation)

3. Straw man

5. Straw man

6. Ad hominem (pseudorefutation)

8. Begging the question (in the last sentence)

9. False dilemma (perfectionist fallacy)

Exercise 6-4

2. Begging the question

3. Burden of proof, in Moe's second remark

5. Slippery slope

6. False dilemma. Clearly, there are other things going on in this passage, too.

8. Ad hominem: personal attack (circumstantial)

9. Burden of proof (third sentence); ad hominem (personal attack) of a hypothetical sort that's easy enough to see

Exercise 6-6

2. False dilemma (perfectionist fallacy)

3. False dilemma

5. False dilemma (perfectionist fallacy)

6. Ad hominem (pseudorefutation)

8. Ad hominem (personal attack/circumstantial)

9. Begging the question

Exercise 6-9

2. The fact that Seltzer and Sterling received millions for their research projects from the tobacco industry should make us very suspicious indeed of their objectivity in interpreting data. But we would be guilty of ad hominem pseudoreasoning if we rejected their data as false just because they were paid by the industry. What makes us reject their data in this case—and we certainly should reject it—is the fact that so many more studies *do* show that tobacco use causes health problems and that most of this research has not been sponsored by anybody who stands to gain from the result.

3. There are obvious elements of nonargumentative persuasion here; the whole thing smacks of straw man.

6. Reagan's remarks do count as something—if they are both true and indicative of his actual views, then they are evidence that he is personally not hostile to blacks. Beyond that, however, and especially with regard to the issue mentioned at the beginning of the passage, his remarks are a red herring (or, if you like, a smoke-screen). They are clearly irrelevant to whether White House policy is hostile to black viewpoints or whether it finds them unwelcome.

7. We take the issue to be whether the deaths of so many civilians were justified, and we think that the speaker is doing something very much like begging the question (in the next-to-last sentence) and evading the issue (in the last sentence). Actually, what the last sentence does is *downplay* the issue, although not in the way that slanters do it (See Chapter 4).

8. The reference to the university is a red herring or smokescreen. The developers are in the business of making a buck, presumably, and one way to do that is to encourage people to stay around and buy a house.

10. A couple of elements here: The "good guys" reference smacks of a straw man; the whole thing can be seen as a false dilemma: Either sanctions turn Beijing leaders into good guys by now, or the sanctions should be lifted.

Chapters 5 & 6 Test Question/Exercise Banks

Note to instructor: As mentioned at the beginning of this chapter division, there is only one bank of exercises for these two chapters. It should allow you to cover nearly any ground you like, however. For best results, as they say, we recommend that you mix these examples with cases of legitimate reasoning. Otherwise, students come to expect that *every* item is pseudoreasoning, and they miss the most important kind of practice—distinguishing real reasoning from its impostors. We've included an example of relevant support for a conclusion here and there, but those are easy enough to find or make up so we've left that mainly to you.

Identify instances of pseudoreasoning in the following passages either by naming them or, where they seem not to conform to any of the patterns described in the text, by giving a brief explanation of why the pseudoreasons are irrelevant to the point at issue.

1. "People in Hegins, Pennsylvania, hold an annual pigeon shoot in order to control the pigeon population and to raise money for the town. This year, the pigeon shoot was disrupted by animal rights activists who tried to release the pigeons from their cages. I can't help but think these animal rights activists are the same people who believe in controlling the human population through the use of abortion. Yet, they recoil at a similar means of controlling pigeons. What rank hypocrisy."
   —Rush Limbaugh

   Ad hominem

2. "Several senators on the [Ted Koppel] show agreed with Maxine Waters that there should be more women in the Senate. Paul Simon clucked about the inequity. So did Bill Bradley. Well, guess what? Both of those senators defeated women in their last elections. If Bill Bradley wants more women in the Senate, why doesn't he give up his seat to Christine Todd Whitman, who almost beat him? The same with Paul Simon, who ran against Lynn Martin, now the Secretary of Labor."
   —Rush Limbaugh

   Ad hominem

3. "When [Nidal] Ayyad [convicted of conspiring to blow up the World Trade Center in 1993] complained that 'human rights advocates' had not monitored his treatment during months of detention, [U.S. District Judge Kevin T.] Duffy interjected: 'Did human rights organizations monitor the people whom you killed?'"
   —Robert L. Jackson, in the *Los Angeles Times*

   Duffy commits an ad hominem

4. Yes, people convicted of violent felonies for the third time oughta go to prison for life. Can you think of a single reason why they shouldn't?

   Burden of proof

5. No, I do NOT believe that a murderer ought to be allowed to live. No way! Murderers have forfeited the right to live because anyone who murders another person has lost that right.

   Begging the question

6. No, I do NOT believe that a murderer has a right to live, and here's why. The criminal justice system in this country has gotten completely out of control, what with rapists, murderers, you name it—all getting off scot-free. It's gotta change!

Red herring

7. No, I don't believe we ought to reinstate the death penalty in this state. Doing it isn't going to prevent all crime, and you know it.

Perfectionist fallacy

8. No, I don't think I believe in "three strikes and you're out" for convicted felons. Next thing it will be two strikes, then one strike. Then we'll be sticking people in jail for life for misdemeanors. It's not good policy.

Slippery slope

9. You show me when a fetus wasn't a person, just show me! Tell me exactly when it is. When the baby is born? Well, why not just a day before that? Or the day before that? Or the day before that? Where you gonna draw the line? You gotta say life begins with conception.

Line-drawing fallacy

10. You show me when an embryo becomes a human person, just show me! Tell me exactly when it is. When it's just an egg, the size of a pin head? When it divides once? Twice? Three times? When? Where you gonna draw the line? An embryo is not a person, and that's that.

Line-drawing fallacy

11. All this talk about secondhand smoke causing cancer, I just don't get it. How does it happen? WHEN does it happen? The first time you take a breath in a smoky room? The second time? The third? You can never pin it down exactly.

Line-drawing fallacy (assuming the conclusion is that indirect smoking doesn't cause cancer)

12. "And certainly, our soldiers must never be forced to accept homosexuality or any grand social experiment that has little support outside the White House and the extremist liberal community. . . . Your hard-earned dollars will be used effectively in one of the many Republican National Committee candidate support programs."
—Solicitation for the Republican Party from Senator Bob Dole

There isn't anything unreasonable about sending money to organizations that endorse causes you believe in. This wording, however, seems to play on fear as a "reason" for believing that the reader's money will be used effectively (analyzed that way, call it "scare tactics"); or on the reader's indignation (appeal to indignation).

13. Gays in the military? Either let 'em in, or keep out all minorities; take your choice. I'm for letting them in. The alternative is ridiculous.

False dilemma

14. Gays in the military? If we allow that, then next we'll be letting women into the men's barracks. And the next thing you know, women, men, gays, everyone— they'll all be showering together and sleeping in the same bunks. Get real.

Slippery slope

15. Gays in the military? Are you familiar with the expression "OVER MY DEAD BODY"?

Ridicule

16. Gays in the military? No way. The president's promoting the idea just to get the homosexual vote.

Red herring

17. Gays in the military? Yes. There are no valid grounds for opposing the measure, as can be seen in the fact that policies of nondiscrimination to gays are common practice throughout Western democracies.

Common practice

18. Gays in the military? Yes. Maybe you favor excluding everyone except for white Anglo-Saxon males with adolescent personalities, but not me.

Straw man

19. From a defense attorney's closing statement at a trial: "In conclusion, ladies and gentlemen of the jury, there can be absolutely no doubt that this defendant committed these terrible murders. Look at the mother of the victim, sitting over there, and the father—their lives are forever destroyed by this evil deed. Never again will they know the peace and happiness that was their due. Put yourselves in their shoes, and you will know whether or not this man is guilty."

Appeal to pity

20. "The second group that has latched on to the environmentalist movement . . . wants to preserve the earth at all costs, even if it means that much of the Third World will be forever condemned to poverty. Rather than elevate the Third World, they want to move us closer to Third World conditions. That's somehow cleaner, purer. It's the way things were before Western white people came along and terrorized by the earth by inventing things. They want to roll us back, maybe not to the Stone Age, but at least to the horse-and-buggy era."
   —Rush Limbaugh

Ridicule/straw man/even ad hominem (depending on what you focus on)

21. Is the president guilty of sexual harassment, as the Republicans are yelping? Hey, give me a break! What's important is jobs, health care, welfare reform.

Red herring

22. Bob, I certainly do feel I have earned a promotion. My record speaks for itself, and the way I look at it, I'll just look for a new position if the company thinks it can step all over me.

   Scare tactics

23. Of course that can't be a legitimate proposal. They're just trying to get the city council to pass a regulation that will stir up some business for them.

   Ad hominem

24. The next speaker is gonna speak in favor of the idea. But she works for the gun lobby. Don't even bother listening to what she's gonna say.

   Poisoning the well

25. Preferential treatment in hiring is something we must support; after all, can you think of a reason why we shouldn't?

   Burden of proof

26. Free speech in China? Of course they have free speech in China. You are guaranteed the freedom to speak; it's just that you're not guaranteed freedom after you've spoken!

   Ridicule

27. Letter to the editor: "In rejoinder to your July 21 editorial, I certainly don't see how you can criticize the striking Springfield Unified School District teachers who carried their own signs. Let us not forget that you endorsed and supported city council members Holt and Donazetti, who not only paraded up and down Main Street with their own placards, but also got young children out of school to parade with them."
   —*North State Record*

   Ad hominem (pseudorefutation)

28. No, I don't believe that Uncle Bob is really gone forever. He was like a father to me, and I believe that someday, somehow or other, we'll see one another again; I don't think I could go on if I didn't believe that.

   Wishful thinking

29. You know very well I don't care what Mason says about investments or, for that matter, anything else. That guy is the most money-grubbing creep I've ever run into; all he ever cares about is where his next dollar is coming from. He can take his opinions and stick 'em in his ear.

   Ad hominem (personal attack)

30. Listen, friends, it's *our* money the board of supervisors wants to spend putting sewers and other improvements out there in that Antelope Creek development. And you know who's going to profit from it the most? The developers, who don't even live around here. I tell you, we have sat back and done nothing long enough! It's high time we told these out-of-town interlopers or antelopers or whatever they are to go mess with somebody else's town. I won't stand for it any more!

Appeal to indignation (There is a relevant appeal here, but the speaker is clearly trying to evoke outrage from his audience as well.)

31. I'll tell you why a hundred dollars is enough child support. You go into court and ask for more, and I'll have my lawyer file a countersuit that will set you back a bundle in legal fees!

Scare tactics

32. I know it was not very nice to overcharge them like that for the room, but all's fair in love, war, and business, my dear. Besides, if the situation were reversed and *we* were desperate for lodging, they would have bled us for all we're worth.

Two wrongs make a right

33. George, I speak for the rest of the neighbors on our street. Frankly, your front yard is a mess, and we'd appreciate it if you would do something about it. We put the time and money into making our places look nice, but the effort is largely ruined by one awful looking place right here in the middle of the block. We hope you'll do something about it.

This might look like peer pressure or common practice, but we don't believe it's pseudoreasoning at all.

34. Letter to the editor: "Your food section frequently features recipes with veal, and you say veal is a wholesome, nutritious dish. I disagree. Do you know how veal comes to be on your plate? At birth a newborn calf is separated from its mother, placed in a dark enclosure, and chained by its neck so that it cannot move freely. This limits muscular development so that the animal is tender. It is kept in the dark pen until the day it is cruelly slaughtered."
—*Cascade News*

Appeal to pity

35. Overheard: "When it comes to the issue of growth in this town, you're either part of the solution, or you're part of the problem."

False dilemma (Clever-sounding remarks like this one often disguise one type of pseudoreasoning or another.)

36. Letter to the editor: "President Reagan continued to support Star Wars even after the Congressional Office of Technology Assessment Report found that the system probably wouldn't work and would be hideously expensive. Unfortunately, after Reagan publicly committed himself so strongly to Star Wars that it was impossible for him to reverse his position."
—*Chilton County Register*

Ad hominem (circumstantial)

37. This business of American car manufacturers having joint ventures with foreign car makers really stinks. Think of the consequences of not being able to buy American-made cars. No jobs for American car workers, no big cars, no ready supply of parts, no consumption of American steel. I think we should prohibit joint ventures.

Straw man

38. John, I just know you would make a wonderful and successful doctor. It's what your father wanted for you, and I know he would have been very proud if you were to go to medical school.

Appeal to loyalty, or a variation on the theme

39. In spite of its hypocritical announcement that North Korea has ceased nuclear testing, it is safe to assume that the North Koreans have done no such thing, for at present we have no means of verifying their so-called moratorium.

Burden of proof

40. Ad for a store that sells pianos: "Pianos are our *only* business. You'll get the best deal at the piano experts."

Pseudoreasoning, although not of one of our patterns. (That they sell nothing but pianos is irrelevant to how much they sell them for.)

41. You bet I'll explain why FantasyLand [an adult bookstore] should be closed down! You go in there, and we'll send your license plate number to the newspaper. You going to like people knowing what kind of stuff you read?

Scare tactics

42. This river has been changing its course every couple of years for the past few thousand years. Now they've decided that the banks need to be stabilized. Who does the Army Corps of Engineers think it is to come in here and decide they know something Mother Nature doesn't?

This kind of pseudoreasoning is of the "if it's been going on like this for a long time, then this is the way is should continue" variety—not one of our forms in the text. Sometimes the mere fact that something has happened in a certain way can provide reasons for leaving well enough alone, but the mere fact that this is the way it has happened is not itself such a reason.

43. Frankly, I don't think you would be satisfied with anything less than our Model 24, which allows for more expansion than any other personal computer in its class. The way you catch on to things—something I can tell just from the questions you've asked here in the store—you're not going to be happy with a machine whose limits you'll soon reach.

Apple polishing

44. Are you telling me that you're twenty-one years old and still a virgin? I'd keep quiet about that if I were you—you'd be the laughing stock of the dorm if that were widely known.

Peer pressure

45. "I certainly don't think much of the totalitarian form of government. A so-called free election with only one candidate is not free at all."
    "Oh, I don't know. I don't think it's all that bad."
    "Why not?"
    "Just look at our elections. Sure, we have more than one person running, but the candidates are all alike. They might just as well be one person, for all the difference there is among them."

Straw man, we trust

46. "I say let's splurge and buy seats on the fifty-yard line. I know a place we can get them for twenty-five dollars apiece."
    "Good grief! Maybe you want to spend every last cent we make on a football game, but not me. Are you nuts?"

Straw man

47. Well! Finally, after all these years, the telephone company makes an error on my bill in my favor! And I'm surely not going to point it out to them. They've been gouging me since telephones first came into existence.

Two wrongs make a right

48. So they came along and made me take my sign down because it was in violation of the city sign code. But look at the signs down in the next block, will you? They're under the same code, and they're just like the one I had to take down.

This may *be an appeal to common practice, but there may be a reasonable appeal here as well, an appeal to fair play or equal treatment.*

49. Of course they have legal elections in Chicago. They just have to postpone certifying the results sometimes because the ballots get . . . uh . . . lost.

Horse laugh, ridicule

50. Why do I spend so much on clothes? Well, it's either that or look like a bum, and I know which of those I prefer.

False dilemma

51. Hey, Charley! Get a load of this: Frank thinks the Chargers will make it all the way to the Superbowl next year. Can you beat that?

   Ridicule

52. Sure, driving after you've been drinking can get you into trouble with the law, but if you're careful I don't think there's anything wrong with it. After all, everyone does it, right?

   Appeal to common practice

53. Hank "Icebox" Gallagher, defensive lineman for the Tigers, knows his hamburgers—he orders them a half dozen at a time. If *he* eats at Big Al's, then shouldn't you?

   Pseudoreasoning as a result of a misuse of authority—see Chapter 3 on expertise

54. When he was twelve, Walter Polovchak and his family were permitted to emigrate from the Soviet Union to the United States. Walter's father, however, eventually decided to return to Russia and was pressured by the Soviet Embassy to take Walter with him. The American Civil Liberties Union sided with Walter's father, rather than with Walter, who wished to remain in Chicago. When the case reached the courts, the legal arguments of the ACLU were criticized by some editorial writers on the grounds that in most other instances involving the rights of children, the ACLU had always sided with the child. Commented one law professor: "The ACLU's actions regarding Walter can be understood only in terms of 'an unwillingness to criticize communism.'"

   Ad hominem (pseudorefutation)

55. I don't see how you can possibly think Snellrod's Groceries has a good selection of fruit. Don't you remember that when he first moved here, it was you who lent him the money to get started? Sure, he paid you back, but did he ever do any favors for you? And now it's Snellrod, not you, who's getting all the business, all the attention.

   Appeal to spite

56. I don't like postmodern expressionism. It's another style spawned by the East Coast art establishment, and, frankly, I'm tired of that group's dictating to the rest of the art world.

   Ad hominem (genetic fallacy)

57. Getting on Senator Davis's case about the propriety of some of his financial dealings strikes me as just plain carping. Davis made a considerable economic sacrifice when he left private industry and entered politics; the people of this district are lucky to have him there.

   Generic pseudoreasoning: Red herring

58. From a letter to the editor: "They're wrong again, the doctors who say that the sun causes cancer. The four substances for all life are water, food, air, and sun. Everybody knows the sun opens the pores of your skin to release poisons; it cannot cause cancer. Cancer is caused by the toxins man puts in the air, not by sunlight."
—*Cascade News*

Appeal to belief

59. Overheard: "I don't know why Barbara won't go out with me. She must think I'm too intense for her."

False dilemma (could be she finds him boring, if this remark is any hint)

60. "Doesn't the fact that very few first-rank economists accept Marxist economic ideas suggest to you that there may be something wrong with those ideas?"
   "Not at all. Those economists are all tools of the ruling capitalist parties. I dismiss their views out of hand."

Ad hominem (personal attack)

61. I just learned why all those theories about nonhumans building the Great Pyramids and the Easter Island statues and so on are full of baloney. The guy who wrote about them was once a hotel manager somewhere in Switzerland, and he was once convicted of embezzlement. No wonder those theories smelled fishy!

Ad hominem (personal attack)

62. Yeah, sure the Los Angeles district attorney believes that O.J. Simpson can get a fair trial in California. But before you sign on to something like that, you might notice that O.J. is a black man and that the Los Angeles district attorney is a white man. That tells you all you need to know about his opinion of fair trials. *(Similar to remarks widely heard during and just after the preliminary hearing, in which it was determined that Simpson would stand trial for the murder of his former wife and another person.)*

Ad hominem (circumstantial)

63. After his return to India, Bhagwan Shree Rajneesh remarked that "Russia is far better than the United States." When the *New York Daily News* learned that the 53-year-old multimillionaire vowed never to leave India again, it said the following about his remark concerning Russia: "Shucks. It would have been a gas watching him accumulate umpteen Rolls-Royces and four battalions of aging flower children in the exurbs of Vladivostok." What technique was the *Daily News* using to "refute" the guru?

Horse laugh

64. From a defense attorney's closing remarks at a trial: "This young man isn't guilty of a crime. No, ladies and gentlemen, it's *society* that's guilty of a crime, a crime against the very person on trial here. The society that wants to send him to prison for half his life is the same society that produced the rotten neighborhood in which he was born and grew up, that saw to it that he got a fifth-rate education, that

gave him pimps and drug dealers for role models, and that offered him the choice between street crime or jobs nobody else would take. This jury—you—can do something to right the wrong that has been done to this young man. . . ."

Red herring. The jury's job is to determine guilt or innocence; these remarks may be relevant to the kind of sentence that is deserved.

65. Listen. As long as you're going to live here at home and let your mother and me support you, you can rest assured that you're going to cooperate. And that goes for your opinions as well as for your behavior.

    Scare tactics

66. What is the name of the mistake in reasoning committed by people who dismiss the policies of former President Reagan on the grounds that he is a former actor with a "cowboy mentality"?

    Ad hominem (pseudorefutation). The important thing is to notice that the reason given for dismissal of Reagan's policies is so very weak that it approaches irrelevance.

67. I know there are people who think that Sarah is too impetuous and flighty. But these qualities only make her exciting to me and make me love her all the more.

    This is really as much a case of self-induced self-deception as it is pseudoreasoning. We suppose wishful thinking is as close as our categories come to it. (Instances of this sort seem almost absurdly silly to most of us most of the time, but we must remember that reasoning about certain subjects becomes much more difficult when romance puts one's brain chemistry inconveniently, if pleasantly, out of kilter. It is part of the human condition that we are sometimes called on to make crucial decisions at such times.)

68. Letter to the editor: "Should people on welfare be allowed to play the lottery? I say no. It's time we did something about the welfare rip-off in this country. I believe in charity for the poor, but free-loading parasites who are too lazy to get out and do an honest day's work—I say cut them off at the knees!"
    —*North State Record*

    This piece of vitriol is certainly pseudoreasoning; it seems to have one foot in straw man and one in appeal to spite or indignation, though it doesn't fit neatly into either category. There's plenty of Chapter 4 stuff here, too!

69. Another letter to the editor on the same subject: "It is positively disgraceful that welfare recipients can spend some of their checks on lottery tickets. If they can afford to spend their monthly allowances on the lottery instead of things that are essential, such as food, shelter, and clothing, then they don't need public assistance. Why should I, a taxpayer, shell out my money to them for that purpose?
    —*North State Record*

    False dilemma, with one horn of the dilemma a straw man

70. I know it probably puts me in the unfashionable minority these days, but I really don't care for Hank Williams's music. Ever since I learned that he drank a lot and took drugs, I've felt that way.

While this may be ad hominem pseudoreasoning of the personal attack sort, it may also be a psychological explanation about somebody's reaction to Hank Williams and his music. It becomes more clearly the former if the person goes on to claim that the music in question is bad because of its creator's personal habits.

71. "Because of [Abraham] Lincoln's policies the cemeteries of the nation were sown with 600,000 premature bodies, long turned to dust now, but in their time just as open to the promise of life as any young draft dodger of the 1960s."
—From Tom Landess, "The Dark Side of Abraham Lincoln," *The Southern Partisan*

The reference to draft dodgers of the 1960s is an appeal to spite or indignation.

72. In response to the woman who felt that Chicago Honeybear cheerleaders were being exploited by men who viewed the Honeybears as sex objects, *Chicago Tribune* columnist Mike Royko devoted a column to the subject, suggesting that such women are hypocrites. The most sexually motivated of all sports fans, he said, are females, who gather in front of the TV screen solely to gawk at the muscular thighs and lean hips of the "hunks."

Ad hominem (pseudorefutation)

73. *Revenge of the Nerds* was really a funny movie. I know, because I was a nerd myself, and that's really the way it was!

Plain vanilla pseudoreasoning of no particular category. There may be two independent reasons here (see Chapter 8 on independent premises) for seeing the movie, but neither of them supports the other. (Wonder what he means, "was" a nerd?)

74. THERESA: Hey! Take it easy with the salt. Don't you know too much of it is bad for you?
DANIEL: Aw, come on. They say that about everything.

The fact that many things are said to be bad for you is not relevant to the question of whether this thing is bad for you. Making that association is pseudoreasoning. However, if Daniel means that since many of the claims about things being bad for you are false, this claim is probably false, then he is not guilty of pseudoreasoning; he has given an argument, although a weak one. Discussion of such arguments is found in Chapter 11.

75. Look, you can argue about it all day long, but I believe that Carmichael is the best person for the job, and I hope he gets it. That's my opinion, and it's as good as any other opinion, so we may as well change the subject.

A version of the subjectivist fallacy. One person may be as good as another, and one may have as much right to an opinion as another, but not all opinions are created equal; those with better reasons are better opinions.

76. You can't trust the arguments you find in that magazine. It's well known as a right-wing apologist for the wealthy.

Genetic fallacy. As noted in the text, arguments stand on their own feet; their origins are not important.

149

77. Toads do too cause warts. People have known that for centuries.

   A version of appeal to belief

78. "It says here that smoke from wood-burning stoves, no matter how airtight they're supposed to be, gets into your house and is a health hazard."

   "No way. We just spent close to a thousand on this new stove; what you're reading can't be true."

   Wishful thinking

79. It isn't so important how they're made or how long they last or how much they cost. These are the best jeans because they're incredibly popular right now. Sometimes I think you just don't understand style.

   Peer pressure (bandwagon), if the issue is whether the jeans are the best. There is also a danger of begging the question here (the question of what criteria should be used to determine the best jeans). If the issue is simply what jeans should you wear to be like everybody else, then of course there's no pseudoreasoning at all—and no real need for the remark in the first place. And it may be that, as the speaker says, your authors just don't understand style.

80. "Greyhound reminds you that when you travel by car, you take chances, especially if you are traveling alone. Anything can happen: dangerous thunderstorms [sound effect: thunder], engine trouble [sound of car failing to start], blowouts [tire blowing out, car screeching to a stop]. Next time [upbeat music] don't take chances. It's time to go Greyhound and leave the driving to us."
   —Greyhound advertisement

   This may look like scare tactics, but the points made are relevant to the claim that alternatives to the automobile may be safer. Of course it doesn't follow that Greyhound is the best alternative.

81. You shouldn't wear anything made of white harp seal fur. Do you know how they get that fur? Baby harp seals, which are among the sweetest-looking creatures on earth, are clubbed to death right in front of their mothers when they are just days or weeks old.

   This is not so clearly pseudoreasoning. Compare with item 34, which associates cruel treatment of calves with the value of veal as food. Truly, the killing of young harp seals arouses a great deal of pity, but if the issue is whether they should be killed— including whatever uses their fur is put to—then the appeal to pity is quite relevant. Extended discussion of this item usually requires careful separation of the two issues: (a) whether harp seals should be killed for human use and (b) whether harp seals should be killed in this particularly brutal fashion.

82. Don't give me reasons where feelings are concerned; I can't be argued out of my feelings.

   This interesting remark is more complex than it looks. It's probably true that a person—at least sometimes—can't do much about his or her feelings. But this issue is different from the issues of whether a person should act *on those feelings and whether the feelings themselves are proper, appropriate, based on fact, and so on. That a person has certain feelings, and may be stuck with them, is irrelevant to the other two questions. To offer the former as a reason for a position on the latter issues is to commit pseudoreasoning of a form that at least vaguely resembles our subjectivist fallacy category.*

83. News report: The city council's internal affairs committee voted to allow public access to the city's five creeks. But Councilwoman Shelly Harvard voiced strong opposition to the public access requirement. "Why do we want to allow access to the creek?" she asked. "Are we going to turn this into a town where anyone can walk across a person's lawn?"

    Straw man

84. In a letter to the editor of a newspaper, a certified nutritionist criticized an editorial that had appeared earlier in the paper advocating a ban on raw milk. He wrote, "You call for an 'outright ban on commercial sales' of raw milk. Yet, by your own figures, you relate about 123 California cases of *Salmonella dublin* [food poisoning], which represents a miniscule danger compared to the lives lost by smoking cigarettes."
    —Sacramento Bee

    Ad hominem (pseudorefutation)

85. Did Amundsen beat Scott to the South Pole? Hardly, sir! 'Twould be disastrous indeed for the Empire if we allowed ourselves to believe Norwegians with dogs could ever best red-blooded English Males!

    Appeal to the consequences of belief

86. In an advertisement entitled "The Second Best Smokescreen," the R.J. Reynolds Tobacco Company comments on the claim that cigarette smoke in the air may be harmful to nonsmokers. The ad first asks whether this charge is "wholly motivated by concern for the nonsmoker" or whether it is "the same old war on smoking in a new guise." It then quotes a spokesperson for the American Lung Association, who says that probably the only way we can reduce smoking is to make it nonacceptable socially. "Obviously," the ad concludes, "one way to make smoking 'nonacceptable socially' would be to suggest that secondhand smoke could cause disease."

    This doesn't seem to fit any of our categories precisely, except the generic one of red herring. Still, it's clear-cut (and rather clever) pseudoreasoning. Here's a way to spell it out: The cigarette company says, "If the Lung Association wanted to accomplish X (some rotten thing), then the way they would do it is by saying Y. And, sure enough, they're saying Y. Therefore, the reason they're doing Y is to accomplish X. Of course, the Lung Association may have other reasons for saying Y. In this case, the fact is that Y is pretty clearly true.

87. Cheryl is deciding which of the girls who are rushing her sorority she wants most to join. Pearl and Maria are trying to convince Cheryl that Debra is the best of the rushees and that Cheryl should vote for Debra when the time comes.
    "Debra has a wonderful personality, and she'll fit right in," Pearl says. "All the other sisters are going to vote for her."

"And she'll be really hurt if you don't support her," Maria points out. "She thinks you like her a lot."

"Besides," Pearl says, "she and I are very close. She's just about the best friend I ever had."

In the last three speeches, we find (1) a bandwagon, (2) an appeal to pity, (3) some apple polishing, and (4) an appeal to loyalty.

88. "Proposition 99 is a prejudiced proposition—flat-out prejudiced. It takes one group of people and punishes them for their choice of life-style. You know Proposition 99 as the Cigarette and Tobacco Tax Initiative. But it doesn't punish tobacco companies—it punishes people who happen to smoke. Once we start passing propositions limiting people's freedom, we've got a big problem. Suppose they start picking on you because of some choice you make—or the way you look. History tells us pretty soon that kind of thing gets out of hand . . . there are a lot of good reasons to vote no on 99. . . ."

—Text of political commercial urging people to vote no on Proposition 99 (which raised taxes on cigarettes) on the November 1988 California general election ballot. The ad was sponsored by the tobacco industry.

There's an obvious slippery slope present and some nonargumentative persuasion ("punishing" people); the business about who suffers, the smoker or the tobacco companies, is a red herring.

89. "To the people who brought you 'The Great American Smokeout,' we make The Great American Challenge. We challenge the American Cancer Society to clean up the air in its 'smoke free' offices. We are willing to bet there isn't much cigarette smoking at American Cancer Society offices. But, according to a recent study from the National Institute for Occupational Safety and Health (NIOSH), cigarette smoke also wasn't the problem in 98 percent of 203 buildings reported to have indoor air problems. . . . Indoor air inspections resulting from worker complaints typically find viruses, fungal spores, bacteria, gases, closed fresh air ducts, and ventilation systems in need of maintenance."

—Full-page ad in *USA Today,* sponsored by the Tobacco Institute

A real, literal smokescreen! The Tobacco Institute is playing off reports of dangerous office environments, but the ad is meant to divert attention away from the even greater dangers of cigarette smoking. The ad may also hint that those who feel ill at the office should not blame the smoker; but the "Smokeout" was directed to actual smokers.

90. MARTY: If we keep on the way we are going, we will destroy civilization on this planet.
TRACY: That's so depressing. I think we need to think well of things.

Wishful thinking

91. "Sure, driving after you've been drinking can get you into trouble with the law, but if you're careful and stay in control I don't think there's anything wrong with it. What makes something like that wrong is endangering others; so as long as you haven't drunk enough to impair your control, you aren't doing anything wrong."

This is interesting. Regarding the issue of whether drinking and driving will get you into trouble with the law, the whole thing is irrelevant—a red herring. But stating that driving after drinking moderately is not wrong because it does not endanger others (and perhaps should not be against the law) is an argument. Given that most or at least many people find it difficult to tell when they've had too much to drink, it isn't a very good argument.

92. Here's a "common practice" from the world of sports, overheard during the 1988 Olympics: "Oh, I don't know. All athletes use some type of steroids in training and competition."

93. In its July 1988 issue, *Consumer Reports* criticized the Suzuki Samurai as unsafe and dangerously easy to roll over. In the next issue, a reader wrote in response, "In order to completely idiot-proof our society, we would have to surrender all freedom. Your suggestion that the government protect us from this evil vehicle is just another step in a journey that could ultimately lead to an erosion of freedom in this country."

This could be viewed as a slippery slope combined with a straw man, a false dilemma, or both.

94. Evaluate the following: Rubwald went to the fights Saturday night. Outside the arena he ran into Bagan, a man he knew. Bagan was taking bets on the main event, a bout between Svit Onion, a top-ranked contender, and Alf Granstan, an unknown fighter. Rubwald remembered that he went to high school with Granstan and decided he should bet on his old schoolmate; he put down $100 against the favorite.

Appeal to loyalty, although it's less an "appeal" than a reliance on loyalty

95. I am absolutely sick of seeing the videotape of those L.A. police beating Rodney King. It's time for the press to lay off and give law enforcement officers a break. There are a lot of very good police officers out there, and they aren't recognized nearly as often as they should be.

Red herring

96. "There's no reason to investigate something that never happened."
—Bush administration spokesman Marlin Fitzwater, when asked what he thought about an investigation of charges that the 1980 Reagan campaign made a deal with Iran to delay release of American hostages until after that year's presidential election.

Begging the question

97. [The state of Nevada has a law that allows water that is going unused in one part of the state to be claimed by parties from another part of the state. Because of growth in Las Vegas, the law has caused serious disputes over water.] "Look. We in Las Vegas aren't trying to take water from anybody else's bathtub or kitchen faucet. The water we're talking about out in rural Nevada will either come to us and be put to good use, or it'll simply go to waste."

False dilemma and straw man—water that isn't "put to good use" by a city does not necessarily "go to waste."

98. "A preliminary economic analysis suggests that federal government proposals to protect the northern spotted owl will cost the Pacific Northwest about 40,000 jobs—and the effect on the spotted owl population is pretty much unknown. But, hey, what do the livelihoods of 40,000 human beings matter when the government is responding to pressure groups?"
—*Orange County Register*

This appeal is to indignation; alternatively it could be described as a sarcastic horse laugh.

99. Overheard somewhere and paraphrased: "The statistics that show you are better off wearing a seatbelt are completely flawed and can safely be ignored. Forcing people to use seatbelts, like making motorcyclists wear helmets, is just one more case of Big Brother infringing on personal liberty."

Red herring

100. PROF: I gave you a D on your essay because your grammar was faulty and your organization was difficult to follow.
STUDENT: That's just your opinion!

Subjectivist fallacy

101. Obviously it was right for us to attack Iraq. Polls showed that over 90 percent of Americans thought the war was justified.

Appeal to belief

102. HE: Well, things didn't work out quite the way I wanted, but that's the way life often is.
SHE: That's not my philosophy. Your dreams *will* come true if you want them to, but you really have to want them to.

Wishful thinking

103. SOCIAL CRITIC: Don't call it the Persian Gulf War. Call it the Persian Gulf Massacre. We killed over 300,000 Iraqis, most of them conscripts and many just plain civilians. The war against Iraq wasn't for the sake of world peace; it was for the sake of Big Oil.
TRUE PATRIOT: Oh, c'mon. Take some pride in your country, for a change. When was the last time you said the Pledge of Allegiance, anyway?

Bandwagon (Appeal to loyalty)

104. FIRST SPEAKER: Think about it. A seven-day waiting period to buy a gun would give people a chance to cool off; it would also give police a chance to make background checks. Are seven days that much of an inconvenience?
SECOND SPEAKER: I wouldn't talk that way around here, friend. Lots of people 'round here own guns, and they don't take kindly to people who want to make 'em register their guns.

Scare tactics

105. CITY SUPERVISOR: Schools need support, yes, but, unfortunately, to balance the city budget we need to reduce spending by around $13 million. Some of that reduction will have to come from the schools.

CITY RESIDENT: I don't see why. You supervisors should visit schools and talk to teachers. Teachers already work sixty to seventy hours a week. When other people are home relaxing in front of their TV set, Mr. and Mrs. Teacher are grading tests, attending meetings, or rearranging their classroom. The next time you are out fishing or playing golf, think of teachers at home preparing for next week's classes. They work very hard for very little money and rarely get any recognition for the job they've done.

Red herring. Could also be an appeal to pity.

106. After the Washington riots in the spring of 1991, Mike Royko, *Chicago Tribune* columnist, wrote that he assumed that the rioters had suddenly been overwhelmed by a craving for fried chicken, since they had smashed "into a chicken joint and were looting it of every last wing and drumstick." When a spokesperson for the Latino community stated that the rioting was to protest intolerable living conditions, Royko retorted: "And what better way to do it than to smash into a chicken joint and make off with all the chicken?"

Ridicule

107. "Re: 'New York taxes soak the poor.' The article stated that a family of four with an income of $11,000 pays over 14 percent of its income on state taxes. So what? The only way that could be done is if they spent half their income on high tax items such as liquor and cigarettes and movies. I, for one, won't shed any tears."
—from a letter to the editor

Appeal to spite

108. In the spring of 1991, presidential chief of staff John Sununu was charged with using Air Force executive jets for frequent trips to vacation spots. In a letter to a major newsmagazine, Rita Rech observed: "What is all the fuss about? Everyone does it."

This is not an appeal to common practice. The letter writer is wryly lamenting that such practices are common.

109. When Lebanon and Syria signed a treaty on May 22, 1991, aimed at ending sixteen years of Lebanese civil war, Israel stated that the treaty was tantamount to annexation of Lebanon. Syrian President Hafez Assad responded, "It seems that the Israelis have found it beneficial to use the treaty to cover up their rejection of peace [i.e., to cover up Israeli opposition to U.N. Security Council resolutions calling for Israel to give up occupied Arab lands]. They want to create a cause to talk about it, thinking they would thus divert the world's attention from the ongoing efforts for peace in the region."

Assad's response is a smokescreen. What's interesting is that his smokescreen amounts to calling Israel's statement a smokescreen.

155

110. What do I think about Scientology's belief in reincarnation? I think Scientology is run by a high school drop-out who doesn't know any science at all—except the science of fleecing people.

Personal attack

111. The article "Race and the Death Penalty" is just another liberal diatribe aimed at convincing people that there is racial bias in capital punishment. The whole point of the so-called statistics it mentions is to get people to be against the death penalty.

Genetic fallacy

112. Did you ever notice how the people who favor abortion on demand are the same people who are against the death penalty? How inconsistent can you get?

Pseudorefutation, assuming this is supposed to be a "refutation" of the abortion-on-demand position

113. I wouldn't pay too much attention to what you read there. *Reader's Digest* is known for its right-wing political bias.

Poisoning the well

114. SPEAKER: In sum, despite the military's claims for the accuracy of smart weapons, over 70 percent of allied bombs missed their intended targets.
PERSON IN AUDIENCE: What's your documentation? Can you prove that you are right about that?
SPEAKER: Can you prove I'm wrong?

Burden of proof

115. Pop, a new car may be expensive, but do you want me to drive around in this junk pile the rest of my life?

False dilemma

116. HE: They're nice speakers, but we can't really afford them.
SHE: Why in heaven not?
HE: If we buy them, next thing you know we'll want to buy a new receiver to go with them, then a CD player, then a new tape deck, and on and on. We can't afford all that stuff.

Slippery slope

117. BIG L: I like the new civil rights bill, especially the provision that prohibits indirect discrimination practices, such as height and weight requirements that could exclude women.
LITTLE C: It may sound fine to you, but not to me. We are almost to the point already that employers are forced to hire blacks just because they are black and women just because they are women, and that's just reverse discrimination.

Could be analyzed as a straw man (Little C is distorting the provision that Big L supports) or as a slippery slope (if Little C is arguing that the provision will lead to the situation he describes) or as a red herring.

118. I wouldn't take a course from anyone in the Polysci department, if I were you. They are all anti-U.S., ultraliberal types, at least that's what I hear.

Poisoning the well

119. You know how some people against gun control say that making guns illegal won't stop anyone who wants one from getting one? Ever notice how the same people are usually against legalizing drugs because they don't want drugs made available? Funny how they think that law won't work for guns but will work for drugs.

No fallacy as it stands, but if it is supposed to refute arguments against gun control or drug legalization, it is a pseudorefutation.

120. One person, speaking to her friends before they attend a political fund-raising party: "Now listen, folks, before we go into this party. You should be prepared to hear all kinds of flattery as they butter you up before they try to pick your pockets. Remember, all they're after is your money."

Poisoning the well (of course, there may be a wee grain of good advice in there, too.)

Here is a bunch of ad hominems.

121. SHE: We'd do well to get a Zenith. Their salesman told me they have the best repair record of any brand on the market.
HE: Well, forget that. He *sells* Zeniths, for crying out loud; of *course* he'd tell you they have the best record.

122. Overheard: "There's absolutely no point in asking a conservationist if toxic wastes are contaminating Butte County well water. As a conservationist, of course he'll say that they are."

123. From a letter to the editor: "The secretary of defense claims we cannot cut defense spending by so much as a jot. Right. What the generals want, the generals get. What the secretary is, is just another lawyer. It's not what's right that matters, it's what you can get. No wonder his relations with Congress are so poor."

124. Are you really going to believe her about librarians' salaries not being excessive? I'll have you know she herself is a librarian, or don't you think that matters?

125. Ann Landers did an informal survey on sex. Many people responded, some of them favorably, but a lot unfavorably. In a follow-up column, she wrote, "Comments by Erica Jong, Andrew Greeley, Helen Gurley Brown, Gay Talese, and Gloria Steinem showed insight and understanding. A few so-called sex experts who called the survey 'dangerous' demonstrated incredible ignorance and missed the point completely."

126. In one of his columns, Mike Royko had a word or two to write about Sylvester Stallone. According to Royko, after completing the movie *Rambo: First Blood Part II,* Stallone explained that it was an attempt to secure some credit for Vietnam veterans. Royko quoted Stallone as saying, "The people who pushed the wrong

button all took a powder. The vets got the raw deal and were left holding the bag. What Rambo is saying is that if they could fight again, it would be different."

Royko went on to observe that during the Vietnam War, when Stallone could have been a "real-life Rambo," he spent his time first at American College of Switzerland "teaching rich girls how to touch their toes" and then as a drama major at the University of Miami "improving his tan."

127. From a letter to the editor: "The *Times* editorial headed 'The Murder of Innocents' deplored the motive behind the Air India tragedy by posing the following question: 'What possible reason could there be for killing 329 innocents, so many of them children . . . ?' The writer then urges Americans never to accept some 'maniacal logic' that offers an excuse for such a heinous crime.

"Below this editorial followed a second, which urged the governor to strike from a family-planning bill awaiting his signature a stipulation prohibiting state funding for any family-planning agency that provides abortions, or incentives or referrals to obtain them.

"What an incongruous position—to condemn the murder of 80 innocent children in a plane over the Atlantic, but to condone the murder of 4,000 children nationwide per day in the womb.

"Isn't this the very same 'maniacal logic' that permits constant slaughter under the guise of 'family planning,' a euphemistic term to obscure another form of 'murder of the innocents'?"

128. Although I've not read much of Jean-Paul Sartre's existentialism, I'm pretty confident that its influence will be bad in the long run. I don't know how you could possibly expect anything else, really. Maybe you weren't aware of it, but the philosophy of Martin Heidegger was the single biggest influence on Sartre, and Heidegger was a dues-paying member of the NSDAP (the Nazi Party) from 1933 until 1945.

129. A lot of senators are crabbing about everything the president does these days. But if you look at the party those senators belong to, you'll notice that nearly all of them are members of the opposition party. So you can safely bet these criticisms are just partisan politics rather than the kind of thing we should take seriously.

The rest of these all beg the question.

130. The ACLU? Yeah, I know about them, and I don't like them very much. They're the ones who furnish free lawyers for criminals.

131. Every event has a cause other than itself, since if it didn't, it would have to have caused itself, which is impossible.

132. HE: I believe everybody should be permitted to cheat.
SHE: That's absolutely ridiculous.
HE: Why do you say that?
SHE: Well, assume that everyone were permitted to cheat. To say they are permitted to cheat means that it's all right for them to cheat, right? And if it's all right for them to cheat, then there's nothing wrong with cheating. But then, if there's nothing wrong with what they're doing, they wouldn't be cheating. So your suggestion is absurd.

This one takes careful explanation when you do it for a class!

133. "Opponents to Proposition 102 say that contact tracing will lead to 'witch hunts.' We say it's time to stop peddling such fear and panic."

—Rebuttal to argument against Proposition 102, 1988 *California Ballot Pamphlet*

134. Reconstruction of a remark heard at a faculty meeting: "The quality of teaching performance cannot be measured. No matter what administrators at campuses around the country might say, teaching performance is simply not the kind of thing to which you can assign measurable variables and then compare a bunch of numbers at the beginning of a course and again at its end. That isn't the way it works."

135. Clearly Mexico desperately needs financial help in handling its $96 billion foreign debt, since without any aid Mexico cannot possibly reduce that enormous sum, and it is urgent that it be reduced.

Chapter 7
Explanations

Students sometimes find it very difficult or even impossible to tell whether a passage contains an argument, an explanation, or some combination of the two. Often, the student simply doesn't recognize the different objectives of arguments and explanations—one of the ways in which they sometimes fail to appreciate the underlying presumptions of discourse. Hence there are a few pretty obvious exercises as well as some tough ones.

The two categories do overlap: There are arguments that explain, and there are explanations that attempt to convince. (There are also arguments the conclusion of which is that one explanation is better than another, which is a different matter, of course.) We've accommodated this overlap in the exercises, and we've added the further complication of distinguishing explanations from justifications, which are a species of argument.

Our idea is to foster in students some sense of what explanations are and how they operate, including an ability to evaluate them, without making them experts in explanation theory, action theory, or metaphysics (or requiring such expertise of the instructor). This aim turns out not to be as easy as it sounds, certainly not as easy as we'd like.

You may have students who think that the criteria for evaluating explanations provided in the text are a set of precise conditions that together are sufficient for determining the correctness of an explanation. They should understand that this is not the case; that is, these criteria are not the analogue of, say, the rules for syllogisms. The criteria are a set of considerations that, if kept in mind when one encounters explanations, help one distinguish explanatory claims that merit further consideration from those that don't. Acquiring the ability to make this distinction is an important step toward becoming a critical thinker.

Exercises Unanswered in the Text

Exercise 7-1

2. Argument

3. Argument

5. Explanation (We think the truth of the claim that you don't hear as much about jazzercise is being taken for granted.)

6. Explanation

8. Explanation

9. Argument

Exercise 7-2

2. Explanation

3. Explanation

5. Explanation

6. Explanation

7. Explanation

9. Argument with unstated conclusion: It isn't God who's telling him those names.

11. Argument (premise needs restating in declarative mood).

13. Explanation

14. Argument; justification

16. Argument

17. Argument (same note applies as in item 11).

19. Explanation or argument, depending on whether the orange has yet been tasted.

20. Explanation

22. Argument; justification

23. Argument

24. Explanation

Exercise 7-3

2. Behavioral explanation

3. Functional explanation; although it contains a bit of physical "how it works" explanation

5. Behavioral explanation

6. Behavioral explanation

8. Physical explanation

9. Functional explanation

11. Behavioral explanation

12. Behavioral explanation

13. Behavioral explanation

15. Behavioral explanation

17. Functional explanation

Exercise 7-4

2. Our knowledge and interests

3. Asking for too many links in a causal chain; imputing motives in physical explanations; giving an explanation at the wrong level for the audience

4. Physical theory

6. Yes

7. Usually, but not always

8. These are easily found in the text.

11. Functional explanation

12. No

13. A theory in the social sciences

15. The first provides an argument; the second provides an explanation

Exercise 7-6

2. This is a circular explanation. It also is untestable.

3. Uh huh, right. This explanation is too vague. It is also circular, if the sole criterion of biological "strength" is longevity.

5. Circular explanation

6. Vague, untestable, unnecessary assumptions, and, with some reflection, circular

8. Vague, untestable, unnecessary assumptions, and lacking in explanatory power

9. Ignoring a common cause—could be it was a good movie

11. Circular explanation

12. Requires unnecessary assumptions and is unreliable

14. Vague, untestable, unreliable, and requires unnecessary assumptions

15. A better explanation of Blackmore's negative results is the nonexistence of ESP. The given explanation requires the unnecessary assumption that psychic phenomena (a vague concept, of course) exist, and it is weaker in explanatory power than the other explanation.

16. The explanation is nontestable, contains unnecessary assumptions, and is not consistent with well-established theory. Notice that three misfortunes out of a *thousand* who defied the curse would indicate that Pele isn't very thorough, is she?

18. Relevance, reliability, and vagueness too.

20. It is more plausible that the Walters photo is of a model. In terms of our criteria, the UFO explanation requires unnecessary assumptions.

Exercise 7-7

The explanations, call them R and D, compete with one another and are incompatible, since both are set forth as the primary cause of the drop in the inflation rate. The inflation rate's remaining low despite a reversal in or elimination of those factors cited in R would favor D. The rate's remaining low despite an elimination of the factors mentioned in D would favor R. Alternatively, a rise in the inflation rate despite a continuation of the factors mentioned in R would favor D, while a rise in inflation despite a repetition of the factors mentioned in D would favor R. One might look to history or to other economies for situations analogous to these.

Exercise 7-9

3. The most credible, in our view, are Professor Shore and his associate and James Randi, because they can be expected to have the most experience in detecting trickery in similar cases. Roll also has some credibility and could be expected to have experience in spotting trickery, but one would expect a professional magician (Randi) to be especially qualified to sniff out chicanery. However, the CSICOP team was not allowed to observe Tina (though it does not follow from this fact that we must accept a paranormal explanation of the phenomena).

5. The RSPK explanation comes in a distant second when compared with the natural explanation. The former is vague (what kind of "power" or "energy" are we talking about here?), a feature that contributes to a serious lack of testability. The explanation may be circular, depending on how it is described—is the "power" in question manifested in situations other than those that seem inexplicable? The existence of strange powers requires a suspicious assumption, and their existence conflicts with well-established theory, which does not support forces of the sort the explanation requires.

6. We don't think so. We find the second explanation easier to accept. In fact, we expect that cases of "average teenagers" hoodwinking adults are rather common.

Chapter 7 Test Question/Exercise Banks

Bank 7-1

Consider the following: Chris says to Lynn, "The car won't go because the battery was stolen."

1. If Chris was giving an argument, what was the conclusion?

   The car won't go.

2. If Chris was giving an explanation, what was the fact taken for granted that was being explained?

   The car won't go.

3. Suppose Chris and Lynn had just got in the car to go to the store, tried to start it, and noticed that when Chris turned the key nothing happened. Chris got out, looked under the hood, came back, and made her statement to Lynn. If this was the context of the statement, was it an argument or an explanation?

   Explanation

4. Suppose Chris and Lynn live together and share the car. They were talking about going to a movie and whether they should ride their bikes or take the car. Lynn doesn't know the car won't go, but Chris does and has found out why. If this was the context of the statement, was it an argument or an explanation?

   Argument

5. Could Chris have made this statement to argue that the battery was stolen?

   No

Bank 7-2

Parker is on the phone to Moore, lamenting, "I couldn't get to sleep last night before 4 A.M., because our new dog kept yelping all night long. As a result, I didn't get up till noon. So I'm a little behind in the work I promised I'd get done."

6. True or false: Parker is giving an argument, the conclusion of which is that his new dog kept yelping all night long.

   False

7. True or false: Parker is offering a justification for being a little behind in his work.

   True

8. Is Parker (a) arguing that he didn't get up till noon, (b) explaining why he didn't get up till noon, or (c) doing neither?

(b)

9. Is Parker (a) arguing that he couldn't get to sleep last night before 4 A.M., (b) explaining why he couldn't get to sleep last night before 4 A.M., or (c) doing neither?

(b)

10. Suppose Moore says, "Hey, I thought you were allergic to dogs!" and Parker says, "I am, but we got one anyway." Is Parker now (a) arguing that he got a new dog, or is he (b) explaining why he got a new dog, or is he (c) justifying getting a new dog, or (d) none of these?

(d)

Bank 7-3

Determine which of the following passages contain arguments, which contain explanations, and which contain neither.

11. I did well in medical school in part because I was a philosophy major as an undergraduate.

Explanation

12. There must have been fire, because there was smoke.

Argument

13. Marijuana should be legalized because it is much less dangerous than alcohol or nicotine.

Argument

14. ". . . women are not creating culture because they are preoccupied with love."
—Shulamith Firestone, *The Dialectic of Sex*

Explanation

15. "A witty experiment by Philip Goldberg proves what everyone knows, having internalized the disesteem in which they are held, women despise both themselves and each other. This simple test consisted of asking women undergraduates to respond to the scholarship in an essay signed alternately by one John McKay and one Joan McKay. In making their assessments, the students generally agreed that John was a remarkable thinker, Joan an unimpressive mind. Yet the articles were identical; the reaction was dependent on the sex of the supposed author."
—Kate Millett, *Sexual Politics*

Argument

16. The reason he looks so awful is that he was up all night.

Explanation

17. He must have been up the entire night, since his eyes are red and swollen and his clothes are all wrinkled.

Argument

18. It is a very good idea to buy term life insurance rather than whole life insurance, because when you buy the latter you are in effect investing in a savings account that doesn't give you a very good return on your money.

Argument

19. Your staff is having trouble learning to use your new computer system because the commands they have to type in are numerous, complicated, and not related to the machine's operations in any obvious way.

Explanation

20. You really ought to relax a bit more with a good novel or something else you like doing.

Neither argument nor explanation

21. Kim is really a terrifically talented photographer. Incidentally, did you know that he's just got a brand new 35-millimeter camera?

Neither argument nor explanation

22. Even if the weather is clear tonight, you won't be able to see Halley's comet. The reason is that we're too close to the lights of the city to see anything that faint in the sky.

Combination argument/explanation

23. Nevadans have traditionally opposed zoning ordinances because of their fierce individualism.

Explanation

24. "But despite its enormous popularity, the Falcon did not bring in as much money as we had hoped. As an economical small car, its profit margin was limited. Nor did it offer many options, which would have greatly increased our revenues."
—Lee Iacocca, *An Autobiography*

Explanation

25. Possibly the reason you have trouble sleeping is all that coffee you drink.

Explanation

26. "On the morning of his great 'peace' speech, Hitler had promulgated in the greatest secrecy the Reich Defense Law, which completely reorganized the armed forces and introduced a spartan war economy. While talking peace to lull the outside world, he was going to make ready for war as rapidly as he could."
—William L. Shirer, *The Nightmare Years*

Neither

27. Steve never calls Elisa. But she forgives him; she knows how busy he is.

Explanation

28. Of *course* the mining industry depends on government subsidies. Just look at how hard the mining lobby fought to preserve those subsidy programs.

Argument

29. A recent study shows that you are three times as likely to suffer a heart attack just after you wake up in the morning than at any other time. It is theorized that this may be due to the blood's having a greater tendency to clot when you first wake up.

Explanation

30. "As a matter of logical necessity, if someone is certain of something then there never is anything of which he or anyone else is more certain. . . . Thus, if it is logically possible that there be something of which any person might be more certain than he now is of a given thing, then he is not actually certain of that given thing."
—Peter Unger, *Ignorance: A Case for Scepticism*

Argument

31. If you are seventy-five years old, the light you see when you look at the Big Dipper originated the year you were born.

Neither

32. Directed by the solar wind, a comet's tail always extends away from the sun. Hence, when the comet itself is heading away from the sun, its tail precedes it.

Argument, although in certain circumstances this could be put forth as an explanation

33. "Eskimos have a lower incidence of heart disease than do other populations, even though their high-fat, high-cholesterol diet ought to make them a high-risk group for heart disease. How do the Eskimos get away with it?
    "The answer lies in the kind of fat they eat. The Eskimo diet consists mostly of fish, seal, and whale. Fat from these animals contains 'omega-3 fatty acids,' which are structurally distinct from the 'omega-6 fatty acids' that most Westerners get from domestic meats."
—Jennie Dusheck, *Science News*

Explanation

34. " 'Crash' is not a word pilots ever use. I don't really know why the word is avoided in describing what happens when several tons of metal plows itself and its pilot into the ground. Instead, we might say, 'He augured in.' Or, 'He bought the farm.' "
—Chuck Yeager, *Yeager, An Autobiography*

Neither

35. ". . . nothing in the universe occurs haphazardly; there is a cause-and-effect pattern to all phenomena, including weather. It follows, therefore, that . . . weather is predictable."
—*The Old Farmer's Almanac*

Argument

36. Even though fifty million American adults still smoke, the rate of cigarette smoking has declined over the past twenty years. Experts believe that the decline in smoking is responsible at least in part for the decline in cardiovascular mortality.

Explanation

37. Although the case of the computer is double-insulated, as are the casings on the interface cables, the pins in the cable connections are not insulated. In fact, they are connected directly with the motherboard inside the machine. So if you are carrying a charge of static electricity and you touch those connector pins, you risk frying the logic circuits of your computer.

Argument

38. The dietary laws of Moses forbid eating pork because pigs do not chew a cud and are therefore deemed unclean. But the babirusa, a pig native to Indonesia, was thought for a while to be kosher—it has a pinched stomach that, biologists believed, enables it to chew cud like cows, sheep, and other multiple-stomached animals.

Explanation

39. Unfortunately for those who wish both to eat pork and to follow Jewish dietary laws, the babirusa turns out not to be a cud-chewing kosher pig. This was determined after long observation of the animals produced not one sighting of a babirusa chewing its cud.

Argument

40. "All the major Modern movements except for De Stijl, Dada, Constructivism, and Surrealism began before the First World War, and yet they all seem to come out of the 1920s. Why? Because it was in the 1920s that Modern Art achieved social chic in Paris, London, Berlin, and New York. Smart people talked about it, wrote about it, enthused over it, and borrowed from it."
—Tom Wolfe, *The Painted Word*

Explanation

41. "More than half of all mothers with children under age six have jobs, and the number is increasing. Whatever its problems, day care is indispensable."
—Dorothy Wickenden, in *The New Republic*

Argument

42. Ralph Nader practically invented the issue of automobile safety when he published *Unsafe at Any Speed* over twenty years ago. It's true beyond doubt that hundreds, maybe thousands, of today's yuppies would not have survived to pursue their individual interests had Nader not put the interests of the public above his own.

Neither

43. The history of metaphysics in Western philosophy began with speculations by the Ionian cosmologists in the sixth century B.C. about the origin of the physical universe, the matter or stuff from which it is made, and the laws or uniformities everywhere present in nature.

Neither

44. "This year's election scares me. It was conducted with a brutality and lack of attention to basic issues which appalled, and the success of its ugly strategies flashed signals that this was the kind of electioneering we should expect during the next two national campaigns of this century."
—James A. Michener, on the 1988 presidential campaign

May plausibly be viewed as either an explanation or an argument

45. "In California, without necessarily very much effort, almost everyone changes his life."
—Herbert Gold

Neither

We find that students tend to see arguments in passages about current, controversial topics even when such passages contain no arguments. Fresh examples from your daily newspaper make for good practice in class. If they can get those right, they can probably get the others.

Bank 7-4

Identify any phenomena explained in the following passages, and determine for each what kind or kinds of explanation are employed.

46. The class decided on four quizzes instead of two because two quizzes would have required that each one be quite long.

Behavioral explanation

47. The skin of some people is darker than that of others because of a greater amount of melanin present in the former.

Physical explanation

48. Flowers have bright colors so that bees and insects can see them.

    Functional explanation

49. Owls have large eyes so that they can hunt at night.

    Functional explanation

50. Flying in an airplane when one has a head cold can be painful because changes in air pressure produce internal pressure in the sinus cavities.

    Physical explanation

51. The plane's departure has been delayed because of fog.

    Physical explanation, although a behavioral explanation is implicit: presumably someone decided that the fog provided a sufficient reason for delaying the departure.

52. "The United States plans to renounce its security obligations to New Zealand because of that nation's intention to ban visits by U.S. ships carrying nuclear weapons."
    —*Washington Post*

    Behavioral explanation

53. The Washington Redskins didn't make it to the playoffs because they had too many injuries.

    Physical explanation

54. " 'The ranch lies in the swamps,' he warned me as we set forth, and this seemed an unlikely statement, since one visualizes a bull ranch as occupying hard, rough soil which strengthens the bull's legs, 'a common misunderstanding,' the matador assured me. 'It's the nature of the grass, the minerals in the water . . . something in the essence of the land and not its hardness. That's what makes a good bull.' "
    —James Michener, *Iberia*

    Physical explanation

55. The large roller with spikes on it that the tractor is dragging around the campus is a soil aerator. It pokes holes in the soil so that air and water can get through the surface.

    Functional explanation

56. Halley's comet was producing water vapor at the rate of four tons per second on November 5, 1985, when the comet was 170 million miles from the Sun. This explains why it was unusually bright.

    Physical explanation

57. Sam gave up running because, in his words, "I'm bored with the park, and I'm bored with my neighborhood, and there's no other safe place to run in this city."

Behavioral explanation

58. "Nairobi, Kenya (UPI)—The killer famine has ended in most of Africa but long-term recovery has been jeopardized by the reluctance of Western nations to supply cash and farm equipment instead of food aid, the U.N. Food and Agricultural Organization reports."

Behavioral explanation

59. There's too much yellow in the photograph because you didn't take the filter off the lens before you snapped the picture.

Physical explanation

60. "It is noteworthy that the negative reaction to the Soviet peace initiative came at the time when major experiments are to be performed within the framework of the U.S. 'Star Wars' program."
   —Yuri Romantsov, deputy director of Tass, the Soviet news agency

Implied behavioral explanation

61. That little hole is there at the front of the disk drive so that if all else fails, you can eject a disk by poking a paper clip into it.

Functional explanation

62. The reason Edward Kennedy withdrew from the 1988 presidential race is that his own privately commissioned polls indicated that he would have a difficult time winning the election.

Behavioral explanation

63. Highlighters don't really make a marked bit of text any easier to read; they simply call one's attention to the marked passage.

Physical explanation

64. In a report prepared at the request of the New Zealand AIDS Foundation, Dr. John Seale, British expert on sexually transmitted diseases, said that the AIDS virus might have been manufactured and released either deliberately or by mistake from a biological warfare research laboratory. There are serious flaws in theories that AIDS developed from spontaneous mutations of a human virus or was transferred to humans from animals, he said.

   Physical explanation. Had reasons for a deliberate release of the virus been given, we would add psychological explanation.

65. The *cejilla,* or capotraste, both raises the tone of the guitar, producing a more brilliant sound, and makes rapid playing somewhat easier by lowering the action of the strings.

This complex little passage is primarily a functional explanation, although a physical explanation of ease of rapid play is also given. Would you say that the raising of tone is a physical explanation of the more brilliant sound, that a desire to produce a more brilliant tone is a behavioral explanation of raising the tone, or neither?

66. According to a letter to the editor of the *Athens Courier,* the last three winters in the United States have been unusually harsh "to test our faith in a power beyond ourselves."

Functional explanation

67. Question: Why doesn't the Moon rotate? Answer: The Moon does rotate, but in synchronicity with its revolution around the Earth, once every 27.32 days, so that the same face of the Moon always faces us.
   —adapted from the *New York Times*

Physical explanation

68. The reason behind the "spite fence" ordinance against fences more than six feet tall is the prevention of one person's effectively "walling up" a neighbor by obstructing the latter's view.

Functional explanation

69. "Here is what made Francine think he was becoming happier: Dwayne began to sing songs which had been popular in his youth, such as 'The Old Lamp Lighter,' and 'Tippy-Tippy-Tin,' and 'Hold Tight,' and 'Blue Moon,' and so on. Dwayne had never sung before."
   —Kurt Vonnegut, Jr., *Breakfast of Champions*

Behavioral explanation

70. Dense fog can sometimes be dissipated by seeding the fog with dry ice pellets from airplanes. If the fog is cold enough, the pellets freeze the droplets of water in the fog, which then form together as ice crystals that drop from the sky.

Physical explanation

71. The round thing is a thermostat. It's a switch that turns current on when the temperature falls below a set level and off when it rises above another set level; the thermostat does that so that the coffee in the pot stays hot but never reaches the boiling point.

Functional explanation

72. The reason chronic abusers of cocaine suffer sleeplessness is that sustained use of the drug inhibits the body's production of serotonin, a substance known to be important in inducing sleep.

Physical explanation

73. I don't think Louise is losing her voice at all; I think she sang that song badly so that they wouldn't ask her to sing another one.

Behavioral explanation

74. The main reason ragtime music was frowned upon during the early twentieth century—the American Federation of Musicians passed a resolution condemning it in 1901—was simply that it was the music of black people and that it was first heard in sporting-houses, saloons, and honky-tonks.
   —adapted from Max Morath, *Music Journal Magazine*

Behavioral explanation

75. ". . . the cause of the Challenger accident was the failure of the pressure seal in the aft field joint of the right solid rocket motor."
   —From the report of the Presidential Commission on the Space Shuttle Challenger Accident

Physical explanation

76. "Synthetic rubber 'O-rings' . . . were emplaced around the circumference of the joints where the booster segments were mated to seal the joints against hot gas leakage. . . ."
   —Richard S. Lewis, *Challenger: The Final Voyage*

Functional explanation

77. "The Presidential Commission on the Space Shuttle Challenger Accident investigated pressure put upon NASA officials at the Kennedy Space Center as a contributing factor in the disaster. 'Satellite customers requested changes in scheduled launch dates because of development problems, financial difficulties, or changing market conditions,' the report said. As Kennedy processing people complained, this was no way to run a trucking business."
   —Richard S. Lewis, *Challenger: The Final Voyage*

Physical and psychological explanation

78. "The sight of a single bloody, mangled body horrifies us. But if we see such bodies all around us every day, day after day, the horrible becomes normal and we lose our sense of horror. We simply tune it out. Our capacity for horror becomes blunted. We no longer truly see the blood or smell the stench or feel its agony. Unconsciously we have become anesthetized."
   —M. Scott Peck, *People of the Lie*

This is one of those explanations, noted at the beginning of this chapter, that fit into the cracks between physical and behavioral explanations.

79. "Employees gossip to explain a situation that they don't understand, one that might have a direct and personal impact on their own lives. They spread news where none exists. . . . Having some understanding gives everybody a sense of control over her or his life."
   —Jack Levin and Arnold Arluke, *Gossip, The Inside Scoop*

Psychological explanation

80. Athletes take anabolic steroids to help build muscle and stamina during training.

Behavioral explanation, though many students will say that it's a functional explanation

Bank 7-5

Evaluate the explanations in the following passages against the criteria listed in the text.

81. A water dowser can't locate water and blames it on the presence of skeptics who, he says, are confusing the psychic signals. "This only works if everyone around believes it works," he maintains.

Untestable

82. Moore complains about how hot it has been all week. Parker observes that "this is only to be expected, what with global warming and such."

Parker's explanation that this particular hot spell is due to global warming (i.e., is the result of a rise in the mean global temperature) is unreliable. You couldn't predict any localized "hot spell" from information verifying global warming.

83. Mr. Ted claims he can hear colors. "I can hear the difference between red, green, and white," he maintains. Sure enough, when he is blindfolded, he can identify which of the three colors somebody holds up.

The explanation of how Mr. Ted identifies which color is help up—through hearing—almost surely is unreliable. Under rigorous test conditions, Mr. Ted would not be able to identify colors through hearing, contrary to what we would predict if he really could hear colors.

84. Psychic Joseph Klar, as reported in the *Weekly World News,* predicted in 1992 that during 1993 injuries would force the NFL to switch to two-hand touch football. Evaluate this explanation: "The reason the prediction didn't come true is because the event didn't happen."

Circular

85. Clarissa changes her mind at the last moment and flies to Miami, rather than Arizona, for a vacation. Felmer's uncle dies, and Felmer drives to Miami for the funeral. Clarissa and Felmer stay at the same motel, meet, fall in love, and get married. Fate or coincidence?

Well, what's the difference between the two explanations? Perhaps the fate-explanation is that events are arranged by a knowing intelligence, an idea that, among other things, is untestable. A person who argues for coincidence is probably just denying that events are so arranged. We haven't tried this one out in a class, yet, but it looks like it would be best for a discussion.

86. According to *Shape* magazine, "research shows that regular exercisers have far fewer diseases than their inactive counterparts." Dr. Joseph Cannon, a University of Michigan researcher, believes that the explanation may be that exercise raises body temperature, *Shape* reports. According to the magazine, Cannon maintains that the high temperature may benefit the body in the same way that fevers do, namely, by making protective white blood cells work faster, by increasing the number of antibodies in the blood, and by decreasing blood levels of iron, which microorganisms need for growth.

Measured against the criteria in the text, Cannon's conjecture is reasonable (but not necessarily correct, of course).

87. Alcoholics find it difficult to give up drinking because they have become physiologically and psychologically addicted to it.

    Circular

88. Maria drove up from Austin today because I dreamed about her a few nights ago.

    Irrelevant

89. "Question: I have two healthy, vigorous Gravensten apple trees with trunks about 8 inches in diameter. . . . [E]very year they drop their fruit before it ripens." "Answer: Gravensten apples are a short-stemmed variety, and the falling of fruit before and during harvest sometimes results from the apples actually pushing themselves from the spurs as they increase in size."
    —Dick Tracy, University of California master gardener

    A reasonable explanation. Note that this is not a case of "they fall off because they fall off."

90. According to some psychologists, we catch colds because we want to. Most of the time we are not aware of this desire, which may, therefore, be said to be subconscious. Viruses are present when we have a cold, but unless we desire to catch cold, the viruses do not affect us.

    Untestable; requires unnecessary assumptions

91. Even though Elmore Leonard is arguably the best living writer of detective fiction, his books were selling no more than 20,000 copies each. But 200,000 copies of *Glitz* were in stores in a very short time, the result of hard promotional work aimed primarily at chain stores by Leonard's publisher, Arbor House.
    —adapted from a story in *Newsweek*

    Reasonable explanation

92. "People suffering from rheumatism often complain that their aches increase as bad weather approaches and barometric pressure falls. Some scientists believe that the decreased pressure of the air causes the air in the cells of the body to exert an increased outward pressure. This pressure may cause pain in the sensitive tissues of rheumatic persons."
    —New York Times

    Reasonable explanation

93. After a record-breaking rise over the course of several months, the stock market took a substantial nosedive during the first couple of weeks in January. Wall Street analysts noted that this was an expected technical adjustment.

    If indeed this is intended to be an explanation, it isn't a very good one. It's marked by vagueness, a possible lack of testability, and possible circularity.

94. According to projections by the American Cancer Society, both the chance of developing cancer and the chance of dying of cancer have gone up over the past decade. Investigators have offered this explanation of these discouraging statistics: As infectious diseases and heart disease are better controlled, people are surviving longer; they are then more vulnerable to cancer, because their immune systems may be weakened by age.

In terms of the text's criteria, the explanation is reasonable. But it does create a minor (but not unsolvable) puzzle: If people are more vulnerable to cancer because of a weakened immune system, then they should also be more vulnerable to infectious disease. We presume that these other diseases are to some extent controllable even for persons with weakened immune systems.

95. The current crisis among American farmers is not all bad news. One reason our farmers are having a difficult time selling their crops is the fact that many countries that were incapable of feeding themselves only a decade ago are now self-sufficient and no longer require American imports. China is exporting both cotton and corn, and Bangladesh is now self-sufficient in food grains.

Reasonable explanation

96. One reads almost nothing good about the Soviet Union in the American press and hears nothing good about it from our politicians. This contrasts sharply with what I've seen on my five trips to Russia. Why the contradictions between what I've read about Russia and its people and what I've seen? The answer can be traced to nationalism, compounded by forty years of Cold War. Nationalism—patriotism carried a little too far—tells us we're the "best." This attitude makes it awkward to admit publicly that foreign nations can do some things as well or better.
—adapted from Brian Kahn, "What We Don't Know About the Russian People," *Sacramento Bee*

Reasonable, but vague

97. The reason you should continue to use unleaded gasoline in your late-model car is that leaded gasolines, even though they now contain less lead than they used to, still contain enough to cause serious damage to your car's emission system.

Reasonable explanation by our criteria

98. They beat us as badly as one team could beat another in this league. We had some momentum at the beginning of the game, but we just lost it and never got it back.

Vague, circular

99. The reason we like some people and dislike others is because of our experiences with similar personalities in an earlier life.

Untestable; involves unnecessary assumptions; reincarnation may conflict with well-established principles of biology

100. Why have some people claimed to have seen UFOs or reported being kidnapped by aliens? According to Sebastian von Herner, Ph.D., of the National Radio Astronomy Observatory in Green Bank, West Virginia, "only a few hundred years ago, many people, the well educated included, reported seeing the devil. . . . People tend to see things which 100 or 200 years later are believed to be nonsense." And Alvin Lawson, a professor of English at California State University, Long Beach, has speculated that people who claim to have been aboard a UFO are in fact recalling their own births.

The first "explanation" is not an explanation at all but a way of saying that UFO sightings are nonsense. The second remark is an explanation but a defective one in lots of ways: "recalling" is vague and ambiguous; depending on what it means, the explanation may be untestable and unreliable, and it may conflict with what we have reason to believe about our powers of remembering.

101. FIRST ECONOMIST: Prices keep going up and up.
SECOND ECONOMIST: Yeah, that's the result of inflation.

Circular

102. I heard a feature on *All Things Considered,* the show on National Public Radio, on Donna Reed. I hadn't thought about her for years and years, although I used to be a big fan of her television show. That was on January 13th, 1986. The next day, January 14th, she was dead from pancreatic cancer. I'm telling you, that's scary.

No it isn't. If there is an explanation intended here, it's most certainly an irrelevant one.

103. "One study that showed an unexpectedly high prevalence of AIDS antibodies in Zairian patients sick with malaria led researchers to speculate that screening tests for AIDS antibodies may be less accurate in Africans or that malaria does something to the blood that produces positive AIDS tests results."
—Paul Raeburn, Associated Press science editor

The correlation between malaria and positive AIDS tests may both be the result of a common cause: transmission of AIDS and malaria by mosquitoes. Instructor please note: Research after the date of this writing may rule out this possibility (or it may confirm it).

104. Janice has never done well in mathematics, and she never will. She just doesn't have the head for it.

This is either circular or no explanation at all.

105. The area along this part of the coast is especially subject to mud slides because of the type of soil that's found on the slopes and because of an insufficient amount of mature vegetation with root systems to provide stability.

Reasonable explanation

106. Women usually have little solidarity because they've accepted the idea that life without a man is a failure and that they thus have to compete with each other for the scarce resource, men.

    Vague; untestable

107. Americans have the reputation of being the worst lovers in the world because they are the worst lovers in the world.

    Vague; untestable

108. Human beings have noses so that they look more like God.

    Lacking in explanatory power and reliability; requires unnecessary assumptions and is untestable

109. Robin got what she worked so hard for, money; but she died unhappy. That's because of karma, an undetectable force permeating the universe that affects people's lives.

    Vague, untestable, lacks reliability and explanatory power, requires unnecessary assumptions, and may be circular

110. Why is Tracy a Buddhist? Because she couldn't stand Baptists.

    Lacks explanatory power

111. Lots of people go to that restaurant because the local newspaper reviewed it and was very positive toward it.

    May be reasonable but may ignore a common cause

112. White males control most of the world's wealth because of the way things have worked out in history.

    Circular, lacks explanatory power

113. The reason physics, astronomy, and geology all have evidence that the Earth and universe are more than four billion years old is that God wants to test our faith in the Bible.

    Untestable, lacks explanatory power

114. The price of commodities has actually declined over the past six months. That's the happy result of deflation.

    Circular

115. Julie dreamed about Jim, and about that time Jim was involved in a traffic accident. Coincidence? Impossible. Julie must have psychic powers.

    Requires unnecessary assumptions

116. This state is up to its ears in red ink, and the explanation is simple: It spends more than it makes.

    Circular

117. The Trailblazers did much better than the Knicks in the second half. That's because the Knicks allowed the Blazer fans to get into the game.

    But then again, maybe the fans got into the game because the Blazers did much better. We'd fault this explanation on its reliability and testability. Still, this question is best used for discussion because it will be controversial. Although the crowd cannot score any points or block any shots, in some sports teams do much better at home—maybe because the support of the fans makes the players play better, but we'd say the explanation lies elsewhere.

118. Prices are going up because people are charging more for their products than they used to. If you want to stop inflation, impose price controls!

    Circular

119. It's not too difficult to understand why she belongs to all those fringe groups. She's rich and has too much time on her hands.

    Vague and unreliable; also lacks explanatory power

120. The Scorpions are beating the Tarantulas this quarter, Jack, because they just want to win more.

    Untestable; unreliable; lacks explanatory power

121. You wonder why the economy is in such bad shape? Haven't you heard that we're in a recession?

    Circular

122. You should have expected her to be emotional. She's a woman.

    Unreliable

123. The reason American education is in a state of decline is not difficult to understand: in a single word, it's television.

    Vague, unreliable, and lacks explanatory power

124. It's Friday the 13th. No wonder things are going so badly!

    Unreliable; lacks explanatory power

125. You didn't get what you prayed for? That's because your faith is weak. You have to pray harder.

    Untestable

126. "A certain Canon Bourne and his two daughters were out hunting, and the daughters decided to return home with the coachman while their father went on. 'As we were turning to go home,' say the two Misses Bourne in a joint account, 'we distinctly saw my father waving his hat to us and signing us to follow him. He was on the side of a small hill, and there was a dip between him and us. My sister, the coachman and myself all recognized my father and also the horse. The horse looked so dirty and shaken that the coachman remarked he thought there had been a nasty accident. As my father waved his hat I clearly saw the Lincoln and Bennett mark inside, though from the distance we were apart it ought to have been utterly impossible for me to have seen it. . . . it took us very few seconds to reach the place where we had seen him. When we got there, there was no sign of him anywhere. . . . We all reached home within a quarter of an hour of each other. My father then told us he had never been in the field, nor near the field in which we thought we saw him, the whole of that day. . . .'"
—G. N. M. Tyrrell, *The Personality of Man,* originally published in the *Journal of the Society for Psychical Research* in 1893

Tyrrell's explanation is that the two girls and the coachman had a telepathic vision: "The cause which set the telepathic machinery in motion in this case is obscure. No accident had happened to Canon Bourne. It more often happens that the vision coincides with some accident or peculiar event happening to the agent. . . . [Apparently] Canon Bourne unconsciously imposed the pattern or theme of his presence in that particular field, with details of horse, etc., on the minds of his two daughters and the coachman."

A different explanation is that of C. E. M. Hansel, who views the incident as probably a case of simple mistaken identity: "It would appear likely that the witnesses saw something they thought was Canon Bourne although, in fact, it was not Canon Bourne—that is, if his statements about where he had been that day were truthful or if he had had no lapse of memory. They reported that the horse looked dirty, but at a distance they would not recognize dirt as such; they would only infer its presence from the appearance of the horse. They apparently saw a horse that was similar, but not identical, in appearance to Canon Bourne's; they assumed it to be the Canon's and that its changed appearance was due to dirt."
—C. E. M. Hansel, *ESP and Parapsychology: A Critical Re-evaluation*

Hansel goes on to explain psychological experiments in which a drawing is exposed briefly to a subject who is then asked to draw exactly what he has viewed. Most subjects introduce changes and add details that were not present in the original drawing, Hansel says. The same phenomenon would account for one of the party "seeing" the Lincoln and Bennet label inside the hat, he hypothesizes. In addition, he believes that the members of the party would have conversed with one another and thus would have influenced the others by suggestion.

Lack of space prevents detailed analysis. The most glaring defects of Tyrrell's telepathic explanation are that it requires us to make unnecessary (and implausible) assumptions and that it conflicts with well-established psychophysical theory (e.g., that telepathy presumably is a transference of information that does not involve physical media and does not utilize any known sense organ). Incidentally, it can be

180

pointed out in connection with this item that a shorter explanation that conflicts with well-established theory, like Tyrrell's, should not be favored over a more complex theory, like Hansel's, that does not make for such conflicts.

127. There's a reason that putting is the worst part of Curtis's golf game. You see, he lacks confidence in his putting, and that part of the game depends as much on your mental attitude—especially your confidence in your stroke—as it does on anything physical. Mark my words: If Curtis ever gains confidence that he's going to make those putts, he'll start making them.

There's probably something to this explanation; confidence does seem to play a great role in things like putting. Still, the explanation is quite vague, and, partly because of its vagueness, it's not easily testable. Lack of explanatory power is also a problem here.

128. SPEAKER 1: Caleb is late. Do you know why?
SPEAKER 2: Oh, he's late every now and then; you just never know about that guy.

Irrelevant; lacks explanatory power

129. It's been years now since the famous Tienanmen Square massacre in Beijing, and the Chinese government has still not done much to improve its human rights record. The main reason is that the Chinese leaders know our current administration will give them anything they want whether they do anything about human rights or not.

There is some relevant information in this explanation, but it still has problems of reliability—few people are in a position to do more than speculate about the motives of officials in both governments. Also, the explanation is vague.

130. Sheila lost her job because of this recession.

The relevance of this explanation is dubious. Knowing there's a recession is probably not enough to enable us to predict that Sheila would lose her job. Also, the explanation is excessively vague. Notice, though, that if the original phenomenon to be explained were a general fact, such as a rise in overall unemployment, then the explanation would not strike us as so vague. The rule seems to be that more specific events require more specific explanations.

131. NEW DOG OWNER: "I bought heartworm medicine for my dog the other day, and it cost me a fortune! How do they get away with charging so much for that stuff?"
OLD DOG OWNER: "Only one company makes that stuff, because they own the patent and won't license it to anybody else. This means they're in a great position to rip everybody off and make as much as they can until the patent finally expires."

Actually, this is not an unreasonable explanation, at least up to a point. It's highly slanted, of course, but we don't deal with slanting until the next chapter. For now, we can question the reliability of the second speaker's views: Can we really presume that they're trying to "rip everybody off," or could it be that this drug is especially expensive to manufacture?

132. From some angles, a quarter will be seen as elliptical; while viewed from straight on it will be seen as round. The explanation is that the quarter changes its shape as the viewer changes vantage point.

For those instructors so inclined, here is an opportunity to do a little epistemology.

Bank 7-6

Propose an explanation for each of the following phenomena. (Students can share their results with other students for identification and evaluation.)

133. The death rate from coronary artery disease (mainly heart attacks and sudden coronary death) has fallen abruptly since 1968.

134. Sometimes you call a friend and discover that he or she was thinking about you just before you called.

135. Despite strong evidence that cigarette smoking is a major health threat, one-third of American adults are smokers.

136. Prenatal and birth complications occur more frequently in babies who are born between January and April.

137. A road seems shorter the second time you travel on it.

138. During the 1970s, nearly one out of every two marriages broke apart.

139. There were 9,100 fewer highway traffic fatalities in 1975 than in 1974.

140. If your fireplace smokes for a while when a fire is lit, you can stop it by burning a couple of sheets of newspaper on *top* of the wood when you light the fire.

141. The presence of oil pressure gauges and warning lights on the dashboards of automobiles.

142. People with back trouble tend to find that sleeping on hard mattresses results in less pain than sleeping on soft mattresses.

Bank 7-7

Here are some explanations for identification, analysis, or appraisal. (We've also included a couple of items that look like explanations but really are arguments, in case you want to construct another "Argument or Explanation?" exercise.)

143. "What makes our marriage work is that we talk so much. That and the fact that he's so funny."
—Barbara Bush

144. "The Nixon administration authorized the Watergate break-in and cover-up because it screwed up."

145. SHE: "Why on earth would that guy get up at 4:00 A.M. to deliver newspapers, do you suppose?"
HE: "He probably just likes getting up early."

146. Six years after running unsuccessfully for the U.S. Senate, former California governor Jerry Brown decided to plot a return to politics by seeking the chair of the state Democratic Party. When asked why, Brown replied, "The party needs some thrust. It needs rapprochement between the grass roots and the elected people. It needs to really become effective."

Note that this explanation is really a justification offered by Brown for seeking the Democratic Party chair.

147. "As we have seen, the evidence for creation is enormous. Why, then, do many people reject creation and accept evolution instead? One reason is what they were taught in school. Science textbooks nearly always promote the evolutionary viewpoint. The student is rarely, if ever, exposed to opposing arguments. In fact, arguments against evolution are usually prevented from appearing in school textbooks."
—*Life—How did it get here? By evolution or by creation?*

148. "Does California really need 3,700 new laws? Only the most passionate advocate of big government would answer yes. In fact, I vetoed hundreds of those bills because I don't believe it is wise or necessary for government to extend its reach into every aspect of our lives. Nor do I believe that government should spend money it can't afford to spend."
—former California governor George Deukmejian

Comment: This could be viewed as an argument or as an explanation. Either way, it's not very good.

149. On October 19, 1987, the New York stock market crashed, sending markets around the world plunging the next day. A rally beginning in the early part of the year had inflated stock prices and lowered their values. Meanwhile, the yield on bonds was rising as prices weakened. The yields gap became too great, and people sold stocks and bought bonds, thus producing the crash.

Comment: This doesn't seem defective on our criteria. (It's pretty plausible on any criteria, as a matter of fact.)

150. "Yes, there are unemployed people who steal to live—because of taxes, government regulations, and labor laws that keep businesses from creating jobs."
—Rebuttal to Argument in Favor of Proposition 80, 1988 California Ballot Pamphlet

151. The reason for the housing shortage is the massive influx of illegal immigrants into Texas, New Mexico, Arizona, and California.

152. "The Red Cross first abandoned its legendary discretion in 1983 and publicly denounced Iran and Iraq for violating humanitarian accords. As a rule, based on very strict criteria of impartiality, the Red Cross never criticized anyone (a practice harshly condemned in the Nazi era). But faced with an Iranian declaration that

prisoners who do not convert to Iran's brand of Islam offend God and do not deserve to live, there was little choice."

—Mauro Suttora, *Europeo*

Note that this is an explanatory justification.

Bank 7-8

True/False

153. Explanations are designed to provide reasons for believing that a claim is true.

    False

154. A bad explanation is usually more helpful to someone than no explanation at all.

    False

155. There are only three kinds of explanations: physical, behavioral, and functional.

    False

156. Physical explanations of specific events always refer to events that happen or happened earlier than the one being explained.

    True

157. It is often incorrect to evaluate an explanatory comparison in terms of its correctness.

    True

Bank 7-9

Short answer

158. One type of behavioral explanation explains specific instances of behavior. What does the second type explain?

    Regularities or recurring patterns of behavior

159. One type of physical explanation explains specific events. What does the second type explain?

    Regular occurrences

160. What have we produced when we give a series of physical causes of the following sort: W caused X, X caused Y, and Y caused Z?

    A causal chain

161. Aside from the causal role it plays in the production of an event, what factors determine what we identify as the *direct* cause of the event?

Our own knowledge and interests

162. Why do we generally have somewhat less confidence in a good behavioral explanation than we do in a good physical explanation?

The generalities referred to in behavioral explanations are somewhat less reliable.

Bank 7-10

Evaluate the following explanation in a brief essay.

163. The correlation between heavy smoking and lung cancer is not to be explained by claiming that smoking causes lung cancer. There is a chemical substance, known as phenomenthasorbitol, that is secreted in the brain of some individuals, disposing them to take up smoking. This same substance triggers the growth of cancer cells, usually (though not always) in the lungs. However, phenomenthasorbitol cannot be detected in a person who has lung cancer, because the human immune system, in reaction to the unwanted cancer cells, destroys all traces of the substance.

We would especially want students' answers to refer to unnecessary assumptions and to testability.

164. An interesting phenomenon has occurred in a number of American cities. A large number of the employees in a new, modern office building will begin to exhibit a set of symptoms ranging from sneezing, itchy eyes, and sore throats to dizziness and fainting. There will be no simultaneous outbreak of these symptoms in neighboring buildings.

    One explanation for these occurrences is that a large variety of chemicals are used in the manufacture of new buildings (in insulation, paint, adhesives, and so on) and the furniture that is placed in them. While the building and interior fixtures are new, they go through a period of "off-gassing," that is, throwing off gases from the chemicals into the building environment. Then, since modern buildings are built to be energy-efficient and hence are sealed from outside air, the ventilation system recirculates the gases over and over through the building before they are vented to the outside. Thus people working in the building are exposed to the gases, some of which can be low-level toxic, for a considerable period of time.

We'd expect this explanation to get high marks from students. A really good answer might mention that there are other ways in which pollutants can get into a ventilation system besides off-gassing from new materials. (Many products, such as copy machines, use chemicals that can also release gases into the environment, and a source of pollution near the system's outside intake can produce the same effects.)

Chapter 8
Understanding and Evaluating Arguments

This chapter is our principal introduction to argument. Instructors with backgrounds in logic will find this territory familiar; others will find that the basics come fairly easily.

We've made two main changes in the chapter for this fourth edition. First, we've moved the section that lists basic deductive argument forms to the back of the book; it's now Appendix 3. Everything on the list can be found in Chapters 9 and 10, which can be taught selectively as well as systematically. The idea of merely producing *lists* of valid and invalid forms does not get across to a student the idea of *what makes* an argument valid or invalid. The idea of validity is difficult enough for some students, no matter how it's approached; simply to say, "Here are some valid arguments, and here are some invalid ones," leaves the whole notion a mystery to many of these students. But, of course, the entire list is intact in Appendix 3, and will remain so in future editions, for those who are able to make good use of this approach.

The second change results from some tampering with the distinction between deduction and induction. We've downplayed the significance of this distinction in favor of discussing arguments as valid or invalid, and invalid ones as strong or weak. These are, we're quick to admit, the most important things to know when evaluating arguments. But—and we're sure this will chagrin some of our reviewers—we still draw a distinction between deduction and induction in terms of a speaker's or writer's intentions. If we let matters rest *entirely* on the valid/invalid–strong/weak business, we'd have to give up the distinction and the words "deductive" and "inductive," and we'd like not to have to think up new titles for Chapters 9, 10, and 11 just yet. Some writers have given up the "intention" distinction entirely in favor of the valid/invalid treatment and have then gone on to mention deductive and inductive arguments as if there were still a way to tell a difference between them. We're keeping the distinction, even if we're deemphasizing it. That enables us to keep around a couple of words that have served us long, and for the most part, well.

Exercises Unanswered in the Text

Exercise 8-2

2. Premise: The Lakers almost didn't beat the Jazz.
   Conclusion: They'll never get past Dallas.

3. Premises: If the butler had done it, he could not have locked the screen door. The door was locked.
   Conclusion: The butler is in the clear.

5. *We've broken this one down into two arguments, with part of each unstated.*

   Premise: His mother's daughter has only one brother.
   Conclusion (from preceding) and premise (for remainder): [Unstated:] He *is* his mother's daughter's brother.
   Premise: [Unstated:] He can't be older than himself.
   Conclusion: He can't be older than his mother's daughter's brother.

6. Premises: The state police have a weight limit.
                Moscone is over the weight limit. (These two premises could be combined into a single conjunctive premise; see Chapter 10.)
   Conclusion: Moscone will never make it into the state police.

8. Premise: He wastes his time watching daytime TV. (Although stated as a question, the claim is clear enough.)
   Conclusion: He doesn't have a thing to do.

9. Premises: There are more injuries in professional football today than there were twenty years ago.
                If there are more injuries, then today's players suffer higher risks.
                If today's players suffer higher risks, then they should be paid more.
   Conclusion: Today's players should be paid more.

Exercise 8-3

We've left out "probably" and other such qualifiers that occur in some of the conclusions. These phrases tell us whether the person presenting the argument intends it to be taken inductively or deductively. They *could* be included as introductory phrases to the conclusions; it's your choice.

2. Premises: Kera, Sherry, and Bobby were all carded at JJ's.
                They all look as though they're about thirty.
   Conclusion: I'll be carded too.

3. Premise: Seventy percent of the freshmen at Wharfton College come from wealthy families.
   Conclusion: About 70 percent of all Wharfton College students come from wealthy families.

5. Premises: She wears the finest clothes.
                She orders the most expensive dishes.
                When she goes on vacation, she stays at the best resorts.
                [Unstated:] Anyone who wears the finest clothes, and so on, will be interested only in our top line.
   Conclusion: She'll be interested only in our top line. (Show her the Ferraris.)
                [The parenthetical remark can be taken as a further conclusion, with the unstated premise "Anyone interested only in our top line is someone to whom we should show the Ferraris."]

6. Premises: According to *Nature,* today's thoroughbred racehorses do not run any faster than their grandparents did.
                Human Olympic runners are at least 20 percent faster than their counterparts of fifty years ago.
   Conclusion: Racehorses have reached their physical limits but humans have not.

8. Premises: If this bucket has a hole in it, then it will leak.
                It doesn't leak.
   Conclusion: It doesn't have a hole in it.

9. Premises: The last person we hired from Alamo Polytech was a rotten engineer, and we had to fire him.

   Conclusion: This new candidate [from Alamo Polytech, presumably] is somebody I won't take a chance on [that is, somebody who will not be a good engineer and will have to be fired].

Exercise 8-4

2. Independent

3. Dependent

5. Dependent

6. Independent

8. Dependent

9. Independent

Exercise 8-5

2. Dependent

3. Dependent

5. Dependent (In our opinion. Notice that the comparison of Hubbard with Jesus, even though it's preceded by an "also," is actually evidence for the differences in the views of Christians and cultists.)

6. Dependent

7. Dependent

9. Independent (These may be related, depending on what the physicists' reasons are, but what we have here is a nutshell version of the teleological argument on one hand and an appeal to authority on the other.)

Exercise 8-6

1. False

2. False

4. False

5. True

7. True

8. False

10. True

11. False (Helms is from North Carolina, and he's a Republican. The argument is valid but unsound—both premises are false.)

12. True

Exercise 8-7

(Refer to Exercise 8-2.)

2. Invalid

3. Valid

5. Valid

6. Valid

8. Invalid

9. Valid

(Refer to Exercise 8-3.)

2. Invalid

3. Invalid

5. Invalid

6. Invalid

8. Valid

9. Invalid

Exercise 8-8

Our opinions (which we hope agree with yours):

2. Probably true

3. Possibly true and possibly false

5. Probably true, but not something we'd bet on

6. Probably true and possibly false. There are plenty of other reasons for the differences in GRE scores.

8. Probably true

9. Probably true

Exercise 8-9

Note: For a conclusion of the sort "A is a Y," the type of premise we supply is "All Xs are Ys," where the other premise states that "A is an X." One could also make a truth-functional inference by supplying the premise "If A is an X, then A is a Y."

2. Everybody who is pretty sharp will get a good grade in this course.

3. There are puddles everywhere only when it has rained lately.

5. No party that produces tons of leftovers could have been very successful.

6. If the lights are bright, then the battery is in good condition.

8. All good senators would make good presidents.

9. All people who don't own guns are for gun control.

Exercise 8-10

(Refer to Exercise 8-9.)

2. Most people who are pretty sharp will get good grades in this course.

3. About the only times there are puddles everywhere is when it has rained lately.

5. Most parties that produce tons of leftovers are not very successful.

6. If the lights are bright, then the battery is probably in good condition.

8. Most good senators would make good presidents.

9. Most people who don't own guns are for gun control.

Exercise 8-11

2. Everybody who has a C going into the final and gets an A on the final will make at least a B in the course.

3. All students of Pepe Romero are good guitarists.

5. If the Federal Reserve Board chair is an experienced hand at monetary policy, then the board will make sure inflation doesn't reach 10 percent again.

6. Nobody who is well known to have a liberal policy on most matters stands a chance of getting elected in this county.

8. If half the people in the front row believe in God, then half the entire class believes in God.

9. If every Montezuma State student I ever met was career-oriented, then so are all the rest of them. (*There are other possibilities—one is that the speaker has actually met every Montezuma State student.*)

Exercise 8-12

(Refer to Exercise 8-11.)

2. Most people who have a C going into the final and get an A on the final will make at least a B in the course.

3. Most of Pepe Romero's students are good guitarists.

5. It's very likely that if the Federal Reserve Board chair is an experienced hand at monetary policy, then the board will make sure inflation doesn't reach 10 percent again.

6. Almost nobody who is well known to have a liberal policy on most matters stands a chance of getting elected in this county.

8. If half the people in the front row believe in God, then most likely half the entire class believes in God. (*Or, simply replace the premise with something like this:* "Of half the class [or more, depending on the size of the class] asked, half of them believed in God.")

9. If every Montezuma State student I ever met was career-oriented, then it's very likely that all the rest of them are, too. (*Or:* I've met most of the students at Montezuma State.)

Exercise 8-13

2.

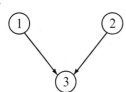

3.

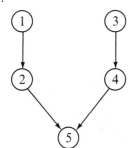

5.

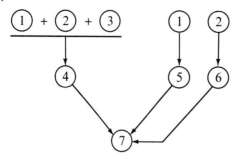

We've duplicated (1) and (2) to keep lines from crossing.

Exercise 8-14

These exercises can be assigned with directions to include unstated claims or not to include them. We've diagrammed them as they are presented—that is, without any unstated claims. The unstated claims are given in the answers above and can be inserted as appropriate.

(Refer to Exercise 8-2.)

2. 1. The Lakers almost didn't beat the Jazz.
    2. They'll never get past Dallas.

3. 1. If the butler had done it, he could not have locked the screen door.
    2. The door was locked.
    3. The butler is in the clear.

5. 1. He is not older than his mother's daughter's brother.
   2. His mother's daughter has only one brother.

6. 1. Moscone will never make it into the state police.
   2. The state police have a weight limit.
   3. Moscone is over the weight limit.

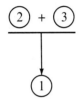

8. 1. He doesn't have a thing to do.
   2. He wastes his time watching daytime TV.

9. 1. There are more injuries in professional football today than there were twenty years ago.
   2. If there are more injuries, then today's players suffer higher risks.
   3. If [today's players] suffer higher risks, then they should be paid more.
   4. Today's players should be paid more.

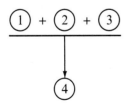

(Refer to Exercise 8-3.)

2. 1. Kera, Sherry, and Bobby were all carded at JJ's.
   2. They all look as though they're about thirty.
   3. I'll be carded too.

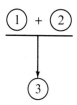

3. 1. Seventy percent of freshmen at Wharfton College come from wealthy families.
   2. Seventy percent of all Wharfton College students come from wealthy families.

5. 1. She wears the finest clothes.
   2. She orders the most expensive dishes.
   3. When she goes on vacation, she stays at the best resorts.
   4. She'll be interested only in our top line. (Show her the Ferraris.)

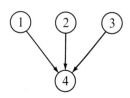

6. 1. According to *Nature,* today's thoroughbred racehorses do not run any faster than their grandparents did.
   2. Human Olympic runners are at least 20 percent faster than their counterparts of fifty years ago.
   3. Racehorses have reached their physical limits but humans have not.

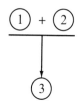

8. 1. If this bucket has a hole in it, then it will leak.
    2. It doesn't leak.
    3. It doesn't have a hole in it.

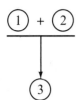

9. 1. The last person we hired from Alamo Polytech was a rotten engineer, and we had to fire him.
    2. This new candidate [from Alamo Polytech, presumably] is somebody I won't take a chance on [that is, somebody who will not be a good engineer and will have to be fired].

(Refer to Exercise 8-4.)

2. 1. You should drive me to the airport. *(Requires paraphrase)*
    2. I'll pay you twice what it takes for gas.
    3. You're my friend. *(Requires paraphrase)*

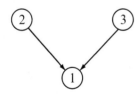

3. 1. If you drive too fast, you're more likely to get a ticket.
    2. The more likely you are to get a ticket, the more likely you are to have your insurance premiums raised.
    3. If you drive too fast, you are more likely to have your insurance premiums raised.

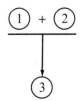

5. 1. If Jackson were president, he'd have lowered taxes by now.
    2. If taxes were lowered, we'd have more money. *(Requires paraphrase)*
    3. If we had more money, we'd be happier.
    4. If Jackson were president, we'd be happier. *(Requires paraphrase)*

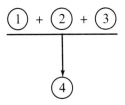

6. 1. The cat's food hasn't been touched in two days.
    2. The cat's water hasn't been touched in two days.
    3. The cat has run away.

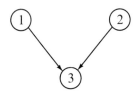

8. 1. By trying to eliminate Darwin from the curriculum, creationists are doing
       themselves a great disservice.
    2. Darwin's discoveries only support the thesis that species change, not that they
       evolve into new species.
    3. Darwin actually supports the creationist point of view.

9. 1. The Supreme Court's ruling that schools may have a moment of silence but not
       if it's designated for prayer is sound.
    2. Nothing stops someone from saying a silent prayer at school or anywhere else.
    3. A moment of silence will not favor one religion over any other.

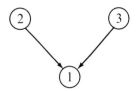

(Refer to Exercise 8-5.)

2. 1. Jones won't plead guilty to a misdemeanor.
   2. If he won't plead guilty, then he will be tried on a felony charge.
   3. Jones will be tried on a felony charge.

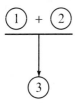

3. 1. John is taller than Bill.
   2. Bill is taller than Margaret.
   3. John is taller than Margaret.

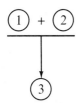

5. 1. It is false (that all religions are basically the same and fraudulent).
   2. The beliefs of Christianity and the cults are different.
   3. There is a big difference between Ron Hubbard, who called himself God, and Jesus Christ, who said, "Love your enemies. . . ."

We can see doing this either of the following two ways:

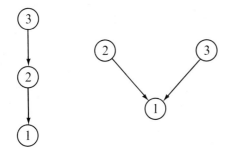

6. 1. We've interviewed two hundred professional football players.
   2. Sixty percent of those interviewed favor expanding the season to twenty games.
   3. Sixty percent of all professional football players favor expanding the season to twenty games.

Numbers (1) and (2) can be put together as a conjunction, as in the original passage.

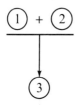

7. 1. Exercise may help chronic male smokers kick the habit.
    2. Thirty young male smokers were put on a three-month program of vigorous exercise.
    3. A year later only 14 percent of them still smoked.
    4. Thirty young male smokers who did not exercise were checked a year later, and 60 percent still smoked.

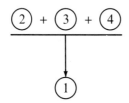

9. 1. God exists. (I believe in God.)
    2. The universe couldn't have arisen by chance.
    3. More and more physicists believe in God. . . .

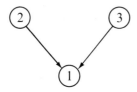

Exercise 8-15

We've made the unstated claims in items 3 and 5 explicit.

2. 1. The federal deficit must be reduced.
    2. It [the deficit] has contributed to inflation.
    3. It [the deficit] has hurt American exports.

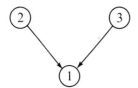

3. 1. Professional boxing should be outlawed.
    2. Boxing almost always leads to brain damage.
    3. Anything that leads to brain damage should be outlawed.
    4. Boxing supports organized crime.
    5. [Unstated:] Anything that supports organized crime should be outlawed.

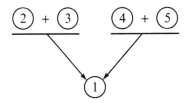

5. 1. One shouldn't vote for Jackson.
    2. Jackson is too radical.
    3. Jackson is too inexperienced.
    4. Jackson's lack of experience would have made him a dangerous president.
    5. [Unstated:] One shouldn't vote for anybody who is too radical.
    6. [Unstated:] One shouldn't vote for anybody who would be a dangerous president.

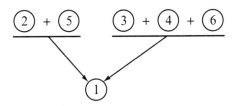

Claim 3 is included, but, given claim 4, it's redundant.

Exercise 8-16

2. 1. You should listen to loud music only when we are not at home.
    2. It [loud music] bothers us.
    3. We're your parents.
    4. [Unstated:] You shouldn't do things that bother your parents.

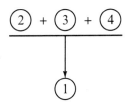

3. 1. The 1948 version of *The Three Musketeers* is a much better movie than the 1993 version.
    2. Lana Turner is luscious (in the 1948 version).
    3. Vincent Price is dastardly.

4. Angela Lansbury is regal.
5. Nobody has or will portray D'Artagnan with the grace, athleticism, or skill of Gene Kelly.
6. You should rent the 1948 version of the movie.

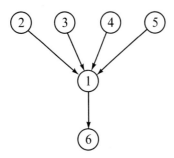

5. 1. Too many seniors . . . are paying far too much . . . for housing.
   2. Proposition 168 will help clear the way for affordable housing for these groups.
   3. Proposition 168 reforms the . . . requirements for an election before . . . approved.
   4. Requiring elections . . . wastes money.
   5. No other state constitution puts such a roadblock. . . .
   6. Please support Proposition 168. [I.e., you should support Proposition 168.]

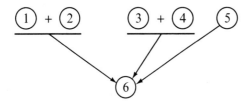

6. 1. Thirty years after . . . it's no easier to accept . . .
   2. There is no credible evidence to contradict the Warren Commission finding . . .
   3. It is time to accept the conclusion [of the Warren Commission].
   4. The nation pays a heavy price for chronic doubts and mistrust.
   5. Confidence in the government has declined.
   6. Participation in the voting process has steadily slid downward.
   7. The national appetite for wild theories encourages peddlers to persist.
   8. Evil is never easy to accept.

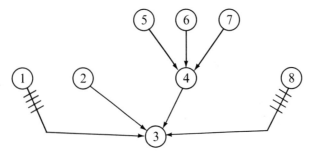

Notice that claims 1 and 8 could easily be considered window dressing and simply ignored.

8. 1. The nation's cities reel under staggering murder totals.
    2. Kids use guns simply to get even after feuds.
    3. Children are gunned down by random bullets.
    4. This is not exactly the weapon of choice for deer hunting or for a homeowner seeking protection.
    5. It is an ideal weapon for street gangs and drug thugs in their wars with each other and the police.
    6. To legalize fully automatic machine guns is to increase the mayhem that is turning this nation—particularly its large cities—into a continual war zone.
    7. Doesn't the NRA have something better to do [than wanting the Court to throw out the ban on private ownership of fully automatic weapons]?

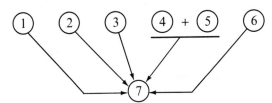

9. 1. Our right to move about freely is more important than having a checkpoint system for drunk drivers.
    2. If the checkpoint system continues, there will be checkpoints for drugs, seat belts, and so on.
    3. We'll regret it later if we allow the system to continue.
    4. [Unstated:] We'll regret it if we get checkpoints for drugs, seat belts, and so on.

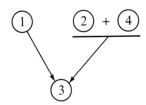

Since no evidence is given for claim 2, this has the distinct aroma of slippery slope pseudoreasoning.

11. 1. The constitutional guarantee of a speedy trial prevents crime.
    2. More than a third of those with serious criminal records . . . are arrested for new offenses while free on bond awaiting . . . trial.
    3. The longer the delay, the greater the likelihood of further violations.

12. *Clearly, this one requires some rephrasing to bring it down to size:*

1. A real town should be named after the one in which *The Andy Griffith Show* was set, Mayberry, only if some real town could live up to the image of Mayberry in the program.
2. No real town could live up to that image.
3. No real town should be named after the fictional Mayberry.

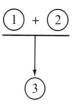

14. 1. Recycled water in automatic carwashes may dump salt and dirt from one car to the next.
2. Brushes and drag cloths hurt the finish.
3. [Unstated:] ICA-sponsored tests don't really prove that automatic carwashes are easier on cars than home washes.
4. The home washes in the tests may not have been "average."
5. The automatic washes in the tests were surely in perfect working order (that is, in better condition than the "average" automatic wash).
6. Most automatic carwashes may not be properly maintained (we can't tell).
7. If you follow a mud-caked pickup through the wash, there may be dirt in the brushes or cloths that are dragged over your car.
8. You should wash your own car. (*Or:* You're better off washing your own car; *or:* Home washing is easier on your car than automatic carwashes.)

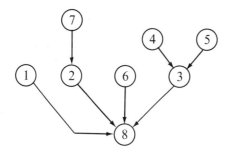

15. 1. The worst disease of the 1990s will be AIDS.
2. AIDS has made surgery scary.
3. In the last ten years several hundred Americans got AIDS from contaminated blood in surgery.
4. It is predicted that within a few years more hundreds of people will receive AIDS blood each year.

5. No one can feel safe receiving blood.
6. We should be tested for AIDS (by a very sensitive test) before we give blood.

There is more than one way to set this out. It's possible to leave out claims 1, 2, and 5 at no substantial loss to the argument.

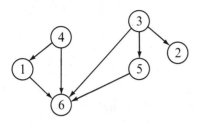

17. 1. A project with 3,000 houses and 7,000 new residents cannot properly be called a "village."
 2. Citizens of Chico will be better off if they vote no on Measure A. [Vote no on Measure A.]
 3. The project will not protect agricultural land.
 4. The Greenline protects valuable farmland.
 5. With the Greenline, there is enough land in the Chico area available to build 62,000 new homes.
 6. The project's park dedications will not reduce use of Bidwell Park.
 7. The developers want to attract 7,000 new residents [who will use the park].
 8. The developers will not provide a school site [without cost to the taxpayers].
 9. The developers intend to sell the site to the school district, which will pay for it with taxpayers' money.

One could include the claim "Chico does not need the Rancho Arroyo project" as the conclusion of a subargument—in the place of claim 2 in the diagram—and let it support the final conclusion: One should vote against Measure A. (Chapter 13 discusses getting "ought" conclusions from "is" premises—we won't complicate the example here by introducing an additional premise.)

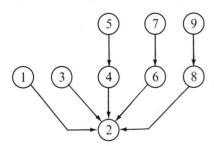

18. 1. My relative's client, who was serving a life sentence for murder, escaped and murdered someone else.
 2. It's a waste of taxpayers' money to try this man [or others like him] again.
 3. Murderers should be executed. [The death penalty should be restored.]
 4. We are the most crime-ridden society in the world.
 5. Someone is murdered every 27 minutes in the U.S.

6. There is a rape every 10 minutes.
7. There is an armed robbery every 82 seconds.
8. According to the FBI, there are 870,000 violent crimes a year, and the number is increasing.
9. Only 10 percent of those arrested are found guilty.
10. A large percentage of those found guilty are released on probation.
11. There aren't enough prisons to house the guilty.
12. The death penalty would create more room in prisons.
13. The death penalty would reduce the number of murders.
14. If a robber knew before he shot someone that if he's caught his own life will be taken, [he wouldn't do it or would be less likely to do it].
15. [Murderers] deserve to die.
16. [Murderers] sacrificed their right to live when they murdered someone.

We see the last claim in the passage as polemical window dressing. Also, we're not sure whether claim 11 is supposed to support claim 9 as well as 10.

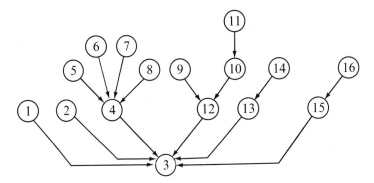

Chapter 8 Test Question/Exercise Banks

Bank 8-1

Only some of the following passages contain arguments. Identify those that do, and underline the sentence that contains the conclusion (or state the conclusion in your own words). If any passage contains more than one argument, underline the sentences that contain the conclusions (or state them in your own words), and indicate which is the principal argument.

1. Bamboo can grow up to four feet a day, but only after it is well established. This can take from three to five years, depending on the type of bamboo.

No argument

2. The Burnhams have invited the performers home for a reception following the recital. But <u>it would be wise to let them know if you plan to attend,</u> because space is limited.

   Argument

3. Feldspar works at a restaurant at night and teaches during the day. I'd have to bet <u>he's tired most of the time,</u> and that's a good reason for thinking <u>he won't do well in school this term.</u>

   Two arguments present; "He won't do well . . ." is the conclusion of the principal argument.

4. It is a very nice clock, but as you can see, <u>it doesn't really go very well on that wall.</u> For one thing, it's too large for the space. For another, it's red, and the wall is green. <u>The best thing you could do with it, I'm afraid, is take it back.</u> Walmart is good about giving refunds.

   Two arguments present; "The best thing you could do . . ." is the conclusion of the principal argument.

5. "Hey, what IS that stuff you're cooking, anyway? It smells like fish."
   "Fish! What do you mean, 'fish'? That's a pot roast I'm cooking."
   "Oh . . . say, you don't mind if I open a window, do you? No, it's not the fish— uh, roast; it just seems sorta warm in here."

   No argument. In the last passage the speaker is explaining—actually, pretending to explain—why he or she wants to open a window, not giving an argument that a window should be opened.

6. The market for Jackson Pollock paintings has collapsed virtually overnight. Reason: A lot of them were bought during the 1980s, and 1990s investors figure that 1980s prices were too high.

   No argument

7. Imagine yourself naked, without weapons, and running after a deer. If you were to catch this deer how would you eat it? Humans are not equipped with the canine teeth in order to eat meat without tools. A carnivore's teeth are long and sharp, and its jaws move up and down. Humans, by contrast, use their molars to crush and grind their food. Have you ever noticed that so many Americans are overweight and unhealthy? That's because they eat meat.
   —From a student paper

   Argument; the conclusion is that meat isn't an appropriate or healthy diet for humans.

8. Is Bill Clinton's behavior prior to his becoming president relevant to how he should be judged in office? Yes: 22% No: 71%
   —From a telephone poll of 800 adult Americans taken for *Time*/CNN by Yankelovich Partners, Inc.

   No argument

9. "Hey, see that bald dude over there? You know how old that guy is? He's my teacher."

"I dunno, fifty, maybe."

"He's not fifty, he's almost seventy!"

"Must eat a lot of Grow Pup."

"I guess! He's a good teacher, too. He really communicates. Makes you remember stuff. I forget now what the course was. . . ."

Argument; the conclusion is that he's a good teacher.

10. "If you don't mow your lawn at least once a week, what happens is that when you do mow it, it'll turn brown later."

An argument in most contexts, for the unstated conclusion that you ought to mow your lawn at least once a week.

Note to instructor: The following argument passages can be treated in any number of ways: You can ask students to specify the issues they address, identify their premises and conclusions, classify them as inductive or deductive, determine whether their premises are dependent or independent, supply missing premises, separate the arguments themselves from their window dressing, or diagram them. You can also return to them from later chapters or appendixes for examples or exercises. We've grouped them and included diagrams for some. Claims that we suggest leaving unstated are given in square brackets.

Bank 8-2

Deductive arguments with dependent premises

11. We'll be better off in the dark than driving on ice in the fog. So let's wait a while. [If we're better off in the dark than driving on ice in the fog, then we should wait a while.]

12. It isn't too late. The bars haven't closed. [If the bars haven't closed, then it isn't too late.]

13. I'd advise you not to vote for Melton. Melton is very radical. [You shouldn't vote for radicals.]

14. The almond trees have not blossomed. It is not yet the middle of February. [The almond trees do not blossom before the middle of February.]

15. Computer networks are immune from computer viruses only if they're completely isolated from other machines and stray software. So, as I told you, this network is not safe from viruses. [This network is not completely isolated from other machines and stray software.]

16. No floor with 2 × 4 joists on two-foot centers is strong enough. So this floor isn't strong enough. [This floor has 2 × 4 joists on two-foot centers.]

17. The only time you can count on dry weather in Seattle is the first week of August. So, since you need to count on dry weather for your trip, you'll have to plan it for next week. [Next week is the first week of August.]

Bank 8-3

Deductive arguments with independent premises (or independent sets of premises). Diagrams are provided for some items.

18. If your shoes are too small, then you shouldn't wear them, and those are much too small. Besides, they're worn out. [If the shoes are worn out, then you shouldn't wear them.]

19. You shouldn't buy a television set that costs over $300, and that one costs $450. And that television set is much too big for your living room anyway. [You shouldn't buy any television set that's too big for your living room.]

20. Tony's car is dangerous. It has bad brakes, and the tires are nearly worn out. [Any car that has bad brakes is dangerous. Any car with tires that are nearly worn out is dangerous.]

21. Look, (1) there's no sign of smoke from the cabin. (2) If he were there, he'd have a fire, and we'd see the smoke, unless he couldn't find any dry wood. (3) But there's a lot of dry wood around. Notice also that (4) you don't hear his dog. (5) He's not there. [(6) If you don't hear his dog, he's not there.]

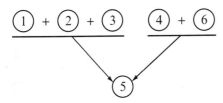

22. If she really thought those clothes were unflattering, she wouldn't be caught dead in them. Anyway, she told me herself she thought she looked good in them, and she wouldn't say that unless she believed it, so she obviously does. [She wears those clothes.]

23. You've got to take Math 3. First of all, it's a required part of the general education program. Second, it's a prerequisite for several courses in your major. [You've got to take all required parts of the general education program. You've got to take all prerequisites for courses in your major.]

24. (1) Toyota is raising its prices by 3 percent on January 1, and (2) we won't be able to afford one if we wait until then. Besides that, (3) the old heap won't make it to the first of the year. (4) We'll have to buy now. [(5) If we cannot afford a Toyota after January 1, we'll have to buy now. (6) If the old heap won't make it to the first of the year, we'll have to buy now.]

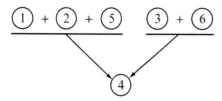

25. (1) Either there's a burglar outside, or there's a dog in the garbage. (2) There can't be a dog in the garbage because of the fence. So, (3) it must be a burglar. Besides, (4) I think I saw a flashlight beam, and (5) it could only be a burglar that would make such a light.

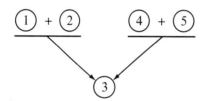

26. (1) Congress will allow the construction of more than 50 MX missiles only if the Air Force finds a way to protect them; otherwise, we'll get more Midgetman missiles. Furthermore, a study has just been done that shows that (2) the Midgetman is more efficient than the MX, and it's clear that (3) Congress will allow building more of whichever of the two missiles is more efficient. And (4) the Air Force could never protect the MXs anyhow. Therefore, (5) Congress is going to authorize building more Midgetmen rather than more MXs.

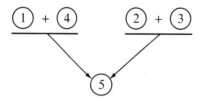

Bank 8-4

Inductive arguments with dependent premises

27. I've already won a hundred dollars in the state lottery, and hardly anyone wins that much twice. So I'm not likely to win that much again.

28. It's Monday, so the mail carrier will probably arrive after noon today. He usually comes in the early afternoon on Mondays.

29. The blasted hedge clippers aren't working again. Must be the switch. That's usually the problem.

30. "Sixty Minutes" has been in the top ten in the Neilsen ratings for the last ten years. It's a safe bet to be there this coming season as well.

31. I'll bet a dollar that (1) Booth picks Chapman as his new vice-president. (2) Booth and Chapman have been on a first-name basis for a long time, and (3) Booth usually rewards his friends.

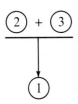

Note: Booth's picking Chapman is the latter's reward, of course. You may want to make this clear with additional premises.

32. I've been looking at the available literature on the trial of Julius and Ethel Rosenberg, and the great majority of writers on the subject have grave doubts about the Rosenbergs' guilt. It seems clear that they may well have been innocent.

33. (1) I'm pretty certain she wouldn't be happy as a police officer. (2) Just watching a crime movie makes her nervous, and (3) if she can't tolerate simulated violence, (1) she most likely won't like the real thing.

Note: The way we've chosen to indicate that the first and last claim are essentially the same is simply to assign them the same number in the passage. Another way to do this is to give them different numbers and indicate their sameness in the diagram.

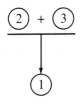

34. (1) People who read more tend to have better vocabularies than those who don't, and (2) having a good vocabulary makes you a better speaker and writer. Since (3) good speaking and writing are important job skills, (4) you are probably a better job candidate if you read a lot.

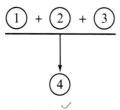

35. (1) It seems pretty likely that all the smaller food stores around town are going to have trouble staying open. (2) Jack's Market has closed, and the 5th Street Market has closed, and now I hear that the Cash And Carry across town is going to fold up, too. (3) You'd best get used to the idea of shopping at the big supermarkets, since (4) those are probably going to be all that's left in another six months.

Bank 8-5

Inductive arguments with independent premises

36. Sal is probably going to be late, since the traffic is so bad. And he said he had an errand to run on his way over here.

37. The MiniMax video camera: It's the lightest in weight, it's the least expensive, and it comes with the longest warranty in the business—all good reasons for making it the one you take home.

38. For one thing, (1) every movie Stallone has made in the past decade has made money. For another, (2) blood-and-guts patriotism is selling big these days. So (3) the combination of a second film of that kind from Stallone is very nearly a certain money-maker.

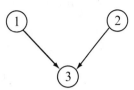

39. (1) Automobile air bags substantially reduce the chances of being hurt in a crash, and (2) unlike seat belts, you can't forget to use them. What's more, (3) there is not one case on record of a bag inflating when it shouldn't have and causing an accident. So, (4) you're much safer buying a car with air bags than one without them.

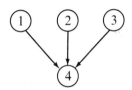

40. Let's see. (1) I know our policy covers us if our car is stolen or if the windows are broken, so (2) chances are it'll cover us if someone steals the stereo, too. Besides that, (3) our homeowners policy covers stereos, and (4) our car policy seems to cover a lot of the same stuff the homeowners policy covers.

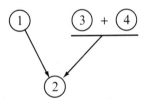

Bank 8-6

Miscellaneous problems

41. The competition employs a sliding mechanism. (1) But a hinged door is lighter and easier to operate and (2) ensures a better fit and seal with the body than a sliding mechanism, thus (3) keeping the cabin's interior noise level to a minimum. And (4) it allows for greater freedom in the shape of the vehicle. [Unstated conclusion: (5) A hinged door is better than a sliding door.]
—Adapted from Mazda truck product manager Bernie Chaisson, arguing that the new Mazda MPV's door setup is superior to that of Chrysler minivans.

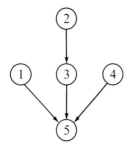

42. (1) The Gallup people estimate that most Americans believe that physicians' fees are excessive, so (2) probably most of them do. I know (3) everyone I talk to thinks that. But (4) we'll never have socialized medicine in this country. (5) Americans will pay any amount for the freedom to choose their own doctors; (6) that's what history tells us.

Note that this one has arguments for two separate conclusions.

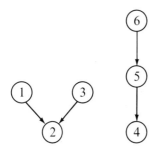

43. (1) I think we should ask Bill to take care of the house while we're gone. (2) He took good care of Kent's house, according to Kent. In addition, (3) he's always been responsible about other things. (4) I'm sure he'll do a good job.

Bank 8-7

Fill in the blanks

44. Arguments whose premises are intended to provide absolutely conclusive reasons for accepting the conclusion are _deductive_ , and arguments whose premises are intended to provide some support but less than absolutely conclusive support for the conclusion are _inductive_ .

45. Sound arguments are _deductive_ arguments that are _valid_ and whose premises are all _true_ .

True/False.

46. A valid argument cannot have any false premises.

False

47. If a strong argument has a false conclusion, then not all its premises can be true.

False

48. If a valid argument has a false conclusion, then not all its premises can be true.

Chapter 9
Deductive Arguments I: Categorical Logic

Some students find the "logic" section of our courses much more to their liking than the rest. We presume the reason is that many of the answers are pretty cut-and-dried: If you have a basic knowledge of the material, you ought to get most of the answers right. This contrasts with much of the "critical thinking" part of the course, where the material can be a good bit slipperier. Lots of other students, however, especially the mathophobes, find any kind of technical work a real chore to learn. The best solution is practice and more practice—preferably practice that's guided by an experienced tutor. Simply watching an instructor work a problem on the chalkboard does only a little more to teach a student logic than listening to Itzhak Perlman play the violin teaches the listener to fiddle.

Students are often surprised to learn that so much can be said by using nothing but the four standard-form categorical types of claims. Much of what can be said must be said awkwardly, of course—in "logician's English"—but it can be said nonetheless.

If we were especially careful (and a little less worried about confusing students unnecessarily), we would say more about the distinction between a categorical claim and a categorical claim *form*. "All Xs are Ys" is not a claim at all, but a claim *form* (or an open sentence, or a propositional function), since it contains variables for the subject and predicate terms. Such expressions can't be true or false; only their instantiations can have truth values. We've discovered that, technically correct or not, the distinction between claims and forms can be glossed over most of the time. You and your students don't have to be so careful when you're talking about the material, and students usually don't miss the distinction. If a student *does* remark that a form can't be a claim because it can't be true or false, we simply identify the distinction and point out that we're ignoring it most of the time in the interest of economy. You, of course, are welcome to be more careful if you like.

An understanding of the usual categorical inferences, both immediate and syllogistic, is valuable to a student. But we believe that learning to translate from informal English claims to standard-form claims serves an equally valuable purpose. We can hardly help but wonder how deeply students are thinking about the claims they hear and make themselves when they have great difficulty deciding whether a claim should be translated as "All Xs are Ys" or "All Ys are Xs." Requiring such translations must, at a minimum, get students to think a little harder about the kinds of sentences they use all the time.

Regarding the square of opposition, sharp students may notice that contraries *could* both be true if the subject class were empty and that subcontraries could both be false under the same condition. True enough, we have to tell them. Contradiction is the only inference on the square that does not require the assumption of at least one member of the subject class. So every other inference tacitly begins, as it were, with, "On the assumption that there is at least one S. . . ." Since we rarely reason about the empty set outside a math or symbolic logic course, this shouldn't offend the sensibilities of the rigorous. And this "existential" interpretation of the square does allow "All Xs are Ys" and "No Xs are Ys" to be conflicting claims. Any other view is counterintuitive to most students. There's no point in beginning their study of formal logic with a gross counterintuition, we figure.

Another note about the square of opposition: We don't discuss subalternation (the relationship between an A-claim and its corresponding I-claim and between an E-claim and its corresponding O-claim). This is just more terminology to learn, and students find that going from an A-claim to an E-claim and then to an I-claim—that is, going across the top of the square and then diagonally—is just as fast and intuitive as learning a new relationship up and down the sides of the square. Things are complicated enough without throwing in everything that's been tacked onto categorical logic since the time of Aristotle. (The same holds true for syllogistic "mood" and syllogism names, although some students are amused to learn that they have names like "Barbara." Those are probably students whom *anything* would amuse.)

Exercises Unanswered in the Text

Exercise 9-1

When we ask students to turn in exercises like these, we make them put parentheses or brackets around the subject and predicate terms—doing this helps students keep their answers straight, and it helps us read them.

2. Some lizards are not salamanders.

3. All lizards are reptiles.

5. Some members of the suborder Ophidia are not snakes.

6. No burrowing snakes are poisonous snakes.

8. All frogs are amphibians.

9. All places where there are snakes are places where there are frogs.

11. All times the frog population decreases are times the snake population decreases.

12. All people who arrived are cheerleaders.

14. All people who got seats are people who arrived early.

15. Some home movies are things that are as boring as dirt.

17. No people identical to the bank robber are people identical to Jane's fiancé.

18. All automobiles built before 1950 are antiques.

20. Some examples of corn are not stuff that makes good popcorn.

Exercise 9-2

2. No students of mine are students who are failing.

3. No people who live in the dorms are people who can own cars. (*If there is something about the addressee of this claim that makes it apply to him or her but not to all others, this one should be rephrased:* "No people *like* you *who live in the dorms are people who can own cars.*")

5. All times Joan sings are times people make faces.

6. All tests George fails are tests George takes.

8. All people who can be members are people over fifty. (*Notice the difference between this and the claim, "All members are over fifty." The latter doesn't capture the requirement that one be over fifty to be a member.*)

9. All people who catch on are people who study. (*Or, the converse of the obverse may seem more natural: "No people who fail to study are people who catch on."*)

Exercise 9-3

2. E-claim: No drugs are harmless substances. (True)
   Corresponding O: Some drugs are not harmless substances. (True)
   Corresponding I: Some drugs are harmless substances. (False)
   Corresponding A: All drugs are harmless substances. (False)

3. I-claim: Some wars are just wars. (True)
   Corresponding A: All wars are just wars. (Undetermined)
   Corresponding E: No wars are just wars. (False)
   Corresponding O: Some wars are not just wars. (Undetermined)

5. A-claim: All woodpeckers are birds that sing well. (False)
   Corresponding E: No woodpeckers are birds that sing well. (Undetermined)
   Corresponding O: Some woodpeckers are not birds that sing well. (True)
   Corresponding I: Some woodpeckers are birds that sing well. (Undetermined)

6. E-claim: No mockingbirds are birds that can sing. (False)
   Corresponding O: Some mockingbirds are not birds that can sing. (Undetermined)
   Corresponding I: Some mockingbirds are birds that can sing. (True)
   Corresponding A: All mockingbirds are birds that can sing. (Undetermined)

7. I-claim: Some herbs are medicinal plants. (False)
   Corresponding A: All herbs are medicinal plants. (False)
   Corresponding E: No herbs are medicinal plants. (True)
   Corresponding O: Some herbs are not medicinal plants. (True)

8. A-claim: All logic exercises are easy exercises. (False)
   Corresponding E: No logic exercises are easy exercises. (Undetermined)
   Corresponding O: Some logic exercises are not easy exercises. (True)
   Corresponding I: Some logic exercises are easy exercises. (Undetermined)

Exercise 9-4

We looked it up: The prefix "non-" is combined with other words with a hyphen only when the other word is capitalized or is itself a compound word (e.g., "non-Greek" and "non-ablebodied," but "nonreligious").

2. Some Arabs are not non-Christians. (Equivalent)

3. No Sunnis are non-Muslims. (Equivalent)

216

5. No Muslims are Hindus. (Equivalent)

6. Some non-Hindus are not non-Indians. (Equivalent)

8. All non-Christians are non-Catholics. (Equivalent)

9. All Christians are Protestants. (Not Equivalent)

Exercise 9-5

2. All students who wrote poor essays are students who were not admitted to the program. (Equivalent)

3. Some students who did not score well on the exam are not students who were not admitted to the program. (Equivalent)

5. All students who did not write good essays are students who were not admitted to the program. (Equivalent)

6. All students of mine are registered students. (Equivalent)

8. All people whose automobile ownership is restricted are noncommuters. (Equivalent)

9. Some students who do not do poorly (*or* who do all right) in history classes are students with no short-term memory problems. (Not Equivalent)

Exercise 9-6

1. Some percussion instruments are clarinets.

3. Some non-Celts are not non-Englishmen.

5. All freshwater fish are nonsharks.

Exercise 9-7

1. Equivalent to (b).

3. Equivalent to (e).

Exercise 9-8

Note: There is often more than one way to do problems like this.

2. Contrapose (a) to get: "All non-Westerners are non-Europeans".

3. Obvert claim (a), then convert the result, to get: "No non-Europeans are Greeks.".

5. Contrapose claim (a) to get: "All people who did not take the exam are members of the club."

6. Obvert claim (a) to get: "Some cheeses are products that are not high in cholesterol."

8. Convert claim (a), then obvert the result to get: "All people with name tags are participants."

9. Convert claim (b), then obvert the result to get: "Some perennials are not plants that grow from tubers."

Exercise 9-9

Some students find these among the most difficult exercises in this chapter. Work on such problems needs to be divided into two parts: making the claims correspond, if possible, then using the square of opposition. We do these exercises by putting the first claim high on the chalkboard and the second one near the bottom, then working toward the middle (using only equivalent-producing operations of conversion, obversion, and contraposition) until the claims correspond, if they can be made to correspond. If they can, the square of opposition produces the answer; if they can't, the second claim remains undetermined. In hopes of making this clear, we've laid item 2 out this way.

2.   (a) Some students are not ineligible candidates. (T)

   obverts to   (a_1) Some students are eligible candidates. (T)

   converts to   (a_2) Some eligible candidates are students. (T)

   by sq. of opp.   (b) No eligible candidates are students. (F)

Begin by writing (a) and (b), leaving space between; then, ask students what needs doing. One term needs to be changed into its complement, and the terms are in the wrong places. So, we obvert (a) to get (a_1), then convert (a_1) to get (a_2). Since (a_2) corresponds to (b), the square of opposition gives us the answer: Since (a_2) is true, (b) must be false. We expect this is overkill and will give just answers and a note or two for the remainder.

4. False. Obvert (a), convert (b), and use the square of opposition.

6. Undetermined. From a true I-claim, nothing follows about the O-claim.

7. True. Translate (a) as "Some of Gary Brodnax's novels are novels in which the hero gets killed." The square of opposition tells us the corresponding O-claim must be true.

8. Undetermined. These cannot be made to correspond without converting an A- or an O-claim. So, there isn't enough information to tell what (b)'s truth value is.

10. True. Translate (a) as "All persimmons that have not been left to dry are astringent persimmons," and then contrapose this claim. Obvert; then convert (b). It's now an I-claim that corresponds to the contrapositive of (a).

This one is a killer. Notice, though, that there's nothing unusual about the original claims—they're the sort students use all the time. Most students can't stare at them and tell you what follows about (b), and this inability justifies learning this technique:

They need some way of determining just exactly what they're talking about if they're ever going to do things like sign contracts.

Exercise 9-10

2.

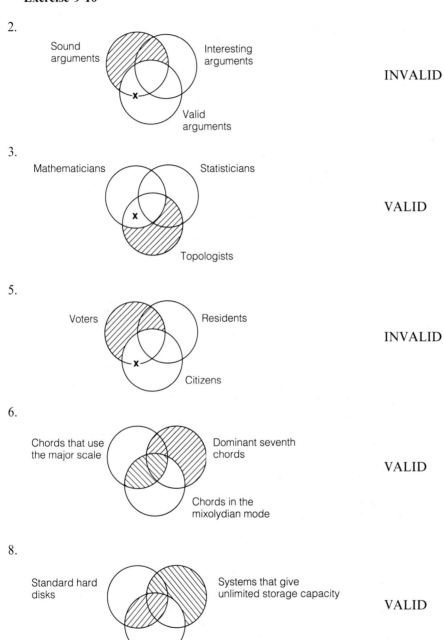

INVALID

3.

VALID

5.

INVALID

6.

VALID

8.

VALID

9.

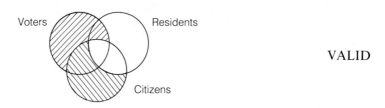

Voters   Residents

Citizens

VALID

Before diagramming this argument, the term "citizens" must be turned into "noncitizens" or vice versa. The easiest way to do this is to change the second premise, "No noncitizens are voters." If we convert it and then obvert the result, we get "All voters are citizens."

Exercise 9-11

Some of these exercises can be done more than one way. You may prefer to use obversion and the other operations on different claims from the ones we've worked on.

2. No ears with white tassels are ripe ears.
   <u>Some ripe ears are not ears with full-sized kernels.</u>
   Some ears with full-sized kernels are not ears with white tassels.

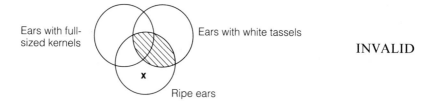

Ears with full-sized kernels   Ears with white tassels

x

Ripe ears

INVALID

3. No prescription drugs are drugs that can be taken without a doctor's order.
   <u>All OTC drugs are drugs that can be taken without a doctor's order.</u>
   No OTC drugs are prescription drugs.

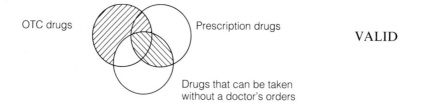

OTC drugs   Prescription drugs

Drugs that can be taken without a doctor's orders

VALID

5. Some compact disc players are players that use 4x sampling.
   Some players that use 4x sampling are players that cost under $100.
   Some compact disc players are not players that cost under $100.

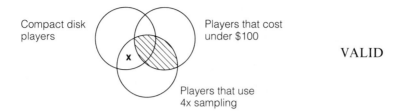

VALID

6. All things that Bob won are things that Pete won.
   All things that Bob won are junk.
   All things that Pete won are junk.

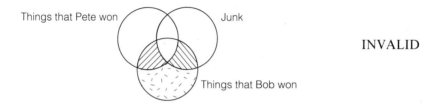

INVALID

Problem 6 is really a good one. Lots of students manage to do it incorrectly even though it's about as straightforward as can be—a good example to show them that they really need to be careful and that they need a technique to help them.

8. No off-road vehicles are vehicles allowed in the . . . park.
   Some off-road vehicles are not four-wheel-drive vehicles.
   Some four-wheel-drive vehicles are vehicles allowed in the . . . park.

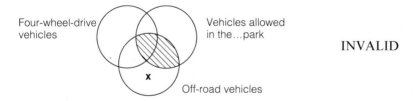

INVALID

9. Some people affected by the drainage tax are residents of the county.
   Some residents of the county are people paying the sewer tax.
   Some people paying the sewer tax are people affected by the drainage tax.

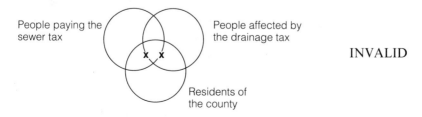

INVALID

Exercise 9-12

Whether the answers below fit the questions will depend on the shape of the argument after the appropriate obversions, and so on, are carried out. If you modify different claims, an invalid syllogism may break a different rule. Still, if a syllogism breaks a rule in one version, it'll break *some* rule in any other version. We have presumed the versions of the syllogisms found above and in the answer section of the text.

(Refer to Exercise 9-10.)

1. Valid; breaks no rule

3. Valid; breaks no rule

4. Valid; breaks no rule

6. Invalid; breaks rule 3

9. Invalid; breaks rule 2

10. Valid; breaks no rule

(Refer to Exercise 9-11.)

1. Valid; breaks no rule

3. Valid; breaks no rule

4. Valid; breaks no rule

6. Invalid; breaks rule 3

9. Invalid; breaks rule 2

10. Valid; breaks no rule

Exercise 9-13

Some of the answers to Exercise 9-13 follow. We're putting the arguments into standard form and using the rules. (Diagrams require that we wrestle with that graphics program.) We've shortened some of the terms to save space.

1. All creationists are religious.
   <u>All fundamentalists are religious.</u>
   All creationists are fundamentalists.

   Invalid; breaks rule 2

2. All sportscasters are athletes.
   <u>No athletes are college professors.</u>
   No sportscasters are college professors.

   Invalid; breaks rule 3

3. All Democrat-voters are people who favor expansion. . . .
   <u>All people who favor expansion . . . are people who favor higher taxes.</u>
   All Democrat-voters are people who favor higher taxes.

   Valid

4. All cave dwellers are people who lived before radio.
   <u>No people alive today are cave dwellers.</u>
   No people who lived before radio are people alive today.

   Invalid; breaks rule 3

5. No conservationists are Republican-voters.
   <u>All environmentalists are conservationists.</u>
   No environmentalists are Republican-voters.

   Valid

8. All philosophers are skeptics.
   <u>No philosophers are theologians.</u>
   No skeptics are theologians.

   Invalid; breaks rule 3

9. All philosophers are skeptics.
   <u>No philosophers are theologians.</u>
   No theologians are skeptics.

   Invalid; breaks rule 3

10. All peddlers are salesmen.
    <u>All confidence men are salesmen.</u>
    All peddlers are confidence men.

    Invalid; breaks rule 2

11. No addicts are decent people.
    <u>All criminals are decent people.</u>
    No addicts are criminals.

    Valid

Hereafter, we'll abbreviate terms.

12. C = critical thinkers
    R = people who recognize invalid syllogisms
    L = logicians

    All C are R.
    <u>All L are R.</u>
    All C are L.

    Invalid; breaks rule 2

17. M = Mohawk Indians
    A = Algonquins
    C = Cheyenne

    All M are A.
    <u>All C are A.</u>
    All C are M.

    Invalid; breaks rule 2

18. I = idiots
    P = people who support the measure
    S = members of the school board

    All P are I.
    <u>No S are I.</u>
    No S are P.

    Valid

20. A = cases of aesthetic surgery
    L = surgery designed to make a patient look better
    R = reconstructive surgery

    All A are L.
    <u>No A are R.</u>
    No R are L.

    Invalid; breaks rule 3

Exercise 9-14

2. R = rats
   D = disease-carrying pets
   C = creatures that should be eradicated

   All R are D.
   <u>All D are C.</u>
   All R are C.

   Valid

3. *Note: These terms are easily confused, since it's natural to represent two of them with "C."*

M = masterpieces
C = pieces that can still be found on cassettes (*or* that have been recorded on cassettes in recent years)
R = parts of the classical repertoire

All M are R.
No R are C.
No M are C.

Valid

5. P = parties the police have to break up
C = campus parties
O = parties that get out of control

Some C are O.
All O are P.
Some C are P.

Valid

6. F = fundamentalist Christians
E = evangelicals
R = revivalists

All F are E.
All R are E.
Some F are R.

Invalid; breaks rule 2

8. I = intramural sports
O = Olympic sports
C = intercollegiate sports

No I are O.
Some C are not O.
Some C are I.

Invalid; breaks rule 1

9. M = moas
D = Dinornithidae
E = creatures that still exist

All M are D.
No M are E.
No D are E.

Invalid; breaks rule 3

11. P = software in the public domain
     S = software that may be copied without permission or fee
     C = software under copyright

     All P are S.
     No C are S.
     No C are P.

     Valid

12. D = countries that have been living under dictatorship
     F = countries familiar with social requirements of democracy
     T = countries that will make a successful quick transition to democracy

     No D are F.
     All T are F. (After contraposition)
     No D are T

     Valid

14. I = investor-held utilities
     R = companies that should be allowed to raise rates
     P = public utilities

     All P are R.
     No P are I.
     No I are R.

     Invalid; breaks rule 3

15. I = things that are important to learn
     U = things that are not useful
     C = chemistry (things identical with chemistry)

     All C are U.
     No U are I.
     No C are I.

     Valid

17. *Getting students to represent this one correctly can be instructive, but it sometimes reminds you of pulling teeth.*

     W = stockholders' information about a company's worth
     M = information that must come from the managers of a company
     B = information that must come from the very people who are trying to buy the stock from stockholders

     All W are M.
     All M are B.
     All W are B.

     Valid

19. C = China (countries identical to China)
    R = countries with a bad record (of human-rights violations, and so on)
    S = countries on whom Congress should impose sanctions

    All C are R.
    All R are S.
    All C are S.

    Valid

Exercise 9-15

Different instructors will require different levels of rigor in constructing arguments for these claims. We'll give a middling version that should satisfy all but the hardest noses. Some students find these fun. Those who don't tend to look puzzled a lot.

2. False. Anything like this shows it to be false: Some Xs are Ys; no Ys are Zs; so, some Xs are not Zs.

3. True: Imagine a syllogism, S, that's valid and has an E-claim for a conclusion. It must distribute its middle term (because of rule 2), plus both minor and major terms (because of rule 3). Therefore, three terms must be distributed in the premises, and the only way to do this without having two negative premises is to have an A-claim and an E-claim as premises.

5. False, as the preceding answer shows. However there are *some* things you can't do, such as break rule 1 both ways (i.e., have two negative premises *and* an affirmative conclusion) *plus* break both of the other rules. The proof of this is left to the reader.

Exercise 9-16

The passage contains an invalid argument that can be cast as a syllogism. Here it is:

S = people they saw
H = homeless people
W = people wearing worn-out hippy gear

All H are W.
All S are W.
All S are H.

The last sentence begs the question, a fault covered in Chapter 6: Anyone who doesn't think the people in question chose for themselves certainly won't accept the premise "If they didn't choose for themselves, who did?"

Exercise 9-17

P = instances or examples of pornography
D = things that carry demeaning messages about a woman's worth
R = things that violate women's rights

All P are D.
[All D are R.]
All P are R.

Valid

Now, add:

B = things the Minneapolis City Council is justified in banning

[All R are B.]
All P are R.
All P are B.

Valid

Chapter 9 Test Question/Exercise Banks

Bank 9-1

Translate the following into standard-form categorical claims.

1. Not every product that's organic is actually a chemical-free product.

   Some organic products are not chemical-free products.

2. The only organic products are chemical-free products.

   All organic products are chemical-free products.

3. Chemical-free products are the only organic products.

   All organic products are chemical-free products.

4. Only organic products are chemical-free products.

   All chemical-free products are organic products.

5. Chemical-free products are not the only organic products.

   Some organic products are not chemical-free products.

6. It's not only chemical-free products that are organic.

   Some organic products are not chemical-free products.

7. Not all savings institutions are banks.

   Some savings institutions are not banks.

8. Banks are the only savings institutions.

   All savings institutions are banks.

9. Banks are not the only savings institutions.

   Some savings institutions are not banks.

10. Only banks can be savings institutions.

    All savings institutions are banks.

11. People always leave when Tony plays the accordion.

    All times Tony plays the accordion are times people leave.

12. People always duck when Richard picks up a golf club.

    All times Richard picks up a golf club are times people duck.

13. Whenever Tony plays the accordion, people leave.

    All times Tony plays the accordion are times people leave.

14. People duck whenever Richard picks up a golf club.

    All times Richard picks up a golf club are times people duck.

15. Tricia's dog goes wherever she goes.

    All places Tricia goes are places her dog goes.

16. Except for members of the Lucero family, there's nobody in the park.

    All people in the park are members of the Lucero family.

17. There's nobody in the park except members of the Lucero family.

    All people in the park are members of the Lucero family.

18. Lydia is the only person in our group who sold stock before the crash.

    All people in our group who sold stock before the crash are {people = Lydia} (that is, people identical to Lydia).

19. The morning star is actually the evening star.

    All {things = the morning star} are {things = the evening star}.

20. Mr. Ashcroft isn't at home.

    No {people = Mr. Ashcroft} are people at home.

21. Only athletes play in the National Basketball Association.

    All who play in the National Basketball Association are athletes.

22. Not every gambler is a criminal.

    Some gamblers are not criminals.

23. Exceptional employees are always rewarded.

    All exceptional employees are recipients of rewards.

24. Few voters think critically.

    Some voters are not critical thinkers.

25. Many Democrats are conservative.

    Some Democrats are conservatives.

26. Wherever there's smoke, there's fire.

    All places there is smoke are places there is fire.

27. Mechanics make great lovers.

    All mechanics are great lovers.

28. The only people who vote are members.

    All voters are members.

29. Angels aren't real.

    No real things are angels.

30. Richard Nixon was not impeached.

    No {people = Richard Nixon} are people who were impeached.

Bank 9-2

Using the square of opposition and the truth value of the first claim, determine what, if anything, follows about the truth values of the other claims.

31. a. True: All surprises are unpleasant events.
    b. No surprises are unpleasant events. *False*
    c. Some surprises are unpleasant events. *True*
    d. Some surprises are not unpleasant events. *False*

32. a. True: Some winters are dry seasons.
    b. No winters are dry seasons. *False*
    c. All winters are dry seasons. *Undetermined*
    d. Some winters are not dry seasons. *Undetermined*

33. a. False: No guppies are egg-layers.
    b. All guppies are egg-layers. *Undetermined*
    c. Some guppies are egg-layers. *True*
    d. Some guppies are not egg-layers. *Undetermined*

34. a. False: Some frozen dinners are nutritious meals.
    b. All frozen dinners are nutritious meals. *False*
    c. No frozen dinners are nutritious meals. *True*
    d. Some frozen dinners are not nutritious meals. *True*

Bank 9-3

Assume that the original claim is true, and follow the directions given. What follows about the truth value of the claim you wind up with?

35. Some uninsured investments are risky deals.
    (Convert this claim, then obvert the result.)

    Some risky deals are not insured investments. (True)

36. All people who win lotteries are people who get lots of mail.
    (Find the contrapositive, then convert.)

    All people who do not win lotteries are people who do not get.lots of mail. (Undetermined: requires converting an A-claim)

37. No medical books are inexpensive books.
    (Convert, then find the contradictory.)

    Some inexpensive books are medical books. (False)

38. Some plutonium-contaminated soil storage areas in New Mexico are not areas that are isolated from drinking-water supplies.
    (Find the obverse, convert that, then find the subcontrary.)

    Some areas that are not isolated from drinking-water supplies are plutonium-contaminated soil storage areas in New Mexico. (Undetermined)

39. All nonisolated computer systems are systems that are at risk from computer viruses.
    (Find the contrapositive, then find the contrary of the result.)

    No systems that are not at risk from computer viruses are isolated computer systems. (False)

40. No public television stations are stations that broadcast commercials.
(Obvert, then convert, and then find the contradictory.)

   Some stations that do not broadcast commercials are not public television stations. (Undetermined: cannot convert an A-claim)

Bank 9-4

Treat these items like those in Exercise 9-9: Determine the truth value of the second claim based on that given for the first. The first few are given as forms, which makes the relationships between terms easier to see. Translation into standard form will be required for most of the remainder. (Many students find this type of problem pretty tough.)

41. a. No Xs are non-Ys. (True)
    b. Some Xs are Ys. *True*

42. a. All Xs are non-Ys. (True)
    b. Some Ys are Xs. *False*

43. a. Some non-Xs are not Ys. (False)
    b. No Xs are non-Ys. *False*

44. a. Optical disks never wear out. (False)
    b. Some disks other than optical disks do sometimes wear out. *Undetermined*

45. a. Some fish from the river have been found to contain toxic levels of trace minerals. (True)
    b. No fish in which toxic levels of trace minerals have not been found have come from the river. *Undetermined*

46. a. Every editorial that Smathers has written has been one in which he attacks the city council. (True)
    b. At least one of the editorials that has not attacked the city council was not written by Smathers. *True*

47. a. British comedies are always more sophisticated than American comedies. (False)
    b. Some comedies that are no more sophisticated than American comedies come from Britain. *True*

48. a. None of the clothes that were bought at Severn's lasted very long. (True)
    b. Some of the clothes that lasted a long time are clothes that were were not bought at Severn's. *True*

49. a. Not everybody who was indicted by the grand jury went to trial. (False)
    b. Some of the people who did not go to trial are people who were not indicted by the grand jury. *True*

50. a. Not everybody who was indicted by the grand jury went to trial. (True)
    b. Some of the people who did not go to trial are people who were not indicted by the grand jury. *False*

Bank 9-5

Reconstruct these as standard-form syllogisms; then, using either Venn diagrams or the rules of the syllogism, determine whether they are valid.

51. All législatures are more influenced by the legal profession than by any other, but it is legislatures that make the rules by which the legal profession operates. So the result is that the bodies that make the rules for the lawyers' profession are bodies most influenced by that very profession.

    All legislatures are bodies influenced most . . .
    All bodies that make rules . . . are legislatures.
    So, all bodies that make rules . . . are bodies influenced most . . .

    Valid

52. Anyone who wants recordings of music that are faithful to the original will find that CDs cannot be surpassed; so, you, too, will find that CDs cannot be surpassed.

    F = people who want recordings of music that are faithful to the original
    C = people who will find that CDs cannot be surpassed
    Y = you

    All F are C.
    [All Y are F.]
    Therefore, all Y are C.   *Valid*

53. Only those courses that are in the schedule will be offered. Among the courses that will not be offered is History 105, History of Europe. Therefore, History 105 is not in the schedule.

    S = courses in the schedule
    O = courses that will be offered
    H = History 105

    All O are S.
    No H are O.
    Therefore, no H are S.   *Invalid*

54. "No country can vote for a man as President who aims to destroy the system he heads. That's why we didn't support [Stipe] Mesic."
    —Borisav Jovic, former president of Yugoslavia

    S = countries that support Mesic
    P = countries that can vote for a man as president who aims to destroy the system he heads
    T = this country

All S are P.
No T are P.
Therefore, no T are S.   *Valid*

55. "Not necessarily, Mr. Dalgliesh. Suppose it's a double bluff. Suppose he's saying in effect, 'Look, I can prove I knew the Whistler was dead. Whoever killed Hilary Robarts didn't know. So why aren't you looking for someone who hadn't been told that the Whistler's body had been found?'"
—P. D. James, *Devices and Desires*

I = I
W = people who knew the Whistler was dead
K = people who killed Hilary Robarts

No W are K.
All I are W.
Therefore, no I are K.   *Valid*

Bank 9-6

Determine whether the following arguments (or, in the case of the first few, forms of arguments) are valid by using either the diagram method or the rules of the syllogism.

56. No Xs are Ys.
Some Ys are not Zs.
So, some Xs are not Zs.   *Invalid*

57. All Xs are Ys.
No Ys are Zs.
So, no Xs are Zs.   *Valid*

58. Some Xs are Ys.
No Zs are Ys.
So, some Xs are not Zs.   *Valid*

59. No coinsurance policies are policies that cover the full value of the property.
Some policies that cover the full value of the property are discounted policies.
So, some discounted policies are not coinsurance policies.

                                           Valid

60. Some early Christians were rationalists.
All early Gnostics were rationalists.
So, some early Gnostics were Christians.   *Invalid*

61. Everybody who exhibits hubris is an arrogant person, and some arrogant people are not sympathetic people. So some people who exhibit hubris are not sympathetic people.

                                           Invalid

62. All the networks devoted considerable attention to reporting poll results during the last election, but many of those poll results were not especially newsworthy. So the networks have to admit that some unnewsworthy items received quite a bit of their attention.

Valid

63. Only people who have lost a job can appreciate the difficulties the loss can cause. Some of the people in this room have lost jobs in the past, so there are people in this room who can appreciate the resulting troubles.

Invalid

Bank 9-7

Here are a few more with term variables defined and the forms supplied.

64. Evergreen trees can't be hardwood, because they aren't deciduous. Hardwood trees are all deciduous.

E = evergreen trees
H = hardwood trees
D = deciduous trees

No E are D.
All H are D.
Therefore, no E are H.   *Valid*

65. In this country, nothing counts except success on the job. And since traditional women's work has not counted as a "job," such work has not been properly appreciated.

X = work that counts (i.e., is appreciated)
Y = successful work "on the job"
Z = traditional women's work

All X are Y.
No Z are Y.
Therefore, no Z are X.   *Valid*

66. From a letter to the editor: "Any project that gets taxpayers' money ought to be one that the taxpayers get some sort of benefit from, don't you think? So if the Federal Aviation Authority is going to pour millions in public funds into automated flight centers at all privately owned airports, then justice can only be served by forcing those airports to begin offering services to the public as well as their current wealthy patrons."

X = automated flight center projects at private airports
Y = projects that get taxpayers' money
Z = projects taxpayers should get some benefit from

All Y are Z.
All X are Y.
Therefore, all X are Z.   *Valid*

67. God, by definition, possesses all perfections. Existence, by definition, is a perfection. Therefore God, by definition, exists.

P = perfections
A = attributes or characteristics of God
E = the class of things identical with existence

All P are A.
All E are P.
Therefore, all E are A.   *Valid*

68. The new dean at Stratford Business School initiated many new policies after taking office. All of the new policies emphasized employee and customer satisfaction. After a conversation with the new dean, an associate dean remarked that since none of the policies of the old curriculum was among those initiated by the dean, the associate dean had to conclude, to his surprise, that none of the old curriculum emphasized employee and customer satisfaction.

X = new policies initiated by the dean
Z = policies that emphasize employee and customer satisfaction
Y = policies of the old curriculum

All X are Z.
No Y are X.
Therefore, all Y are Z.   *Invalid*

Bank 9-8

Here is a batch of syllogisms with unstated premises (or with an unstated conclusion).

69. Whoa, don't enroll in that class, man. That's a physics class; all those people must be brains.

All people in that class are people in a physics class; [all people in a physics class are brains]; therefore, all people in that class are brains. Valid.

70. Nobody can fall off a bike like that and not be injured, so he's injured.

All persons who fall off bikes in that manner are injured persons; [he is a person who fell off a bike in that manner]; therefore, he is an injured person. Valid.

71. It seems like everyone who goes to lots of movies loves Julia Roberts; I guess Becky must go to lots of movies.

All people who go to lots of movies are Julia Roberts fans; [Becky is a Julia Roberts fan]; therefore, Becky is a person who goes to lots of movies. Invalid.

72. Nobody gets married around Christmas except people who don't care about making their friends fight the holiday travel rush, and she couldn't care less about her friends. Draw your own conclusion.

   All people who get married around Christmas are people who don't care about their friends; she is a person who doesn't care about her friends; [therefore, she is a person who will get married around Christmas.] Invalid.

73. Robert Stewart actually thinks computers get in the way of true scholarship. He thinks they make people lazy.

   All people who use computers are people who are lazy; [no people who are lazy are good scholars]; therefore, no people who use computers are good scholars. Valid.

74. The guys must have gone home early, since none of them were at the Bear.

   All members of the guys' group are people not at the Bear; [all people not at the Bear are people who went home early]; therefore, all members of the guys' group are people who went home early. Valid.

75. Granita is a good mood. It's her birthday.

   All people whose birthday it is are people in a good mood; [Granita is a person whose birthday it is;] therefore, Granita is a person in a good mood. Valid.

76. Some family men are not gamblers, since no gamblers are prudes.

   No gamblers are prudes; [some family men are prudes]; therefore, some family men are not gamblers. Valid.

77. If you miss class, you fail the course, because you can't learn anything if you miss class.

   No people who learn something are people who miss class; [all people who pass the course are people who learn something]; therefore, no people who miss class are people who pass the course. Valid.

78. Anyone who missed class failed the course. Therefore, Cecile missed class.

   All people who missed class are people who failed; [Cecile is a person who failed;] therefore, Cecile is a person who missed class. Invalid.

Chapter 10
Deductive Arguments II: Truth-Functional Logic

When students first confront truth-functional logic, some recoil from the symbolizations. They get the idea that there will be a lot to memorize—an idea that can cause trouble if they're not disabused of it right away. In fact, the basic truth tables for the truth-functional symbols are very easy to learn. But a student who doesn't learn them immediately, of course, is going to get absolutely nowhere. We like to give a brief quiz on the basic truth tables as soon as possible to keep students from getting behind.

We said in Chapter 9 that we believe the translation of informal claims into standard-form categorical claims gets students to do some hard thinking about their language. And, when they get things wrong, they realize that things are not as obvious as they had thought. The same holds true for the display of claims' truth-functional forms, the result of the type of symbolization we do in this chapter. We try to make this point early by calling students' attention to items like those found in Bank 10-3, below. This is sometimes unpleasant news, since more students miss those questions than one might think. Things look better after students do their first successful symbolizations. Most of the symbolizations in Exercises 10-1 and 10-2 in the text are not difficult, and students learn quickly that if they're careful, they can learn this stuff.

Exercises Unanswered in the Text

Exercise 10-2

Note: We've given the most obvious symbolizations, but we feel obliged to take anything that's truth-functionally equivalent as correct.

3. $(P \& Q) \to R$

4. $P \& (Q \to R)$

6. $(P \to Q) \& (R \to Q)$

7. $(P \lor R) \to Q$

8. $P \lor (Q \to R)$

9. $(P \lor Q) \to R$

10. $P \to (Q \lor R)$

13. $Q \to P$

14. $\sim Q \lor P$ or: $Q \to P$

15. R v Q or: ~R → P

17. P → Q

18. P → Q

19. Q → R

Exercise 10-3

The following is a selection of truth tables from some of the items in Exercise 10-2. To save space and the tedium of repeating the reference columns, we've laid these items out horizontally.

		#2	#3	#4	#6
P Q R		P → (Q & R)	(P & Q) → R	P & (Q → R)	(P → Q) & (R → Q)
1. T T T		T	T	T	T
2. T T F		F	F	F	T
3. T F T		F	T	T	F
4. T F F		F	T	T	F
5. F T T		T	T	F	T
6. F T F		T	T	F	T
7. F F T		T	T	F	F
8. F F F		T	T	F	T

	#7	#8	#9	#10	#11	#15	#20
	(P v R) → Q	P v (Q → R)	(P v Q) → R	P → (Q v R)	~P → Q	R v Q	~(P v Q)
1.	T	T	T	T	T	T	F
2.	T	T	F	T	T	T	F
3.	F	T	T	T	T	T	F
4.	F	T	F	F	T	F	T
5.	T	T	T	T	T	T	F
6.	T	F	F	T	T	T	F
7.	F	T	T	T	F	T	F
8.	T	T	T	T	F	F	T

Exercise 10-4

For items that are invalid, we've produced only as many rows as are necessary to demonstrate invalidity; that is, when we come across one row in which the premises are true and the conclusion false, we stop. If the item is valid, we just say so, since no row will produce true premises and a false conclusion.

2. Valid

3. Valid

5. Invalid; the second row shows it:

P Q R	P v (Q → R)	Q & ~R	~P
1. T T T	T	F	F
2. T T F	T	T	F

6. Invalid; the fourth row shows it:

P Q R	(P → Q) v (R → Q)	P & (~P → ~R)	Q
1. T T T	T	T	T
2. T T F	T	T	T
3. T F T	F	T	F
4. T F F	T	T	F

8. Valid; the premises are both true in only the second row, and the conclusion is true in that row as well.

9. Invalid; the first row shows it:

L J R	L v ~J	R → J	L → ~R
1. T T T	T	T	F

10. Valid; the table for this one, which is sixteen rows long, demonstrates the virtues of the short truth-table method.

Exercise 10-6

2. 1. P → S   (Premise)
  2. P v Q   (Premise)
  3. Q → R   (Premise) /∴ S v R
  4. S v R   1,2,3, CD

3. 1. R & S   (Premise)
  2. S → P   (Premise) /∴ P
  3. S   1, SIM
  4. P   2,3, MP

5. 1. (P v Q) → R   (Premise)
  2. Q   (Premise) /∴ R
  3. P v Q   2, ADD
  4. R   1,3, MP

6. 1. ~P   (Premise)
  2. ~(R & S) v Q   (Premise)
  3. ~P → ~Q   (Premise) /∴ ~(R & S)
  4. ~Q   1,3, MP
  5. ~(R & S)   2,4, DA

8. 1. P → ~(Q & T)　　　(Premise)
　　2. S → (Q & T)　　　(Premise)
　　3. P　　　　　　　　(Premise)　/∴ ~S
　　4. ~(Q & T)　　　　1,3, MP
　　5. ~S　　　　　　　2,4, MT

9. 1. (P v T) → S　　　(Premise)
　　2. R → P　　　　　(Premise)
　　3. R v Q　　　　　(Premise)
　　4. Q → T　　　　　(Premise)　/∴ S
　　5. P v T　　　　　2,3,4, CD
　　6. S　　　　　　　1,5, MP

Exercise 10-7

2.　4.　. . . . .　1, 3,　DA
　　5.　. . . . .　2,　　SIM
　　6.　. . . . .　4, 5,　MP

3.　4.　. . . . .　1,　　CONTR
　　5.　. . . . .　3,4,　CA
　　6.　. . . . .　2,5,　CA
　　7.　. . . . .　6,　　IMPL
　　8.　. . . . .　7,　　EXPORT

5.　4.　. . . . .　1,　　DEM
　　5.　. . . . .　4,　　SIM
　　6.　. . . . .　2,5,　MT
　　7.　. . . . .　4,　　SIM
　　8.　. . . . .　6,7,　CONJ
　　9.　. . . . .　8,　　DEM
　10.　. . . . .　3,9,　MT

Exercise 10-8

Note: The level of formality you hold your students to is of course up to you. We allow combining double negation with other steps (CONTR, IMPL, and so on). In the items that follow, we've indicated such combinations in the annotation. We probably don't need to indicate that there is usually a different, and equally correct, way of constructing a derivation.

2.　1. ~P v S　　　　(Premise)
　　2. ~T → ~S　　　(Premise)　/∴ P → T
　　3. P → S　　　　1, IMPL

4. S → T	2, CONTR	
5. P → T	3,4, CA	

3.
1. F → R	(Premise)	
2. L → S	(Premise)	
3. ~C	(Premise)	
4. (R & S) → C	(Premise) /∴ ~F v ~L	
5. ~(R & S)	3,4, MT	
6. ~R v ~S	5, DEM	
7. ~F v ~L	1,2,6, DD	

5.
1. (S & R) → P	(Premise)	
2. (R → P) → W	(Premise)	
3. S	(Premise) /∴ W	
4. S → (R → P)	1, EXPORT	
5. R → P	3,4, MP	
6. W	2,5, MP	

6.
1. ~L → (~P → M)	(Premise)	
2. ~(P v L)	(Premise) /∴ M	
3. ~P & ~L	2, DEM	
4. ~L	3, SIM	
5. ~P → M	1,4, MP	
6. ~P	3, SIM	
7. M	5,6, MP	

Note: Students usually hit on such things themselves, but we'll mention it anyhow: When it isn't clear how to proceed, the best strategy sometimes is to work backwards—"I could get *this* if I had *that,* and I could get *that* if I had such-and-such."

8.
1. Q → L	(Premise)	
2. P → M	(Premise)	
3. R v P	(Premise)	
4. R → (Q & S)	(Premise) /∴ ~M → L	
5. P v R	3, COM	
6. ~P → R	5, DN/IMPL	
7. ~P → (Q & S)	4,6, CA	
8. P v (Q & S)	7, IMPL/DN	
9. (P v Q) & (P v S)	8, DIST	
10. P v Q	9, SIM	
11. M v L	1,2,10, CD	
12. ~M → L	11, DN/IMPL	

9.
1. Q → S	(Premise)	
2. P → (S & L)	(Premise)	

3. ~P → Q	(Premise)
4. S → R	(Premise) /∴ R & S
5. P v Q	3, IMPL/DN
6. (S & L) v S	1,2,5, CD
7. S v (S & L)	6, COM
8. (S v S) & (S v L)	7, DIST
9. S v S	8, SIM
10. S	9, TAUT
11. R	4,10, MP
12. R & S	10,11 CONJ

Exercise 10-9

2. ~C v B

3. B v (~D → C)

5. C → ~D

6. ~(D v B) or: ~D & ~B

8. ~C → (D & ~B)

9. ~C → D

Exercise 10-10

2. c

3. a

5. e

6. b

8. d

Exercise 10-11

Be careful with this exercise—some of these require a tricky step.

2.
1. (P v Q) & R	(Premise)	
2. (R & P) → S	(Premise)	
3. (Q & R) → S	(Premise) /∴ S	
4. R & (P v Q)	1, COM	
5. (R & P) v (R & Q)	4, DIST	

243

6. (R & P) v (Q & R)	5, COM
7. S v S	2,3,6, CD
8. S	7, TAUT

3.
1. P → (Q → ~R)	(Premise)	
2. (~R → S) v T	(Premise)	
3. ~T & P	(Premise) /∴ Q → S	
4. P	3, SIM	
5. Q → ~R	1,4, MP	
6. ~T	3, SIM	
7. ~R → S	2,6 DA	
8. Q → S	5,7 CA	

5.
1. (P → Q) & R	(Premise)
2. ~S	(Premise)
3. S v (Q → S)	(Premise) /∴ P → T
4. Q → S	2,3, DA
5. ~Q	2,4, MT
6. P → Q	1, SIM
7. ~P	5,6, MT
8. ~P v T	7, ADD
9. P → T	8, IMPL

6.
1. P → (Q & R)	(Premise)
2. R → (Q → S)	(Premise) /∴ P → S
3. (R & Q) → S	2, EXPORT
4. (Q & R) → S	3, COM
5. P → S	1,4, CA

This next one could be shortened if you combine double negation with other steps.

8.
1. ~P v ~Q	(Premise)
2. (Q → S) → R	(Premise) /∴ P → R
3. ~R → ~(Q → S)	2, CONTR
4. ~ ~R v ~(Q → S)	3, IMPL
5. R v ~(Q → S)	4, DN
6. R v ~(~Q v S)	5, IMPL
7. R v (~ ~Q & ~S)	6, DeM
8. R v (Q & ~S)	7, DN
9. (R v Q) & (R v ~S)	8, DIST
10. R v Q	9, SIM
11. Q v R	10 COM
12. ~Q → R	11 IMPL

| 13. P → ~Q | 1, IMPL |
| 14. P → R | 12,13, CA |

9.
1. S	(Premise)
2. P → (Q & R)	(Premise)
3. Q → ~S	(Premise) /∴ ~P
4. ~~S	1, DN
5. ~Q	3,4, MT
6. ~Q v ~R	5, ADD
7. ~(Q & R)	6, DᴇM
8. ~P	2,7, MT

Exercise 10-12

2.
1. P → Q	(Premise)
2. R → Q	(Premise) /∴ (P v R) → Q
③ P v R	CP Premise
4. Q v Q	1,2,3, CD
5. Q	4, TAUT
6. (P v R) → Q	3–5, CP

3.
1. P → (Q → R)	(Premise) /∴ (P → Q) → (P → R)
② P → Q	CP Premise
③ P	CP Premise
4. Q → R	1,3, MP
5. Q	2,3, MP
6. R	4,5, MP
7. P → R	3–6, CP
8. (P → Q) → (P → R)	2–7, CP

5.
1. ~P → (~Q → ~R)	(Premise)
2. ~(R & ~P) → ~S	(Premise) /∴ S → Q
③ S	CP Premise
4. ~~S	3, DN
5. ~~(R & ~P)	2,4, MT
6. R & ~P	5, DN
7. ~P	6, SIM
8. ~Q → ~R	1,7, MP
9. R → Q	8, CONTR
10. R	6, SIM
11. Q	9,10, MP
12. S → Q	3–11, CP

6. 1. P → (Q → R)   (Premise)
    2. (T → S) & (R → T)   (Premise) /∴ P → (Q → S)
    3. P   CP Premise
    4. Q   CP Premise
    5. Q → R   1,3, MP
    6. R   4,5, MP
    7. R → T   2, SIM
    8. T   6,7, MP
    9. T → S   2, SIM
   10. S   8,9, MP
   11. Q → S   4–10, CP
   12. P → (Q → S)   3–11, CP

8. 1. (P v Q) → R   (Premise)
    2. (P → S) → T   (Premise) /∴ R v T
    3. ~R   CP Premise
    4. ~(P v Q)   1,3, MT
    5. ~P & ~Q   4, DEM
    6. ~P   5, SIM
    7. ~P v S   6, ADD
    8. P → S   7, IMPL
    9. T   2,8, MP
   10. ~R → T   3–9, CP
   11. R v T   10, IMPL

9. 1. P → ~Q   (Premise)
    2. ~R → (S & Q)   (Premise) /∴ P → R
    3. P   CP Premise
    4. ~Q   1,3, MP
    5. ~S v ~Q   4, ADD
    6. ~(S & Q)   5, DEM
    7. ~ ~R   2,6, MT
    8. R   7, DN
    9. P → R   3–8, CP

Exercise 10-13

2. U → (Q v D)
   J → ~D   /∴ ~J v Q

Invalid: The following assignment of truth values (which would occur in the next-to-last row of the truth table for the argument) makes both premises true and the conclusion false:

$$\frac{U \quad Q \quad D \quad J}{F \quad F \quad F \quad T}$$

3. *Valid, as per the following derivation (in which, in step 4, we start combining DN and other steps—in this case, CONTR):*

1. ~R v A	(Premise)
2. A → E	(Premise)
3. M → ~E	(Premise) /∴ ~R v ~M
4. E → ~M	3, DN/CONTR
5. A → ~M	2,4, CA
6. R → A	1, IMPL
7. R → ~M	5,6, CA
8. ~R v ~M	7, IMPL

5. V → O
   T → O   /∴ V → T

Invalid, as per the following:

$$\frac{V \quad O \quad T}{T \quad T \quad F}$$

6. (C & (N & T)) → E
   E → P
   ~P & C   /∴ ~N & ~T

Invalid:

$$\frac{C \quad N \quad T \quad E \quad P}{T \quad F \quad T \quad F \quad F}$$

8. *Valid, as per the following deduction:*

1. G → (L → D)	(Premise)
2. L & ~D	(Premise) /∴ ~G
3. ~~L & ~D	2, DN
4. ~(~L v D)	3, DEM
5. ~(L → D)	4, IMPL
6. ~G	1,5, MT

9. *Here's the symbolization, with an assignment of claim letters:*

   C = The creation story in Genesis is compatible with the theory of evolution.
   L = The creation story is taken literally.
   E = There is plenty of evidence for the theory of evolution.
   T = The creation story is true.

   C → ~L
   E → (~C → ~T)   /∴ L → ~T

   Invalid:

C	L	E	T
F	T	F	T

11. *Valid, as per this deduction:*

1. ~M → H	(Premise)	
2. (H → I) & (I → C)	(Premise) /∴ ~M → C	
3. H → I	2, SIM	
4. I → C	2, SIM	
5. ~M → I	1,3, CA	
6. ~M → C	4,5, CA	

12. *Valid:*

1. ~T v N	(Premise)
2. ~T → W	(Premise)
3. N → D	(Premise) /∴ D v W
4. T → N	1, IMPL
5. ~D → ~N	3, CONTR
6. ~N → ~T	4, CONTR
7. ~D → ~T	5,6, CA
8. ~D → W	2,7, CA
9. D v W	8, IMPL

14. *Valid, as per the following deduction. The symbolization can be confusing; here's how we did it:*

    B = Jane goes on eating binges for no apparent reason.
    F = Jane looks forward to times when she can eat alone.
    S = Jane eats sensibly in front of others.
    A = Jane makes up for it when she's alone.
    D = Jane has an eating disorder.

    In the first premise, the parentheses look more confusing than they actually are. You can help students by building the symbolization up from its parts.

1. (B v (A v (S & M))) → D	(Premise)
2. B	(Premise) /∴ D

| 3. B v (A v (S & M)) | 2, ADD |
| 4. D | 1,3, MP |

15. *Valid:*

1. I & (I → M)	(Premise)
2. (M → G) & (G → C)	(Premise) /∴ C
3. M → G	2, SIM
4. G → C	2, SIM
5. I	1, SIM
6. I → M	1, SIM
7. M	5,6 MP
8. G	3,7, MP
9. C	4,8, MP

Chapter 10 Test Question/Exercise Banks

Bank 10-1

Symbolize the following claims, using the letters indicated.

P = We plant perennials.
A = We plant annuals.
S = We plant from seed.
C = We plant from cuttings.

1. If we plant from seed, we'll have to plant annuals.

   S → A

2. We can plant perennials only if we plant from cuttings.

   P → C

3. The only way we can plant from seed is to plant annuals.

   S → A

4. If we plant both annuals and perennials, then we can plant from both seed and cuttings.

   (A & P) → (S & C)

5. We cannot plant perennials if we plant from either seed or from cuttings.

   (S v C) → ~P

6. If we don't plant from seed, then we can't plant either annuals or perennials.

   $\sim S \rightarrow \sim (A \vee P)$

7. We can't plant perennials unless we plant from cuttings.

   $\sim P \vee C \quad or \quad P \rightarrow C$

8. The only way we can plant both annuals and perennials is by planting from both cuttings and seed.

   $(A \& P) \rightarrow (C \& S)$

9. Either we will plant from cuttings, or, if we don't plant perennials, we can plant from seed.

   $C \vee (\sim P \rightarrow S)$

10. We can plant neither perennials nor annuals if we don't plant from both cuttings and seed.

    $\sim (C \& S) \rightarrow \sim (P \vee A)$

Bank 10-2

Follow the same directions given in the preceding bank.

W = Wildlife are (or will be) threatened.
A = Agricultural production is increased.
P = The use of pesticides is continued.

11. The only way we can avoid threatening wildlife is to avoid increasing agricultural production.

    $\sim W \rightarrow \sim A$

12. We cannot both increase agricultural production and avoid threatening wildlife.

    $\sim (A \& \sim W)$

13. If we are to increase agricultural production, we'll have to continue the use of pesticides, but if we do that wildlife will be threatened.

    $(A \rightarrow P) \& (P \rightarrow W)$

14. Wildlife will not be threatened provided we do not continue the use of pesticides.

    $\sim P \rightarrow \sim W$

15. Wildlife will be threatened if either agricultural production is increased or pesticide use is continued.

    $(A \vee P) \rightarrow W$

16. The continuation of pesticide use will be sufficient to ensure that wildlife will be threatened.

    $P \rightarrow W$

17. The continued use of pesticides is necessary for increased agricultural production.

    $A \rightarrow P$

18. Together, the continued use of pesticides and the increase in agricultural production will guarantee that wildlife will be threatened.

    $(P \ \& \ A) \rightarrow W$

19. Agricultural production will not increase even though the use of pesticides will continue.

    $\sim A \ \& \ P$

20. While pesticide use will continue, agricultural production will not increase.

    $P \ \& \sim A$

Bank 10-3

Determine which of the lettered claims is equivalent to the numbered ones. You will have to use one letter twice. (These are easy to do if students symbolize the claims first and have some familiarity either with truth tables or with the group II rules for derivations—the truth-functional equivalences.)

A. If Steve can give blood, then he has been tested.
B. If Steve has been tested, then he can give blood.
C. Steve cannot give blood, and he has not been tested.
D. Steve has not been tested, but he can give blood.

21. Steve can give blood if he has been tested.

    Equivalent to B

22. Steve cannot give blood unless he has been tested.

    Equivalent to A

23. Although Steve can give blood, he has not been tested.

    Equivalent to D

24. It's necessary for Steve to be tested in order for him to give blood.

    Equivalent to A

25. Steve can neither be tested nor give blood.

    Equivalent to C

Bank 10-4

For each of the following argument symbolizations, assign truth values to the letters to show the argument's invalidity. (There is only one such assignment for each— one counterexample—so these are easy to grade.)

26. Q v P
    ~Q → ~R   /∴ R → P

    P = F
    Q = T
    R = T

27. ~Q → P
    R v S
    Q → ~S   /∴ R

    P = T
    Q = F
    R = F
    S = T

28. P v Q
    P → R   /∴ R → Q

    P = T
    Q = F
    R = T

29. ~R → ~Q
    ~P → (R & Q)   /∴ P

    R = T
    Q = T
    P = F

30. (Q & P) → R
    S → ~R   /∴ S → ~Q

    Q = T
    P = F
    R = F
    S = T

31. S → (P v R)
    Q → S   /∴ Q → P

    S = T
    P = F
    R = T
    Q = T

32. T → ~S
    S v ~Q
    ~T → (Q v R)   /∴ ~Q → R

    T = T
    S = F
    Q = F
    R = F

33. (Q & S) → (P v R)
    T → Q
    ~T v S   /∴ T → R

    Q = T
    S = T
    P = T
    R = F
    T = T

34. P → (Q → S)
    Q v R   /∴ (P & R) → S

    P = T
    Q = F
    S = F
    R = T

35. P → (Q v R)
    ~(Q → R)
    S → P   /∴ ~S

    P = T
    Q = T
    R = F
    S = T

36. P v Q
    (Q & R) → S
    ~P → ~R   /∴ R → S

    P = T
    Q = F
    R = T
    S = F

37. P v (Q → R)
    S → ~(P v R)   /∴ S → Q

253

$P = F$
$Q = F$
$R = F$
$S = T$

38. ~L & ~S
    (P v Q) → L   /.∴ Q v S

    $L = F$
    $S = F$
    $P = F$
    $Q = F$

39. P → (T & R)
    (R → S) v T
    ~(S & Q)   /.∴ Q → ~P

    $P = T$
    $T = T$
    $R = T$
    $S = F$
    $Q = T$

40. ~P v (Q → R)
    Q → (R v S)   /.∴ Q → (~P v S)

    $P = T$
    $Q = T$
    $R = T$
    $S = F$

Bank 10-5

Use the short truth-table method to determine whether these are valid or invalid.

41. P → Q
    Q → R
    R → S
    P   /.∴ S v T

    Valid

42. A → B
    C → D
    B v D   /.∴ A v C

    Invalid: $A = F$
                 $B = T$
                 $C = F$
                 $D = T \text{ or } F$

254

43. A → B
    ~D → ~C
    ~D
    ~C → ~B   /∴ ~A

    Valid

44. A → B
    ~C v D
    E → F
    G → H
    A v C
    E v G   /∴ (B v D) v (F v H)

    Valid

45. A → B
    C → D
    ~(~A & ~C)   /∴ ~B → (D & ~B)

    Valid

46. ~E v ~D
    ~(A → C)
    ~(~B v ~E)
    ~(A & B) v (C → D)   /∴ ~A

    Invalid: A = T
                B = T
                C = F
                D = F
                E = T

47. P → Q
    ~Q v R
    ~(R & ~S)
    ~P   /∴ ~S

    Invalid: P = F
                Q = F
                R = F
                S = T

48. P → (Q & R)
    R → (T v S)
    ~T v (U & ~W)
    P   /∴ ~W

255

Invalid: $P = T$
$Q = T$
$R = T$
$S = T$
$T = F$
$U = T \text{ or } F$
$W = T$

49. M → (N → O)
(~N v O) → ~P
P   /∴ ~M

Valid

50. P → Q
~(Q & ~R)
~R v S
~(S & ~T)
T   /∴ P

Invalid: $P = F$
$Q = F$
$R = F$
$S = F$
$T = T$

Bank 10-6

Using only rules from group I, construct deductions to prove the following symbolized arguments valid. (These are pretty simple, but they're good for getting students used to formatting deductions, seeing complicated cases of simple symbolizations ("substitution instances"), and realizing that group I rules can be used only on entire lines—three of the main problems encountered early in this kind of work.)

51. 1. P → (Q & R)   (Premise)
     2. (Q & R) → S   (Premise) /∴ P → S

     3. *P → S*   *1,2, CA*

52. 1. P → Q   (Premise)
     2. P v R   (Premise)
     3. R → (S & T)   (Premise) /∴ Q v (S & T)

     4. *Q v (S & T)*   *1,2,3, CD*

53. 1. (P & Q) → (R v S)   (Premise)
     2. (R v S) → T   (Premise)
     3. P & Q   (Premise) /∴ T

4. R v S	1,3, MP
5. T	2,4, MP

54.
1. (R v Q) & S	(Premise)
2. (R v Q) → ~P	(Premise)
3. P v T	(Premise) /∴ T
4. R v Q	1, SIM
5. ~P	2,4, MP
6. T	3,5, DA

55.
1. P → (S v T)	(Premise)
2. S → Q	(Premise)
3. P	(Premise)
4. T → R	(Premise) /∴ Q v R
5. S v T	1,3, MP
6. Q v R	2,4,5, CD

56.
1. ~P & Q	(Premise)
2. R → P	(Premise) /∴ Q & ~R
3. ~P	1, SIM
4. ~R	2,3, MT
5. Q	1, SIM
6. Q & ~R	4,5, CONJ

57.
1. P → M	(Premise)
2. ~M v ~Q	(Premise)
3. S → Q	(Premise)
4. (~P v ~S) → R	(Premise) /∴ R
5. ~P v ~S	1,2,3, DD
6. R	4,5, MP

58.
1. Q → (P → R)	(Premise)
2. ~R & Q	(Premise) /∴ ~P
3. Q	2, SIM
4. P → R	1,3, MP
5. ~R	2, SIM
6. ~P	4,5, MT

59.
1. (P v Q) → (X & Z)	(Premise)
2. (X → W) & (Z → Y)	(Premise)
3. P	(Premise) /∴ W & Y

4. P v Q	3, ADD
5. X & Z	1,4, MP
6. X	5, SIM
7. X → W	2, SIM
8. W	6,7, MP
9. Z	5, SIM
10. Z → Y	2, SIM
11. Y	9,10, MP
12. W & Y	8,11, CONJ

60.
1. (P v Q) → M	(Premise)
2. S v ~M	(Premise)
3. L	(Premise)
4. L → ~S	(Premise) /∴ ~(P v Q)
5. ~S	3,4, MP
6. ~M	2,5, DA
7. ~(P v Q)	1,6, MT

Bank 10-7

Using rules from both group I and group II, construct deductions to prove that the following are valid.

61.
1. P & Q	(Premise)
2. R v ~(P & Q)	(Premise) /∴ R
3. ~~(P & Q)	1, DN
4. R	2,3, DA

62.
1. ~(P v Q)	(Premise) /∴ ~Q
2. ~P & ~Q	1, DEM
3. ~Q	2, SIM

63.
1. (P v Q) & (P v R)	(Premise)
2. ~P	(Premise) /∴ Q & R
3. P v (Q & R)	1, DIST
4. Q & R	2,3 DA

64.
1. P v Q	(Premise)
2. Q → R	(Premise) /∴ ~P → R
3. ~P → Q	1, IMPL
4. ~P → R	2,3, CA

65. 1. P → Q   (Premise)
    2. R → Q   (Premise)
    3. P v R   (Premise) /∴ Q

    4. *Q v Q*   *1,2,3 CD*
    5. *Q*   *4, TAUT*

66. 1. P v ~Q   (Premise)
    2. R → Q   (Premise) /∴ R → P

    3. *~Q v P*   *1, COM*
    4. *Q → P*   *3, IMPL*
    5. *R → P*   *2,4, CA*

67. 1. P v (Q & R)   (Premise)
    2. Q → ~R   (Premise) /∴ P

    3. *~Q v ~R*   *2, IMPL*
    4. *~(Q & R)*   *3, DEM*
    5. *P*   *1,4, DA*

68. 1. (M v P) → Q   (Premise)
    2. Q → (~L v R)   (Premise)
    3. (L → R) → S   (Premise) /∴ (M v P) → S

    4. *(M v P) → (~L v R)*   *1,2, CA*
    5. *(M v P) → (L → R)*   *4, IMPL*
    6. *(M v P) → S*   *3,5, CA*

This item shows the advantage of the deductive method for proving validity over even the short truth-table method: Only a modest familiarity with CA and IMPL is required to do this problem in one's head.

69. 1. P → ~(M & R)   (Premise)
    2. ~P → Q   (Premise) /∴ ~Q → (~M v ~R)

    3. *~Q → P*   *2, DN/CONTR*
    4. *~Q → ~(M & R)*   *3,1, CA*
    5. *~Q → (~M v ~R)*   *4, DEM*

70. 1. P v (Q & P)   (Premise)
    2. P → R   (Premise) /∴ R

    3. *(P v Q) & (P v P)*   *1, DIST*
    4. *P v P*   *3, SIM*
    5. *P*   *4, TAUT*
    6. *R*   *2,5, MP*

259

71. 1. P → (Q → R)   (Premise)   /∴ Q → (P → R)

     2. *(P & Q) → R*   *1, EXPORT*
     3. *(Q & P) → R*   *2, COM*
     4. *Q → (P → R)*   *3, EXPORT*

72. 1. (P → Q) & (R → S)   (Premise)
     2. Q → ~S   (Premise)
     3. ~T → (P & R)   (Premise)   /∴ T

     4. *P → Q*   *1, SIM*
     5. *R → S*   *1, SIM*
     6. *~Q v ~S*   *2, IMPL*
     7. *~P v ~R*   *4,5,6, DD*
     8. *~(P & R)*   *7, DEM*
     9. *T*   *3,8, MT/DN*

73. 1. P → (Q & R)   (Premise)
     2. ~S → ~(Q v R)   (Premise)   /∴ P → S

     3. *~P v (Q & R)*   *1, IMPL*
     4. *(~P v Q) & (~P v R)*   *3, DIST*
     5. *~P v Q*   *4, SIMP*
     6. *(~P v Q) v R*   *5, ADD*
     7. *~P v (Q v R)*   *6, ASSOC*
     8. *P → (Q v R)*   *7, IMPL*
     9. *(Q v R) → S*   *2, CONTR*
     10. *P → S*   *8,9, CA*

Examples like the next one are not designed to show off the deductive method, obviously; but you can't have a rule for everything, can you?

74. 1. P → (Q & R)   (Premise)
     2. R → (S v T)   (Premise)   /∴ ~(~P v S) → T

     3. *~P v (Q & R)*   *1, IMPL*
     4. *~P v (R & Q)*   *3, COM*
     5. *(~P v R) & (~P v Q)*   *4, DIST*
     6. *~P v R*   *5, SIM*
     7. *P → R*   *6, IMPL*
     8. *P → (S v T)*   *2,7, CA*
     9. *P → (~S → T)*   *8, DN/IMPL*
     10. *(P & ~S) → T*   *9, EXPORT*
     11. *(~~P & ~S) → T*   *10, DN*
     12. *~(~P v S) → T*   *11, DEM*

75. 1. P → (Q & R)   (Premise)
     2. ~(S & Q)   (Premise)
     3. (R → S) & Q   (Premise)   /∴ ~P

     4. ~S v ~Q   2, DEM
     5. ~Q v ~S   4, COM
     6. Q → ~S   5, IMPL
     7. Q   3, SIM
     8. ~S   6,7, MP
     9. R → S   3, SIM
     10. ~R   8,9, MT
     11. ~R v ~Q   10, ADD
     12. ~(R & Q)   11, DEM
     13. ~(Q & R)   12, COM
     14. ~P   1,14, MT

Bank 10-8

The following examples can be used for symbolization practice, for determining invalidity, or for constructing deductions. We've indicated which ones are valid and which invalid, and we've produced counterexamples or deductions for some. Sample directions:

Symbolize the following arguments, and test them for validity. For those that are valid, construct a deduction; for those that are invalid, assign truth values that show that the premises can be true while the conclusion is false. Use the following letters for (76) through (80):

D = The drought will continue.
S = We get an early storm.
M = Managers of the ski areas will be happy.
F = There will be great fire danger next year.

76. The drought will continue if we don't get a storm. If we do get a storm, the managers of the ski areas will be happy. Since we'll either get a storm or we won't, it follows that either the drought will continue or the ski area managers will be happy.

   Valid
   1. ~S → D   (Premise)
   2. S → M   (Premise)
   3. S v ~S   (Premise) /∴ D v M
   4. D v M   1,2,3 CD

77. Unless an early storm moves in, the drought will continue, and there will be great danger of fire next year. But the drought is not going to continue. Therefore, there will not be a great danger of fire next year.

   Invalid

   $\sim S \rightarrow (D \,\& \, F)$

   $\sim D$ /∴ $\sim F$

   $S = T;\ D = F;\ F = T$

78. If there's no early storm, the drought will continue. And if the drought continues, there will be a great danger of fire next year. So, if there is to be no great danger of fire next year, there must be an early storm.

   Valid

   1. $\sim S \rightarrow D$ (Premise)
   2. $D \rightarrow F$ (Premise) /∴ $\sim F \rightarrow S$
   3. $\sim S \rightarrow F$ 1,2, CA
   4. $\sim F \rightarrow S$ 3, CONTR/DN

79. There will be a great danger of fire next year only if the drought continues, and it will continue unless we get an early storm. However, if we do get an early storm, the ski area managers will be happy. So if the ski area managers are not happy, it'll mean that there's going to be a great danger of fire next year.

   Invalid

   $(F \rightarrow D) \,\& \, (\sim S \rightarrow D)$

   $S \rightarrow M$ /∴ $\sim M \rightarrow F$

   $F = F;\ D = T;\ S = F;\ M = F$

80. Either there will be an early storm, or the drought will continue. If there's no continuation of the drought, then the managers of the ski areas will be happy and there will be no great danger of fire next year. So if we're both to avoid any great danger of fire next year and to make the ski area managers happy, it will be necessary for there to be an early storm.

   Invalid

   $E \lor D$

   $\sim D \rightarrow (M \,\& \sim F)$ /∴ $(F \,\& \, M) \rightarrow S$

   $E = T$ or $F;\ D = T;\ M = T;\ F = T;\ S = F$

81. If a flyer is on one of the bulletin boards, then you know it was approved by the Associated Students, and that flyer was approved. Therefore, it's on one of the bulletin boards somewhere.

   Invalid

82. If it's going to be a cool spring, then the azaleas will need extra fertilizer. Indications are, however, that it's not going to be a cool spring.

    Invalid [Unstated conclusion: The azaleas won't need extra fertilizer.]

83. If she can play the tuba, then she can darn well play the baritone. And if she can play the baritone, then she can play the French horn. We can conclude that she can play the tuba, therefore, she can play the French horn.

    Invalid

84. If we don't see the movie tonight, we won't be able to talk about it in class. And if we can't talk about it in class, we won't make Ms. Schmidt very happy. So let's see the movie. Then Ms. Schmidt will be happy.

    Invalid

85. Look, if the check bounced, then you're right: Two things happened. First, we'd owe a penalty. And second, our records would be out of whack. Now, if our records are out of whack or if we pay a penalty—either way—then we're in big trouble, just like you said. The check isn't gonna bounce, though. So relax. We're not in any trouble.

    Invalid

86. If he doesn't think he'll pass the class, then either he'll be talking to someone, or he won't be paying attention, or both. Well, look at him. He's talking to someone. And he's not paying the least bit of attention. Clearly he doesn't think he'll pass the class.

    Invalid

87. Either she ordered the eggplant, or she ordered the calamari, though possibly she might have ordered both. Well, she ordered the eggplant. So, she didn't order the calamari.

    Invalid

88. She must not have ordered the eggplant, 'cause if she ordered it, then she wouldn't be eating any dessert like she's doing right now.

    Valid

89. It's easy enough to do logic if you think logically. Fortunately, I have no trouble doing logic, so I guess I think logically.

    Invalid

90. It's time to leave when they start putting up the chairs, as they're doing right now.

    Valid [Unstated conclusion: it's time to leave.]

91. In a class like this, it's necessary to work a lot of problems on your own in order to be familiar with the material, and such familiarity is necessary to do well on the exams. So if you work a lot of problems on your own, you'll do well on the exams.

    Invalid

92. It's not true that Alberto and John will both attend the meeting. I did learn, however, that if either Susan or Allene goes, John plans to go for sure. Therefore, If Alberto goes, it means neither Susan nor Allene is going.

    Valid

93. If the current economic policies were to put an end to the recession, then the administration would deserve a round of applause. But there can be no end to the recession without the creation of a large number of decent-paying jobs. It follows, then, that the only way the administration is going to get a round of applause is if a large number of decent-paying jobs get created.

    Invalid

94. I finally discovered the mystery of why hard beds are good for you. Here's the story: If you have a hard bed, then you cannot stay comfortable for long periods, and when you can't stay comfortable for long periods you roll around a lot. If you roll around a lot, then your joints don't ache from being in one position too long. Therefore, if your joints ache in the morning from sleeping too long in one position, then you don't have a hard bed.

    Valid

95. Either the bank made a mistake, or none of this month's deposits has been recorded. If our accountant is correct, then all the accounts have been reconciled. If it is not the case that none of the month's deposits has been recorded, then all the accounts could not have been reconciled. I have checked with our accountant, and he is indeed correct. Therefore, the only alternative is that the bank made a mistake.

    Valid

Chapter 11
Inductive Arguments

This chapter of the text presents a series of questions that we think a reasonable person should consider when encountering inductive arguments. Not all of the arguments in the text's exercises or in the ones below—or in daily life—respond tractably to all the questions. So students should not be led to think that the questions should be applied unthinkingly and mechanically, as if the result of doing so will be an easy final evaluation of the argument at issue. The purpose of the questions is to help students deal thoughtfully with these types of arguments—to help students understand the arguments (which is crucial to everything else, of course) and to help uncover their strengths and weaknesses.

One point we think is worth emphasizing is that technical arguments—for example, the polls discussed in this chapter and the scientific studies discussed in the next—depend for their reliability on exactly the same kinds of considerations our everyday reasoning depends on. Students often get the idea that "serious" thinking is something foreign to their everyday affairs. It may help if they realize that a person who shouts, "Okay, try to start it again, but this time don't touch the gas pedal," is trying to do the same thing—isolate a variable's effects—just as a technician might in a fancy laboratory study.

Then again, it may not help. Some semesters, it's hard to tell.

Exercises Unanswered in the Text

Exercise 11-1

2. Our five previous visits

3. 100 percent

5. You would want diversity regarding the season, which the argument provides.

Exercise 11-2

2. Clifford's previous four attempts

3. 100 percent

5. The argument would be even stronger if the rides took place in different terrains and under different conditions and if Clifford had ridden different types of bicycles and had been in various states of readiness.

6. This weakens the argument.

8. This strengthens the argument.

9. This strengthens the argument.

Exercise 11-3

Arguments like the ones in Exercise 11-3 confirm the claim that a little learning is a dangerous thing—or at least it can be confusing. In particular, knowing that one factor is relevant to a conclusion can confuse the issue of whether its addition makes a given argument stronger or weaker. Let's consider a supposition similar to the one in item 3 of this exercise, namely, that this year will be a wetter year than the three previous years. Now, people who know about mildew can tell you that wetter weather will *increase* the likelihood that the artichokes will get it, and it is thus correct to say that the conclusion is *more* likely. But is this not the same as saying that the original argument is stronger. Added to that argument, the consideration about wetter weather produces a *difference* between the sample and the target, which *weakens* the original argument. It's hard to get students to keep in mind that the idea behind the original argument is that, *ceteris paribus,* similarities between sample and target make the argument stronger; dissimilarities weaken it.

What's confusing about the current case, of course, is that the additional consideration provides an *additional argument for the same conclusion:* Wetter weather increases the likelihood of mildew; this year is wetter; therefore, this year the likelihood of mildew is greater. But the fact that this argument makes the conclusion of the original argument *more likely to be true* is different from saying that it makes the original argument *stronger.*

2. Relevant, stronger

3. Relevant, stronger

5. Relevant, weaker

6. Irrelevant, as far as we can see

8. Irrevelant, weaker

9. Not relevant

Exercise 11-4

1. Claghorn's senatorial performance is the sample; his potential presidential performance is the target. Excellence is the characteristic in question, whatever the speaker means by "excellent." The sample is diversified and it is indeed a reasonable bet that the speaker will be pleased with Claghorn as president.

3. Homer's appearance is the sample; the state of the Barneses' house upon their return is the target. Whatever the Barneses find "neat and tidy" is the characteristic. The important differences between the sample and target make this a weak argument.

4. The seven presidential elections from 1968 to 1992 are the sample; some future election is the target. The characteristic in question is victory for the more conservative candidate. The conclusion of the argument is that the next election will be won by the more conservative candidate. The argument is not particularly strong, since social, economic, and political circumstances can change dramatically and since the

personalities of candidates can have an important effect on elections. Also, the sample is small, and the percentage of its members with the property is small.

6. The sample is a household budget, and the target is the federal budget. The characteristic is "asking for trouble," and what it is for something as complicated as the federal budget to have this characteristic is altogether too vague for the argument to be much good. Also, there are enormous differences between the federal budget and a household budget; further, a temporarily unbalanced budget in some households does not produce the "trouble" that seems to be claimed here.

7. I am the sample, you are the target, and the characteristic is experiencing the same thing that we both refer to with the same word, that is, "pain." (We tend to emphasize the difficulties in this argument, because lower-division university students are not apt to see them straight off.)

9. Oregon's bottle law is the sample; Michigan's bottle law is the target. The characteristic is "cleaned up the highways and provided extra jobs." There are differences between the states, but these do not seem particularly relevant to the issue. The argument is not a weak one.

10. The sample is existence in fish bodies. The target is existence is nonmaterial "bodies" or environments. The characteristic is retention of personal consciousness or identity. The strength of the argument depends on the similarities and differences between the two cases. Those who believe in a disembodied afterlife will see enormous differences between sample and target (e.g., the desire and support of God for the disembodied survivors); those who don't so believe won't see such differences. The item could also be analyzed as a persuasive comparison.

Exercise 11-5

2. A generalization whose conclusion is stated in terms of a percentage of the target is a statistical generalization.

3. The target is the class the conclusion is about.

5. A random sample is one in which every individual in the population has an equal chance of being selected.

Exercise 11-6

2. Students from Tulare State

3. Belief in God

5. Yes. They should diminish our confidence.

6. Yes. It should diminish our confidence, because many people may change their views (either way) during the course of their college careers. Such changes might result from their college experience, from other kinds of experience, or simply from becoming older or more mature.

8. Yes. It should increase our confidence.

9. Yes. It should diminish our confidence (since more people with one view may choose to respond).

Exercise 11-12

Something like, ". . . which means the poll is consistent with as few as 49 percent in favor of the ban, which means the poll does *not* show that a majority favor it."

Exercise 11-13

2. No

3. Yes

5. No

6. Yes

Exercise 11-14

2. Students in Professor Ludlum's history classes

3. That a majority find him lacking

5. Yes: Students with an animus toward Ludlum may be more likely to write evaluations.

6. No

8. It is much too small.

Exercise 11-15

2. Hasty generalization

3. Hasty generalization

5. Biased generalization

6. Hasty generalization

7. No fallacy

8. Hasty generalization, biased generalization

9. Anecdotal evidence

11. Biased generalization

13. Hasty generalization

14. Hasty generalization

Exercise 11-16

1. Over the long haul, a given number will come up once in every 38 spins. When the number comes up, a one-dollar bet on it will win thirty-five dollars—as if the chances were 1 in 36 instead of 1 in 38. This 2-in-38 difference is the house advantage; it computes to 5.2 in 100— a little over 5 percent. (For nongamblers—in case anybody asks—the house also collects all bets made on red, black, odd, even, and other "outside" bets when the zeros come up; these bets work out to the same 5.2% advantage to the house.)

2. One source for this sort of thing is *Playboy's Book of Games* (Chicago: 1972), by Edwin Silberstang. The odds can be calculated for any bet, however, by comparing the likelihood of a win against the amount paid off should one win. Leaving aside cases of 21 (blackjack), where the odds change with each play because of the change in the cards remaining in the deck, the best bet a person can make in an American casino is in the game of craps. Bets made on the "pass," "don't pass," "come," or "don't come" line favor the house somewhat, but "odds bets" (bets placed behind the original bet) are dead-even: They pay off at exactly the same rate as one has of winning. (I.e., if the chances of winning are 5 against 6, the house pays winners six dollars for each five wagered.) That makes craps the best "no-skill" game.

    We've seen several books on gambling that, after identifying the mathematical odds and the best way to bet, note that dice run in "streaks" and that it's a good idea to bet more heavily when they're running in your favor. This is a straightforward example of the gambler's fallacy.

3. Lottery games have proliferated, so we'll just take a typical example: In a lottery where there is a 1-in-14,000,000 chance of winning a jackpot (as is currently the case in California's lottery) and the payoff is one million dollars, the "house" advantage is 140%. Obviously, this is not a way to invest any significant portion of one's fortune!

Exercise 11-17

1. The larger the number of chance-determined repetitive events we consider, the closer the alternatives will approach predictable ratios. For example, the more times we flip a coin, the closer to 50 percent heads and 50 percent tails we can expect to get. The more times we roll dice, the closer to 16.67 percent they'll come up 7.

    The phrase "a priori odds" has been used to describe what we call "predictable ratios." We know "a priori" that a fair coin has a 50-50 chance of coming up heads.

2. The problem here, of course, is that we would have to determine that 50-50 is the predictable ratio for male/female births. This depends on whether the number of gender-determining gametes a male produces are equally male- and female-producing, whether they are equally viable, and whether human ova, once fertilized, have equal chances of developing to birth if they are male or female. Because of the huge number of unknowns, we cannot arrive at such a predictable ratio.

What we know about the male/female birth ratio is the result of looking at how many of each have been born—we have to deal with *observed* ratios.

3. He's just exactly as "due for" the coin coming up heads this time as he is any other time it is flipped; it is the gambler's fallacy to think that how the coin has come up in the past will affect how it will come up next time. (This is on the presumption that the coin and flip are fair, of course.)

Chapter 11 Test Question/Exercise Banks

Bank 11-1

Analogical arguments for evaluation.

1. Can I recommend a good mechanic? Sure—Brott's Automotive. I've been taking my car there for years, and I've never had a single complaint. Of course, I have an old Chevy, and you drive a Mazda—one of those rotary-engine jobs, isn't it?

   It is reasonable to expect good service from a mechanic who has given years of good service to a friend, but you cannot be certain that the mechanic who knows Chevys will be very good with your rotary-engine Mazda—as the speaker implies.

2. Hey, Coach! I know somebody good for our volleyball team. Her name is Stacy, and she hasn't played much volleyball, but she's a great basketball player.

   Someone good at basketball is unlikely to be terrible at volleyball. Good analogical argument.

3. Rank the following analogical arguments:

   A. Look, our stereo is a Panasonic and so is our TV, and we've never had any trouble with either of them. Let's get the Panasonic answering machine. Why take chances?

   B. Look, our stereo is Japanese and so is our TV, and we've never had any trouble with either of them. Let's get the Japanese answering machine. Why take chances?

   C. Look, Frank's answering machine is a Panasonic and so is Heather's, and they both say they've never had trouble with them. Let's get the Panasonic answering machine. Why take chances?

   C (the strongest), then A, then B.

4. The thing that worries me is that we're going to get bogged down in Haiti just as we got bogged down in Vietnam. The situations are exactly the same: It's us against a Third World nation that is determined to win and doesn't play by the rules our military thinkers understand.

   Weak argument. The situations certainly aren't exactly the same.

5. HE: Let's leave Cincinnati for the golden West! Why don't we move to Los Angeles?
   SHE: Well, for one thing, we couldn't afford to buy a house there.
   HE: Don't be such a pessimist. We bought this house here, didn't we? How much more expensive can houses in L.A. be?

Even if he is not aware of the difference in the cost of housing in the two cities, he should realize there are important relevant differences between such different parts of the country that could profoundly affect housing costs. Furthermore, if they bought their Cincinnati house quite a while ago, the changes that have since occurred in the real estate market can make a great difference in either or both localities. Note that the argument would be just as shaky if the inference were from Los Angeles to Cincinnati. (The fact that housing costs are currently higher in L.A. than in Cincinnati is irrelevant to the strength of the argument, though it proves that the implied conclusion is false.)

6. The Cowboys easily made it into last year's Superbowl. They'll have almost the same personnel next year, so I'm putting my money on the Cowboys to be back next year.

The Cowboys' having almost the same personnel next year helps the analogy some, but too many other relevant factors have to be considered before this argument would be a safe one—the other teams may not have the same personnel they had last year, for instance. Notice that it's easy to confuse what a person is betting on in cases like this: It's one thing for the Cowboys to be the team most likely to play in the championship game; it's another for it to be more likely that they'll play than that they won't.

7. Six months ago, several of Molly's friends joined the Trimtime Fitness Center. Each of them participated in Trimtime's weight-reduction and fitness regimen. All reported substantial weight reduction, and all are visibly slimmer. Molly is convinced. She joins Trimtime and enrolls in the same program, hoping and expecting to see the same results. She is especially delighted to learn that Trimtime had adjusted its program to make it even more effective in a shorter period of time.

Molly should consider potential differences between her and her friends. From our outsider's point of view, though, we would have to say that if she followed the original program just as they did, then we would expect her to get similar results. But without knowing the details of the changes in the program or the evidence for believing that the changes will be an improvement, Molly should not be delighted to learn that the program has been "adjusted"; the change in the program weakens the argument. (Trimtime might, of course, be able to give Molly good reason for thinking that the change will be an improvement.)

Items 8 through 11 are based on the paragraph in item 8.

8. Juanita has taken six courses at Valley Community College, and she has a grade average of B so far. All the courses she has taken have been in sociology and psychology. She's thinking of enrolling in another course next term, and she expects to make at least a B in whatever she takes. If we don't know yet what subject she

will take, would her argument be stronger, weaker, or neither if her previous six courses had been in four different subjects rather than two?

Stronger. The more diversification among the sample, the more likely that at least some of its members will resemble the new course.

9. Would Juanita's argument be stronger, weaker, or neither if we knew that the new course will be in psychology?

Stronger. If her new course is in a subject that we know is included in the sample, that tells us of at least one relevant similarity.

10. Would you assess Juanita's argument as stronger, weaker, or neither if you knew that she had made a B in each of her previous courses and not just that she has a B average?

Stronger. She could have a B average even though she had made Cs in several of her previous courses, and such a possibility weakens the argument.

11. Suppose that when she took the previous courses, Juanita had done all her studying alone because she didn't know any of the other students at Valley but that now she knows several good students and plans to study with them when she takes her next course. Would her argument be stronger or weaker?

Weaker. This may seem paradoxical, but we're thinking of a separate argument *(which might go something like this: Juanita studies better when she studies with other good students; she did not study with other students for her previous courses, but she'll study with other good students for the next course; therefore, she'll study better for the next course). This other argument would support the conclusion, provided that its premises are true. But the original analogical argument is weakened because of the addition of a relevant difference between the target and the sample. (See answers for Exercise 11-3.)*

12. Mr. Naphal has read in an authoritative science report that a dye commonly injected into Florida oranges is carcinogenic. He resolves not only to avoid Florida oranges until he learns that they no longer are dyed with the same chemical, but also to avoid California oranges and all grapefruit as well.

We'd avoid California oranges too, unless we had some reason to think they weren't dyed with the same dye. But the fact that grapefruit are yellow (and thus would require different colored dyes) weakens the argument.

13. In Great Britain, savings of between 20 and 40 percent in costs have resulted from selling government-run programs and business to individuals and companies in the private sector. This argues well for the administration's interest in selling such U.S. government entities as the Bonneville Power Administration, the Tennessee Valley Authority, and various parts of the postal service.

The terms of the analogy are not clear: Which (or at least what kind of) British programs and businesses were sold off? Would the sales be handled similarly (with regard to terms of payments, for example)? Would the government subsidize private ownership for a period of time after the sale? How would general differences in the economic structures of the United States and Great Britain affect the argument? There are too many differences between the sample and the target to put too much confidence in this argument.

14. Wolfgang has been to America, once visiting New York and once visiting Columbus. *(Why is it always "Columbus, Ohio"?)* Now his friend has an opportunity to visit New Orleans and wants to know what Wolfgang's recommendation is. Wolfgang tells her to stay away from New Orleans. "Based on my experience, it will be awful—you'll find crime, violence, poverty, rude people, drug addicts—every kind of unpleasantness."

Wolfgang's reasoning is really to this effect: He didn't like New York or Columbus, so he wouldn't like any other U.S. city—and she won't, either. And we would expect Wolfgang not to like New Orleans, even though there are tremendous differences among the cities mentioned in the exercise.

15. "He won the Silver Medal of Honor, has a Purple Heart, and was an Eagle Scout. I find it difficult to believe that it was he who committed the robbery."

Even though few of us know people who have won all these awards, most of us do have experience with people who have earned acknowledgement for dedication, respect for others, courage, conscientiousness, and so on. These people are the "sample." Because we know (and know of) few such people who also commit deeds that deny these virtues, we reason that this individual is unlikely to have done so. The analogical reasoning encountered here is inherently weaker than any direct evidence that bears on the person's evidence.

16. A conversation:
    "You going to vote for Spankey or Howard in the city council election?"
    "Howard. As far as I can make out, their experience is the same, and they both take about the same position on the issues. But Spankey was a student of mine. I caught him cheating once."

Our experience tells us that most people who are dishonest in one situation are more apt to be dishonest in another; so, everything else being equal between the two candidates, it is reasonable to give the nod to Howard. (Seldom is everything else equal, of course.)

17. Hank ("The Flailin' Australian") Kingscote has won every one of his fifteen previous prizefights by knockouts. The chances are that the poor fellow who's going to fight him next will wind up stretched out on the canvas.

Prizefights are a lot like snowflakes and political elections: The next one is not necessarily going to look like the last one(s). We know nothing about the opponents in Hank's previous fights (the sample) nor about his upcoming opponent (the fight with whom is the target).

18. Washburn has read that it is good to include cabbage in one's diet. He doesn't care much for cabbage, but he likes brussels sprouts. Since the latter look like small cabbages, he assumes that their nutritional benefits will be about the same as those of cabbage.

Obviously there may be differences between cabbages and brussels sprouts that are highly important from a nutritional standpoint. Nevertheless, the clear physical similarities between the two vegetables make this a fair analogical argument.

19. From a letter to the editor: "Harry Kryshnah lost the last election because he supported handgun control. So now he's changed his tune and claims he'll be the first one to oppose handgun control. I voted for him last June, but I won't vote for him this time, and it's not because I favor handgun control. I just don't want a governor who can talk out of both sides of his mouth like that."

This is not an ad hominem. This is the writer's argument: Experience shows that most people who are unprincipled in one way are apt to be unprincipled in others; therefore, Kryshnah, who is a member of this class, is apt to be unprincipled in other ways, too. Given the premises, the argument is not a weak one; however, a premise that assigns a person to a class of unprincipled people because of a change in position is one that needs close examination. Is the change due to a lack of principle? Or was it occasioned by legitimate reasoning that was not self-serving?

Bank 11-2

Passages for the identification of fallacies.

20. Overheard: "You don't think this country is in a slump? Get real. George here was laid off before Memorial Day, and Howie's wife and a whole bunch of other people lost their jobs when the Safeway over on Jeffrey closed down. These are tough times."

Hasty generalization

21. We're gonna have trouble with that new paper boy, Honey. He's been late twice already.

We'd call this a biased generalization. After all, the new fellow is new.

22. Hey, let's start shopping at Musgrave's. It's a whole lot cheaper. I stopped in there yesterday on the way home and found strawberries there for 79¢ a basket and ground beef for $1.29 a pound. And they weren't even on sale!

Hasty generalization

23. You can't decide between a Macintosh and an IBM for word processing? Well, it's the mid 1990s, you are forty years old, and you're still using a typewriter! Looks to me that you'd rather spend your time doing other things than learning how to use a computer. You'd probably be happiest with the most user-friendly system, which is still the Mac.

We'd call this a reasonable generalization. The purchaser apparently does prefer other activities to learning how to use computers. Students may have trouble spotting the sample and the target and understanding that the generalization is what is stated in the third sentence.

24. Invest in real estate! Buy a house! It's the best investment you will ever make. Despite occasional temporary dips, home prices have always gone up. You can't go wrong if you buy a house.

Despite the "size" of the sample, there are important differences between it and the target, for example; the number of additional homebuyers is declining, consumer debt

274

has risen dramatically; discretionary income has been shrinking. Can you expect entry-level university students to know such things? Maybe not. But you can expect them to understand the importance of carefully checking out arguments like this before they contract a major debt.

25. Housing is far too expensive in this country. Why, the median price of a home in San Francisco is now over $200,000.

    If the speaker is generalizing from San Francisco to the entire country, then the argument is hasty generalization, and, if you are aware of typical housing costs in San Francisco, you could also call it a biased generalization. But perhaps the speaker only means that when the median price of a home has gone over $200,000 in some place—San Francisco or wherever—then housing has just gotten too expensive in this country. If the passage is viewed this way, it's not clear that the speaker is even offering an argument.

26. I certainly did not enjoy the first meeting of that class. I think I'll drop it; I don't want a whole semester of meetings like that.

    Whether this is a hasty generalization depends on exactly what the student didn't like about the first class. There are some things, such as an instructor's manner of presentation, that a person can reach legitimate conclusions about after only a small sample. Further, if the student is referring to the instructor's overview of the course, he may have a good inductive argument: "She said she was going to cover such-and-such material; instructors usually cover what they say they're going to cover; therefore, she will probably cover the material she said she was going to cover. And I have neither need nor inclination to study that material."

27. Remark made while driving on the Pennsylvania Turnpike: "We've seen nine cars with licence plates from west of the Mississippi today, and six of them have been from Texas. Texans must travel more than other people."

    Hasty generalization

28. FIRST BICYCLE RIDER: How come when we coast downhill you always go so much faster than I?
    SECOND BICYCLE RIDER: Because I'm heavier. Heavier things fall faster.
    THIRD BICYCLE RIDER: Wait a minute. I thought that was what Galileo proved wrong.
    SECOND BICYCLE RIDER: C'mon! That's only common sense. Heavy things are bound to fall faster. Just look at how fast I coast—and I'm the heaviest.

    This is something between hasty generalization and anecdotal evidence. Begging the question would also be a straightforward analysis.

29. If you think the people of Phoenix are going to give up their rights to water from the Colorado River to Los Angelenos, you'd better think about it some more. Read the letters to the editors of the Phoenix newspapers, and you'll see what I mean. People are really hot under the collar about the issue.

    Biased generalization

30. A reliable statewide study found that one western town (which we won't name) had an unusually high rate of death from cancer. The study, done during the 1970s, showed the cancer death rate for white females to be 175.4 per 100,000, compared to 154.9 for the state. One resident dismissed the finding as follows: "Statistics! You can prove anything you want with statistics! There's no more cancer here than anywhere."

Hasty generalization: Some statistical conclusions aren't trustworthy, so none of them are.

31. I went into that office supply store on Jackson Avenue the other day, and I can tell you that I'm not ever going back. They're the rudest people I've ever seen in a retail business. The guy who waited on me griped constantly about it being inventory time, and he was of no help at all in finding what I wanted to buy.

Biased and hasty generalization

32. From a letter to the editor: "The news media can never be trusted. Shortly before the Geneva summit, the *Washington Post* decided that a news scoop concerning a confidential letter from the secretary of defense to the president was more important news than a coordinated posture by our negotiating team."

Hasty generalization

33. Goldman may have won the Supervisor of the Year award, but that just means they didn't look very hard for a winner. I know a couple of people who work in Goldman's division and they say that he's a real pain to work for. I'd sooner trust my friends than some awards committee.

Anecdotal evidence

34. I watched "Nova" on public television the other night, and it was great! I'm going to be in front of the tube every week for it from now on.

If one "Nova" was good, that's not a bad reason for believing that they're generally pretty good. Still, this generalization may be just a bit hasty.

35. I've seen brochures depicting the scenery in the Ozark Mountains, and it's beautiful. I'm even thinking of retiring to Arkansas, since it's clearly such a beautiful state.

Biased generalization

36. The photographs from the first roll of that new Kodak film were really good. I'll tell you, that film is good stuff.

This is okay, since one roll of Kodak film can be expected to be much like every other roll of the same type.

37. Bill bought one of those Burn-Rite wood stoves last year, and it smoked up his house all winter. Those stoves are not worth the high prices they get for them.

Hasty generalization

38. According to one of the leading consumer magazines, the best-built cars these days are Japanese. Cars built by foreign manufacturers have just outclassed those built in the United States, it appears.

   Biased generalization: What holds for Japanese cars may not hold for all foreign-built cars.

39. "Sharon's father thinks the idea of a space-based laser missile defense is entirely feasible, and he should know—he's a physicist who specializes in laser technology, and he has a degree in computer science."

   "Yeah, well, he may be right, but he also works for the defense industry. There's a pot of gold in it for him if people believe that. He's probably not the most reliable source."

   No fallacy

40. "A Prairie Home Companion" must be a pretty popular radio program around here. About half my friends have copies of the book the program's host recently published.

   A hasty, and quite likely biased, generalization. The speaker's friends may not resemble the general population in its taste in radio programs.

41. "Hello Mom? Yeah, it's me. . . . Fine. Great, in fact. Massachusetts is super— I've never had so much fun. . . ." No. . . . Yes! And listen, I've just met the most wonderful guy. And I'm *sure* he's rich. You should just *see* the expensive car he drives. . . ."

   Hasty generalization

Bank 11-3

Generalizations for evaluation. Identify sample, target population, property in question, and the extent to which the claims involved are knowable. Consider carefully the size and diversification of the sample and the extent to which the target differs or may differ from the sample. Remember, what's important is that the sample be representative.

42. Stratton takes one look at his new teacher and concludes he is going to like the course. "You can just tell," he says to his girlfriend later, "it's gonna be a great course. The teacher brought up all these interesting subjects—and it was only the first day."

   Hasty generalization, although we don't think the reasoning is all *bad. Even from one meeting, Stratton is probably able to tell a good bit about whether he likes to listen to this particular teacher, and such things can make a course more enjoyable.*

43. The cocktail Beatrice orders before dinner is watery, so she decides not to eat there after all. "Don't see how they can fix decent dinners if they can't even make a decent martini," she thinks.

   Hasty generalization

44. Parker recommends the latest Larry McMurtry novel to Moore. Moore decides not to bother, since every other novel Parker has recommended turned out to be a dud, in Moore's opinion.

If the list of duds is a long one, no fallacy.

45. Fong notes that the pavement deteriorates as he crosses into the next county. "Guess they don't keep up their roads very well," he thinks.

Hasty generalization

46. Stortz has heard from his friends that the folks in North Carolina are pretty friendly, so he looks forward to going through it on his bike trip to Florida.

Biased generalization, because the sample of opinion isn't likely to be representative; most people he's heard from are likely to have been reporting on their friends in North Carolina.

47. Agnes has read that blonde, blue-eyed, fair-skinned people are more likely to develop problems from overexposure to sun, but she discounts these reports. "After all," she reasons, "my uncle Schleef works on a boat and I never heard of him having any problems, even though he's blonde, blue-eyed, and fair."

Anecdotal evidence

48. Noting that recent scientific research suggests that a daily glass of wine or two might be good for the heart, Mr. Laub decides to tank up. "Why in hell not," he says. "If one glass of wine is good for you, most likely five or six is *really* good for you."

Hasty generalization

49. "How come the people in these big motor homes always have a couple of midget dogs with them," Jasper wonders.

Hasty generalization

50. Victor has just heard somewhere that regular injections of testosterone help improve the memories of men his age, but he can't recall where he heard it. "Probably was on the TV news," he figures. "I don't read the newspaper very often."

No fallacy

51. Gridley has been going to the Silver Dollar Fair every year for the past fifteen years. An acquaintance suggests they go to the fair, but "For God's sake, let's don't eat there, we'll die." Gridley knows better; he's never even once gotten sick from Silver Dollar food.

No fallacy

52. SUSANVILLE—Fewer than 20 percent of college professors consider themselves shy, according to a new study by two psychologists. "We were surprised by this

278

result because other studies have reported that almost 50 percent of adult Americans think of themselves as shy," said Elliot Smalley, professor at Colusa State University. "College professors are sometimes thought to be an introverted lot and so we expected perhaps a majority to think of themselves as shy," he said.

Smalley and his associate, John Mahmoud, interviewed 150 college professors who were identified by administrators at twenty-five American universities as typical faculty. The universities were selected by a random procedure from a list of American colleges and universities, Smalley said.

This is a poor generalization. University administrators might be apt to state the first professors who come to mind, and professors selected in this manner might tend to be among the more outspoken faculty. Truly shy, introverted faculty might well be unknown to most administrators at a large university.

53. A random survey of 1,000 callers to a drug hotline number produced the following results: 535 of the callers were heavy users of either cocaine freebase, amphetamines, or heroin; 220 were "recreational" users of cocaine or hashish, 92 were not drug users at all, and the remainder refused to answer the survey questions. This should put to rest the claim that most people who take drugs are of the occasional, "recreational" type.

The sample in this argument is badly biased. A typical heavy user of a drug is much more likely to get into a crisis situation and thus call a hotline number than a typical "recreational" user.

54. ATLANTA (UPI)—A long-term federal study by the National Centers for Disease Control of 13 million U.S. births shows increases in the rate of eleven different types of birth defects, including a 17.5 percent yearly average increase in patent ductus arteriosus and a 10.8 percent increase for ventricular septal defects, over a fourteen-year period. The study was conducted by the Birth Defects Monitoring Program of the CDC, which collected its data from hospitals across the country. From 1970 to 1983, over 13 million births were monitored. [An adaptation]

"Hospitals across the country" is vague, but this is almost certainly a reputable scientific study, and the sample is extremely large. A generalization from these results to the American population as a whole should be sound.

55. A survey was made in 1948 in which a large number of names was randomly selected from the telephone book of a large city. The individuals called were asked whether they preferred Truman or Dewey in the presidential race. Over half of the respondents named Dewey, so the pollsters concluded that Dewey would carry the city and region.

The principal problem with this survey is that in 1948 many voters did not have telephones and thus had no chance of being selected. Since possession of a telephone was linked with a person's economic status, and economic status helps determine political views, the sample was badly biased.

56. As part of his work for NASA, Dr. Murdock was asked to find out what percentage of Americans saw Halley's comet when it was visible in 1985–1986. He randomly selected three cities, Seattle, Cleveland, and Boston, and polled several hundred randomly selected individuals from these cities. His findings are that fewer than 5 percent of Americans saw the comet.

It makes no difference whether the cities and the individuals were randomly selected. Inhabitants of large cities, especially northern big cities, would be less likely to see the comet because of city lights, clouds, air pollution, and latitude.

57. Haslett wanted to know what percentage of students at his college votes in local elections. He asked each of his professors (he was a political science major) to ask for a show of hands in his classes so he could make a count. He found that 45 percent of the 120 classmates polled vote in local elections. He concludes that about 45 percent of the students at his college vote in those elections.

The sample is large enough to be somewhat reliable, although Haslett should not be surprised by a substantial deviation from his 45 percent projection. A more serious problem is that Haslett's poll may have been taken in political science classes (or at least mainly in political science classes) and that people who take such classes may be more interested in political matters and hence more likely to vote in any election. The possibility of bias is substantial.

58. Seventy-two percent of those interviewed at a luncheon sponsored by the Camellia Chamber of Commerce favored local tax incentives to attract new businesses. Would this finding generalize to the Camellia population?

No. This is not likely to be a representative sample.

59. Let's say that according to statewide studies done in Montana and Virginia, the infant mortality rate for these two states averaged 10.5 per thousand live births. Could this figure be generalized to the infant mortality rate in the United States? What factors might be relevant to the generalization?

Montana and Virginia provide a large and reasonably good sample, although there may be a bias toward rural areas and small towns over large urban areas. We would want to know about Montana's and Virginia's resident-to-doctor ratio, its ratio of residents to hospital beds, the level of prenatal education available in the two states, and similar matters. The more similar these possibly relevant factors are in Montana and Virginia to the remainder of the country, the stronger the argument.

60. A majority of Americans think that tobacco companies should be prohibited from advertising their products. In a survey of 1,213 adults, 86 percent said that prohibiting tobacco advertising would lower smoking rates. The results of the nationwide telephone survey, conducted by American Opinion Research, Inc., were published in this week's edition of *Research Fact*. Spokespersons for the American Tobacco Council had no immediate comment on the findings.

It is not clear from this passage whether a majority of the respondents actually think that tobacco advertising should be prohibited. The 86 percent said something else: that doing so would lower smoking rates. Whether they would outlaw tobacco advertising is not known.

61. Osteoporosis is a degeneration of bone tissue that afflicts between fifteen and twenty million Americans and leads to approximately 1.3 million bone fractures every year. The condition is found mainly among women. A conference sponsored by the National Institutes of Health in 1984 reported that calcium was one of the "mainstays of prevention and management of osteoporosis." In a localized study designed to help predict the future incidence of osteoporosis in women in a midwestern community, a county hospital did a survey on calcium intake. It selected five hundred women at random and asked them to keep a record of their food and dietary supplements for one month. The data were analyzed to determine the amounts of calcium each woman received. It was determined that 85 percent of the surveyed women received less calcium than the recommended amount of 1,000 to 1,500 milligrams per day. County medical authorities concluded that about 85 percent of the community's women were getting less than the recommended intake of calcium. They also concluded that local medical facilities would soon see an increase in the number of cases of osteoporosis as the calcium deficiency showed its effects. Given just the information presented here, how much confidence would you have in these conclusions?

The first conclusion is less solid than it might appear. The survey was done during one month, and diets change during the course of a year. More dairy products may be consumed during one time of the year than others; certainly some vegetables are consumed on a varying seasonal basis. Hence, the study may accurately reflect only the calcium intake in the population during that month of the year. Another problem with the survey is that the women were categorized by age. Women of different ages may consume different amounts of calcium, and since osteoporosis is a degenerative condition, it is likely to affect women of different ages much differently. (Women who take too little calcium at age twenty-four but who increase their intake by the time they are thirty-five may be no more likely to suffer osteoporosis than those whose intake is high during their entire lives.)

The second conclusion does not follow at all. The insufficient intake of calcium may have been going on for years; so the incidence of osteoporosis may remain exactly the same in the future.

62. FRESNO—In a new study of dangerous Halloween pranks, Fresno State University sociologist Joel Best has documented the exact number of American children killed or seriously injured by anonymously given, booby-trapped Halloween treats. Best reviewed supposedly real Halloween horror stories appearing from 1958 to 1984 in the *New York Times,* the *Chicago Tribune,* the *Los Angeles Times,* and the *Fresno Bee.* He did not find a single case in which a Halloween treat anonymously given to a child caused serious harm. He concluded that the infamous Halloween sadist is an "urban myth."
—Adapted from a McClatchy News Service release

The question is whether the "exact number" of American children killed or seriously injured by anonymously given Halloween tricks can be determined by looking at the incidents reported in the four newspapers mentioned. There may have been a few incidents not reported in these newspapers, but we'd be surprised if there were many. Events of this type tend to attract too much attention not to be reported in at least one of these sources.

63. A poll of fifty weight lifters at a southern California gym determined that thirty-three payed close attention to their diets as well as to their exercise. Of those thirty-three, twenty-five (50 percent of the original fifty) made it a point to eat more than the minimum daily amount of protein for large adults, and twenty (40 percent of the original fifty) took vitamin pills and other dietary supplements. The chain of health food stores that took the pool concluded that weight lifters constitute a substantial market for its products, since it is likely that 40 percent of all weight lifters across the country take vitamin pills and supplements and that an additional 10 percent are at least highly conscious of their diets.

The health-food chain had best not invest too much in attracting this new market. The first flaw in the survey is technical: The sample is too small to give a very detailed picture of weight lifters' habits—even if nothing else were wrong with the survey, strong confidence (95 percent) would be justified only in the claim that from about 36 to 64 percent of the weight lifters nationwide make sure to eat more than the usual amount of protein—not a very precise conclusion (see the error margin table (Table 11-1) in the text, page 340). A more important flaw in the survey is that the interviews are confined to clients of only one gym. Information is often passed around among people who frequent the same establishments, and there may be trends or fads or a particular bit of useful information that is current at one gym but not in others. The sample is biased, in other words.

64. NEW YORK (AP)—Women who read "bodice-rippers," a sexy, violent genre of historical romance novel, have sex 74 percent more often than nonreaders, according to a survey by two psychologists from the Emory Medical School in Atlanta, who interviewed 72 middle-class women in Atlanta, an equal number of them housewives, working women, and college students. Women who read the romances reported making love an average of 3.04 times a week, compared to 1.75 for nonreaders.

Our concern here is whether the 3.04 and 1.75 times a week figures generalize from the Atlanta sample. First, we'd not be at all surprised if there were an important discrepancy between reports of frequency and actual frequency (the article runs the two together). Further, a sampling of Atlanta women may not be representative of American women even in regard to reporting the frequency of sex. There may be cultural differences between urban and nonurban areas, southern and other areas of the country, and so forth, that affect attitudes about sex and reports about sexual activity. Also, does the distribution in the sample among housewives, working women, and college students reflect the distribution in the population as a whole? Are one-third of American women college students, for instance? Only if they were would this sample be representative.

The following four exercises are all based on the two paragraphs in item 65.

65. A college professor converted one room of her house into a home office and intended to deduct her expenses on her federal income tax return. She wondered how many other college faculty had done the same, thinking that the more who deducted

home offices, the less likely her own return would be noticed by the IRS and hence the less likely she would be audited. So she decided to do her own informal survey of her colleagues to see how many of them had home offices. She sent out a questionnaire of three questions to all 1,200 instructors at her campus, and she received 950 responses. (Her promise to share the results of the survey apparently motivated faculty to respond.)

As it turned out, 32 percent of her respondents answered yes to the question, "Do you maintain an office at home?" Half of these also answered yes to the question, "Do you deduct your home office expenses on your federal income tax return?" And 24 percent of the entire group of respondents answered yes to the question, "Is your campus office adequate?"

Would our professor's conclusion, "About 32 percent of college faculty nationwide maintain home offices," be more likely if she had included faculty from other institutions among her survey? Why?

It would be much more likely to be accurate. Faculty at different kinds of colleges (community colleges, state colleges, state universities, and private universities) have different requirements and hence a different level of need for offices at home—the more research a faculty does, the more likely the need for home offices.

66. Would our professor's conclusion, "Sixteen percent of faculty nationwide deduct home office expenses on their federal income tax return," be more accurate if she restricted it to faculty in her own state?

Yes. Different states may have different state income tax rules, and it may be more worthwhile, for tax reasons, to have a home office in some states than in others. A faculty member who does not find it worthwhile to have a home office in one state may find it advantageous in another.

67. Is it reasonable for our professor to conclude that faculty office space on the campus is inadequate?

Yes; at least, it is reasonable for her to conclude that her faculty colleagues believe it is inadequate, and by a large majority. Her sample not only is large enough to guarantee reliability in such a conclusion, but also includes almost all of the target population.

68. Do you find any flaw in our professor's reasoning about the usefulness of the survey for her own purposes? Should she believe that the more people who have home offices, the more likely her own will escape attention from the IRS?

This is not a question about the criteria for evaluating statistical generalizations, but rather about the assumption that motivated the study. It does us no good to produce studies to answer questions if they are the wrong questions to begin with. In this case, it may be that the IRS will turn more attention to home office deductions if there are enough of them to constitute a large total of deductions. Our professor has done a good job of answering some questions (about office space, about the number of home offices maintained by her colleagues and at other campuses similar to hers) but she had best be careful not to let her enthusiasm at having produced some reliable figures rub off on her initial assumption; such a mistake could be costly at tax time.

69. Seventeen percent of Winchell State students intend to pursue careers as computer programmers or analysts. That's what a recent survey of WSU students conducted by psychology major Jack Nafarik shows. Nafarik passed out questionnaires to students who voted in the March student election as they exited from the polling stations in the student union. "The results didn't surprise me," Nafarik said. "The figure may seem fairly high, but you'd expect that in a technical school like Winchell State."

Do student voters constitute a representative sample of the students at Winchell State? Probably not. Upper-division students may vote in larger numbers than freshmen and sophomores, and there may be correlations between class standing and career goals. There may also be a direct correlation between types of major and participation in student elections. Can you think of any other possible sources of bias?

70. Thirty percent of American women ages nineteen to thirty-nine diet at least once a month, according to a news syndicate poll released last November. These findings are based on telephone interviews with a random sample of women listed in the Los Angeles telephone directory.

We wouldn't trust a generalization about the subject based on a sample of women who list themselves in the telephone book, especially if they live in southern California, which may have more than its fair share of aspiring models and actresses, beach-goers, and other figure-conscious women.

71. According to a study published by Dr. William P. Newman III of Louisiana State University Medical Center in the January 16, 1986, edition of the *New England Journal of Medicine,* physicians in Bogalusa, Louisiana, conducted autopsies on thirty-five youngsters ranging in age from seven to twenty-four (the average age was eighteen) who had died mostly from accidents, homicides, or suicides. They found that all but six of the young people had fatty streaks on their aortas, the body's main artery. Fatty streaks are the earliest gross recognizable lesions of atherosclerosis (hardening of the arteries), according to Newman. Since there was a direct link between the number of fatty streaks and the cholesterol levels in the young people, Newman recommended that all schoolchildren be checked for high cholesterol levels.

Newman is generalizing from the sample of thirty-five young people to all schoolchildren. However, he probably would not say that the sample indicates that a majority of all young people have the early signs of atherosclerosis. Rather, he would say that the sample suggests that a sufficient number of young people may have that disease to make monitoring the cholesterol levels of all children worthwhile. Interpreted this way, this is a reasonable generalization: The Bogalusa study does warrant concern and further investigation.

72. Ronald is driving across the country when his car develops a minor mechanical problem. He can fix the trouble himself, but he'll need a wrench of a size he doesn't have. He resolves to stop at the next Sears retail store he sees to purchase one. He's been in four or five Sears retail stores in the past, and all of them have carried automotive tools. So he is confident that all Sears retail outlets stock them.

His sample is small, but very representative: Ronald has made a sound generalization. Note that the argument could also be construed as analogical.

73. Well, I did rotten in Algebra I last semester, so I expect I'll do poorly in the rest of the math classes I'll have to take.

    There may be enough differences between last semester and the rest—we'd like to think—to make the argument a weak one: different instructor, new study habits, and so on. Still, we'd bet against his doing well before we'd bet against somebody who did well in Algebra I.

74. Don't buy any Australian wine. I've had Australian wine before and, believe me, you won't like it.

    Well, maybe she will. This is too hasty. That one kind of Australian wine was not very good doesn't mean that there aren't good varieties. Every country that makes wine makes at least a little bad wine.

75. Mr. Smythe has closed each of the last four contracts with France International. Seems to me he'd be likely to do well with the rest of our overseas deals.

    This may be a biased sample. Did Mr. Smythe work with the same people on the four France International contracts? More diversity in the sample would make this a stronger argument.

76. Hamilton City was considering annexing a portion of land adjacent to the city limits where construction of a subdivision was planned. To determine what the residents of the town thought about this annexation and about municipal growth in general, the city council had a poll taken. One thousand of the city's fifteen thousand registered voters were randomly selected and asked three questions: (1) Do you favor no growth, modest growth, or accelerated growth for Hamilton City? (2) Do you favor annexation of the eight-hundred-acre Osborne parcel north of town and its planned subdivision? (3) Should the city enter into agreements with developers promising to supply city services, such as sewers and street maintenance, in return for the added tax revenue the developer's projects will produce? The results of this survey were taken to be the "official" opinion of the voters of Hamilton City.

    There is clearly nothing wrong with the sample size, and, if the selection was indeed random, this poll can be taken as a reliable indicator of what the voters of Hamilton City think about the questions asked. The problem is the questions: The first is much too vague (we'd bet the great majority of responses favored mdoest growth, whatever that means); the second can be intelligently answered only by voters who understand the implications of annexation—we can imagine a voter responding yes to the question and living to regret the annexation later (or responding no and living to regret that). The third question is also too vague to be helpful. How expensive will the services be? How much tax revenue will be generated? What kinds of commitments would the agreements involve, and over how long a period? Without carefully thought-out questions, no adherence to the rules of statistical generalization can produce a reliable result.

77. Memo: "We interviewed Haddow and found that she could handle each of the problems we gave her. I recommend we hire her."

The speaker is betting that because Haddow can solve certain kinds of problems, she'll be able to solve all those she's given. If the problems she solved really are representative of the problems she will encounter, then it's a good bet. If they're not, it's not.

78. A New York newspaper stopped theater goers as they exited from a performance of *La Tragédie de Carmen* and asked them whether they thought that Broadway theater was better or worse than it was ten years ago. When the majority of the respondents answered that they thought it was worse, the paper printed an article with the headline "Public Thinks Broadway Is Going Downhill." Does the poll justify the headline?

No. "Public" is misleading, since it could be taken to refer to the general public and not just the theater-going public. More important, the poll is highly biased in at least two ways: it may be that the production mentioned does not draw a typical theater audience, and hence the sample may be biased; and the effects of the performance attended may bias an individual respondent (whether he liked this particular performance may have unduly influenced his answer).

79. Readers of *Consumer Reports* can write in their opinions of movies they have seen. Each month, *CR* reports the total number of opinion votes it receives in this way. In one issue, the average rating of a certain movie is 4 on a scale of 1 to 5, with 5 the bad end of the scale. The total vote on the movie is 107. How sound would a generalization from this sample to American moviegoers in general be?

Not very. We know that maybe 107 people who know about the CR *movie poll didn't like the movie very much (we say "maybe" because some may have voted more than once), but that's about all we know. There is no assurance that the sample is representative of the population mentioned in the question.*

Bank 11-4

Fill-in-the-blank; true/false; miscellaneous.

80. When you add a group of quantities together and divide the result by the number of quantities, you get an average known as _the mean_ .

81. In the premises of an inductive generalization, a thing is said to be characteristic of a _sample_ of a class of things. And in the conclusion the same thing is said to be a characteristic of the entire class, or _target_ .

82. No generalization based on an unrepresentative sample is trustworthy.

True

83. A statistical inductive generalization cannot establish that some precise percentage of a target population has a given characteristic.

True

84. "In a study done by a University of Pennsylvania psychologist, 29 suburban and 38 inner-city children from the Philadelphia area, ranging in age from 3 to 12 years, were asked to consume foods mixed with 'disgusting' substances, like apple juice stirred with a used comb or containing a dead grasshopper. Almost two-thirds of the children from 3 to 6 sipped juice in which a grasshopper floated. There were no differences between city and suburban children."

—published in *Developmental Psychology*

Would it be safe to say, on the basis of this study, that the same percentage of *all* American children from ages three to six would be willing to sip juice in which a disgusting object floats? Explain in a brief essay.

The essay should clarify what the sample and target classes are and what characteristic is attributed to each (note the shift from "apple juice in which a grasshopper floats" to "juice in which a disgusting object floats"). Further, the essay should address the "knowability" of the thesis, given the latter's vagueness, and show that the writer remembered the cautions in the chapter about making inferences in statistical inductive generalizations. The essay should also consider the size, diversity, and representativeness of the sample.

85. Critically discuss the following analogical argument.

Economic sanctions simply do not work. As a weapon on international persuasion, they are about as effective as popguns.

The United Nations imposed drastic sanctions upon Rhodesia; they failed utterly.

We imposed sanctions upon Poland; nothing happened.

Our government has forbidden trade with Cuba for the past twenty-five years; Cuba goes its way. Most recently, the president has laid heavy sanctions upon Libya; our noble allies have pooh-poohed the effort.

You can count on the same kind of result if economic sanctions are imposed on North Korea.

We think that a good evaluation should identify the sample, the target, and the characteristic attributed to both. The last of these is vague in this example—the phrases "failed utterly," "nothing happened," and "goes its own way" are not clear. The claim that "our noble allies pooh-poohed the effort" attributes a characteristic to the Libyan case that is different from that attributed to the others. Is the author trying to say that economic sanctions never have an effect whatsoever? His remarks don't say so (Cuba may "go its own way," but American sanctions were very detrimental to the Cuban economy). How knowable is such a claim? Does he mean that sanctions don't destroy a country? Are we talking about American sanctions or sanctions imposed by all of America's allies as well? Any relevant differences between North Korea and the other countries mentioned would add to a critical evaluation.

Chapter 12
Causal Arguments

We continue to be happy with the bare-bones scheme of just two patterns of specific-event causal arguments: "X is the common thread" and "X is the difference." Most everyday arguments fall into one or both of these patterns, and the simplicity of the scheme compensates for any leftovers. Mill's methods still claim ancestral credit, of course.

Do remember the treatment of causal explanations in Chapter 7. When causal explanations are given without support, students should keep in mind the principles and questions discussed in that chapter (circularity, testability, and so on). When they are offered with supporting argumentation, then the *supporting arguments* are to be analyzed and evaluated in accordance with the guidelines in the current chapter.

Exercises Unanswered in the Text

Exercise 12-2

2. a. Water brings the worms out of the earth.
    b. X is the common thread.
    c. If the heavy watering is the only relevant common factor preceding the emergence of the critters; if independent causes are responsible for the various occurrences of the worms' emergence; and if the phenomenon and the heavy watering came about coincidentally or as the result of a common cause.
    d. We can't think of any.
    e. None appears.
    f. Yes. It's possible that independent causes are responsible for the various occurrences of the worms' emergence, but the fact that worms *always* come out after a rain *or* heavy watering seems to make this possibility remote. For the same reason, it's also unlikely that the events are coincidental. That the water and the worms' appearance are both the result of some third cause is most unlikely, since sometimes the water comes from rain and sometimes from Mr. Mahlman's faucets. There could be another relevant common factor—that is, perhaps Mr. Mahlman always fertilizes before he waters and before it rains. But, assuming that the combination of events has been observed by Mrs. Mahlman over a long period of time, these possibilities seem unlikely too. (Of course, if he fertilized every time he watered, he wouldn't water long—he'd kill everything. We also presume nobody is running an electrical charge through the ground; somebody told us this would bring out the worms, too.)

3. a. Your choice of two alternatives: (i) Getting into a lane causes the other to go faster. (ii) The GTC in the Sky is causing my lanes to move slowly. (We intended the first of these but got a couple of letters from people who gave it the second interpretation.)
   b. (i) This is a feeble attempt at common thread; (ii) is an even feebler assumption of a common cause.
   c. The important question, clearly, is whether the events are purely coincidental.
   d. There are as many explanations for the changes in speed as there are variables in traffic, which are practically without end.
   e. Post hoc.
   f. No good at all, of course, although we'll bet we're not the only ones who've wondered about it when we're in a hurry to get someplace.

5. a. The cat isn't hungry because it has been catching and eating mice.
   b. X is the difference.
   c. Are there other events or circumstances that might have made the difference?
   d. Cats just go off their feed sometimes, for reasons known only to cats. It could be the cat has been working up an appetite chasing those mice around in the attic: When they left, the cat stopped getting exercise. (We're grasping at straws here, of course.)
   e. Sounds like post hoc to us.
   f. No. It *may* be that the cat ate the mice, but we think this is a long shot.

6. a. El Niño caused the abnormally wet winters on the Pacific Coast.
   b. X is the common thread.
   c. Is El Niño the only relevant common factor that has accompanied the wet winters? Did the wet winters result from some independent cause?
   d. It may be that tidal movements or atmospheric conditions caused the wet winters and possibly El Niño as well. We are not told whether each occurrence of El Niño has been accompanied by a wet winter (only the other way around). If there have been occurrences of El Niño that have not been accompanied by wet Pacific Coast winters, then that fact makes the argument weaker and increases the likelihood of some other cause.
   e. None appears.
   f. This one gets a rating of fair.

9. a. The clickety-click sound in Egmont's bicycle is caused by the pedal mechanism.
   b. X is the difference: When the pedals stop going around (as he coasts), the sound stops.
   c. Is the operation of the pedal mechanism the only relevant factor that distinguishes the situation in which the sound is present from situations in which it is not?
   d. If the claim that the sound has to be due to something that revolves is correct, then the only remaining explanation with any plausibility is that the chain is causing the sound, since the sound stops when the chain stops as well as when the pedals stop.
   e. None of the fallacies named are present, provided it is true that only something that revolves could be causing the sound. There is a chance, of course, that the account provided by the chain is really the correct one.
   f. The argument is pretty good.

10. a. The disinfecting solution is causing Judith's contact lenses to bother her.

    b. & c. This looks like a case of post hoc, ergo propter hoc, but we can sometimes convert such an argument into another variety that is more likely to be reliable. If we ask the question suggested—"Is the earlier event the only thing that could have resulted in the later event?"—we find that this argument is a good candidate for the "X is the difference" pattern. What is required is that Judith has considered the possibility of other causes of the irritation and ruled them out.

    d. If the lenses themselves were new, they might be the cause, but since no mention is made of this possibility, we presume such is not the case. It may also be that Judith has been in an area lately where there is an abnormal amount of dust in the air and that the dust is causing the irritation. Windy days could account for the same phenomenon. If such possibilities have not been considered and determined to be unlikely, then the reliability of the argument becomes much more questionable.

    e. None.

    f. This is a fairly good argument, especially if possibilities like those mentioned in (d) have been ruled out.

Exercise 12-3

1. The claim in question: Eliminating coffee caused the drop in pulse rate. The pattern is X is the difference (X is the common thread is another possible analysis). Is the elimination of coffee from her diet the only relevant difference between situations when her pulse rate was higher and situations when it was lower? What if Malvina's exercise has resulted in a more efficient cardiovascular system, and her heart does not have to beat as fast now to recover from the exercise?

    This is not a very likely account, since the passage indicates that the drop in pulse rate happened more or less suddenly; the drop would have been gradual were this account correct. Another possibility is that Malvina dropped other stimulants from her diet at the same time as she dropped coffee. The elimination of any of these could be a contributing factor. Provided that the considerations raised above are taken into account, this argument is a good one.

2. The claim in question: The radio is the source of the problem. This is pretty decent common-thread reasoning. Unfortunately, though his reasoning is reliable, Hong has overlooked another plausible alternative explanation: that the problem is in the ignition system, through which current flows whenever the car is running.

5. The claim in question: TV violence has caused violence in society. This is rather like common thread (the violence on television has been going on during the time violence in society has been going on), but there's a version of post hoc here, too. Mainly, though, there are simply too many other potential causes of violence in society to put all the blame on television. It may be a contributing factor, but this "argument" doesn't give us reason to think so.

8. The claim in question: Drinking coffee or playing basketball is the cause of his chest pains. The pattern is X is the difference. Elroy should ask: Are coffee and basketball the only relevant differences? Maybe he took aspirin (or other medication) when he had a cold.

    This is not a strong argument. There are other possible relevant differences between the situation with the chest pains and the situation with the cold and no chest pains. Nevertheless, Elroy might test his hypothesis by giving up basketball and coffee while he has no cold; if the pain abates, he should see his physician. Probably he should see his physician anyway.

9. The claim in question: Dipping snuff caused Marsee's death. Since the connection between tobacco use and cancer is well known and since post hoc reasoning is unreliable, it may seem strange to call this post hoc, but that's what it is. Our knowledge about the correlation between cancer and tobacco comes not from evidence supplied by individual cases like this one but from studies done on large numbers of such cases. There *is* a good argument that Marsee's tobacco use caused his cancer and death, but it's not *this* argument; it's this: "Heavy tobacco users who get certain characteristic forms of cancer get it as a result of their use of tobacco; Marsee was a heavy tobacco user who got a characteristic form of cancer; therefore, Marsee got cancer as a result of his use of tobacco." The first premise of this argument is itself the result of studies of the sort discussed later in the chapter.

   Our post hoc argument at hand gets its credence from its association with the argument just described. If we had no information about cancer-tobacco correlations, the argument at hand would not seem nearly so convincing. Yes, Marsee used a lot of snuff, and yes, Marsee got cancer. Maybe Marsee also drank lots of hot coffee from an early age and bit his tongue a lot. Any of these would make plausible accounts (and do make moderately plausible accounts), but they are less plausible than the tobacco argument because of the abundance of evidence linking tobacco usage to cancer.

   Incidentally, Marsee was a promising high school athlete in the early 1980s, and his death resulted in a well-publicized lawsuit.

10. The claim in question: High unemployment caused retail sales to drop. This is post hoc thinking. There is a high potential for a common cause in issues like this as well. As a matter of fact, there is good reason to think that high unemployment *does* cause lowered retail sales, but more than is said here needs to be said to make the case.

Exercise 12-4

2. a

3. b

5. b

6. a

8. b

9. b

11. b

12. a

13. b

15. b

16. c

18. b

19. a

Exercise 12-6

2. a. Taking aspirin every other day reduces the risk of heart attack.
   b. Men
   c. The use of a placebo indicates that this was a controlled cause-to-effect experiment.
   d. Experimental and control groups each had about 11,035 members; the first took an aspirin every other day while the second took a sugar pill placebo.
   e. 104 of the experimental group (0.0094 percent) and 189 (0.0171 percent) of the control group had heart attacks, a difference of 0.0077 percent. While this is a tiny percentage difference, it is balanced by the enormous size of the sample: over 22,000 people. (It sounds more impressive when reported, as in the article, as a 47 percent reduction in the risk of heart attack. Results can be misleading when the occurrence of E in one group is reported as a percentage of its occurrence in the other. If there had been two heart attacks in the control group and only one in the experimental group, we'd have a case of a "whopping" 50 percent reduction in heart attack risk, but with practically no statistical significance, since *one* more heart attack in one of the groups is certainly attributable to chance.)

      This report does indicate statistical significance: The source (the *New England Journal of Medicine*) is reliable, as is the sponsor (the National Heart, Lung and Blood Institute), and the fact that the study was cut short so that members of the control group could benefit from aspirin-caused reduction in risk says something about the sponsor's confidence in the study.
   g. None that we can think of
   h. The report seems to support the claim in (a); but before we all go reaching for the aspirin bottle, we want to remind you that aspirin can riddle your duodenum if you tend toward ulcers.

3. a. Cigarette smoking can cause (vascular-associated) impotence; nicotine causes an immediate reduction in sexual arousal.
   b. Men
   c. The South African, French, and Canadian studies are nonexperimental effect-to-cause studies. The Southern Illinois–Florida State study is experimental cause-to-effect.
   d. The South African study mentions no control group. We can only presume that something less than 93 percent of the South African male population are smokers (but see below). In the U.S. study, we assume that the forty-two-member sample was divided into three groups of equal size to be administered high-nicotine cigarettes, low-nicotine cigarettes, and mints.
   e. The frequency of cause in the South African study is 93 percent, which, as noted, is probably higher than the incidence of smokers in the target population. No difference is specified in the U.S. study, although the report leads one to believe that slow arousal was universal among the high-nicotine cigarette smokers.

f. There is no specific indication of significance in the report, except on the "universal" reading given to the U.S. study.

g. Based on this passage, we're not sure how much confidence we'd have in the results, especially because of the nonexperimental nature of the South African, French, and Canadian studies. It may be, for instance, that the percentage of alcohol drinkers among smokers is higher than normal, and that alcohol plays a significant role in some kinds of impotence.

h. The report gives some support to the claim in (a), but we'd give that claim more credence only after more confirmation.

4. a. Certain cloned human genes can repair damaged cells (in hamsters; that it would do the same in humans is indicated but still speculative).

b. Damaged cells in hamsters

c. Experimental cause-to-effect

d. Cells in hamsters in which the cloned genes were inserted form the experimental group; cells in untreated hamsters are the control group. No figures about the sizes of either one are given.

e. Two-thirds of the experimental group were repaired, compared to one-tenth of one percent in the control group.

f. There is a huge difference of frequency; even if the sample were relatively small, we'd expect it to be statistically significant.

g. None that we can spot; information about the sizes of the groups would have been helpful, however.

h. The report supports claim (a). Lawrence Livermore National Laboratory has had its troubles in recent years, but not in areas like this. We're willing to give credence to the report.

6. a. Circumcision causes pain (and, possibly, prolonged effects on neurological and social development) in infants.

b. Male infants

c. Both studies seem to be experimental cause-to-effect. (Presumably, the attending physicians did not select infants to be circumcised at random, but we can probably assume the next best thing, since there's no reason to think that the circumcised infants were more susceptible to pain than the others.)

d. No sizes are given for either experimental (circumcised) or control (uncircumcised) groups in the first study. The same is true of the second study, although here both groups were composed of circumcised infants, with members of the experimental group given anesthetic before the operation.

e. & f. The "almost all" indicates a significantly large difference in frequency of effect in the first study cited; the second study reads as if the effect (less irritability, better motor responses, and so on) were universal among the experimental group.

g. & h. No weaknesses that we can think of, although the entire report is pretty vague. It's difficult to assess just what's going on in an infant, of course, but we'd as soon trust the folks at Harvard Medical School as anybody. Frankly, we're surprised (and a little put off) by the fact that physicians knew no more about infant pain than they seem to have known. We wonder what other "medical school myths" may be floating around.

7. a. & b. High doses of androgens reduce HDL levels in the blood of adult human males.

c. Nonexperimental cause-to-effect study

d. The experimental group consisted of sixteen healthy, "well-conditioned" men in their early thirties who took androgens for four weeks as part of their weight-training program. The control group consisted of the same men before using androgens, all of whom had normal levels of HDLs.

e. The HDL levels in the experimental group decreased by 60 percent.

f. We don't know what normal HDL levels are, expressed in numerical terms, so we don't know what a "60 percent drop" amounts to, or whether a drop of 60 percent from a normal level produces a level that's too low. However, the implication of the article is that the drop is medically important.

g. It certainly would be nice to know something more about the "self-prescribed and self-administered use" of steroids. Was the overall drop in HDL due to a very large drop on the part of two very heavy users? Well, probably not, given the source of the study and where it was published.

h. The study warrants caution on the part of anyone contemplating taking androgens for medically unnecessary reasons.

12. a. A medical self-care problem of the sort described reduces visits to the doctor by families that use it.

b. American families

c. Controlled cause-to-effect experiment

d. A group of families of unspecified size randomly chosen from the Rhode Island Group Health Association cared for their medical needs with self-care literature, with backup telephone counseling available ("in some cases") from a nurse. The control group was of unspecified size; the families in it received no special educational help.

e. The frequency of the effect is unstated for both groups.

f. There is no reason to believe that these results are statistically significant.

g. Details concerning the telephone hot line are much too obscure.

h. The first sentence of the item states very nicely the claim that is warranted by the report.

13. a. Pap smears are effective in reducing the incidence of cancer of the cervix.

b. Women

c. Nonexperimental cause-to-effect study

d. The total of both control and experimental groups is 207,455 Swedish women. How many were in the control group and how many in the experimental group is not stated.

e. The frequency of the effect is not given for either group, only that it was "two to four times higher" in the control group. (This way of phrasing casts cases of cervical cancer as the effect. Since the study investigates the effects of Pap smears, it may be better to identify the effect as a *failure to contract* cervical cancer, in which case we would say that the frequency of the effect was "two to four times higher" in the *experimental* group.) The "two to four times higher" claim does not tell us anything about the actual frequencies; however, the study is clearly a reputable one, and the coauthor's remark implies that the difference in frequency was significant.

f. Yes, the report quotes a coauthor of the study to this effect.

g. None that are obvious

h. Same as (a)

15. a. Vaccine made of living cancer cells from a patient's colorectal cancer can slow or prevent the subsequent appearance of cancer elsewhere.
    b. Humans
    c.–f. This is a modified cause-to-effect experiment, in which there is no control group *per se*. The experimental group consists of twenty patients with colorectal cancer; four had recurrences in the two to four years they were followed, but none of the group has died. The significance of these findings can be determined only by comparison with recurrence statistics in cancer victims who have not received such a vaccine. Unfortunately, no such statistics are mentioned. This was clearly a reputable scientific experiment, and the report does not state or imply that the study proves that the vaccine prevents a recurrence of cancer in victims of colorectal cancer. In fact, the opposite is stated in the last sentence of the report. The experiment does support the claim that the vaccine and its effects should be studied further.

Exercise 12-7

To begin with, there's the matter of "rounding upward" by $10 to $50 billion. But that was done by fiat and involved no pretense of reasoning.

There remain two very serious reasons for doubting the $26 billion figure for "reduced productivity." First, the NIDA contractors grouped people *who had ever* smoked marijuana regularly and people who had not, but they compared their *current* incomes; not the incomes of the two groups at the times the marijuana smokers were actually using the drug. This means that low income now is being attributed to marijuana use that may have occurred decades ago.

The second, and more important, criticism of this study is the obvious failure to control for other causal factors, including common causes and even reverse causation. We expect there are more people who come into regular contact with drugs because they are poor than who become poor because they come into regular contact with drugs.

If the remaining $21 billion figure for drug-related crimes, accidents, and so on, was arrived at with the same carelessness as the $26 billion figure, our opinion is that the government wasted our money on such a poorly done study.

Chapter 12 Test Question/Exercise Banks

Bank 12-1

The following arguments can be evaluated in accordance with the questions listed in the directions for Exercise 12-2 in the text, or they can be discussed more informally. We'll provide only brief comments here.

1. Parker's mimosa tree is getting yellow and dropping leaves. He figures it must be the tiny little caterpillars he sees on it, since before he saw them the tree seemed fine.

   X is the difference, and a reasonable conjecture; Parker probably would have noticed the changes in the tree previously had they been due simply to a change of season.

2. Sharon has observed that her teacher sometimes seems to be in a bod mood and speculates why. "Well," she thinks, "it seems to happen only when people haven't done their assignments. That must be it."

Common thread, though if this is the cause, then Sharon's teacher may be in a bad mood a lot of the time.

3. Studies indicate that older women who attempt weight training seem to be in better shape physically than those who don't. This is a good reason for older women to lift weights.

Could be reversed causation

4. Cheryl and her new acquaintance, Ted, have just walked into Target when in comes her steady boyfriend, Lemmy. "Oh, for crying out loud," Cheryl thinks. "Why would he come into Target, of all places? I must be being punished for something I did, and I know what."

Cheryl is using some type of X is the difference reasoning, but this is probably just coincidence.

5. Ever since the Brady Bill was passed, it seems like violent crime has skyrocketed—a good reason to repeal the bill, I'd say.

Post hoc reasoning

6. "Four years ago, nonfat milk sold for 95 cents per half gallon. Today I paid $1.45 per half gallon from one of our low-priced supermarkets. That's a 52 percent increase in just four years for an average of 13 percent per year, while the official government inflation rate is less than 3 percent. Why is this? It's not coincidence that four years ago we got our first Republican governor in this state in a long time."
—from a newspaper call-in column

Post hoc reasoning; it probably is a coincidence

7. Have you noticed how yellow the Doerrs' lawn has gotten? They started fertilizing it, too, I understand. Must be cheapo fertilizer, to make it turn yellow like that.

Consider reversed causation

8. See? When she has a good day at the store and sells lots of clothes, she always is in a good mood. It just shows you how effective a good mood can be in the sales busines.. The customer eats that stuff up.

Consider reversed causation

9. Have you ever noticed how successful businesspeople always wear expensive clothes? There's a moral there: Watch what you wear if you want to be a success.

Consider reversed causation

10. Studies indicate that close to 85 percent of university professors are liberal Democrats. It only stands to reason, therefore, that if you want to get a job as a college instructor, register as a Democrat.

    Could be an instance of ignoring a common cause (the same traits of mind that are likely to get a person a job as a college instructor are also likely to make a person favor the Democratic party); or, more likely, college professors tend to think their interests are best served by the Democratic party.

11. February 2 is Groundhog Day. If the groundhog sees his shadow, there'll be six more weeks of winter. If he doesn't, spring is right around the corner.

    Groundhog Day claims are not causal: No one thinks the groundhog's seeing or not seeing his shadow causes *whatever happens to the weather afterward. (A dark February 2 in Pennsylvania—where Punxsutawney Phil, the official groundhog, lives— might be* correlated *with an exceptionally short winter, for all we know. If it is, look for some sort of meteorological phenomenon as a common cause.)*

12. Every time I play tennis my wrist hurts for several days afterward. If my doctor can't help me figure what to do about it, I may have to give up the game.

    X is the common thread. Probably okay, although the likelihood is that tennis is only part of the cause; some underlying condition is being exacerbated by playing tennis.

13. A lottery winner, asked why he thought he had won a major prize, pulled a small rhinestone four-leaf clover out of his pocket and said, "I think this had a lot to do with it."

    Post hoc: "I carried my lucky charm, and I won."

14. I had a lot of noise on my car stereo when the engine was running, until I read in an old Champion Spark Plug publication that the way to fix the problem is to install a 4MH choke coil in the hot wire from the battery to the stereo. I did it, and it cured the problem.

    X is the difference, and in this case just fine.

15. I'd wash the car but for the fact that we don't need any more rain.

    This is probably best construed as a bad case of X is the difference.

16. The car usually makes it over the hills between here and the lake without any trouble. The only time it makes any trouble is when we have to pull the boat and trailer; they must make too heavy a load for the car's small engine.

    X is the common thread, although reading the first part of the second sentence as "The car makes trouble if and only if the boat is pulled" allows an X-is-the-difference interpretation as well. (That isn't what the sentence says*, but . . .)*

17. Before every voyage, we toss a drink to the old man in the sea.

    That is, doing so brings good luck; not doing so brings bad luck. The superstition probably originated as a faulty application of X is the difference or X is the common thread, or both. (Before every airplane flight, your authors toss a drink down the hatch, but not from superstition.)

18. "Of course he was outdoors Wednesday, Watson. That's the only day there has been rain, and he had a good bit of dried mud on the heels of his boots."

    Wednesday's rain caused the mud to be on the boots: X is the difference. Note: Sherlock Holmes examples are as nice for the first part of this chapter as they are for truth-functional inferences.

19. "I'm over seventy years old and got all of my natural teeth but one. The secret is to eat a dollop of raw veal bone marrow every day."
    —Attributed to Mrs. Keller [a "wise old woman of Ohio"] by Robert L. Tubbesing, *Old Farmer's Almanac* (1986)

    This item is probably best analyzed as post hoc (I ate veal marrow every day and have all my teeth save one; therefore, the former caused the latter). A case for common thread can be made for this one, but not a very good case; there are too many other possible variables.

20. The only packages that suffered damage during the trip were the ones we packed with newspaper instead of that styrofoam packing stuff. I learned a lesson: Make sure you have enough of the proper packing material.

    X is the common thread. Our packer might consider, though, whether the materials that were damaged were more fragile than the others—that could be another relevant factor besides packing material. (See remarks at end of item 16; they apply here, too.)

21. Raphael is troubled by the fact that when he purchases new guitar strings, they seem always to go dead after just a few weeks of use. A friend suggests that he boil the strings in vinegar when they lose their resonance. Raphael tries it, and the strings sound almost like new again. After a few weeks, the strings go dead again, and Raphael boils them in vinegar and gets the same results. He resigns himself to a session with boiling vinegar every few weeks.

    X is the difference; because of the second treatment, common thread may be a possibility, but a far-fetched one. (Does anyone know whether this really works? The smell of boiling vinegar wouldn't be worth a failed attempt.)

22. When Halley's comet hovered over Jerusalem in A.D. 66, the historian Josephus warned it meant the destruction of the city. Jerusalem fell four years later, thus confirming the power of the comet.

    Post hoc. Somebody applied Josephus's prediction again in 1988, this time to Los Angeles. Didn't work this time. At least not yet.

23. A terrible squeaking noise from my tape recorder got so bad I couldn't stand to listen to my tapes anymore. I was sure the machine had developed a problem—and just a month after the warranty expired, too. So I cleaned the heads, the capstan, and all the moving parts, hoping I could make the noise go away. It remained. Then, just as I had decided I was going to have to take it in for repairs, I played some tapes belonging to a friend of mine, and the squeak wasn't there. So the problem is with my tapes, not my machine. I'm not sure I like that any better, since I've got dozens of them.

X is the difference. This is a fairly good argument; of course his problem could lie in the combination *of the tapes and the machine.*

24. Less than twenty-four hours after seeing the movie *Glade's Corner,* which depicts the brutal knife-slaying of an elderly man by teenagers, fifteen-year-old Mark Striker attempted to kill his sixty-five-year-old great uncle. His weapon: a knife.

Post hoc, but keep in mind the question that should be asked about this type of argument.

25. Fund-raising director for a public radio station: "I know that our music director gets hysterical when we play a lot of tired stuff like the *1812 Overture* and the Grieg piano concerto. But go back and look at our most successful fund drives; every big day has been a day heavily loaded with those 'classics.' "

X is the common thread.

26. If you don't want your kids to smoke tobacco, keep them away from marijuana. It has been estimated that 75 percent of pot smokers do use other drugs, including tobacco.

This argument may ignore a common cause. Also, if there is causation, the argument may have it reversed.

27. Between 1984 and 1989, American consumption of oatmeal at breakfast went up 56 percent. Meanwhile, the consumption of coffee dropped 11 percent. For some reason, oatmeal must make coffee taste bad.

Probably there is a common cause. The statistics cited might even be coincidence.

28. "Being happy and having a positive outlook may help people with heart disease avoid heart attacks and other health problems. Approximately one in five coronary heart disease patients is seriously depressed, so be on guard against depression in yourself and your loved ones."
—Sharon Faelten, *Vitality*

This could be a case of reversed causation.

29. "After four years as an associate and brokerage manager with the New York life insurance consulting firm Kramer-Helgans, Sharon Brick noticed that she was being taken more seriously. It wasn't just because she'd done a great job, says Brick. She had changed her hair color from a dull brown to a lighter, more flattering sandy blond. Several months later, Brick was offered a partnership in the firm."
—*Working Woman*

Post hoc

30. Are body lice a cause of good health? So it seemed to the people in New Hebrides Islands, according to John Allen Paulos's comment in his book *Innumeracy*. After all, when body lice departed, people became ill.

   As Paulos in effect observed, this is an instance of ignoring a common cause. The good health and the lice both departed because of a fever. (Of course, the fever doesn't actually cause the illness, but it causes some of the discomfort of the illness.)

31. Since the taxes [on cigarettes] have been going up in Canada, cigarette smoking has been going down, particularly among the young. The lesson here is plain: The best way to reduce smoking is simply to raise the price of cigarettes.

   X is the difference, though are the higher taxes the only thing that's different from times when the young smoked more? We doubt it.

32. The price of a pack of cigarettes in Norway is $4.95, with taxes making up at least 70 percent of the total cost. Contrast that to the United States, where a pack sells for about $1.70. That's why per capita consumption here is 2,200, whereas in Norway it is 700.

   X is the difference. $4.95 a pack? Wow. We're glad we quit years ago.

Bank 12-2

The following are for informal analysis or for applying the questions in the directions for Exercise 12-6 as a guide. Once again, we'll provide brief comments.

33. "You don't need to become a complete ascetic in order to lower your cholesterol levels. Scott M. Grundy of the University of Texas Health Science Center at Dallas and his colleagues rotated nine men through two-month stints on each of three diets—the American Health Association diet, in which a maximum of 30 percent of the calories come from fat; a 40 percent fat diet; and a 20 percent fat diet. The subjects' average cholesterol level was 210 mg/dl on entry.

   "In all the men, the blood levels of total cholesterol and of the 'bad' form of cholesterol, LDL-cholesterol, fell to around 175. 'There were no significant differences [in cholesterol levels of the men] on these three diets,' Grundy says."
   —*Science News*

   The "control" group consists in effect of the same men before the diets. The article does not make clear what percentage of the calories in the men's former diets came from fat, a defect in the report. (We've heard that in the standard U.S. diet, about 41 percent of calories are fat-derived.)

34. Do sudden heart attacks increase with vigorous exercise? A community-based study investigated this issue and discovered that persons who habitually exercised vigorously had a *reduced* risk of sudden cardiac death as compared with persons who only occasionally exercised vigorously. One hundred thirty-three married men who experienced out-of-hospital cardiac arrest were chosen for the study. They were classified according to their usual amount of activity and the amount of activity at the time of the cardiac arrest. All appeared healthy prior to the heart

attacks. The benefits outweighed the risks for men at the upper levels of habitual high-intensity activity. Their overall risk was 40 percent of that of sedentary men.
—Adapted from "Stress and Health Report," N.T. Enloe Memorial Hospital Stress and Health Center, Chico, California

Since we don't know how many of the men qualified as sedentary or habitually high-intensity active, the 40 percent figure tells us little. Since we have no information on who conducted the study, we can make no inferences concerning how reasonable the definitions of the various activity categories are or whether the 40 percent figure translates into a significant difference. (This kind of report is sometimes the summary of a creditable study. However, too many details are missing in this summary to allow us to attach great importance to it.)

35. BOSTON—AP, UPI reports (adapted). The constant bright lights of hospital nurseries, often two to four times as bright as normal office lighting, may contribute to the blinding of hundreds of premature babies each year, a recent study warns. Doctors kept track of the incidence of retinopathy, a disease of the retina, in two groups of premature babies. One group was kept in incubators covered with acetate that reduced the amount of light by 58 percent. The rest stayed in ordinary incubators. Among the smallest babies, the researchers found that twenty-one of thirty-nine (54 percent) in shielded incubators developed retinopathy, compared with eighteen of twenty-one (86 percent) of those exposed to the bright lights. Dr. Penny Glass, a developmental psychologist at Children's Hospital National Medical Center and Georgetown University Medical Center, who directed the study, recommends that the light levels in hospital nurseries be brought down. "I feel that the increase in light levels has not been demonstrated safe," she said.

Note the researcher's mild conclusion (last sentence). This controlled cause-to-effect experiment offers strong support for such a cautious conclusion.

36. Does learning how to program a computer help first graders to think? Douglas H. Clements and Dominic F. Gullo of Kent State University randomly assigned eighteen first graders from a middle-class, Midwestern school system into two computer groups. The first group programmed an Apple II computer, using the computer language Logo, during two forty-minute sessions a week for twelve weeks. The other group received computer-based lessons in arithmetic and reading for the same time period. It was found that the children who programmed increased their scores on a creativity test in which they had to devise and draw pictures under time restraints and became better at identifying instances when they had not been given enough information to complete a simple task or understand how a magic trick is performed. However, a number of other tests provided no evidence that the programming experience can improve overall thinking abilities.

The investigation was reported in the *Journal of Educational Psychology*.
—Adapted from *Science News*

Based on the report of this cause-to-effect experiment, the extent and the nature of improvement seen on the tests are unclear. Note that the study was published in a respected journal.

37. Each year in the U.S., a surgical procedure known as extracranial-intracranial arterial (EC/IC) bypass is done on three thousand to five thousand people who have had, or are at risk of, stroke. The operation, in which an artery on the scalp is attached to an artery on the brain to bypass a partial or total blockage, costs about $15,000. In a new study, researchers from the University Hospital in London, Ontario examined 1,377 people who had recently had strokes or had signs of impending strokes. They randomly assigned 714 to get standard medical care and 663 to get EC/IC bypasses. The group that had the surgery subsequently had a slightly higher rate of stroke and death than the control group, according to the study.
—Reported in the *New England Journal of Medicine*

Remind us not to spend $15,000 on an EC/IC bypass.

38. In a study designed to test some of the effects of marijuana on the performance of difficult tasks, Jerome A. Yesavage of Stanford University and his colleagues recruited ten experienced private pilots and trained them on a computerized flight-simulator landing task. All subjects had smoked marijuana at some time in the past, though none was a daily user. None smoked marijuana during the test period, except as required by the test. The test period began with a morning baseline flight, after which each subject smoked a marijuana cigarette containing 19 milligrams of tetrahydrocannabinol, the active agent in marijuana. The pilots repeated the landing task one, four, and twenty-four hours later. The worst performances compared with the baseline occurred one hour after smoking the cigarette. Twenty-four hours later, however, the pilots still experienced significant difficulty in aligning the computerized airplane and landing it in the center of the runway. According to the scientists, there were marked deviations from the proper angle of descent in the last six thousand feet of approach to the landing.

The amount of marijuana smoked is comparable to a strong social dose, the researchers said.
—Adapted from *Science News*

The men's baseline performances constitute the control group in this controlled cause-to-effect experiment. One wonders about the pilots' attitudes: Were any out to prove a point?

39. In a study of telephone operators in North Carolina, Suzanne Haynes of the National Center for Health Statistics in Hyattsville, Maryland, compared 278 women who worked all day at video display terminals (VDTs) with 218 clerical workers in the same companies who did not use VDTs. Twice as many VDT users reported chest pains as clerical workers in the same companies—20 percent compared to 10 percent. Perhaps, Haynes commented, "VDTs can be the ultimate nonsupportive boss."
—Adapted from *Science News*

This is a cause-to-effect study, of course. The report is short on details, but the findings are statistically significant. Nevertheless, before indicting VDT use as a cause of chest pain or heart trouble, we would want to know more about the other duties and responsibilities of the VDT users as compared with those of the nonusers.

40. Tiffany Field, a psychologist at the University of Miami Medical School, believes that it is good for premature babies to be given short sessions of body stroking and limb movement. She and her fellow researchers studied forty premature babies in a transitional-care nursery. Although the infants were stable enough to be released from the intensive care unit and none needed extra oxygen or intravenous feedings, they had required an average of twenty days of intensive care, and the heaviest among them was under four pounds. Their average age at birth was thirty-one weeks. Half the group was randomly chosen to receive standardized touch and movement stimulation for three fifteen-minute periods per day over ten consecutive weekdays. Treated infants averaged a 47 percent greater weight gain per day, even though they had the same number of feedings and the same level of calorie intake as did the control babies. The stimulated group also was awake and physically active a greater percentage of the time. "Since the experimental kids were more active, their weight gain was not due to greater energy conservation," Field points out. Infants in the treatment group also outdistanced controls on a number of behavioral measures, and they were hospitalized on the average six days fewer than infants in the control group.

—Adapted from Bruce Bower, *Science News*

This controlled cause-to-effect experiment provides strong support for the conclusion stated by the researcher.

41. In 1960, Dutch researchers from the University of Leiden questioned 852 men and their wives about the men's diets and then monitored the men for the next twenty years. They found that the death rate from heart disease was more than 50 percent lower among men who ate at least thirty grams (one ounce) of fish per day compared with men who ate no fish. Just one or two fish dishes a week, the researchers say, "may be of value in the prevention of coronary heart disease."

—Adapted from *Science News*

Fish in the diet may be of value in the prevention of coronary heart disease, but this study, as reported here, does not show that it is. Unless we know what the death rate actually was, we cannot attach great importance to the "50 percent lower" claim. Given the scope and likely credibility of the investigators, though, the 50 percent figure probably translates into a difference that is significant.

42. A study of 546 men in New Zealand who were identified as leukemia patients between 1979 and 1983 suggests that electrical workers are at increased risk of developing this cancer. Each man was matched with four other men from New Zealand's cancer registry. The study found a significant excess of leukemias among those electrical workers who had been employed as electronic equipment assemblers (4 cases, where only 0.5 would have been expected) and radio and television repairers (7 cases, where only 1.5 would have been expected). The study was conducted by N. E. Pearce and his colleagues at the Department of Community Health, Wellington Clinical School, and National Health Statistics Centre in Wellington, New Zealand.

In a second study, Washington State epidemiologist Samuel Milham, Jr., obtained the death certificates for 95 percent of the 296 deceased Washington members of the American Radio Relay League (amateur radio operators) and 86 percent of the 1,642 deceased California members. Twenty-four of the deaths were due to leukemia; 16 of these were of the myeloid class—nearly triple the 5.7 deaths that would have been expected from this type of leukemia. Milham acknowledges that the difference might be attributable to chance but points out that three other studies have revealed a tendency toward a relative increase in the acute myelogenous type of leukemia in electrical workers.

—Adapted from *Science News*

The first investigation, an effect-to-cause study, suggests that something associated with working with electronics is a causal factor for leukemia in humans. The second, a cause-to-effect study, does not support the same thesis. But given the other studies mentioned, we would not think that further investigation of a possible link between leukemia and electrical work would be a waste of money.

43. "Exercise can temporarily disrupt a woman's menstrual cycle, according to Boston University research published in the May 23 [1985] *New England Journal of Medicine*. The researchers monitored the daily hormone levels in 28 college women who did not exercise regularly and had a history of regular menstrual cycles. The women were then sent to summer camp and participated in a rigorous exercise program—an initial 4-mile daily run, working up to 10 miles a day after five weeks, in addition to three and one-half hours daily of moderate sports such as biking or tennis. Only four, three of whom were on a high-calorie weight maintenance diet, had a normal menstrual cycle during that time. The researchers concluded that, regardless of whether the women lost weight, strenuous exercise disrupted their reproductive function. 'If very active women are having trouble getting pregnant, they probably should slow down intense exercise,' says exercise physiologist Gary Skrinar of BU."

—*Science News*

This is a cause-to-effect experiment, in which the 'control group' is the same women before the exercise regimen. This is a standard and often reliable practice. However, in this instance it is a weakness in the experiment, since menstrual cycles can be affected by nervousness, excitement, going on vacations, and other such things. It would be going out on a limb to conclude, on the basis of this experiment, that women athletes who have menstrual problems owe that fact to their exercise.

Bank 12-3

Here are ten studies for analysis of whatever sort you'd care to assign.

44. As reported in the *Journal of the American Medical Association*, 26 surgeons-in-training were studied to see whether sleep deprivation impaired their patient-care ability. For 18 to 19 days the residents kept a sleep diary and underwent five tests each morning to measure cognition, visual and auditory alertness and hand-eye coordination. Sleep deprivation was defined as less than 4 hours of continuous sleep in the previous 24 hours, which occurred in 89 percent of the on-duty nights studied. When sleep deprivation occurred, total sleep averaged 3 hours, and the longest uninterrupted sleep averaged 2.2 hours.

Residents did show "trivial" improvement on two tests when they obtained some sleep just before testing, but the researchers said repetitive sleep deprivation did not impair the residents' test performances.

The study "does not support arbitrary recommendations to limit working hours of residents," it was said.

—Adapted from *Science News*

45. A study published in the *New England Journal of Medicine* concludes that the number of handgun deaths in Vancouver, British Columbia, between 1980 and 1986 was less than one-fifth that of Seattle, 120 miles to the south. Seattle's population is approximately 490,000, whereas Vancouver's is about 43,000.

In Seattle, handguns may legally be purchased for self-defense. After a thirty-day waiting period, a permit to carry a handgun as a concealed weapon can be obtained. Recreational uses are minimally restricted. In Vancouver, self-defense is not a legal reason to purchase a handgun. Concealed weapons are not permitted, and recreational weapons may be fired only at a licensed shooting club.

Dr. Henry Sloan, chief investigator for the study, said 388 homicides occurred in Seattle during the study period, while 204 occurred in Vancouver. The number of gun-related deaths in Seattle was 139, compared with 25 for Vancouver, he said. He stopped short of saying his findings prove Seattle's less strict gun control laws cause more deaths, but said, "It virtually explains it."

Note: New gun control laws went into effect in 1978. Sloan said Vancouver's laws were made stricter in 1978 but didn't change significantly.

—Adapted from Associated Press

46. Twenty-five two-pack-a-day smokers who had tried unsuccessfully to quit smoking were tested at the University of Tennessee in Memphis. For seven weeks, twelve took doxepin, an antidepressant, and thirteen took placebos. After fifty-six days, nine people on doxepin were no longer smoking, as compared with only one in the other group. The doxepin-takers reported reductions in nervousness, anxiety, and craving for nicotine.

In a second study, Dr. Alexander H. Glassman of Columbia University gave heavy smokers either clonidine, a drug used to treat hypertension, or a placebo. After four weeks, 61 percent of the clonidine group were not smoking, while only 26 percent of the placebo group had stopped.

These studies, reported in *Physician's Weekly,* were given by *Reader's Digest* as grounds for the conclusion that "Two drugs, one for depression, the other for high blood pressure, may help smokers resist cigarettes."

47. We provided evidence that we could prevent myocardial infarction in angina patients, says Pierre Theroux of the Montreal Heart Institute. As reported in the *New England Journal of Medicine* (October 27, 1988), Theroux and his colleagues placed 479 hospitalized patients who had experienced chest pains into four treatment groups receiving either aspirin, heparin, a combination of the two, or a placebo. Heparin therapy reduced the rate of fatal and nonfatal heart attacks by 89 percent as compared with the placebo. It also reduced chest pain by 63 percent. Previous studies of heparin treatment of chest pain have produced questionable results, Theroux says.

Aspirin therapy also helped: The Montreal team found that aspirin reduced the risk of heart attacks by 72 percent as compared with the placebo. But the combination aspirin/heparin treatment showed no particular benefit compared with aspirin alone or heparin alone, and patients getting the two drugs combined had a slightly higher risk of complications, such as bleeding.

The researchers recommend for patients hospitalized with chest pain treatment with heparin upon admission followed by aspirin therapy for long-term management.

—Adapted from *Science News*

48. "Barbara Sherwin, director of a research team at McGill University, found that a small quantity of the male hormone testosterone, in addition to estrogen, led to a spicier sex life for some postmenopausal women. Twenty-two of the McGill team's subjects were given 150 milligrams a month of testosterone with estrogen, 11 were given estrogen alone, and 11 took placebos. The testosterone group reported more desire and arousal and more frequent sexual thoughts than did the women in the other two groups. Though 17 percent of the testosterone recipients developed mild facial hair, this side effect receded when the dosage was reduced."

—Elsie Rosner, *Physician's Weekly,* reported in *Reader's Digest*

49. Smoking greatly increases the likelihood of premature facial wrinkling, according to University of Utah scientists reporting in the *Annals of Internal Medicine.* The scientists studied 109 smokers and 23 people who had never smoked, all between the ages of thirty-five and fifty-nine. The smokers had smoked three to fifty pack-years, with a pack-year equal to smoking one pack a day per year. Each subject estimated the number of hours spent in the sun, and that information was adjusted for pigmentation, place of residence, and use of sunscreen or protective clothing. The subjects' temples were then photographed and the pictures evaluated by two doctors, who did not know whether the subject smoked or not. The reviewers agreed on the degree of wrinkling 81 percent of the time, and disagreements were averaged. The results were adjusted for age and pigmentation. Heavy smokers were nearly five times more likely to show excessive skin wrinkling than their nonsmoking counterparts.

—adapted from *Science News* and AP reports

50. William Elliott, a University of Chicago physician, has found a link between diagonal creases in earlobes and risk of heart disease. He investigated twenty-seven groups of people, each group containing two pairs of individuals matched for age, sex, and race: one pair with established coronary heart disease and another pair of healthy people. A single member of each pair also had creased earlobes. After eight years, a significantly greater number of people with ear creases had died of heart disease, whether or not they were known to have heart disease at the start of the study.

   Elliott, who reported his findings at a meeting of the American Federation for Clinical Research, encourages other physicians to monitor patients with earlobe creases for symptoms of heart disease.

—adapted from *Science News*

51. Dr. Dean Ornish, of the University of California San Francisco Medical School and Pacific Presbyterian Medical Center, wanted to learn whether life-style changes could reverse the progress of heart disease. At first, he found little support for his research, and several of his grant requests were turned down. Eventually he secured funding from private contributors.

   Ornish recruited forty-three men and five women, ages forty-one to seventy-one, all with very serious heart disease. A statistician randomly assigned the subjects either to a group that followed their own doctor's recommendations for diet and life-style changes or to a group that would follow a mild exercise regimen coupled with stress-management counseling and a low-fat vegetarian diet with no meats, poultry, or fish and with restricted intake levels of cholesterol and fat.

   Six people in this group did not complete the testing. Among the remaining twenty-two participants, eighteen showed reversal of the blockages in their coronary arteries after one year. In the comparison group, one person dropped out, and ten of the remaining nineteen developed measurably worse heart disease, while three showed no significant change. Six people in the comparison group showed measurable reversal. This was due, says Ornish, to the life-style changes they made on their own.

Dr. Alexander Leaf, former chairman of the Department of Preventive Medicine at Harvard University Medical School, says, "For the first time, we have a carefully done scientific study that shows, even in advanced stages, this disease can be reversed with life-style changes." Ornish's findings have prompted sizable grants from the National Heart, Lung, and Blood Institute and other foundations.

—adapted from *Reader's Digest*

52. A study from the University of Health Sciences/Chicago Medical School suggests, says psychologist David E. Schotte, coauthor of the study, "that dieters have to learn to cope with stresses and emotional upsets in order to lose weight." Fifteen women who were frequent dieters and fifteen who dieted infrequently were all given a premeasured bag of popcorn, and then saw scenes from *Halloween*. After the screening, each bag was collected and reweighed. The habitual dieters ate more than twice as much popcorn as did the women who dieted infrequently.

—adapted from Sally Squires in the *Washington Post*

53. Women who take one to six aspirin tablets a week can lower their risk of heart attacks, according to a new study conducted at Boston's Brigham and Women's Hospital. The study followed 87,678 female nurses for six years. According to the study leader, Dr. JoAnn Manson, there was a 30 percent reduction in the risk of a first heart attack among women who took one to six aspirin tablets per week. Altogether, about 26 percent of the nurses studied took one to six aspirin a week, she said.

—adapted from an article by Judy Foreman, *Boston Globe*

Bank 12-4

True/False

54. The claim "Fluoridated water prevents tooth decay," if true, implies that fluoridated water would prevent tooth decay in the majority of individuals who use it.

False

55. The claim "Fouled spark plugs kept the car from starting" implies that the car would have started if the spark plugs had not been fouled.

True

56. In a nonexperimental cause-to-effect study, the members of the experimental group are exposed to the suspected causal agent by the investigators.

False

57. In a nonexperimental effect-to-cause study, *none* of the members of the control group show the effect of the cause being investigated.

    True

58. Arguments of the post hoc, ergo propter hoc pattern can sometimes be converted into a reliable version of another pattern.

    True

Bank 12-5

The next five items are based on the following paragraph:

Lin sends away for a hot-cold serving tray she has seen advertised. The tray is promised to keep hot dishes hot and cold dishes cold without electricity. Lin tries it out by placing a pan of hot beans on it. They stay hot throughout dinner. "It works," she tells her husband.

59. What causal claim (if any) is stated or implied in Lin's conclusion?

    Placing the pan of beans on the serving tray kept them hot.

60. What kind of causal claim is this?

    Causation between specific occurrences

61. What type of argument or pattern of reasoning is employed?

    Post hoc, ergo propter hoc

62. Invent at least one plausible alternative explanation of the effect.

    The beans stayed hot all by themselves—that is, they would have stayed hot even if they had been placed on a standard trivet.

63. If you think there could be a better test of the hot plate, explain it in a sentence or two.

    Compare what happens with two pans of beans of the same temperature, one left on the hot plate and the other on a standard surface.

The next five items are based on the following paragraph:

Johnson is hired by a pharmaceutical company to determine whether a new product, Topocal, will promote hair growth on balding men. He runs an ad in the newspaper inviting men with hair loss to participate and gets fifty respondents who participate in a hair growth experiment. He randomly divides the respondents into two groups: half of them (group A) rub Topocal on a preselected, one-inch-square bald patch on their scalps. The other half (group B) apply a mixture of lemon juice and water in a similar manner. At the end of one month, Johnson compares the appropriate patches of each man's scalp and notes the results.

64. What is the causal claim at issue?

Topocal causes hair growth on bald men.

65. What type of argument or pattern of reasoning is employed?

Controlled cause-to-effect experiment

66. Which group is the experimental group?

Group A

67. Suppose that the results were significant at the 0.05 level. That means we could say with a _95_ percent degree of confidence that Topocal produces hair growth in balding men.

68. Briefly criticize Johnson's experiment. Are there things you do not know that you would need to know in order to have confidence that the experiment was reliable?

It is essential that the men from each group be alike save for the fact that group A men are treated with Topocal. Were they? Could their hair losses have resulted from different causes? Age and medical condition of the subjects could also affect the findings. Also, how were the before-and-after scalp areas compared? By hair count? The comparison should not be subjective or impressionistic on the part of the observer.

Bank 12-6

Essay questions

69. It is widely believed that chocolate causes acne, since people susceptible to acne frequently assert that eating chocolate is invariably followed by an outbreak of the skin condition. However, Donald G. Bruns, in a letter to *Science News,* wondered whether those who have the belief that chocolate causes acne might not have things backwards. Some studies indicate that hormonal changes associated with stress may cause acne, he notes. Other studies indicate that people fond of chocolate may tend to eat more chocolate when under stress. Given these studies, Bruns comments, it may be easy to confuse which, the chocolate or the acne, is the cause and which is the effect.

In a brief essay, explain what pattern of reasoning seems to underlie the belief that chocolate causes acne *(probably X is the difference—the only relevant difference between this situation, in which there was an outbreak of acne, and situations in which there was none is that in this situation the person ate chocolate),* and then answer this question: Bruns complains that those who believe that chocolate causes acne may be guilty of the fallacy of reversed causation. Given the studies he cites, has Bruns correctly identified the fallacy? *No. The fallacy is ignoring a common cause.*

70. "An FBI study of thirty-five serial killers [killers of several people, not all at once] revealed that twenty-nine were attracted to pornography and incorporated it into their sexual activity, which included serial rape and murder." This assertion, taken

from an antipornography ad, seems to have been intended to show that pornography is a causal factor of serial rape and murder. Does it show that?

An essay on this question should demonstrate sensitivity to the following points: The assertion about the FBI study would support the causal claim in question only if the frequency of attraction to pornography in the "experimental group" cited above were known to exceed significantly the frequency in a "control group" of people who had not committed serial rape and murder. Further, that condition, while necessary for the FBI study to support the causal claim in question, would not be sufficient. Were the subjects in the "experimental group" different from the control group and the rest of us in some relevant way other than that they were murderers? Almost certainly. Were these biasing differences controlled? The essay should perhaps consider directly the question of whether the attraction to pornography and the propensity for sexual violence were both the result of some other factor or factors. It might also indicate the vagueness of the phrase "attracted to pornography."

Chapter 13
Moral, Legal, and Aesthetic Reasoning

This chapter, which covers the material of Chapters 13 and 14 in the third edition, is the product of Nina Rosenstand and Anita Silvers, whom we thank once again for their fine work.

Exercises Unanswered in the Text

Exercise 13-1

2. Descriptive

3. Prescriptive

5. Descriptive

8. Prescriptive

9. Descriptive

10. Prescriptive

Exercise 13-2

2. Nonmoral value

3. No value (although being well informed is something that we often do attach a nonmoral value to, it isn't done in this claim.)

5. Nonmoral value

8. Nonmoral value

9. Moral value

10. Moral value

Exercise 13-3

1. Borrowers should pay for damages that occur to a borrowed object while that object is in their possession.

3. When one person acts to help another in need, the second person should make a reasonable effort to help when the first is in need.

4. People should abide by the terms of contracts they agree to.

6. People should keep their campaign promises. (We're reading the conclusion as saying that Havenhurst *ought* to produce some results.)

9. People who work overtime should receive bonuses.

10. A majority should not be allowed to dictate to a minority.

Exercise 13-4

1. This item obviously depends upon the moral problem one chooses.

2. a. Roy must ask himself whether he would wish that people *always* hide unpleasant facts in order to complete a sale and whether, if people did so, this would undermine the whole enterprise of selling goods to one another.
   b. His approach will not pass the test, because it would mean Roy must be suspicious of everything he buys from another—something he wouldn't want—and it would indeed undermine the whole idea of selling goods, since that enterprise rests at least in part on good faith.
   c. His approach treats the buyer as a means to an end, namely, getting rid of the car at a price satisfactory to him. Treating the buyer as an end involves taking the buyer's interests into account, which Roy isn't doing if he fails to mention the brakes.

3. Virtue theory would have Jim give Farah a modest present along with an expression of his gratitude and to present both in a timely manner. A bouquet of flowers would be appropriate. Money is probably a bad idea, since it undermines the idea that Farah helped Jim out of friendship.

Exercise 13-5

Answers to the questions in this exercise will vary.

Exercise 13-7

The judges' instruction is closer to a retributivist theory, since a person following the principle of social utility must consider the consequences of a verdict. There are cases where it is tempting to consider consequences, whether large scale or small: The Rodney King case indicates how large-scale consequences might weigh on a juror; consequences on a smaller scale might weigh on a juror in a case where a conviction would leave a defendant's family destitute. Many find both kinds of cases reasonable grounds for considering the consequences of convicting the defendant, especially if the crime is nonviolent, victimless, and generally not threatening to society.

Exercise 13-8

We're not going to presume to write a paradigm for these essay answers; we expect that reasonable people may disagree about the direction of the answers.

Exercise 13-9

3. Both, most likely: Backward-looking because execution is the prisoner's just desert; forward-looking because the only other reasonable alternative is to free them, which may allow them to prey on others

5. Forward-looking. Clearly, there's no reasonable fitting of the punishment to Young Lew's crime; he's to be punished as he is because of the benefit others will receive from it.

Exercise 13-10

2. a. Principle 3
   b. Principle 7

   Incompatible

3. a. Principle 1
   b. Principle 5

   Compatible

5. a. Principle 8
   b. Principle 6

   Incompatible

Exercise 13-11

2. Relevant on Principle 1

3. Relevant on Principle 6

5. Irrelevant

6. Irrelevant

Exercise 13-13

2. e

3. a

5. a

6. c

8. d

9. c

Chapter 13 Test Question/Exercise Banks

Bank 13-1

Identify the following claims as descriptive or prescriptive.

1. Morgan is old enough to have known what would happen if he didn't pay the fine on time.

Descriptive

2. Morgan should have paid the fine on time.

Prescriptive

3. Twenty past ten. We should go home.

Prescriptive

4. Jake will pay Mrs. Sly the money he owes, if he knows what's good for him.

Descriptive (presuming the last clause simply makes a prediction)

5. Hazel owes Bert one hundred dollars and, according to the contract, was supposed to pay him back last month.

Descriptive

6. The program Sam wrote for finding repeating decimals works wonderfully, and it's only thirty-five lines long—that's real elegance.

Prescriptive (at a minimum, it prescribes approval)

7. The dog was clearly in pain, but nobody was doing anything about it.

Descriptive

8. It is wrong for the United States to intervene in local wars outside U.S. territory.

Prescriptive

9. It is not in the best interests of the United States to intervene in local wars outside U.S. territory.

Descriptive

10. It is hard to think of any nostrum that has less to recommend it than rent control.

    Prescriptive

11. There ought to be a law against doing what Selena has done to her hair.

    Prescriptive (even if it isn't literally prescribing a statute)

12. If you don't get rid of your dog's fleas, it's going to be miserable.

    Descriptive

13. You should get rid of your dog's fleas so that it won't be miserable.

    Prescriptive

14. You ought to get to know Samuel.

    Prescriptive

15. Brooke and Richard are pleasant enough fellows, once you get to know them.

    Descriptive

Bank 13-2

State whether the following items express moral values, express nonmoral values, or express no values at all.

16. The paint job on Linda's car is awful—looks as though somebody did it with a brush.

    Nonmoral value

17. Alicia has not been entirely honest with her husband; that much is clear.

    No value, provided that the claim means only that she hasn't been entirely truthful; if more than that is meant, our answer is "moral value."

18. Kelly did the right thing when he turned in the wallet he found.

    Moral value

19. The Pittsburgh Steelers were the best football team of the 1970s, and the Forty-Niners were the team of the '80s. But the Redskins will turn out to be the best of the '90s.

    Nonmoral value

20. Everybody should be as fair as Mario tries to be.

    Moral value

21. All cigarette advertising should be strictly regulated.

Moral value, under most circumstances. (We can imagine one instance in which the statement could express a nonmoral value: when a cigarette manufacturer makes the statement to another cigarette manufacturer, adding, ". . . or else they're going to eliminate it entirely.")

22. The advertising for that "miracle" cleaner is fraudulent.

Moral value

23. It is bothersome to be telephoned after 9:00 P.M.

We think most people would be expressing a nonmoral value by this remark.

24. She was really hurt by the way he treated her.

We think most people would be expressing a moral value by this remark.

25. The regime in China is harshly repressive.

Moral value

26. Everybody has a legal right to an education.

No value

27. I like Beethoven's Third Symphony better than his Ninth.

Nonmoral value

28. His whole lecture was boring.

Nonmoral value

29. It is too my turn to deal!

No value

30. It's no surprise that they've stopped seeing each other.

No value

31. The carpenter did an excellent job of remodeling the kitchen.

Nonmoral value

32. Everybody should be as kind and generous as Janice.

Moral value

33. The judge in this case is a very informed person.

Nonmoral value

34. The judge's decision was the right one, and everybody got just what they deserved.

    Moral value

35. The sketches we got back from the designer were awful.

    Nonmoral value

36. Allison's necklace is very old.

    Nonmmoral value (indicates that the necklace is valuable because of its age)

37. The Rosens' wedding ceremony was the loveliest one I've ever seen.

    Nonmoral value

38. The last set of essays was much better written than the first set.

    Nonmoral value

39. Jim ought to learn to take his hat off when he's in someone else's home.

    Nonmoral value

40. Pat won a free trip to Europe—she's the luckiest person I know.

    No value

Bank 13-3

For each of the following, try to come up with additional premises that will turn the passage into a deductively valid or an inductively strong argument. Usually this requires adding an evaluative claim and, sometimes, an extra nonevaluative claim as well. The idea is to guarantee that the "ought" claim follows from the "is" claim.

41. When Sarah bought the lawn mower from Jean, she promised to pay another fifty dollars on the first of the month. Since it's now the first, Sarah should pay Jean the money.

    People should keep their promises.

42. John has done something terribly wrong. He copied all of the equations on the take-home exam from Tony's paper and turned them in as his own.

    A person ought not to claim credit for the work of others.

43. Scotty's mother not only is getting too old to take care of herself but also is unable to pay for proper care in a nursing home. It seems to me that Scotty should either take her in or otherwise make sure she is taken care of properly.

    One should take care of one's parents when they cannot take care of themselves or afford to pay for someone else to do so.

44. Mr. Thomas ought to treat his pets better. He feeds them so little that they look like they're starving to death.

    People who feed their pets too little ought to treat them better.

45. Mortimer did the right thing when he decided to start a regular deduction from his paycheck on behalf of the United Way.

    Actions that support charities are morally right.

46. Daniel was bad yesterday. He let only one of the two children who live next door ride his new bike.

    A child should treat other children equitably when playing with a new possession.

47. I think Martin's pushing his children into dangerous sports like football and motocross racing is immoral.

    Parents should not push their children into dangerous sports or activities.

48. Harold is obligated to supply ten cords of firewood to the lodge by the beginning of October, since he signed a contract guaranteeing delivery of the wood by that date.

    People should abide by the terms of contracts they agree to.

49. Dr. Shelby is getting away with charging outrageous fees because she is the only physician in town. She really ought to lower her rates so that she won't be taking advantage of the isolation of the community.

    Physicians (or others) should not set fee schedules that take advantage of others.

50. The computer programs we recently received are all "shareware"—they are accompanied by notices saying that anyone who keeps and uses the program should send a small fee to the author. I think it's only right that we send a check to two of the program authors, since we've started getting a lot of use out of two of the programs.

    It is morally correct to compensate others whose work you voluntarily benefit from.

51. If the Simmonses don't begin teaching their son some discipline, he's going to grow up to be an irresponsible adult. That would amount to moral irresponsibility on the part of the Simmonses.

    Morally responsible parents do what they can in order to ensure that their children grow up to be morally responsible adults.

52. Karen and Gina were roommates for about five months, and, as far as Gina knew, they had planned to room together until the end of the school year. But when Gina returned from a weekend at her parents', Karen had moved out. Since she couldn't find a new roommate on such short notice, Gina asked Karen to pay half of the next month's rent, but Karen answered that she didn't owe the rent

since she wasn't living there anymore. I think Karen should pay at least half of one month's rent, since Gina was led to believe Karen was going to be living there and paying half.

When one person acts to produce reasonable expectations on the part of another, the first should compensate the second for failure to meet those expectations when it leaves the second at a disadvantage.

53. Look, Sam! There's been a bad accident up ahead. We really ought to stop and see whether there's any way we can help.

In circumstances where others may desperately need help and one can provide such help at no great disadvantage to oneself, then one should do so.

54. Knowing how to think critically may help save someone's life some day, so you ought to develop your ability to do so. ·

A person should generally be prepared to save lives.

55. You have no right to complain about Stephenson's performance; after all, you voted for him.

Voting for (or otherwise supporting, presumably) a person eliminates one's right to complain about what he or she does later.

56. It's time to restore diplomatic relations with Cuba. Doing so will make the hemisphere a safer place.

One ought to promote safety in the hemisphere.

57. "You shouldn't have criticized David so harshly; his mistake was a trivial one."

The severity of one's criticism should match the severity of the mistake criticized.

58. In 1965, there were 47,000 road fatalities in the United States. By 1984, there were only 44,250 fatalities, but that is still far too many. The reductions between 1965 and 1984 were due primarily to federal requirements for motor vehicle safety. So, even stricter federal safety controls should be required.

Unstated nonevaluative premise: Regulations that have reduced road fatalities in the past will, if strengthened, reduce the present number of fatalities. Unstated evaluative claim: Steps to reduce the number of fatalities should be taken.

59. Galileo's hypothesis should be suppressed. The biblical accou... in Ecclesiastes clearly states that the sun rises and sets and hastens to the place where it will rise again.

Unstated nonevaluative premise: Galileo's hypothesis contradicts a biblical account. Unstated evaluative claim: Any claim that contradicts a biblical account should be suppressed. Here's a somewhat more charitable version. Unstated nonevaluative premise: Galileo's hypothesis is clearly false (because it contradicts the Bible, which is true). Unstated moral principle: Clearly false claims should be suppressed.

60. We ought not to leave the showroom model's accessories off the price tag, since that will really mislead customers.

   One ought not to mislead customers.

61. Smoke from wood-burning stoves has become a serious health hazard. They ought to be banned.

   One ought to promote safety.

62. You shouldn't have included that material on the exam. It was never mentioned in class.

   One ought not examine students on material that has not been mentioned in class.

63. The dog has been out so long she's probably freezing. You ought to let her in.

   One should not allow animals to suffer unnecessarily.

Bank 13-4

At the supermarket, Vickie just ran her cart into a display of jars with jams and preserves, and now the aisle is full of broken glass and jam. She feels like leaving the store as quickly as possible. Is that an acceptable course of action?

Match each of the following statements about this issue with the appropriate moral position.

64. No, it isn't, because Vickie couldn't imagine such a behavior becoming a universal law, allowing everybody to run away from his or her responsibility.

   Duty theory

65. No, it isn't, because a person of integrity and moral responsibility wouldn't act like that.

   Virtue theory

66. No, it isn't, because someone may have seen her knock the display over. If she is caught leaving, she, as well as the store management, will be embarrassed.

   Utilitarianism

67. No, it isn't, because she has caused product loss that necessitates more work for the employee. So the least she can do is report what she has done and pay for damages.

   Utilitarianism

68. No, it isn't; that would be treating the store employees like stepping-stones, as though they were put on this earth just to clean up after Vickie.

   Duty theory

Bank 13-5

Taffy is a university lab chimpanzee; the university has lost its animal research grant and has to decide what to do with Taffy.

Match each of the following statements about this issue with the appropriate moral position.

68. Since Taffy is capable of suffering, it is important that her future be taken into consideration. She should be placed with people who will care for her.

    Utilitarianism

69. Taffy is not a rational being, and the university has no duty to treat her as anything but a mere means to an end. They can sell her or put her to sleep. If anybody cares enough for her to take care of her, that will be that person's choice.

    Duty theory

70. If the researchers have the proper compassion for Taffy, they should make certain that she is placed with people who will care for her.

    Virtue theory

71. It depends on Taffy's condition; if she is healthy and can expect a long life, she should be taken to a place where she can live a full life; if the experiments have impaired her health to the point where she is suffering and won't recover, she should be put to sleep.

    Utilitarianism

72. Only human greed and insensitivity have put Taffy in her present situation. We can hope that by learning about Taffy, people will become more sensitive toward other creatures.

    Virtue theory

Bank 13-6

Below are some positions on the legalization of active euthanasia (doctor-assisted suicide) and abortion. For each item, identify which of the three ethical theories discussed in the text—utilitarianism, duty theory, or virtue ethics—it follows. Note that each theory may encompass several possible viewpoints.

73. Active euthanasia should be legalized. After all, what are the overall consequences in terms of happiness or unhappiness? Euthanasia may not make the patient who wants to die happy, but at least it can end his or her misery. And although the relatives may feel unhappy at the assisted suicide, they too have suffered, and they will grieve whether the patient dies assisted or unassissted. As a matter of fact,

they may grieve less if they know the patient has been spared a substantial amount of suffering.

Utilitarianism

74. Active euthanasia should not be legalized; it is much too dangerous. The consequences could be devastating to our society. If we allow terminally ill people access to euthanasia, what guarantees do we have that such access won't be abused? It would be easy to imagine greedy relatives insisting that it is better for Grandma to die sooner than linger in pain, or to imagine Grandma choosing to die sooner so she won't cost the family a lot of money. Overall, access to euthanasia may cause terrible unhappiness.

Utilitarianism

75. If we can trust doctors and relatives of the patient to be morally responsible people, then active euthanasia could become an option. However, it may be abused by people with a bad character. And we should not forget that the character of the patients themselves may be important: Are they serious in their request, or are they going to change their minds at the last minute? Above all, let us be certain that the decision is right for the patient in his or her special situation, that the manner of euthanasia is appropriate, and that the situation is viewed with a balanced mind-set.

Virtue ethics (virtue ethics has not contributed much to these current debates about issues of conduct, such as euthanasia and abortion, but we imagine that a virtue ethicist might answer like that.)

76. Active euthanasia should not be allowed. One might opt for euthanasia because one believes it might be to one's advantage, but could one truly imagine this access being available to everyone, as a universal law? Besides, one would be using the poor doctor as merely a means to an end, without any regard for his or her professional integrity.

Duty theory

77. Active euthanasia should be allowed. However, one would have to be very specific about stating the circumstances under which one might allow it. In that case, with circumstances strictly identified, it would be possible to imagine it to be a universal law that everyone under these specific circumstances, could be allowed access to euthanasia.

Duty theory (a modern, revised version that allows for exceptions to moral rules such as "don't kill," as long as these exceptions are stated beforehand.)

78. Abortion should not be allowed. Whether abortion is done for the woman's convenience, health, or other reasons, the fact remains that taking a life is wrong. No number of good consequences can alter that fact.

Duty theory

79. Abortion should be allowed. It doesn't matter whether one, as an individual, is for or against it; what matters is that women will be dying in back alleys again if their access to abortion is taken away from them.

Utilitarianism

80. Abortion should be allowed. It is up to the individual to decide whether abortion is the right thing to do for her. Not everybody is ready for parenthood, and it is better that children not be raised by individuals who have no love for them, no stability in their lives, or no sense of responsibility for their actions.

Virtue ethics

Bank 13-7

81. Evaluate the issue of human cloning from the utilitarian viewpoint.

    Possible answer: Overall potential consequences must be examined. If more overall happiness that unhappiness is likely to result from human cloning, then cloning should be an option.

82. Evaluate the issue of human cloning from the viewpoint of a deontologist (duty theorist).

    Possible answer: Human cloning is morally wrong if the cloned persons are created for someone else's purpose. If we can imagine a cloned population becoming a new race of slaves, then cloning should never be allowed.

83. Evaluate the issue of human cloning from the viewpoint of a virtue ethicist.

    Possible answer: If we can ensure that parents of cloned babies are morally responsible and that they will raise the cloned children with respect for their personhood and teach them moral responsibility, then cloning may be an option.

Bank 13-8

In the following bank of items, discuss whether Marina is treating relevantly similar cases in sufficiently similar fashions. Identify any instances in which the cases are not relevantly similar. *(Note to the instructor: You may adjust the circumstances of each case as you see fit. Also, it may be a good idea to emphasize the independence of each item; Marina could not possibly do everything we have her doing here! We offer our comments without much elaboration.)*

84. Marina's will stipulates that her son by birth will receive substantially more of her estate than will her adopted son, even though both sons love her equally, have treated her with similar regard, and have lived with her for about the same amount of time.

    Our view is that she is treating relevantly similar cases differently.

85. Marina is the principal source of financial support for one of her sons at college; the other son won a large scholarship, and Marina sends him a much smaller amount.

From what's said here, we'd count this as sufficiently similar treatment, given the dissimilarities of the cases.

86. She calls it to the clerk's attention when she is overcharged, but not when she is undercharged.

Here she is inconsistent; the cases are relevantly similar but are treated differently.

87. She leaves large tips at a posh restaurant, where meals are quite expensive, but she leaves much smaller tips at another, much plainer and less expensive restaurant, even though the service is as good and the waiters work just as hard.

We think this is treating like cases differently, but we're afraid Marina has a lot of company.

88. She criticizes her brother for expressing racist views but does not criticize Mr. Durban, a business associate, who holds similar views.

Like cases are treated differently.

89. Marina's automobile is a large, gas-guzzling, luxury car, but in some circumstances (such as cocktail parties when she is among strangers), she will make it a point to criticize people who drive such cars.

This is not a case of treating like cases differently; there's another name for this kind of inconsistency: hypocrisy.

90. She instructs her children to always be truthful but lies to her young daughter when the daughter asks if her (the daughter's) illness is running up large medical bills.

The cases are not relevantly similar.

91. Marina tells her children to tell the truth, but she claims deductions on her income tax return to which she knows she is not legally entitled.

This is hypocrisy again: There is an inconsistency between what she says and what she does, but it is not one of treating similar cases differently. She would be treating such cases in dissimilar ways if, for example, she told her children to tell the truth and also told them to lie on their income tax forms.

92. Marina offers her daughter's fiancé a job in the company she owns, but it never occurs to her to do the same for her son's fiancée.

Different treatment of relevantly similar cases

93. She tells her children not to smoke but smokes herself.

Here once again we find her not practicing what she preaches. But this is an inconsistency between word and deed, not between deed and deed or between word and word. She would be guilty of treating relevantly similar cases in a dissimilar way if, for instance, she told her children not to smoke cigarettes but to smoke cigars, if that can be imagined. Note: The issue here is her treatment of the cases; if her children were to reject her advice, they commit an ad hominem (Chapter 6).

94. At election time, Marina votes for the candidate she thinks will do the best job—in every election except one. In that race, she votes for her second choice, because she is certain that the best person for the job has no chance of winning and that her second choice is still better than any of the rest of the candidates.

The cases are different enough to justify the different actions.

95. Marina opposes tyrannical despots in several countries in the world. But even though the government of Almeria is equally tyrannical, she is not inclined to oppose it because she has a friend who works in the Almerian foreign ministry.

Treating like cases differently

96. She criticizes the Japanese for killing and eating whales, but she eats beef.

That is, she approves beef killing but not whale killing. The cases are arguably dissimilar.

97. The company that Marina owns allows the secretarial staff to accumulate one vacation day per month, but managers at the company accumulate 1½ days per month.

We expect our view may be controversial in some quarters, but we think this is treating relevantly similar cases dissimilarly.

98. She says she believes in equality, but she tells lots of ethnic and racial jokes.

Even though it is unlikely, it is not impossible that a person could tell such jokes and believe in equality.

99. Marina is usually a careful shopper, looking for bargains and buying generic products when she's at the market. But she has a weakness for gloves and handbags, and she owns a closet full of elegant and expensive examples.

The opposite of this kind of inconsistency is not injustice; it's tedium.

100. She watches a viewer-supported public television station, but she does not make contributions to it.

She is taking selfish advantage of the public station, but this is not a case of treating relevantly similar cases differently. Perhaps she is perfectly consistent and takes selfish advantage of others every time she gets the chance.

101. Marina's twins, Mary and Myron, have different aspirations. Mary wants to be an engineer. She's good at mathematics and has a good chance of winning a scholarship to a good college. Myron is both inept and uninterested in such matters. He shows signs of artistic talent and wants to study painting. For their seventeenth birthdays, Marina got them a computer.

Unless Myron gets interested in computer graphics, Marina has been somewhat unfair to him in treating his relevantly different case as though it were just like his sister's. This is the other side of the coin.

102. Marina votes against a tax increase for maintenance of her city park even though she uses the park and plans to continue using it whether or not the measure passes.

    The comments on this item should parallel those on item 100.

103. Although she doesn't believe in stealing, Marina uses the office copy machine for personal business and makes person-to-person long-distance calls to fictitious persons as a code to avoid paying for the calls.

    These activities are relevantly similar to stealing.

Bank 13-9

Answer the question in these paragraphs from the point of view of each of the three positions described in the text (or from whatever point of view your instructor asks you to take).

104. An employer who is considering hiring Eva has asked Donna, Eva's former supervisor, for a report on Eva. In truth, Eva's work for Donna has been only average. However, (a) Eva is Donna's friend, and Donna knows that Eva probably will not get the job if she says anything negative about Eva, and Donna knows that Eva desperately needs the job. Further, (b) Donna knows that if the situation were reversed, she would not want Eva to mention her deficiencies. Nevertheless, (c) it has been Donna's policy to reveal the deficiencies of employees when she has been asked for references by employers, and she knows that some of Eva's faults may be bothersome to this particular employer. Finally, (d) this employer has leveled with Donna in the past when Donna has asked for a report on people who have worked for him. Should Donna reveal deficiencies in Eva's past performance?

105. The water pump in Michelle's car isn't working, and her friend Felipe replaces it for her as a favor. Michelle decides to repay Felipe's kindness by promising to buy him a six-pack of beer. Unfortunately, Michelle isn't quite old enough to buy beer legally, so she asks her friend Carol, who is, to buy the beer for her and explains why. Felipe, too, is slightly under the legal age, but Carol knows Felipe and regards him as a responsible and mature individual. Further, (a) Carol knows that Michelle will be embarrassed if she has to tell Felipe she cannot get beer for him after all, and (b) Michelle has recently done something nice for Carol, and Carol owes her a favor. However, (c) Michelle is aware that if Felipe drinks the beer all at once and goes driving—an unlikely event in Carol's opinion—he could be injured or injure others. Carol could be held liable in that event. But (d) Carol knows Michelle's other friends and doubts that any of them are old enough to buy beer for Michelle. If Carol turns Michelle down, Carol will have to live without getting Felipe the beer she promised to give him. Should Carol get the beer for Michelle, everything considered?

106. Lisa's algebra class has a quiz every other Friday. This is the third time she's been so worried about other matters that she hasn't done quite as well on the quiz as she might have otherwise. What has her upset is the fact that the instructor leaves the room while the students take the quiz, and over half the class is taking the opportunity to cheat. She knows and likes several of the other students in the class,

and some of the ones she likes are among those who are cheating. Lisa knows that (a) a failure to speak to the teacher about the cheating will result in her own grade being lower, since the teacher grades in part on the curve. But (b) she will be doing her friends and the others a great harm, since cheating is taken very seriously at the school. If she doesn't "turn in" her classmates, (c) the only other alternative to getting a worse grade than she deserves is to begin cheating herself, something she's never done. What should she do?

107. Jan witnessed a certain Mr. Gaines commit a crime several months ago, but despite his certain knowledge of Gaines's guilt, the charges against him were dismissed because of an error in the investigation. Jan is especially upset about the nature of the crime—(a) Gaines was defrauding a charitable organization that Jan happens to think accomplishes a lot of good. Jan also knows that the crime was committed out of greed, since (b) Gaines owns a large jewelry store and is already well-off. Gaines has spoken to his friends about how he got away without having to stand trial, and (c) he is gloating about it.

One day, Jan is walking up the alley that runs behind Gaines's store, and he notices that the back door has been left unlocked and, from the look of things, it appears that the burglar alarm has not been turned on. One of several vaults in the back room has a half-open door. He realizes that he could make off very easily with a large amount of expensive jewelry. (d) The likelihood of his being caught is very small. It occurs to him that it wouldn't be quite the same as stealing, certainly not as bad as what he saw Gaines do, if (e) he did not keep the loot for himself but gave it away. It occurs to him that (f) if he takes what doesn't belong to him he may not be any better than Gaines, and on the small chance he did get caught, nobody would believe him, and (g) the penalties would be stiff. But (h) this is his chance to see justice done with regard to Gaines, and he can make some deserving people very happy with the proceeds of the burglary. Should Jan grab the jewels?

108. Kevin's mother and father are divorced. Kevin is eight, and he lives with his father, John, for three months every summer. The rest of the time, except for occasional weekends, he lives two hundred miles away with his mother. John is the one with the problem: He and Kevin talked a lot last summer about getting a dog. For the first time, John is living in a house that has a back yard big enough to keep a dog and a fence around it as well. John had always used the "no place to keep it" line to avoid making promises, but that no longer applies. John finally promised to get Kevin a dog at the beginning of the next summer, and he knows Kevin is hoping to get one. In fact, John knows that Kevin is expecting a dog with enough confidence that (a) he'll be very disappointed if he doesn't get one, even though he may not say much about it. Furthermore, (b) not getting a dog will deprive both Kevin and John of considerable pleasure, since John knows how happy it would make his son to get one. But the danger of having a dog around is that John lives alone during most of the year, and having a dog means being responsible for another creature. (c) When John travels, as his job requires him to do from time to time, who will look after the dog? He can't leave it with a friend for a week or two at a time. And he has no neighbors close by who could look after it. It looks like a difficult trade-off: Three months a year of pleasure for John, Kevin, and a dog, balanced against what might be nine months a year of frequent unpleasantness for both John and the dog. What should he do?

109. Shelley and Maurita are both disturbed by their C+ final grades in Mr. Carlton's geography class, and they request that he recheck his grade book. He does so and finds that, indeed, he had made mistakes. Maurita was supposed to get a B− and Shelley was supposed to get a C−. He gives Maurita the B− and allows Shelley to keep the C+.

Should he have lowered Shelley's grade to a C−? Construct one argument whose conclusion is that he should, and construct one argument whose conclusion is that he should not. Be sure to spell out clearly any moral principles in the arguments.

Bank 13-10

True/false and fill-in-the-blanks

110. Legal reasoning and moral reasoning both lead to prescriptions about whether or not certain actions should be done.

True

111. Legal positivists believe that all law ultimately derives from social conventions and practices.

True

112. Appeals to authority in law are not an acceptable form of argument.

False

113. *Stare decisis* is the doctrine that even though a court has pronounced a principle of law applicable to a certain set of facts, other judges should follow common sense in determining whether to apply that principle to other cases in which the facts are substantially the same.

False

114. *Stare decisis* is a defeasible principle.

True

115. In the United States, the supreme law of the land is _____.

The United States Constitution

116. In the United States, each state has its own constitution.

True

117. According to naturalism, the ultimate foundation for law is consensus among lawmakers; as such, it is only natural if laws change.

False

Bank 13-11

In each pair of cases below, the first may serve as precedent for the second. Decide whether the second case is so relevantly similar to the first that it should be decided identically.

118. First case: On the basis of observation and a car license number, police reasonably suspected Mrs. H of possessing stolen radios. Informed by the manager of her apartment that a man living with her was sickly, officers knocked on the apartment door and received no response but heard "moans and groans." When they were admitted by the manager, no one was present, but one of the stolen radios was in plain sight. On the basis of this information, they obtained a search warrant and seized the radio. Mrs. H was later arrested. A court held that the radio was admissible as evidence: The officers testified that they believed someone in the apartment was in distress and had entered for the purpose of giving aid. The court ruled that this justified what would otherwise have been a trespass. Second case: Mr. G was found by police in his car, unconscious and with a severe knife wound. He was taken to a hospital for surgery, and his clothing was searched for identification. Marijuana was found, and he was arrested for possession of narcotics.

Since the search in both cases was legal, the evidence obtained in both cases is admissible even though unconnected with the initial purpose of the search.

119. First case: The owner of an amusement park, believing that homosexual activity was taking place in its pay toilets, authorized police to use an observation pipe leading from the roof to the booths. Officer H regularly visited the roof for surveillance. If he observed illegal conduct, he would notify officers below, who would make the arrest. A court ruled that the evidence of Officer H was illegally obtained and set aside the information. Second case: The management of a department store authorized police to observe suspected illegal homosexual activity in the men's room. An officer did observe such activity and arrested the participants. But in this case, the officer looked through a legitimately installed vent instead of a special spypipe. Furthermore, in this case, the booths, unlike those in the first case, were not pay toilets (and thus were not in the same sense "private"). Finally, unlike in the first case, the observed behavior was committed in the space below the partition, and thus was observable by anyone who might have been in the public, or common-use, portion of the men's room at the time, though nobody was.

In the second case, the court ruled that the evidence was obtained in the same illegal manner as in the first case.

120. First case: Same as the first case in the preceding item. Second case: Same as the second case in the preceding item, except that an officer just happened to open the door of the men's room at the time of the activity and observed it through the doorway.

Second case is importantly dissimilar to the first.

121. First case: Same as the first case in the preceding item. Second case: A motel manager complained to police that his motel was being used for the sale of narcotics. Officers conducting surveillance from an unmarked vehicle observed suspicious activity and, approaching and looking through an unshaded window, witnessed drug use and made arrests.

Second case is importantly dissimilar to the first. In the first case, the officer had no grounds for even suspecting that the individuals had committed or were committing a crime; he was spying on innocent and guilty alike. There are other differences, too. Does looking through a window constitute unreasonable search?

122. First case: Federal and local officers, seeking to arrest Mr. J on a narcotics charge but having no warrant or search warrant, knocked on the door of his apartment. He asked, "Who's there?" and the reply was, "Police." He opened the door partly, keeping the chain latch on, asked what they were doing there, but, before they answered, he tried to close the door, whereupon they broke in and arrested him, seizing as evidence marked money from a narcotics sale. The court ruled that the arrest was unlawful and therefore that the money was unlawfully seized: The authority of officers to break the door of a home to make an arrest is limited; the officers must first state their authority in demanding admission. Mr. J's reaction in attempting to close the door did not show with certainty that he knew that the officers were there to arrest him. Second case: Mr. A was unlawfully arrested on a burglary charge without probable cause and placed in jail. There he was observed attempting to swallow something; he was seized and forcibly searched, and a moist narcotic packet was found on the floor. He was charged with illegal possession of narcotics.

If unlawful arrest carries no right to search in the first case, it carries no right in the second case.

123. First case: Officers on a late-night automobile patrol approached two men parked in a car in a lover's lane, who then drove away at high speed. The officers chased and overtook them, searched the car, and found narcotics. The court ruled that the search of the automobile was lawful even though no arrest had been made: The presence of two men in that place was suspicious, and their sudden flight indicated consciousness of guilt of some crime. Second case: The defendant's car was parked, and officers observed him walking in the middle of the night in a residential area. When they approached him, he made a throwing motion; on interrogation, he admitted prior felonies but made unbelievable explanations of his presence and his car at the place. The officers searched the car and found narcotics.

The court held that the search in the second case, as in the first, was legal and the evidence admissible.

124. First case: Officers arrested D in his living room on a charge of using the mails to transport forged checks. Then they searched the other rooms of his apartment for forged checks, which they did not find. But they did find unlawfully possessed draft cards. D was convicted of possession and alteration of the draft cards. The court held the search was lawful as incidental to a valid arrest. Second case: Federal officers had observed the defendant operating an illegal still. They entered the premises and made a valid arrest without a warrant for a felony committed in

their presence. They seized the still. At trial, the defendant moved to exclude the still from evidence.

On appeal the Supreme Court held that although the arrest was valid, the seizure of the still was illegal because in this case the officers knew what they were looking for and had ample time to obtain a search warrant: They in effect simply ignored the Fourth Amendment. The Court said that if a search was automatically valid whenever a lawful arrest was made, it would be unnecessary to obtain search warrants. However, a couple of years later the Court changed its mind on the point.

125. First case: The U.S. Supreme Court upheld federal regulations that bar abortion counseling at federally funded family-planning clinics in the United States. Second case: The Supreme Court agreed to review a lower-court decision upholding a Bush administration policy that denied federal family-planning aid to a Mexico City clinic that provided abortion counseling.

126. First case: The Pregnancy Discrimination Act of 1978 extended federal antibias protections to pregnant workers. Second case: Johnson Controls, a manufacturer of automobile batteries that uses large quantities of lead in its manufacturing processes, excludes women capable of bearing children from any job where the work carries a high risk of damage to the nervous system of a fetus. Under this policy, eight employees of Johnson Controls were involuntarily transferred to safer but lower-paying work. They sued the company, charging discrimination under the Act.

A point that might be discussed is the company's argument that their guidelines protected them from large damage suits.

127. First case: A court has ruled that victim-impact statements, which document the suffering of the victim and the victim's family that results from the crime, are admissible among the evidence to be considered by a jury during the sentencing phase of criminal trials. Second case: A court is asked to rule whether such statements may be introduced in cases punishable by death.

The Supreme Court held that such victim-impact statements are not admissible in cases in which the death penalty is possible; but as we write this, the Court is reconsidering the issue.

Bank 13-12

Evaluate the following statements: Do they express a backward-looking approach to punishment (retributivist), or a forward-looking approach (utilitarian)?

128. The death penalty should be abolished. It has not been proved that the death penalty has any substantial deterrent effect, and other means of punishment are just as effective in terms of keeping the public safe, provided that they are administered properly.

Forward-looking

129. All over the world, people with terminal illnesses are waiting desperately for organs to become available for transplants. It is only right that criminals on Death Row be executed as soon as possible to make their organs available for these waiting multitudes.

Forward-looking

130. Even though she was not considered a threat to society, Ellie Nessler was convicted of murder and sentenced to prison for her crime, because the jury believed that that was what she deserved.

Backward-looking

131. Harsh punishment may have a considerable deterrent effect, but punishing people in excess of their crime is unfair and inhumane.

Backward-looking

132. Raskolnikov has killed the old pawnbroker, but she was a nasty person, and all her former clients are now relieved that she is gone. Besides, he is young, handsome, intelligent, and able to serve the community in many ways, so he should not be sent to prison for murder. He should be let go to live a useful and fulfilling life.

Forward-looking. (You may want to let your students know that this question is inspired by Dostoyevsky's Crime and Punishment.*)*

Bank 13-14

Evaluate the following statements. Identify which represent the deterrence approach, which the incapacitation approach, which the rehabilitation approach, and which the retributivist approach.

133. A person should be held accountable for his or her crimes and be punished in proportion to those crimes.

Retributivist

134. With the proper approach, a criminal can learn to become a productive and law-abiding citizen.

Rehabilitation

135. Tonight the city can sleep in peace; the Night Stalker is behind bars.

Incapacitation

136. An eye for an eye, a tooth for a tooth.

Retributivist

137. If punishment takes place too long after sentencing, it won't scare anybody straight.

   Deterrence

138. When Sowbelly Sam was hanged in Abilene in 1866, it was quite a show, and many a spectator resolved to live a law-abiding life from then on. Unfortunately, it later turned out that Sam was not guilty, but at least his hanging taught a lot of folks a lesson.

   Deterrence. (Sowbelly Sam is a fictional example, but the situation is not unthinkable.)

The Appendixes

In this edition, we've moved some material from the main text into the appendixes. Appendix 1 and Appendix 2 are much as they were in the third edition, but the discussion and list of valid and invalid elementary argument forms that were previously found in Chapter 8 are now ensconced as Appendix 3.

Not that it matters, but Parker likes to cover the first two appendixes, whereas Moore covers the third in his classes. Each hopes the other will get it right some day.

Appendix 1
Conflicting Claims

Exercises Unanswered in the Text

Exercise A1-1

2. Contradictories

3. Not in conflict

5. Contradictories

6. Contraries

8. Contradictories

9. Contradictories

Exercise A1-2

2. Contraries, on the assumption that Helgren could withdraw, get sick and not complete the term, be hit by a truck, or such.

3. Contraries. Both are false if George passed and if Frank, also in Helgren's class, did not pass the exam.

5. Not in conflict, on the assumption that (a) is not intended as a universal general claim—that it is not intended to apply to every single investor. Note too that these are vague claims, and it's harder to pin down conflicts with vague claims.

6. Contraries

8. Not in conflict

9. Not in conflict

Exercise A1-3

2. If we take Schwarzkopf's earlier remarks to mean "I think we should continue the battle" and his later ones to mean "I think we should stop," and if those do seem to represent his thoughts on the subject, then it's fair to say he is contradicting himself.

4. The remarks identifying two different destinations do conflict; they are contraries.

5. The two positions do conflict, but as contraries, not contradictories.

7. This can be interpreted in two ways: (1) The first reports say there is *this* plan, and the later reports say there is *no* plan. In this case, the two reports are contraries. (2) The first reports are taken to say that there is *some* plan or other, and the later ones are taken to say there is *no* plan. In this case, the two are contradictories.

Appendix 1 Test Question/Exercise Banks

Classify the following pairs of claims as contraries, contradictories, or not conflicting.

1. a. The class began at 8:00 A.M.
   b. The class began by 8:30 A.M.

   Not conflicting

2. a. Maurie's dog is a purebred schnauzer.
   b. Maurie's dog is not a purebred at all.

   Contraries

3. a. There is an infinite number of prime numbers.
   b. There are only 2,497,622,991 prime numbers.

   Contraries

4. a. That cheap pet food you bought contains ash.
   b. That cheap pet food you bought contains no ash.

   Contradictories

5. a. Alekhine was better than Capablanca at simultaneous chess matches.
   b. No, Capablanca was better than Alekhine.

   Contraries (They could have been equally good.)

6. a. Alekhine was better than Capablanca at simultaneous chess matches.
   b. No, he wasn't.

Contradictories

7. a. You can never get something from nothing.
   b. Sometimes you can get something from nothing.

Contradictories

8. a. The least expensive lunch at Le Bistro is eight dollars.
   b. You can get lunch at Le Bistro for five and a half dollars.

Contraries

9. a. Over three inches of rain fell in Caddo Gap last week.
   b. Caddo Gap had at least two inches of rain last week.

Not conflicting

10. a. Babe Ruth's sixty home runs in a season that was much shorter than today's baseball seasons stands as the all-time greatest achievement in hitting home runs.
    b. I don't care how sentimental you are about Babe Ruth, Roger Maris is the home run champion because he hit more than anybody else ever has in one season.

Not conflicting

11. a. You can't get Cuban cigars in the United States.
    b. You can if you smuggle them in through Canada.

Contraries

12. a. Isaac's violin was made by Antonio Stradivari.
    b. Isaac's violin is not an expensive instrument.

These do not conflict as they stand, but given the reasonable assumption "All violins made by Stradivari are expensive instruments," the claims are contradictories.

13. a. No company makes it into the Kopp 500 unless it has annual sales of over $700 million.
    b. Stanton Corporation has sales of over $700 million, and it is not one of the Kopp 500.

Not conflicting

14. a. No company with less than $700 million in annual sales is in the Kopp 500.
    b. Stanton Corporation has over $700 million in annual sales, and it is not in the Kopp 500.

Not conflicting

15. a. Every company that has annual sales of over $700 million is in the Kopp 500.
    b. Stanton Corporation has sales of over $700 million, and it is not one of the Kopp 500.

Contradictories

16. a. An eye for an eye, and a tooth for a tooth.
    b. Turn the other cheek; do not return injury for injury.

Contraries (if both are taken universally—that is, as applying to every case)

17. a. To forgive is divine; a perfect being will always forgive.
    b. Some sins are unforgivable.

Not in conflict, except on one or another assumption about a perfect being

18. a. Love is wonderful, and anything that is wonderful won't hurt.
    b. Love hurts.

Contraries, unless one exploits the vagueness of the notion of love, in which case they can be said not to conflict

19. a. You shouldn't work so hard; don't try to do so much.
    b. Besides everything else you're doing, you should iron my clothes!

Contraries

20. a. "Growing and decaying vegetation in this land are responsible for 93 percent of the oxides of nitrogen."
       —Ronald Reagan
    b. "Industrial sources are responsible for at least 65 percent and possibly as much as 90 percent of the oxides of nitrogen in the U. S."
       —Dr. Michael Oppenheimer of the Environmental Defense Fund

Contraries

21. a. Anything over two hundred micrograms of selenium per day is considered unsafe for a human adult, according to the government standards.
    b. Nobody knows how much selenium it takes to be unsafe for a human adult.

Contraries

22. a. Steve Jobs's new computer will be the biggest seller on university campuses.
    b. I don't think so; it won't sell over a hundred thousand items, because it costs more than most universities can afford.

It may be that a hundred thousand items is all it would take to make it the biggest seller on university campuses, in which case these do not conflict.

23. a. Nicotine makes the body metabolize caffeine faster.
    b. Caffeine makes the body metabolize nicotine faster.

    Not in conflict: both could be true; (a) is in fact true, but we don't know about (b).

24. a. Books are more efficient learning tools than computers, no matter what software is being used with the latter.
    b. Some of the new computer and software combinations are at least as efficient as books as learning tools.

    Aside from obvious vagueness, the difficulty with this one is that such claims as (a) are usually asserted "in general" or "on average," or some such. And, does (b) mean that computers are as efficient as any *book, or as* most *books? If we take each claim to be universal, the claims are contradictories. Otherwise, they may not conflict at all.*

25. a. Most of the savings and loans in this country are in financial trouble.
    b. Most of the savings and loans in this country are in good shape.

    These could both be false and thus contraries, but only in the unlikely event that exactly half the S & Ls are in trouble and the other half in good shape. (We're taking "in financial trouble" and "in good shape" as complementary terms—that every S & L is either one or the other.)

26. a. The United States should support covert actions.
    b. The United States should not support covert actions.

    Contradictories

27. a. Julian Bream is the best contemporary classical guitarist.
    b. No, John Williams is the best contemporary classical guitarist.

    Contraries

28. a. Either Carlos or Julia will pass this course.
    b. Neither Carlos nor Julia will pass this course.

    Contradictories

29. a. Charles is taller than Daniel.
    b. Daniel is at least as tall as Charles.

    Contradictories

30. a. Soccer is the fastest growing sport in the country.
    b. Field hockey is growing faster than soccer in this country.

    Contraries

Appendix 2
Analytic Claims

Exercises Unanswered in the Text

Exercise A2-1

2. Not analytic

3. Not analytic. What is said about hot climates is not part of the meaning of the phrase.

5. Not analytic, at least by the definition in our dictionary.

6. Analytic. Part of the meaning of "eighteen" is that it denotes a number smaller than twenty.

8. Analytic, by a combination of categorical and truth-functional inferences (see Chapters 9 and 10).

9. Analytic. Our notion of matter is of stuff that occupies space, so we think this one is analytic. A different concept of matter may give you a different answer.

11. In the usual sense of "seeing," you can't see what doesn't exist, even though you might *think* you see something that turns out not to exist. In this sense, the claim is analytic.

12. Analytic, by our dictionary's definitions of "love" and "hate." But notice that these two notions, as well as that of time, are quite vague. Very loose interpretations of all three may allow love and hate for a person to coexist in one (rather confused) individual.

14. Not analytic

15. We don't think this is analytic, but it's a controversial matter. Certainly, the claim's negation, "I don't exist," is paradoxical, if not self-contradictory. (The negations of analytically true claims are self-contradictory; this is generally taken as the mark of an analytic truth.) This item can stimulate a nice class discussion. For brushing up purposes, we recommend René Descartes' *Meditations* or the article on Descartes in the *Encyclopedia of Philosophy,* Paul Edwards, editor.

Appendix 2 Test Question/Exercise Banks

Classify the following as analytic or nonanalytic truths. The first five are straightforward, items 6 through 10 require some thinking, and intelligent people can get into arguments about some of the final five. These sometimes make for good class discussions.

1. All baseball players are athletic.

   Nonanalytic

2. The crocodile is a reptile.

   Analytic

3. The juice of some aloe plants has therapeutic value for burns.

   Nonanalytic

4. It's cold at the south pole.

   Nonanalytic

5. Stalagmites are deposits that result from dripping water in caves; they stick up from the floors, whereas stalactites hang down from the roofs.

   Analytic

6. It's impossible to feel a color.

   Analytic

7. Unicorns are mythical creatures.

   Nonanalytic

8. In poker, a flush beats three-of-a-kind.

   Analytic

9. A record that sells a million copies is a bigger financial success than one that sells fewer than a million copies.

   Nonanalytic

10. "Made in Germany the way things are made in Germany."
    —Slogan for Olympia typewriters

    Nonanalytic

11. You can't steal what already belongs to you.

    The authors don't agree on this one; we're leaving it and the remainder to you.

12. Nothing is both red and orange all over.

13. If cats were as smart as people, they wouldn't be cats.

14. You couldn't have been born before your parents were born.

15. Analytic truths are intrinsically uninteresting to anyone who understands what they say.

Appendix 3
Some Common Patterns of Deductive Arguments

If you missed the section on common patterns back in Chapter 8, look no further: Here 'tis.

Exercises Unanswered in the Text

Exercise A3-1

2. Affirming the consequent

3. Modus tollens

5. Modus tollens

6. Chain argument

8. Modus tollens

9. Denying the antecedent

11. This is a chain argument in reverse. It is invalid.

12. Chain argument

14. Modus ponens

15. Affirming the consequent

16. Modus tollens

18. Affirming the consequent

19. Denying the antecedent

20. Modus tollens, if you ignore the difference between tenses; otherwise, the argument is invalid.

Exercise A3-2

2. Invalid syllogism 1

3. Valid syllogism 2

5. Valid syllogism 2

6. Valid conversion 1

7. Invalid conversion 2

9. Invalid syllogism 2

11. Valid syllogism 2 (Reverse the order of the premises, and convert the original first premise.)

12. Invalid syllogism 1

14. Invalid conversion 1

15. Valid conversion 2

16. Unnamed invalid inference

18. Valid syllogism 2, with unstated conclusion

19. Unnamed invalid inference

Appendix 3 Test Question/Exercise Banks

Bank A3-1

All argument patterns in the text are illustrated in the following. You'll know best what to do with them.

1. If the mayor will hire six hundred new police officers, then he must believe that crime is a major problem in New York; and this he does believe. So he will hire six hundred new police officers.

   Affirming the consequent

2. The Bureau of Engraving and Printing is gearing up to print new bills with polyester filament that cannot be duplicated by copiers, so you know that counterfeiting has become a major problem for the government.

   Modus ponens

3. If the allies honor their commitments to pay for the Gulf War, then the war won't cost the U.S. anything. But they won't, so the U.S. will have to pony up.

   Denying the antecedent

4. If the mutual hostility of Arabs and Israelis were not great, then there might be a real chance for peace in the Middle East. Unfortunately, the mutual hostility of Israel and the Arab states is of the severest sort. Therefore, there cannot be any real chance for peace in the Middle East.

   Denying the antecedent

5. You can lease a Cadillac for no more than $469 a month, if you act now. So if you don't, you can expect to pay more.

   Denying the antecedent

6. If people didn't have free will, there wouldn't be much reason to live. Since there is a great reason to live, people do have free will.

   Modus tollens

7. Some of the tribes that aren't in revolt are not opponents of the Mengistu regime. Therefore, as unlikely as it seems, some of the tribes that oppose Mengistu are not revolutionaries.

   Invalid conversion 2

8. Republicans all support tax breaks for corporations in hopes of stimulating economic growth. So those who favor tax breaks for corporations are all Republicans.

   Invalid conversion 1

9. Quiz-game host: "Here, for a new car, is your question. Acuras are all precision crafted for performance, just as the car you may win is. Can you name the car?"

   Invalid syllogism 1

10. America's largest consumer electronics manufacturers all sell computers, and none of America's premier distribution systems for technological products are among the country's largest consumer electronics manufacturers. So, no American computer company is a premier distribution system for technological products.

    Invalid syllogism 2

11. Letter to the editor: "The General Accounting Office says that the average ocean voyage taken by State Department and U.S. Information Agency employees costs the taxpayer on the average of $6,084. GAO investigators were told by foreign service officers that ocean travel is a 'fringe benefit.' If that is true, and I believe the GAO, it's time to trim the fringes."

    Modus ponens, without restatement of the conclusion, "It's time to trim the fringes."

12. The band raised enough money to make it to the Rose Parade. They were only going to be able to go if they could get the funds together, and I read in the paper that they left this morning.

    Modus ponens

13. A universal opportunity to have an education implies 100 percent literacy, and 100 percent literacy, or close to it, is exactly what you find in Denmark, according to the almanac. So, everyone there has the opportunity for an education.

    Affirming the consequent. Note that this could be interpreted as an inductive argument.

14. It's got to be a reasonably short drive from out where Hal lives to downtown Denver, because if it's short, you know you'd find lots of commuters living out there. And look at Hal's subdivision—it's full of commuters.

    Affirming the consequent

15. If war is inevitable, then spies are necessary. They aren't, so it isn't.

    Modus tollens

16. "At the station bookstall, Jim bought himself a *Rude Pravo* and boarded the Brno train. If they had wanted to arrest him, they would have done so by now."
    —John Le Carré, *Tinker, Tailor, Soldier, Spy*

    Modus tollens, with one premise, "They haven't yet arrested him," and the conclusion, "They must not have wanted to arrest him," both unstated.

17. If cutting the federal budget were simply a matter of arithmetic and not one of politics, we would never see the more draconian provisions of the Gramm-Rudman bill put into effect. Unfortunately, though, cutting the budget is much more politics than arithmetic. That means that somewhere down the line, we're going to see Gramm-Rudman's harsh side.

    Denying the antecedent

18. He won't get the tax credit unless he filed before the first, but fortunately he did file before the first.

    Unstated conclusion: "He'll get the tax credit." If the first premise is interpreted as "If he didn't file before the first, then he won't get the credit" (and this is a correct interpretation), then the argument is a case of denying the antecedent. If the first premise is interpreted as "If he gets the tax credit, then he filed before the first" (and this is also a correct interpretation), then the argument is affirming the consequent.

19. Overheard: "If drunk-driving checkpoints continue, then next there will be checkpoints for driver's licenses, infant car seats, you name it. And if we have checkpoints for all those things, we're going to wish we hadn't allowed drunk-driving checkpoints in the first place."

    Unstated conclusion: "If drunk-driving checkpoints continue, then we're going to wish we had not allowed them in the first place." Chain argument

20. You can't get from here to New Orleans without taking the Lake Pontchartrain Causeway, and taking the causeway will bring you in through Jefferson Parish. So you've got to go in through Jefferson Parish in order to get from here to New Orleans.

    Chain argument

21. Jan will start work as an assistant director next fall if she finishes her degree by that time; and she can finish her degree this summer if she goes to summer school. This means she's going to be an assistant director in the fall if she goes to summer school.

Chain argument

22. If Kirkpatrick got his work done before the deadline, he'd have been paid before Phyllis left for Hawaii, and if that had happened, they'd be skiing right now. So they're skiing only if he got his work done before the deadline.

Chain argument

23. There were some people who were disappointed when Ted Kennedy announced he wouldn't run for president, but they aren't what you'd call the old-school liberals. So, none of the old-school liberals were disappointed.

Valid conversion

24. "Nothing that happens is inevitable; therefore, no inevitable events ever happen."

Valid conversion

25. "It really ought to be evident," he lectured. "Wherever that particular type of beetle is present, you'll find exactly that kind of hole in the trees. Therefore, when you see that kind of hole, you know that type of beetle is present."

Invalid conversion

26. All the office people who went to Mexico during the holiday came back with great tans. So, anybody you see around here with a tan was one of the lucky ones who went to Mexico.

Invalid conversion

27. There are a few actors who work for humanitarian causes, so some humanitarians are actors.

Valid conversion

28. A small percentage of the boards he nailed into his fence are nailed so close together they'll buckle when they get wet. Therefore, you can be sure that some of the fence boards that buckle when the rains come are boards he nailed close together.

Valid conversion

29. "At least a few members of the Fatah Revolutionary Council are not terrorists." Does it follow that at least a few terrorists are not members of the FRC?

Nope; invalid conversion

30. Some people who find logic difficult are not good mathematicians, because some good mathematicians are not people who find logic difficult.

    Invalid conversion

31. Jackson won't take the Democratic nomination. He's the front-runner, and the front-runner never captures the nomination.

    Valid syllogism. In effect, it says: "All H are F, and no F are C; therefore, no H are C," where "H," "F," and "C" each denote a one-member class: Jackson, the front-runner, and the capturer of the Democratic nomination.

32. Nobody who showed up had any money left, and everybody who had been to the casino showed up. My earlier estimate of this crowd's luck must have proved to be correct: None of the folks who had been to the casino had any money left.

    Valid syllogism: No S are M, and all C are M; therefore, no C are M.

33. From an editorial: "Any instance of censorship is wrong, and the Soviet attempt to squelch the ABC miniseries *Amerika* is the worst kind of censorship—that imposed by another country. ABC executives should not cave in to the Soviet pressure."

    Valid syllogism: All C are W, and all S are C; therefore, all S are W.

34. Everybody who knows about the violence attending last year's election in the Philippines knows that the election couldn't have been fair, and anybody who reads the papers knows about that violence.

    Unstated conclusion: "Anybody who reads the papers knows that the election couldn't have been fair." Valid syllogism: All K are F, and all P are K; [therefore, all P are F].

35. "Freddy's gone completely wacko. He's nuts."
    "Yeah? Why do you say that?"
    "Because he thinks he's a rock star, and these days all the crazies think they're rock stars."

    Invalid syllogism: All F are R, and all C are R; therefore, all F are C.

36. I'm telling you that every club member can vote. Here are the rules: The only people who can vote are those who are subscribers to the newsletter, and you're automatically a subscriber if you're a member of the club.

    Invalid syllogism: All V are S, and all M are S; therefore, all M are V.

37. Letter to the editor: "I would just like to say, in response to the blatantly anti-Christian letter that appeared on your editorial page on March 11, in which it was alleged that Christians aren't racists but are bigots, just how is that supposed to be? All racists are bigots, so if we Christians aren't racists, then it follows that we aren't bigots either. The writer is not only anti-Christian, he's anti-logic."

    Invalid syllogism: All R are B, and no C are R; therefore, no C are B.

38. Anybody who can speak the local dialect of the Khmer language would have to have been a Cambodian resident at some time, but we believe that none of the new settlers along the Tonle Sap [or Great Lake] are genuine former residents of Cambodia, because none of these new settlers can speak that dialect.

Invalid syllogism: All D are R, and no S are D; therefore, no S are R.

39. If the Syrians really shot down two American jets, then American pilots are not as good as we thought they were. Therefore, the Syrians couldn't really have shot down the American jets, since American pilots are every bit as good as we thought they were.

Modus tollens

40. No performances at which the audience maintains a fixed apparent distance from the performers can be as dramatically powerful as film, in which the audience gets a variety of views, from long, panoramic shots to extreme close-ups. Unfortunately for the theater, stage productions are necessarily performances that keep the audience fixed in the middle distance. For that reason, a play can never be as powerful as a movie. It just doesn't have the equipment.

Valid syllogism: No P [performances . . . fixed apparent distance] are F [performances as powerful as film], and all S [stage productions; plays] are P. Therefore, no S are F.

41. ASPIRING STUDENT: I'm going to get an A in this course.
SKEPTICAL FRIEND: But I thought you got a D on your first quiz.
ASPIRING STUDENT: I did. But I got As on my last three quizzes, and Mr. Garbez said that you get an A for the course if you get one on each of the last three quizzes.

Modus ponens

42. Sure, Professor Bumstead will give you passing marks on all your papers. I know she said she wouldn't pass any papers that didn't analyze the issues, but look: I read your papers, and every one of them contained an analysis of the issues.

Invalid syllogism: All P [passing papers] are A [papers that analyze issues], and all Y [your papers] are A; therefore, all Y are P.

43. "Your honor, I can prove that I'm not guilty."
"I'm listening."
"Okay. Well, if I had broken into the egg chamber, I'd really be sweating it now. I mean, I'd really be nervous, right?"
"I have no idea, but go ahead."
"Right. Well, I'm not nervous. So I *couldn't* have broken into the egg chamber."

Valid, even if unconvincing (modus tollens)

44. I know that all tracks like these in the sand are made by rattlesnakes; my reptile book says that a rattlesnake *always* makes marks just like these.

Invalid conversion

45. Let's start at the top. It had to be Libya that fired at us if it they had surface-to-air missiles. And it *was* Libya that fired at us, right? So they had surface-to-air missiles.

Affirming the consequent

46. Let me explain why beefed-up law enforcement against drug smugglers will be counterproductive. First, if a smuggler has to contend with more enforcement, he's going to turn more to a drug that is easily smuggled into the country than one that's more difficult. That's only good business. Second, if he's looking for a more easily smuggled drug, he's going to choose one with a high value per unit volume, and that means his choice is going to be cocaine, not marijuana. So, in the long run, putting the heat on with more law enforcement will result in cocaine becoming the drug more often brought into the country rather than marijuana.

Chain argument

47. Obviously the next summit, coming as it will around election time, might be politically damaging if the United States breaks the arms control pact. But the president assures us that the United States will not break any arms agreements prior to the summit—and he knows. So it is nonsense to say, as conservatives are inclined to do, that the next summit will be politically damaging.

Denying the antecedent

48. We sympathize with the 3,000 airport workers who staged a strike last week against the Vienna airport. They wanted to have more security. The truth is, the best way to protect airport workers is with an attack against the terrorists themselves. But you can attack terrorists only if you know where they are. And if you know where they are, then you know what government is protecting them. So you can attack terrorists only if you know what government is protecting them—a tall order.

Chain argument

49. We checked all the cheese in the store, and none of it came from the plant that the FDA said may be producing contaminated dairy products. So even if the management and the customers and whoever else want to worry about it, I'm perfectly confident that none of the cheese from the problem dairy plant made it into our store.

Valid conversion

50. Coffee drinkers shouldn't become surgeons. They all have jittery nerves, and anyone with jittery nerves shouldn't become a surgeon.

Valid syllogism

51. It's got to be a case of bad rings if the compression goes up when oil is squirted into the cylinders. And look: The pressure is up by twenty pounds since we squirted in the oil. I'm afraid your fears were well founded; sure enough, it's bad rings.

Modus ponens

52. The drug situation poses a real dilemma. If legalization of certain narcotics would not broaden the population of drug users, then we could decrease the crime and violence that is associated with drug traffic. Most every expert in the field, however, is certain that legalization would certainly increase the number of drug users. That means we can't get at the problem of violence and crime.

Denying the antecedent

53. If your teeth or gums hurt, then you've got a serious dental problem, and if you've got a serious dental problem, then it must be a problem of tooth decay or gum disease. Therefore, only if you have a problem of decay or gum disease do your teeth or gums hurt.

Chain argument

54. From a letter to the editor: "Mr. Weller, like all ultraliberals, can only find harsh things to say about America. But Weller is something besides an ultraliberal. There is another type of person who can only find harsh things to say about America. I am talking about people who allow themselves to be the dupes of the PC crowd."

Invalid syllogism with an unstated conclusion: "Mr. Weller is a dupe of the PC crowd." All W [Weller] are H [people with only harsh things to say . . .], and all D [dupes of the PC crowd] are H; therefore, all W are D.

55. "The Chinese themselves must pronounce the name of their capital 'Pay-King' if indeed that's the way it's really supposed to be pronounced."
    "Well, that's exactly the way the Chinese say it."
    "See there, that must be the correct pronunciation."

Affirming the consequent

56. Now, let me see if I've got this straight: If your brother is moving to Chatooga, then he's moving to Georgia, right? And if he's moving to Georgia, then he's not moving to Chattanooga, which is in Tennessee. So, if he's moving to Chattanooga, then he's not moving to Chatooga. Is that it?

Chain argument

57. I had a friend who was in Port-au-Prince last January during all the uproar. He told me that some news reporters were fooled by the reports that the Haitian government could not fall. So, even though I realize you have all kinds of faith in your fellow correspondents, it appears that at least some of those taken in by the reports were among your colleagues.

Valid conversion

58. I've heard your silly theory before. But if fusil oils and all that other stuff you were talking about were really what gave people hangovers, then they wouldn't get them from vodka, for instance, which doesn't have that stuff in it. However, as you well know, people do get hangovers from vodka. I conclude that your fusil oil theory is just so much bunk.

Modus tollens

59. The rise of the initiatives on state ballots represents an increased demand on the part of the voters for accountability from government. Clearly, therefore, people are demanding, through increased use of initiatives, more accountability from their elected officials.

Valid, but it begs the question

60. All oil is produced from organic matter. For some reason I find this somewhat depressing. Maybe it's the idea of all the world's living things winding up as potential fuel for motor homes and chain saws.

Invalid conversion

61. Sweden has claim to the largest impact structure in Europe, it appears. The area—a twenty-six-mile-wide area about 150 miles northwest of Stockholm—is the largest one in any European country; provided, of course, that the formation known as the Siljan Ring was indeed created by the impact of a meteor, a claim nobody doubts.

Modus ponens

62. From a letter to the editor: "Wood-burning stoves are warm and attractive and are a primary source of energy conservation. The Wood Heating Alliance estimates that wood stoves save about 100 million barrels of oil a year. Yet there is a hidden cost for the savings in oil—our health. The EPA estimates that by the turn of the century wood stoves will be sending 7 million tons of particulate matter into the air. Even now, according to the EPA, residential wood combustion causes 'almost as much airborne particulate matter as all U.S. coal-fired power plants, and more particulate matter than the coal mining, metallic ore mining, iron and steel, cement, and pulpwood industries combined.'
   "Clearly, something must be done. Residential wood burning causes heavy pollution, and sources of heavy pollution, no matter what their other benefits, must be strictly regulated."

Valid syllogism: All W [residential wood-burning] are P [causes of pollution], and all P are R [activities that should be regulated]; therefore, all W are R. The statement of the conclusion is implicit.

63. You could have gotten an A in that critical-thinking course if you had just read over the chapters assigned; since you blew the course, don't tell me you read the chapters!

Modus tollens

64. If the Soviets had built their version of Star Wars, the United States would have redoubled its efforts on SDI. But if that had happened, it would have meant less money for important social programs. So if the Soviets had built their system, Americans would have gone hungry. It's a crazy world!

Chain argument

65. Every politician wants approval, and so does every network anchor. Those anchors had better remember that the next time they snicker at those who lead our country—network anchors are all politicians, too!

Invalid syllogism

66. All professional counselors here in Georgia are licensed, so you can be certain that if the man your mother recommended has a license, he's a professional.

Invalid conversion

67. "Betty, if you were a good girl, you could go outside and play."
   "But, Mommy, you know I got into a fight with my sister."
   "That's right, Betty. And that's why you have to stay inside."

Denying the antecedent

68. With steroids you become very injury-prone. Your muscle insertions can't take that kind of potential strength, and they start to give. That's why you see a lot of minor injuries in players on steroids. And that's why I suspect Jerry uses them. He has a lot of minor injuries.

Invalid syllogism

69. Each presidential candidate can spend up to $23 million in primaries and caucuses. General Foods, by comparison, spends $32 million just advertising Jell-O in a single year. If the American people continue to believe that presidential races are too expensive, then they continue to believe a myth.

This is best analyzed as modus ponens. Students may require a hint, namely, that the last sentence is just a way of saying that presidential races are not too expensive: More is spent advertising such things as Jell-O than the presidential candidates could spend in the primaries and caucuses; [Unstated: If more is spent advertising such things as Jell-O than the presidential candidates could spend in primaries and caucuses, then the presidential races are not too expensive]; Therefore, presidential races are not too expensive.

70. "When we let the fossil record speak, its testimony is not evolution-oriented. Instead, the testimony of the fossil record is creation-oriented. It shows that many different kinds of living things suddenly appeared. While there was great variety within each kind, these had no links to evolutionary ancestors before them. Nor did they have any evolutionary links to different kinds of living things that came after them. Various kinds of living things persisted with little change for long periods of time before some of them became extinct, while others survive down to this day."
   —*Life—How Did It Get Here? By Evolution or by Creation?*

Modus tollens is perhaps the best analysis, since the topic sentence asserts that the fossil record does not support evolution. Thus: If the fossil record supported evolution, then it would not be as the rest of the paragraph asserts. The fossil record is as the rest of the paragraph asserts. Therefore, the fossil record does not support evolution.

71. Before 1917, the United States had a decentralized democracy, the most decentralized government in the West. However, when we entered the war, Woodrow Wilson galvanized the nation into a highly centralized state, in which railroads, shipping lines, and munitions factories were nationalized, other corporations were regulated, and the states turned to the federal government for their instructions. After the war, it became accepted wisdom that if centralization could solve the problems of war, it could help solve peacetime problems as well. Given the sweep of history, it is manifest that we cannot now return to decentralized government. We cannot do so, because the 1980s cannot be the 1900s.

   Looks like question begging to us.

72. Professor Regan thinks that animals can feel pain, and that therefore they have the right not to be experimented on to promote someone else's happiness.

   Valid syllogism: All animals are pain feelers; [no pain feelers should be experimented on to promote someone else's happiness]; therefore, no animals should be experimented on to promote someone else's happiness.

Pre- and Post-Test

About the Test

We offer the following test with numerous caveats.

The test has not been subjected to statistical analysis. We can provide no information at this time about its reliability or validity. We can supply no normative information. Those who have need of a researched test should consider using one of the standard instruments, for example, the Cornell Critical Thinking Test, Level Z, or the Watson-Glaser Critical Thinking Appraisal. The test we provide here can give you a sense of a student's or a class's abilities on some selected critical-thinking skills, but we make no stronger claims for it.

We do not think this test is suitable for a final examination, because it is not sufficiently comprehensive of the material covered in the text. To make it sufficiently comprehensive would make it too long to be a useful pre-test (we give two-hour final exams) and would require the use of certain terms that would not be familiar to all pre-test students. It would perhaps be possible to introduce such concepts as "interdependent premises," "induction," "statistical significance," "prescriptive claim," and so on, on the pre-test itself by use of examples, but the test would then take too long to read.

Incidentally, we do not think any of the usual critical-thinking test instruments, including those mentioned above, adequately test all the skill areas that fall within the scope of critical thinking. So they too are unsuitable as final examinations. It's likely, of course, that subjects who score well in the areas sampled on these tests would also score well in other areas. But a final exam should not assume that this is the case, and it should be comprehensive of all the skill areas attended to in the course. (We think this last point is more important in critical-thinking courses than in certain other kinds of courses.)

As you will see, you are required to use your judgment in scoring certain items in the test. One could adapt the test to a multiple-choice format to save grading time, but we have found it beyond our abilities to devise decent multiple-choice questions and answers on many of the topics covered. We should say, though, that as judgment-graded exams go, this one grades very quickly.

We would like to call your attention to Part III of the test, in which subjects are asked to explain what, if anything, is wrong with each claim in a set of claims. If your pre-test students are anything like ours, some of them will find so few of these claims defective in any way that they will tell you they don't understand what they are supposed to do. You *might* give them an example of a defective claim of some sort, but doing so is likely to result in tunnel vision for the specific type of defect you illustrate. It is better, we think, to elaborate on the instructions a bit (although post-test takers should receive the same instructions).

Finally, whatever the deficiencies of the test, it's not a bad way to begin a critical-thinking course. Students like taking the test. Some have commented that if this indicates what this course is about, they're glad they signed up. Despite our general interest in the truth, we have not checked to see whether they still feel this way at the end of the term.

General Directions

This test can be taken in forty-five minutes or less. (Most students take far less time.) You might tell your students something like the following:

"The test has four parts. Each part is preceded by instructions. When you finish one part, go on to the next. Do not spend too much time on any one question. To help you budget your time, in ten minutes I'll tell you to begin the second part, and then when to begin the third and fourth parts. If you finish a part early, go right on to the next part. If you have not finished a part, you may have time at the end to return to it."

After ten minutes, tell the class to begin working on the second part if they have not already done so. Be sure to tell them that they may go back and finish the first part later if they have time at the end. Remind students of the instructions at the end of each part. Allow the following times:

Part I: ten minutes
Part II: five minutes
Part III: fifteen minutes
Part IV: fifteen minutes

Logic and Critical-Thinking Assessment

Part I (10 minutes)

Each of these items consists of one or more assertions, together with a conclusion that may or may not follow from the assertions. Assume the assertions are true, and then determine whether the conclusion necessarily follows from them. Base your answers only on the information contained in the assertions.

EXAMPLE:

> *ASSERTION:* If Charles was late in paying his rent, then he was evicted.
> *ASSERTION:* Charles was late in paying his rent.
> *CONCLUSION:* Charles was evicted.

Answer: Yes, the conclusion necessarily follows from the information contained in the assertions.

1. *ASSERTION:* If the students from the Ivy League schools perform better, on the average, on the Graduate Record Exam than do students enrolled at Big Ten universities, then it is reasonable to assume that Ivy League students are in general academically more talented than their Big Ten counterparts.
ASSERTION: But we know that Big Ten students are in general at least as talented academically as Ivy League students.
CONCLUSION: The students from the Ivy League schools do not perform better, on the average, on the Graduate Record Exam than do Big Ten students.

   Circle one: YES (The conclusion necessarily follows from the information contained in the assertions.)
   　　　　　　　NO   (The conclusion does not necessarily follow from the information contained in the assertions.)

2. *ASSERTION:* The people who voted for Theodore Roosevelt in the 1896 election of the mayor of New York City were Republicans.
ASSERTION: In 1896, all conservatives were Republicans.
CONCLUSION: The people who voted for Theodore Roosevelt in the 1896 mayoral election for New York City were all conservatives.

   Circle one: YES (The conclusion necessarily follows from the information contained in the assertions.)
   　　　　　　　NO   (The conclusion does not necessarily follow from the information contained in the assertions.)

3. *ASSERTION:* If Charles was evicted, then he was late in paying his rent.
ASSERTION: Charles was late paying his rent.
CONCLUSION: Charles was evicted.

   Circle one: YES (The conclusion necessarily follows from the information contained in the assertions.)
   　　　　　　　NO   (The conclusion does not necessarily follow from the information contained in the assertions.)

355

4. *ASSERTION:* If people trust an individual, then that person will have many friends.
ASSERTION: If a person has many friends, then that person strikes others as sincere.
CONCLUSION: If a person strikes others as sincere, then people will trust that person.

Circle one: YES (The conclusion necessarily follows from the information contained in the assertions.)
NO (The conclusion does not necessarily follow from the information contained in the assertions.)

5. *ASSERTION:* The manned space program will be discontinued if American scientists become convinced that unmanned probes would provide a cheaper, safer, and more efficient means of space research.
ASSERTION: Amerian scientists will not become convinced that unmanned probes would provide a cheaper, safer, and more efficient means of space research.
CONCLUSION: The manned space program will not be discontinued.

Circle one: YES (The conclusion necessarily follows from the information contained in the assertions.)
NO (The conclusion does not necessarily follow from the information contained in the assertions.)

6. *ASSERTION:* People who lived prior to any civilization all lived in caves.
ASSERTION: No cave dwellers had musical instruments.
CONCLUSION: No people who lived prior to any civilization had musical instruments.

Circle one: YES (The conclusion necessarily follows from the information contained in the assertions.)
NO (The conclusion does not necessarily follow from the information contained in the assertions.)

7. *ASSERTION:* People who lived prior to any civilization all lived in caves.
ASSERTION: None of the people who lived prior to any civilization had musical instruments.
CONCLUSION: No cave dwellers had musical instruments.

Circle one: YES (The conclusion necessarily follows from the information contained in the assertions.)
NO (The conclusion does not necessarily follow from the information contained in the assertions.)

Part II (five minutes)

1. What claim or principle, if any, is the author of the following passage taking for granted?

"The United States should not halt the testing and development of nuclear weapons. This is because adversaries will wage war against the United States unless they believe our weapons are modern and sophisticated—and we must continue testing and developing nuclear weapons if they are to believe this."

2. What claim or principle, if any, is the author of the following passage attempting to establish?

"I am writing in response to the recent letters about giving the governor a free hand in keeping killers and rapists behind bars. Killers and rapists are undesirable in society, to be sure. However, I would suggest that perhaps we should take a lesson from history. Power corrupts, and absolute power corrupts absolutely."

Part III (fifteen minutes)

Explain in a sentence or two what, if anything, is wrong with each of the following remarks.

1. People who work hard frequently sleep poorly.

2. The reason she finds it impossible to make a presentation to an audience is that she has stage fright.

3. Women are more tolerant than men.

4. Ninety-seven percent of Chicago's heroin addicts say they smoked marijuana at least once before ever trying heroin.

5. What's wrong with that book? Why, it's trash, that's what.

6. Building a new school will increase my taxes, so I guess it would not benefit the community as much as the school board says.

7. The liberal's answer to every problem is "tax, tax, tax, and spend, spend, spend."

8. How much more time are you going to waste watching that program, anyway?

9. It's true that, just to read them, you would think that Johnson's exam was as good as Carter's; but I've had Carter in several classes before so I gave him the benefit of the doubt on a few items here and there.

10. Dr. Spaulding was once a physicist for the space program, so I believe him when he says that acid rain has become the most serious environmental problem of the decade.

11. That even normal individuals eventually become immune to the degrading aspects of pornography is demonstrated by countless statistics.

12. Said over the telephone by a physician to a patient: "Do you still have some of those capsules I prescribed for you last year? If you do, take some of them every time you feel uncomfortable."

Part IV (fifteen minutes)

Explain in what way, if any, the thinking in each of the following paragraphs is wrong, defective, or otherwise erroneous. Although the selection is about the effects of smoking, you do not need to know anything about smoking to complete this part of the test.

Paragraph 1

The American Medical Association now wants to extend the ban on television advertising of cigarettes and cigars to the print media. The AMA's current view is that smoking is killing people at an alarming rate even though advertising these tobacco products on television has been prohibited for years. But the AMA is not much of an authority on the subject, as it turns out, and it's position ought to be rejected. In the late 1960s, according to a report in the *New York Times,* the AMA promised the tobacco makers that it would *oppose* requiring health warnings on cigarette packages if in return the tobacco lobby would help the AMA fight Medicare.

Paragraph 2

Furthermore, I am not altogether convinced that smoking is the health menace it is commonly believed to be. The economic well-being of millions of people in hundreds of communities depends on tobacco, including growers, sellers, industry workers, and the multitudes who receive indirect benefit from the tax monies collected from tobacco.

Paragraph 3

In addition, I've been a smoker all my life, and I have suffered no ill effects. My father was a life-long smoker too. He died when he was in his mid-eighties, from causes unrelated to smoking. The statistics that purport to show that cigarette smoking is dangerous, therefore, are not as convincing as they appear.

Paragraph 4

One tobacco company has reported on an interesting study. Sixty-one percent of the respondents in a survey of more than one hundred health-care professionals do not believe that smoking increases the risk of a heart attack. You know that there is something wrong with the position taken by the AMA when 61 percent of their own physicians disagree with it.

Paragraph 5

That same report mentions an experiment that shows that, contrary to popular opinion, smoking actually has health *benefits.* A group of smokers was compared with a similarly sized control group of nonsmokers with respect to the number of days of work the members of each group missed during the past month because of illness. It was found that nonsmokers reported missing 20 percent more days than smokers.

For all these reasons, I think it is reasonable to dispute the assertions made by the AMA. If smoking is unsafe, that fact has not yet been proved to my satisfaction.

ANSWER KEY   (With suggested values for correct answers)

Part I

Give one point for each correct answer.

1. Yes

2. No

3. No

4. No

5. No

6. Yes

7. No

Part II

Your judgment is required in evaluating these and the remaining items. Give either one or two points for correct answers.

1. The claim taken for granted is that any step necessary for preventing adverseries from waging war on the United States should be taken. This can be phrased in various ways, of course.

2. The author is attempting to establish the claim that the governor should not be given a free hand in keeping killers and rapists behind bars.

Part III

Give either one or two points for correct answers. The subject need not display mastery of the technical vocabulary used here. Give credit for any unforeseen insights.

1. Structurally ambiguous claim

2. Circular explanation

3. Vague comparison

4. Unknowable statistic

5. Begs the question

6. Rationalizing

7. Stereotyping

8. Loaded question

9. Inconsistency; the speaker's words show that he or she does not treat relevantly similar cases in adequately similar ways.

10. Appeal to illegitimate authority

11. Proof surrogate; vague (As vague as this claim is, it can also be said to be unknowable.)

12. All the following are much too vague for the context in which they appear: "those capsules I prescribed for you last year," "some of them," and "every time you feel uncomfortable."

Part IV

Give either one, two, or three points for correct answers. Once again, credit should be given for unanticipated insights.

Paragraph 1: That the AMA struck a bargain with the tobacco makers in the 1960s has no bearing on its ability to recognize health hazards. However, the fact that the AMA once had an ulterior motive behind its pronouncements is a relevent inductive reason for thinking that it might have an ulterior motive behind its pronouncements now. But the paragraph does more than urge caution or suspension of judgment on the AMA's position; it calls for outright rejection of it. Thus it is an ad hominem.

Paragraph 2: This is what we call "pseudoreasoning": an irrelevance disguised to look like a reason.

Paragraph 3: This is an example of what we call the fallacy of anecdotal evidence. (See Chapters 11 and 12.)

Paragraph 4: Health-care professionals include more than physicians. That 61 percent of the sample of health-care professionals say such-and-such does not warrant the conclusion that exactly 61 percent of all health-care professionals (let alone 61 percent of all physicians) would say such-and-such. No details of the survey are provided, and without them, or a credible authority to vouch for them, no credence can be given to the conclusion drawn from the survey.

Paragraph 5: The 20 percent figure is meaningless without information about the experiment. Further, even if this difference were significant, it would not offer much support for the conclusion. Nonsmokers may miss more days not because they are sicker but because they are more health conscious and take better care of themselves. (Other plausible accounts are also possible.)